D1257555

Canadian POLITICS

Canadian POLITICS

Concise edition

Rand Dyck
Laurentian University

ITP Nelson

an International Thomson Publishing company

Toronto • Albany • Bonn • Boston • Cincinnati • Detroit • London • Madrid • Melbourne
Mexico City • New York • Pacific Grove • Paris • San Francisco • Singapore • Tokyo • Washington

I T P® International Thomson Publishing

The ITP logo is a trademark under licence
www.thomson.com

Published in 1998 by

I T P® Nelson

A division of Thomson Canada Limited
1120 Birchmount Road
Scarborough, Ontario M1K 5G4
www.nelson.com/nelson.html

All rights reserved. No part of this work covered by the copyrights hereon may be reproduced or used in any form or by any means—graphic, electronic or mechanical, including photocopying, recording, taping or information storage and retrieval systems—without prior written permission of the publisher.

To show your appreciation for the time and effort that the author and publisher have invested in this book, please choose **not** to photocopy it. Choose instead to add it to your own personal library. The investment will be well worth it.

Every effort has been made to trace ownership of all copyrighted material and to secure permission from copyright holders. In the event of any question arising as to the use of any material, we will be pleased to make the necessary corrections in future printings.

Cover design: Todd Ryoji
Cover photo (background): The Image Bank / © Jeff Spielman

Canadian Cataloguing in Publication Data

Dyck, Perry Rand, 1943–
    Canadian politics

Concise ed.
Includes bibliographical references and index.
ISBN 0-17-606974-7

1. Canada – Politics and government. I. Title.

JL75.D93 1998   320.971   C97-932335-5

Team Leader and Publisher   Michael Young
Acquisitions Editor   Nicole Gnutzman
Senior Production Editor   Bob Kohlmeier
Project Editor   Jenny Anttila
Interior Design   Peggy Rhodes
Art Direction   Angela Cluer
Composition Analyst   Nelson Gonzalez
Production Coordinator   Brad Horning

Send your comments by e-mail to the production team for this book:
college_arts_hum@nelson.com

Printed and bound in Canada

 3   4   (WC)   01   00

To Michael and Peggy,
two great kids!

Contents in Brief

Contents

Preface

This concise edition of *Canadian Politics* was prepared at the urging of those who liked the second edition of *Canadian Politics: Critical Approaches*, published in 1996, but for whom that version was too long and detailed. In general, this edition is most appropriate for first-year university courses, as well as for community college use.

This book deals with Canadian government and politics in two separate but equal parts, either of which can be studied first. Chapters 2 through 10 could be classified as "politics," while chapters 11 to 16 could be called "government." In this way, the book remains a comprehensive treatment of the whole subject, although it is more factual and less analytical than *Critical Approaches*. It is also backed up by ITP Nelson's political science Web site—polisci.nelson.com—which includes, among other things, key constitutional documents.

This concise edition is half the length of the original but seeks to retain most of the former's virtues. It continues to emphasize the societal setting in which most political activity originates, including regional–economic and class cleavages, the French and Quebec questions, Aboriginal, other ethnic, and gender issues, and external forces. It then turns to linking people to government, including political culture, socialization, and participation, the mass media and public opinion polls, elections and the electoral system, political parties, and pressure groups and lobbying. The third section deals with the constitutional context, including the Constitution as such, the Charter of Rights and Freedoms, and federalism. The final part is called "Governing," and is composed of chapters on the executive, the bureaucracy, Parliament, and the courts.

Like its predecessor, the book aims to be "student-friendly," clearly and engagingly written, and up-to-date. It retains many of the tables and figures from *Critical Approaches* and presents material in digestible chunks. It includes the results of the 1997 federal election and the early returns of the 1996 census, and updates other key variables such as newspaper chain ownership.

ITP Nelson offers a 90-minute videotape featuring two- to three-minute television news clips, compiled from the CTV network archives, that correspond to each chapter of the book. The segments were chosen to amplify some of the concepts found in the book and to provide topical discussion material. More detailed information on these news items, including discussion questions, is provided in the Instructor's Manual.

I continue to feel grateful to the many people who assisted in the production of *Critical Approaches* two years ago, several of whom, including Bob Kohlmeier, helped with updating material for *this* edition. This book involved others at ITP Nelson, however, including Nicole Gnutzman, Jenny Anttila, and Mike Thompson. All were a pleasure to work with. I am grateful also to the reviewers who took time to comment on the manuscript of this edition: Michael Burke, Ryerson Polytechnic University; Robert Keaton, Dawson College; Howard A. Leeson, University of Regina; Doug Long, University of Western Ontario; H.B. McCullough, Okanagan University College; Stephen Phillips, Langara College; Jennifer Schroeder, Seneca College; Peter Silcox, Erindale College; Timothy Thomas, Royal Military College; Neil Thomlinson, Ryerson Polytechnic University; and Sharyn Tyakoff, Douglas College. Their suggestions were appreciated. Above all, as usual, my wife, Joan, provided the most supportive home environment imaginable.

RAND DYCK

Statistics Canada information is used with the permission of the Minister of Industry, as Minister responsible for Statistics Canada. Information on the availability of the wide range of data from Statistics Canada can be obtained from Statistics Canada's Regional Offices, its World Wide Web site, at http://www.statcan.ca, and its toll-free access number: 1-800-263-1136.

Introduction

This first chapter introduces the subject of Canadian government and politics. The chapter's first part outlines a framework, often called the political system, for visualizing how all the ingredients of the subject interact. The second part of the chapter provides a brief sketch of the basic governmental institutions in Canada.

· ·

The Political System
Demands

Perhaps it is best to begin with the 30 million individuals who inhabit the territory called Canada. All of these individuals have an array of needs that they attempt to satisfy, ranging from water and food through security and friendship to self-esteem and self-fulfilment. Political science lumps such needs together with interests, preferences, opinions, and expectations and sometimes calls them "wants." Most of us spend much of our time trying to satisfy such needs or wants.

In the first instance, most of us do so by our own efforts, in pairs, in families, in organizations of all kinds, at work and at play, and do not automatically call for government help. At some point, however, we may begin to feel that the satisfaction of such needs or wants is beyond such personal, interpersonal, family, or group capacity, and come to the conclusion that the government should step in to help us. When we express the opinion that the government should take some action, we are converting a want into a "demand" and crossing the threshold between the private and public sectors. We can therefore say that a demand is the expression of opinion that government take some action.

We must now discover how demands are transmitted from individuals to the government, as indicated in the model of the political system, Figure 1.1.[1] This can be done on a personal basis, by means of a letter, fax, telephone call, or face-to-face encounter. Sometimes such directly transmitted demands will achieve their desired result, but very often they will not. When they do not, it may be time to consider some kind of group action. Canadian society contains many groups, and it is quite likely that a group already exists to articulate the demand any individual decides to transmit. If such a group is not already in existence, it

Figure 1.1   A Model of the Political System

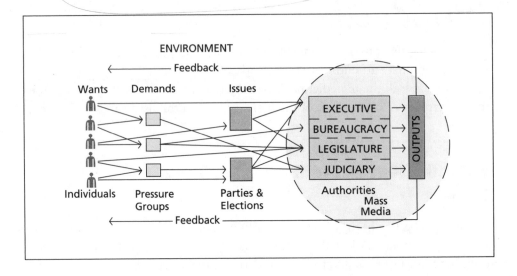

may be worthwhile to create one since, as a general rule, the authorities are more likely to respond to a demand coming from a group than from a single individual. Such groups are usually called *interest groups* or *pressure groups* and constitute an important part of Canadian political activity. The Canadian Chamber of Commerce and the Canadian Labour Congress are two prominent examples. Corporations and other institutions also make demands, either individually or in groups.

A special kind of group that is even more overtly political is the *political party*, and it can also be used to transmit demands to the government. People join a political party or support it financially, and try to get it to recognize their concerns in its platform or policies. If the party comes to power, it can incorporate the demand into government policy; if the party is in opposition, it may be able to use the media to bring the problem to national attention. Parties are particularly responsive to such demands in an election campaign, seeking to attract the support of large numbers of individuals and groups by promising them the action they seek. Those dissatisfied with the manner in which existing parties are responding to their demands can create new parties, such as the Reform Party and the Bloc Québécois.

mass media

Another means of transmitting the demand to the government is, as suggested earlier, via the *mass media* of communication. The media are usually eager to publicize controversial issues and often delight in pointing out problems that the government has failed to resolve. The media give attention to individual and interest group concerns on a regular basis, cover political party activities, and are especially active in election campaigns. But in providing the electorate with most of its information about politics, they also shape the whole nature of political discourse in Canada.

We have assumed thus far that any and all demands actually reach the government. In fact, however, relatively few have any impact. Demands that do not concern very many people or demands for action contrary to the values of the government of the day may be ignored. Since the number of demands under serious consideration at any given time is such a small proportion of the total number being made, it is sometimes useful to distinguish between demands and "issues," the latter including only those demands that the government has taken under serious consideration.

Government authorities are thus bombarded by demands, but what is even more striking than the vast quantity of demands is that there is usually intense conflict among them. The essence of politics and government, therefore, is choosing among competing demands, trying to resolve conflict, or making social choices in the midst of social conflict. *Politics* is said to originate in conflict, and is often defined as the struggle for power and the management of conflict. Here let us say it is activity in which conflicting interests struggle for advantage. It should also be added that the authorities can make their own demands, which sometimes carry more weight than those arising from the wider society.

Government

coercion

Having repeatedly mentioned *government*, we may now define it as the set of institutions that make and enforce collective, public decisions for a society. We must also deal with the concept of *power*, which is often defined in political science as the ability of one actor to impose its will on another. Government, backed up by armed forces, police, and punishments, if necessary, possesses a particular kind of power called "coercion." That is, the government has the ability to impose its will upon us by means of sanctions or penalties. Indeed, as a general rule, *only* the government is allowed to use force or coercive power in society. But if we (or our ancestors) had a hand in the creation of such a government apparatus, as well as

We obey Government

in the selection of the current governors, then we have in a sense agreed to be bound by its decisions, and we have cloaked it with *legitimacy*. Such legitimate power is often called *authority*, and a synonym for government is "the authorities." To some extent we obey the government because of the threat or expectation of penalties if we do not, but we also obey because we accept government decisions to be binding upon us and necessary for the general good. Think of stopping at a red light as an example.

Who are these government authorities? As can be seen in the diagram of the political system in Figure 1.1, we usually divide them into four branches: the *legislature*, the *executive*, the *bureaucracy*, and the *judiciary*. The authoritative decision that a demand seeks can sometimes be made by a single branch of government. If the demand requires the passage of a law, for example, then action of the legislative branch will be necessary. If the demand can be satisfied by an appointment or large monetary grant, then the political executive or cabinet can respond to it. If the demand is for the provision of routine government services or for changes in regulations, then bureaucratic action will probably suffice. Finally, if the demand can only be settled by a judicial decision, then it should be addressed to the courts.

In many instances, however, the demand will require combined actions of any two of the executive, legislative, and bureaucratic branches, or even all three working together, such as in the formulation, passage, and implementation of a new law. The courts normally stand somewhat apart from the other three organs of government, operating on the principle of the independence of the judiciary. Judicial decisions usually follow authoritative actions in other branches of government, such as when the Supreme Court threw out the abortion provisions of the Criminal Code. But they may also lead to subsequent legislative action, as when the government sought to override a Supreme Court decision by introducing a revised law restricting tobacco advertising.

authoritative

Authoritative decisions take many forms—laws, regulations, appointments, grants, contracts, services, and judgments—and are collectively referred to as the "outputs" of the political system. Authoritative decisions are also made in the provinces and in an assortment of regional and local councils and boards, and often require the agreement of two or more levels of government.

Completing the System

Whatever the type of output, it usually sparks a reaction in the rest of the system. This leads us to the concept of "feedback"—that is, a communication of the outputs back into the system, in response to which the pattern of demands is altered. If an output satisfies a particular demand, then that demand will no longer have to be articulated. Think of the federal Official Languages Act silencing the demands for French-language rights. But the bilingualism issue also shows that the satisfaction of one demand may lead those involved to expect even more along the same lines: French-language services at the provincial *as well as* the federal level. On the other hand, a backlash may result, as the Official Languages Act also promoted the articulation of contrary demands among anglophones. This new pattern of demands may well lead authorities to alter their original response.

By now we have established that the political system is a dynamic, circular process in which the authorities react to demands, convert some of them into outputs, and then respond in turn to whatever changes in the pattern of demands have resulted from the feedback from such outputs. Individuals and groups raise conflicting demands, but because there is a consensus on the legitimacy of the government, people generally abide by its authoritative decisions, even when they disagree with them. It is sometimes said, therefore, that politics and government are characterized by both conflict and consensus. The daily conflict normally operates within an underlying consensus about the decision-making apparatus and about remaining together as part of a united political community. Moreover, the authorities usually seek to develop some kind of consensus out of the conflicting demands.

Many of these demands arise from deep, persistent divisions within society that are sometimes called *cleavages*. The cleavages in Canadian society that generally have the greatest political significance are those between the geographic regions, between English, French, Aboriginal, and other ethnic and linguistic groups, and between various socioeconomic classes, as well as cleavages related to gender, religion, and age. The relative importance and nature of these cleavages changes over time.

Beyond the domestic society, the modern world is characterized by a huge number of international and supranational factors, such as other states, international organizations, and transnational corporations. In fact, such external actors increasingly serve as the source of demands on national political systems and as constraints upon domestic policymaking.

....

Foundations of Canadian Government Institutions

The Parliamentary System

It will be useful at this time to outline more specifically the basic institutions of government in Canada. Within the central or national government in Ottawa (often called the "federal government"), the British parliamentary system provides the foundations of these governmental institutions. This system is based on the periodic popular election of the members of the House of Commons. Parliament also has a second or "upper" chamber, the Senate, whose members are appointed by the prime minister. The third part of the British Parliament is the monarch or the Crown; approval of all three parts is necessary for the passage of legislation. Because it was a British colony at the time the Constitution was adopted, Canada automatically shared the British monarch. The current monarch is Queen Elizabeth II. On a practical daily basis, however, the Queen's representative, the governor general, exercises the functions of the Crown.

Although the British system is called *parliamentary government*, and although it is said that Parliament is sovereign or supreme, such labels and descriptions are somewhat misleading. The core of the parliamentary system, even in 1867, was the prime minister and the cabinet. While they must be members of Parliament, they are such an important part of Parliament that they often relegate both the monarch and other members of the House of Commons and Senate to a position of insignificance. On the prime minister and cabinet are conferred the powers to lead the country and make the most important decisions in the political system. But the principle of *responsible government* holds that they retain their position and powers only as long as they are supported by a majority in Parliament. If the House of Commons declares a lack of confidence in the prime minister and cabinet, they must either resign and make way for another group to take their place, or else call an election. Because the prime minister and cabinet ministers have seats in the legislative branch, mostly the House of Commons, the system is often termed a *fusion of powers*—that is, it involves a combination of legislative and executive powers.

In the parliamentary system, then, the prime minister and cabinet ministers, who have seats in Parliament, are given the power to introduce most legislation and the right to control most of the time of the legislature. They are given the exclusive power to introduce legislation of a financial nature—laws either to raise or to spend money. They have other wide powers: of appointment, to draft subordinate legislation under the authority of laws, and in international affairs—essentially all powers necessary to provide effective political leadership for the country. The parliamentary system is executive-dominated, and because the British Parliament operates in the Palace of Westminster, this system is sometimes called the *Westminster model*. Other members of Parliament may criticize, delay, and propose amendments, the monarch (or governor general) may advise and warn, but the prime minister and cabinet almost always get their way. This is so because a majority of the members of Parliament normally belong to the same political party as the prime minister and cabinet, and together they constitute a *majority government*. The cabinet imposes rigid party discipline on its MPs to support its every move. (In a minority government situation, cabinet control is less extensive.)

The significance of the Senate has declined since Confederation because arriving there by appointment rather than election diminishes its members' legitimacy in a democratic age. The powers of the Senate have remained virtually equal to those of the House of Commons (unlike those of the British House of Lords, which have been curtailed), but senators have rarely felt it proper to exercise them. Moreover, independent behaviour has usually been discouraged by the fact that the same party has usually held a majority both in the Senate and in the

Figure 1.2   An Outline of Canadian Political Institutions

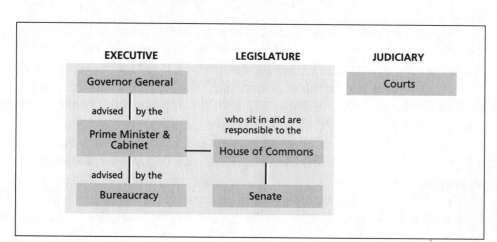

Commons. If for any reason the Senate should ultimately defeat a government bill, it does not affect the constitutional standing of the prime minister and cabinet. The model outlined here is also operational in each of the provinces, except that they now all possess one-chamber (unicameral) legislatures.

Government was small and simple at the time of Confederation, but it has gradually developed another important branch, the *bureaucracy* or public service. The bureaucracy essentially advises the prime minister and cabinet on their decisions and then carries out whatever government programs have been authorized. The current Canadian bureaucracy consists of nearly half a million public servants who make a vast array of government decisions.

The British parliamentary system also incorporates the principle of the independence of the judiciary. Although courts are established by acts of Parliament and judges are appointed by the prime minister and cabinet, the whole judicial system is expected to operate independently of the executive and legislative branches of government. In the case of Britain itself, the judges have considerable discretion in interpreting laws but lack the power of *judicial review*, that is, the power to declare them invalid. The Canadian judiciary soon appropriated to itself the power to invalidate laws that violated the federal–provincial division of powers, but was otherwise quite restrained.

Since the Canadian institutional structure was established in 1867, the only major change has been the adoption of the Charter of Rights and Freedoms in 1982. It added to the scope of judicial review, originally restricted to the federal–provincial division of powers, the new task of protecting civil liberties. Henceforth, the courts could disallow federal or provincial legislation that violated the Constitution in terms of either the division of powers or the Charter of Rights and Freedoms.

The British parliamentary system is distinct in many ways from the presidential-congressional system of the United States. There, the president and the two houses of the legislature are independently elected, and no one is permitted to sit in more than one branch of government. The *separation of powers* means that executive, legislative, and judicial powers are distributed to three separate branches of government: president, Congress, and the courts respectively. Moreover, the U.S. system is also characterized by "checks and balances" designed to ensure that the actions of any one branch of government are subject to veto by another. Members of the House of Representatives and the Senate have much more legislative power than their counterparts in the parliamentary system, in terms of both initiating bills themselves and amending or vetoing those emanating from the president. Party discipline is also much looser, so that even if a majority of the members of Congress belong to the same party as the president, there is no guarantee that the legislature will pass the president's initiatives. The Supreme Court also has the power of judicial review and can overturn any legislation that it feels is in violation of the Constitution. Apart from the name of the upper chamber, the Senate, the Fathers of Canadian Confederation adopted virtually nothing from the U.S. system with respect to the internal operation of the federal and provincial governments.

Federalism

The Fathers of Confederation were dealing with a large piece of territory, and one that they hoped would soon become larger, someday equalling or exceeding that of the United States. They also had to contend with colonies with separate identities and a previous semi-autonomous existence. In this respect, the model of American federalism could not help but influence the design of the new country. It had to be a *federation* of some kind, with a division of powers between the central and provincial governments.

Confederation was to a large extent the work of Sir John A. Macdonald, who went on to become the first Canadian prime minister. Macdonald preferred a unitary state or legislative union in which the new central government would have almost all the powers and the provinces would be little more than municipalities. But Quebec and the Maritimes were not prepared to join such a system. Quebec demanded an autonomous provincial government so that its cultural concerns, such as education and civil law, would be placed in the hands of a French-speaking majority. The Maritimes, too, insisted on provincial governments because they did not want to lose their previously established identities, they had little in the way of municipal government to handle local problems, and they were far removed from the new capital in Ottawa. Hence the logical compromise was a system that contained a central government to deal with common purposes and provincial governments to look after local concerns.

Macdonald accepted a federal form of government, then, allowing the former colonies to retain some of their political and economic independence, but he intended the new country to be a highly centralized federation. He felt that its economic and defensive objectives required a strong central government, a conviction reinforced by the conclusion among most of the other Fathers of Confederation that the American Civil War (ending just as they began their deliberations) had been the result of too much power at the state level.

Besides dividing powers between the two levels of government, constitutional architects in both the United States and Canada had to decide how the provinces or states would be represented at the national level. In both cases, the lower house of the legislature would be based on the principle of representation by population, so that the most populous provinces or states would have the largest number of members in that chamber. To protect the interests of the smaller states, the United States decided that each state, regardless of population, would have two senators at the national level. Some Fathers of Confederation preferred this idea, but others wanted representation by population in both houses of Parliament. The Canadian compromise was to base the Senate on the principle of equal *regional* representation rather than equal *provincial* representation.

Fusing the Parliamentary System with Federalism

Since Canadian politicians were already familiar with divided authority—between themselves and Britain—it might seem that a fusion of the parliamentary system and federalism was not such a constitutional innovation. The colonial division of powers was a somewhat different kind, however, and more importantly, the whole ethos underlying the Canadian and U.S. systems was different. In the parliamentary system, everything is designed to *facilitate* government action by concentrating power in the hands of the executive, whether in terms of its relationship with other institutions of government such as Parliament or the courts, or with territorial units such as local or regional governments. In the American system, everything is designed to *inhibit* government action by preventing the concentration of power in the hands of any government. Institutions of the national government—president, House of Representatives, Senate, and Supreme Court—should be able to veto each other, and they should collectively be kept in line by a division of powers that gives most authority to the states. It is largely because the British system is designed to facilitate government action whereas the American system is designed to inhibit it that the fusion of the two systems in Canadian Confederation was such a distinctive phenomenon. John A. Macdonald saw the contradiction and therefore tried to establish a federal system that was much more centralized than that next door.

. . . .

NOTES

1. Adapted from David Easton, *A Systems Analysis of Political Life* (New York: John Wiley & Sons, 1965).

The Societal Context

The next four chapters deal with the main elements of the societal or socioeconomic context of the Canadian political system. It is widely held that the aspects of Canadian society most relevant to politics are its regional–economic, ethnic, and class features, primarily because they represent deep, persistent divisions called cleavages. Gender issues have also become a prominent feature of Canadian politics. Many of the demands with which the authorities have to contend originate from such cleavages.

Beyond the four factors mentioned are the external forces that also affect the Canadian political system. The world has become a "global village," and international, multinational, transnational, and supranational—that is, "global"—factors are important elements of any national political system. This is especially true of Canada, which has always been open to such external influences.

Chapter 2

Regional–Economic and Class Cleavages

Canada's geographic and economic divisions are some of its most obvious characteristics. The first half of this chapter deals with the regional–economic cleavages that are a daily fact of Canadian political life. Many government decisions are direct responses to such cleavages, and most policies must at least take them into account. Such regional–economic cleavages can be most usefully discussed in terms of distance and division, and regional–economic differences, conflicts, and disparities. The second part of the chapter discusses economic divisions in non-geographic, class terms—that is, disparities and conflicts among individuals with different levels of income.

Regional–Economic Cleavages
Distance and Division

PHYSIOGRAPHIC REGIONS

Canada's tremendous distances have always had a crucial influence on its political system, especially in generating regional–economic demands. The difficulties of dealing with such distances are immensely complicated by divisions caused by natural physical barriers running essentially in a north–south direction. Canada is usually divided into five basic physiographic regions, as shown in Figure 2.1.

TRANSPORTATION AND COMMUNICATIONS SYSTEMS

Apart from the Great Lakes–St. Lawrence water route, transportation and communications systems in Canada had to be constructed across the natural barriers. Demands to overcome distances and divisions have featured prominently in Canadian politics, and the establishment of some of these great transportation and communications projects has dominated whole eras of Canadian history.

Figure 2.1   Canada's Physiographic Regions

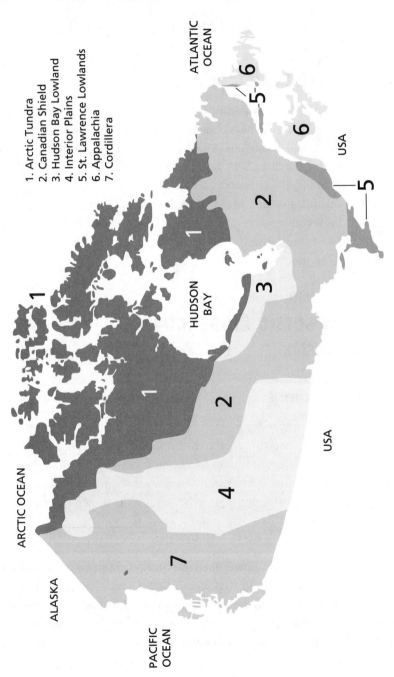

1. Arctic Tundra
2. Canadian Shield
3. Hudson Bay Lowland
4. Interior Plains
5. St. Lawrence Lowlands
6. Appalachia
7. Cordillera

Governments have primarily responded by giving assistance to private corporations, establishing Crown corporations, and creating regulatory agencies.[1]

The major transportation and communications links and agencies with which the government has been associated are as follows:

- Canadian Pacific Railway
- Canadian National Railway
- VIA Rail
- Trans-Canada Airlines/Air Canada
- Trans-Canada Pipeline
- Trans-Canada Highway
- Canadian Broadcasting Corporation (CBC)
- National Film Board
- Canadian Radio-television and Telecommunications Commission (CRTC)
- Telesat
- Teleglobe

POPULATION DISTRIBUTION

Since the people are not spread uniformly throughout this gigantic territory, the distribution of population also complicates the distances involved in Canada. The overall density of the Canadian population is one of the lowest in the world, but it is really more significant that there is no permanent settlement in nearly 90 percent of the country and that 72 percent of the population is huddled together within 150 km of the U.S. border. The population of the various provinces in 1991 and 1996 can be seen in Table 2.1. Provincial population disparities affect the allocation of seats in the House of Commons—indeed, the whole power structure in Ottawa—and the calculation of federal transfer payments. Significantly, Quebec is sensitive to the fact that its proportion of the total Canadian population has fallen below a symbolic 25 percent.

The Toronto–Ottawa–Montreal triangle obviously constitutes the *core*, *heartland*, or *metropolis* of Canada; Ontario and Quebec combined contain over 62 percent of its people. While central Canada forms the political core of the country, it is also the economic heartland, with more large corporate head offices, especially in the Toronto area, than anywhere else in the country. Moreover, it is the communications and cultural core, containing the headquarters of English and French CBC, CTV, Global, and private French television, many other Canadian cultural institutions, and much of the Canadian computer industry.

TABLE 2.1 POPULATION OF PROVINCES AND TERRITORIES

	1991 Census	1996 Census
Ontario	10 084 885 (36.9%)	10 753 573 (37.3%)
Quebec	6 895 963 (25.3%)	7 138 795 (24.7%)
British Columbia	3 282 061 (12.0%)	3 724 500 (12.9%)
Alberta	2 545 553 (9.3%)	2 696 826 (9.3%)
Manitoba	1 091 942 (4.0%)	1 113 898 (3.9%)
Saskatchewan	988 928 (3.6%)	990 237 (3.4%)
Nova Scotia	899 942 (3.3%)	909 282 (3.2%)
New Brunswick	723 900 (2.7%)	783 133 (2.7%)
Newfoundland	568 474 (2.1%)	551 792 (1.9%)
Prince Edward Island	129 765 (0.5%)	134 557 (0.5%)
Northwest Territories	57 649 (0.2%)	64 402 (0.2%)
Yukon	27 797 (0.1%)	30 766 (0.1%)
Canada	27 296 859	28 846 761

Sources: Adapted from Statistics Canada, 1991 Census of Canada, A National Overview—Population and Dwelling Counts, Cat. No. 93-301, and Statistics Canada, INFOMAT (April 18, 1997), Cat. No. 11-002E. Reproduced with permission of the Minister of Supply and Services Canada, 1997.

The rest of the country, the *hinterland* or *periphery*, regularly complains that it is overlooked by both public and private decision-makers, with such a concentration of population at the centre.

PROVINCES AND TERRITORIES

In speaking of regionalism in Canada, then, we begin with great distances complicated by geographic barriers and concentrations of population that cause variations in political and economic power. In addition, it is partly because of such distances and divisions that provinces and territories were created. The constitutional basis of such units is quite different from the natural, physiographic basis of regions, however, and the fit between regionalism and provincialism is not perfect. Feelings of regionalism can exist within a province, such as in the northern parts of many provinces; regional sentiment can cut across provinces, as in the case of people in northwestern Ontario feeling psychologically closer to Manitoba than to southern Ontario; and provinces can be lumped together into regions, such as the Maritimes or the Prairies. Nevertheless, as the 1979 Task

Force on Canadian Unity pointed out, "the provinces ... are the basic building blocks of Canadian society and the logical units on which to focus a discussion of Canadian regionalism, even though they may not be the most 'natural' regions from an economic point of view."[2]

In the 1990s, the province of Quebec came closer than ever before to separating from the rest of Canada. If it were to leave with its existing borders intact (a somewhat debatable issue), Quebec would take almost one-quarter of the Canadian population with it, about 16 percent of its territory, and nearly 23 percent of Canada's gross domestic product. From a strictly geographic point of view, the separation of Quebec would raise the question of continuing transportation links between Atlantic Canada and Ontario, border-crossing impediments, and jurisdiction over the St. Lawrence Seaway.

Regional–Economic Differences

A discussion of the economies of the Canadian regions and provinces reveals striking regional–economic differences that serve to reinforce their geographic distinctiveness and create another pattern of demands facing the Canadian political system.

Regional–economic differences begin with *primary industries* or the natural resource base of the various provinces. The importance of natural resources to the national economy has been a central tenet of Canadian political economy for generations, usually termed the *staples theory* and identified with economic historian Harold Innis.[3] It postulates that Canadian economic development has relied on a succession of resource exports—furs, fish, timber, wheat, minerals, and energy—rather than manufacturing; Canadians are mere "hewers of wood and drawers of water."

Secondary industry consists of manufacturing, construction, and utilities. Manufacturing includes the initial processing and refining of primary products as well as the making of finished goods. Generally, it produces more revenue and more jobs than primary industry, is less seasonal, and commands higher wages.

Economists put transportation and communications, trade, finance, insurance and real estate, private services, and public administration into the *tertiary* or *services* category. While the Canadian economy was never strong on manufacturing, much political attention in this "post-industrial" era is focused on the services sector. By 1996, the tertiary sector had grown to include 72 percent of the labour force, compared to 5.5 percent for the primary and 22 percent for the secondary sectors.

The Atlantic Provinces

How do the provinces differ in their economic bases?[4] The Atlantic provinces have a distinctive and heavy reliance on fishing, but this industry was in deeper trouble in the 1990s than ever before, primarily due to a dramatic reduction in groundfish stocks, especially cod. The three Maritime provinces have a substantial agricultural base, while New Brunswick, Newfoundland, and Nova Scotia also engage in forestry and mining, and Newfoundland possesses great quantities of hydroelectric power in Labrador. Some processing and refining of natural resources takes place in the region, but the small local market and the distance from major population centres have left the region in a state of underdevelopment. Led by New Brunswick, however, a new emphasis on communications technology has revitalized the Atlantic provinces' economies to some extent, for in the modern technological world, physical distance is not the hindrance it was in the past. Newfoundland also hopes that the Hibernia offshore oil project and the prospect of developing the nickel mine at Voisey's Bay will provide badly needed income and employment.

Quebec

The Quebec economy is more diversified than that of the Atlantic region and somewhat more prosperous. Quebec's outstanding primary industries include farming in the St. Lawrence Lowlands, and mining and forestry in the Canadian Shield. The Shield is also traversed by numerous powerful rivers, making hydro-electricity Quebec's most valuable resource. Huge dams have been built on many of its rivers, including the controversial James Bay hydroelectric project. Hydro is the basis of Quebec's aluminum industry, for example, as well as of much other secondary industry. Quebec also stands out in the production of pulp and paper, especially newsprint, and is much stronger than the Atlantic region in the more sophisticated aspects of manufacturing. It also houses a large financial sector. The fact that economic power in Quebec used to rest largely in Anglo-Canadian and foreign hands fuelled the nationalist debate in that province. But since 1960 a major transformation has occurred, and both the public and francophone private sectors in Quebec have repatriated a great deal of industrial ownership.

Ontario

Ontario has always had the most diversified and strongest economy of any region. The province has an abundance of natural resources, including a great expanse of prime agricultural land in the south, and vast stretches of trees and almost every conceivable mineral in the Canadian Shield. Ontario's early development of hydroelectricity and of a steel industry gave it a head start over other regions. A skilled labour force, a large domestic market, proximity to the United States, and the advantage of federal tariff and banking policies also helped to make it the manufacturing heartland of the country. Sparked by the auto industry, it now produces over half of the Canadian manufacturing total. In addition, Ontario leads the country in the tertiary sector, such as finance, trade, and services.

THE PRAIRIE PROVINCES

The Prairie provinces are historically associated with agriculture, especially wheat, other grain, and livestock. Alberta is Canada's petroleum province and has become the richest part of the country by many measures. Petroleum is also of increasing significance in Saskatchewan, in concert with that province's other mineral resources, potash and uranium. Forestry has been of some importance in Manitoba and is just beginning to make a major breakthrough in Alberta, while Manitoba's hydroelectricity complements the petroleum of the other two Prairie provinces. The Prairies are also engaged in an increasing amount of manufacturing, and especially since 1960, the finance, trade, and service industries have expanded rapidly.

BRITISH COLUMBIA

Mountainous British Columbia is the leading forestry province and also specializes in mining, including natural gas, copper, and coal. Several fertile river and lake valleys provide for farming, and, being a coastal province, B.C. also possesses a significant fishing industry. The mountains are the source of several large rivers that have been dammed for the production of hydroelectricity. Manufacturing is primarily related to the forestry, mining, and agricultural bases of the B.C. economy, while Asian immigration has expanded the services sector, especially finance.

THE NORTH

In the North, the inhospitable climate, isolation, small and transient labour force, and poor transportation facilities conspire to retard economic development. Mining has inspired many southerners to venture north over the years, and tourism is on the increase. Northern Natives used to be self-sufficient in hunting, fishing, and trapping, activities that continue to occupy them to some extent, but their lives have been disrupted by the arrival of newcomers. Settlement of some Native land claims and increased autonomy from Ottawa should better allow the Northern territories to respond to local needs in the future.

Regional–Economic Conflicts

As a result of such regional–economic differences, the national government regularly faces demands to assist the economy of a single province, region, or industry. Such demands do not necessarily involve conflict between one region and another, and sometimes benefit them all. More often than not, however, demands from one region *do* conflict with those from another. The most common expression of such regional–economic conflict has undoubtedly been between the Prairie and central regions. Since central Canada's regional interests have historically been persuasive with the federal government, the analysis is usually put in terms of the economic complaints of the West against the central core of the country.[5]

Ownership of Natural Resources

While the Eastern provinces and British Columbia have always had jurisdiction over their own natural resources, Ottawa decided to retain such control when Manitoba was created in 1870, as well as with Saskatchewan and Alberta in 1905. The logic of this discrimination was that the federal government (i.e., central Canada) should control such resources in the national interest, allowing Ottawa to guide the development of the West. The Prairie provinces fought vehemently against this discrimination and were finally successful in gaining control of their natural resources in 1930.

Tariffs

The West complained for generations that Canadian tariff policy was designed in the interest of Ontario at the expense of the Prairies. As early as the 1879 *National Policy*, John A. Macdonald saw the tariff as a means of promoting and protecting the industrial heartland of central Canada. Adding a tariff (an import tax) to the price of imported manufactured goods would raise their price above that of goods manufactured in Canada, and allow domestic goods to be sold more cheaply than imports. Ontario thus gained employment in producing tractors for

Western Canada, for example, but Western Canadians felt that this was contrary to their interests because, in the absence of such a tariff, they would have been able to buy cheaper tractors from abroad. The West demanded lower tariffs at every opportunity, and especially in the 1920s sent its own farmer representatives to the House of Commons to fight on this front. Tariffs among all countries have gradually come down since 1945, but the issue took on a new life in the 1980s with the Western demand for a free trade agreement between Canada and the United States.

TRANSPORTATION

Another aspect of Macdonald's National Policy that displeased the West was the transportation component, especially railway freight rates. Living so far from the central core of the country, Westerners expected to pay additional transportation costs, although many demanded that freight rates be subsidized by Ottawa. Indeed, the Crow's Nest Pass Act (or Crow Rate) of 1897 was an attempt to do just that, and provided a low rate for transporting Prairie grain to eastern ports. After successfully fighting to retain the Crow Rate in the 1920s, many Westerners were greatly upset by the Trudeau government's decision to increase these rates, as well as by the Chrétien government's decision to abolish the subsidy entirely. Another complaint centres on peculiar inequities within the freight rate structure, including higher rates for finished goods than for raw materials (discouraging manufacturing in the West), discrimination against short hauls, and deviations from the principle of distance determining price.

BANKING

Canada deliberately developed a centralized branch banking system in an attempt to construct a sound, stable banking community that would avoid frequent local collapses. The result was a handful of large national banks, usually with headquarters in Toronto or Montreal and with local branches spread across the country. From a hinterland perspective, money deposited in the local branch of a national bank did not remain in the community to be lent out for local purposes, but was sent to headquarters in central Canada to be used in the economic development of Ontario or Quebec. This was another reason for the farmers' revolt of the 1920s, and displeasure with the Canadian banking system had much to do with the rise of Social Credit in Alberta in the 1930s. For many decades Ottawa refused to make any changes to this policy, but in the 1970s, when the

West became stronger in spite of it, the federal government finally allowed regional banks to be established. Several of these new Western financial institutions faltered in the 1980s, however, largely because of a downturn in the Western economy that Westerners blamed on Trudeau's National Energy Program.

TAXATION AND REGULATION OF NATURAL RESOURCES

The original conflict over natural resources re-emerged in the 1970s and 1980s, especially with respect to petroleum pricing. National energy policy in the 1950s and 1960s had actually favoured the West, for Alberta was guaranteed a market for its oil and natural gas as far east as Ontario. But after the OPEC (Organization of Petroleum Exporting Countries) cartel agreed on an artificial rise in the international price of oil in 1973, federal policy began to favour the consumer/manufacturing interest of central Canada at the expense of the producer interest of the West. The height of the regional–economic conflict occurred in 1980 with the Trudeau government's National Energy Program, which imposed new federal taxes, retained a larger share of petroleum revenues for Ottawa, kept the national price below the world level, encouraged frontier development, and promoted Canadianization of the industry, all objectives opposed by most Westerners. Eventually a partial compromise between central and Western interests was reached in 1981, and the Mulroney government later scrapped the NEP entirely. Nevertheless, the NEP had a profound effect on the Western Canadian psyche, especially when combined with the West's simultaneous opposition to Ottawa's constitutional initiatives and official bilingualism policy.

OTHER ASPECTS OF REGIONAL CONFLICTS

These four policy areas—tariffs, transportation, banking, and resources—can be put in a broader context. The metropolitan–hinterland thesis suggests that the West was created as a colony of central Canada and was intended to be held in a subordinate and dependent relationship.[6] The flavour of this relationship is captured in Figure 2.2. Dissatisfaction with both the Liberal and Conservative parties' focus on Quebec issues in the 1980s and early 1990s led to the formation of the Reform Party, whose initial slogan was "The West Wants In." Although it broadened its focus by the time of the 1993 and 1997 federal elections, the Reform Party won the majority of seats west of Ontario, and almost all of them in British Columbia and Alberta.

Figure 2.2   **The Canadian Economy According to Many Westerners**

Source: "The Milch Cow," by Arch. Dale (1882–1962), from the Grain Growers Guide, 15 December 1915. Reproduced courtesy of the Glenbow Archives, Calgary, Alberta.

Many of the Western economic conflicts with central Canada have been echoed by the Atlantic provinces. Nova Scotia and New Brunswick entered Confederation in 1867 as proud and prosperous colonies, but their economies quickly declined. While changes in marine technology (from wooden sailing ships to steel steamships) were probably the principal factor responsible, Maritimers blamed federal economic policy for much of their difficulty. Post-Confederation tariff policy appeared to do the Maritimes more harm than good; the Atlantic provinces shared the West's concerns about freight rates, although they received subsidization in this area, too; and they opposed federal resource policy in the 1980s, prompting them to fight for provincial ownership of offshore petroleum. They also complained of an insufficiently aggressive federal government when it came to protecting Atlantic fish stocks from foreign overfishing.

Smaller-scale regional–economic disputes are also a routine occurrence in Canadian politics. Attempts to support the steel plant in Sydney, Nova Scotia, arouse opposition in Sault Ste. Marie, Ontario; awarding the CF-18 maintenance contract to Canadair of Montreal infuriates supporters of Bristol Aerospace of Winnipeg (and further reinforces Western alienation); extending drug patent protection for multinational pharmaceutical firms in Quebec offends Canadian generic drug producers in Ontario; and promoting frontier petroleum exploration (including federal assistance to Newfoundland's Hibernia project) upsets conventional oil and gas producers in Alberta.

Regional–Economic Disparities

Conflicts between regions are exacerbated in Canada because of regional–economic inequalities or disparities. Whatever the fault of federal policies, Canada's primary resources are not evenly distributed, and the regions have different sizes and populations, and variable distances from key export markets.

Among the available ways to measure regional–economic disparity are provincial gross domestic product (the total value of all goods and services produced), gross domestic product per capita, and provincial unemployment rates. These measures are provided in Table 2.2.

TABLE 2.2 PROVINCIAL GROSS DOMESTIC PRODUCT, GDP PER CAPITA, AND
　　　　　　UNEMPLOYMENT RATE

	1995 GDP (millions)	1995 GDP per Capita	Unemployment Rate 1996
Newfoundland	$ 9 958	$18 047	19.4%
Prince Edward Island	2 591	19 256	14.5%
Nova Scotia	18 760	20 632	12.6%
New Brunswick	15 833	20 218	11.7%
Quebec	174 422	24 433	11.8%
Ontario	315 069	29 299	9.1%
Manitoba	26 333	23 640	7.5%
Saskatchewan	24 281	24 520	6.6%
Alberta	85 411	31 671	7.0%
British Columbia	103 400	27 771	8.9%

Sources: Adapted from CANSIM Database, Matrix Nos. 2623–2631, 4997, 4998, and 6950; Labour Force Annual Averages, 1996, Catalogue No. 71-220, February 1997; and the Statistics Canada Web site: http://www.statcan.ca.

The table generally indicates three categories of provinces: three rich ones, Ontario, Alberta, and British Columbia; four poor ones, the Atlantic provinces; and three intermediate provinces, Quebec, Manitoba, and Saskatchewan. Quebec has a larger economy than any province other than Ontario, of course, but this figure is not so impressive when expressed on a per capita basis.

EQUALIZATION PAYMENTS

In addition to developing national social programs and assisting various industries in a uniform national policy, successive governments have focused on two principal means to deal with the specific question of regional–economic disparities. One is to give federal funding to have-not provincial *governments*, and the other is to provide grants to individual *firms* in designated have-not regions of the country.

In 1957 Ottawa finally responded to repeated demands and began to make *equalization payments*. These annual cash grants to the have-not provinces are designed to allow them to raise their services to an acceptable national level but can be spent for any purpose. In other words, they are unconditional grants, with no strings attached. The sums involved are quite impressive, as Table 2.3 reveals.

TABLE 2.3 EQUALIZATION PAYMENTS, 1998–99

Quebec	$4 108 000 000	New Brunswick	$896 000 000
Nova Scotia	1 211 000 000	Saskatchewan	135 000 000
Manitoba	1 065 000 000	P.E.I.	201 000 000
Newfoundland	976 000 000	Total:	$8 587 000 000

Source: Department of Finance, "Federal Transfers to Provinces and Territories" (February 1997). Reproduced with the permission of the Minister of Supply and Services Canada, 1997.

REGIONAL ECONOMIC DEVELOPMENT PROGRAMS

The second means of trying to reduce regional–economic disparities is to establish federal *regional economic development programs*. The basic thrust of these programs is to designate those parts of the country in need of economic assistance (essentially the whole country except southern Ontario), and then to provide grants to firms that would locate or expand existing operations in such areas. Some grants also go to provinces or municipalities in order to provide the basic infrastructure that might attract industry, such as highways, water and sewage systems, and industrial parks. The latest reorganization of these programs occurred in 1987, creating several separate regional economic development agencies, principally the Atlantic Canada Opportunities Agency (ACOA), Federal Economic Development in Northern Ontario (FEDNOR), the Department of Western Economic Diversification (WED), and the Federal Offices of Regional Development for Quebec and Ontario (FORD-Q and FORD-O). Most observers, however, are increasingly dubious about their effectiveness.

Class Cleavages

Turning from geographic disparities to inequalities in individual incomes, we come to class cleavages. The concept of class is not as clear-cut as that of region, and Canadians are generally more conscious of their regional and ethnic identities. Nevertheless, class is an important generator of political activity in most countries, and Canada has its deep-seated class cleavages as well. This part of the chapter will begin by discussing various definitions and measurements of class and then examine the political role of the different classes.

Defining and Measuring Class

When dealing with the concept of class, it is customary to start with Karl Marx, who predicted that every capitalist economy would produce a class system consisting primarily of the *bourgeoisie*, the owners of the means of production, and the *proletariat*, the workers. The proletariat would sell their labour for a price; the bourgeoisie would pay them as little as possible (and less than they were worth), thereby accumulating profit or surplus value. While religion and the prospect of a pleasant afterlife might keep them content for a while, the workers would eventually come to resent their low wages and their state of exploitation, and finally engage in a violent revolt.

Today's neo-Marxists usually add the *middle class* to Marx's original analysis. The middle class is often divided between the upper middle class, made up of affluent farmers, small business people, and self-employed professionals, and the new middle class—civil servants, teachers, and other salaried professionals.

Those social scientists who are not neo-Marxists commonly divide individuals and families into the upper, middle, and working classes, based on such interrelated factors as income, occupation, and education. Using these measures, the divisions between the classes are less clear-cut than in the neo-Marxist analysis. Although such inequalities both produce and result from inequalities in other characteristics such as education and occupation, income is the simplest measure to use in discussing this subject.

One means of measuring income inequality is to divide the population into five equal groups, or quintiles, from highest to lowest income and to indicate the share of total income received by each group. Table 2.4 presents such proportions for the year 1994; it also shows that the income shares before social program transfers (such as social assistance) were even more inequitable, and how the tax system takes a little away from the rich to redistribute to the poor. Thus, even after taxes and transfers, the highest 20 percent of the population still receive over 40 percent of the total income, while the lowest 20 percent receive just 5.7 percent.

TABLE 2.4 INCOME SHARES BY QUINTILES BEFORE AND AFTER TRANSFERS, AND AFTER TAX, 1994

	Income before Transfers	Total Money Income	Income after Tax
Lowest	0.6	4.7	5.7
Second	7.1	10.2	11.4
Middle	16.4	16.7	17.5
Fourth	26.7	24.8	24.7
Highest	49.2	43.6	40.7

Source: Adapted from Statistics Canada, Income after Tax, Distributions by Size in Canada, 1994, Cat. No. 13-210-XPB, March 1996. Reproduced with the permission of the Minister of Supply and Services Canada, 1997.

Another problem in using the concept of class is the distinction between "objective" and "subjective" class. Objective class refers to the class into which analysts place a person, according to criteria such as type of work or level of income, while subjective class means the class to which people think or feel they belong, even if it contradicts objective standards. Many people who consider themselves to be middle class would be categorized as working class by social scientists.

The Upper Class

Canada possesses many fabulously rich entrepreneurs and some of the wealthiest families on earth. In 1996, *The Financial Post* estimated the worth of Ken Thomson at $8.2 billion, and the Irving family at $7.5 billion.[7] Thomson owns a large number of newspapers in Canada and abroad and many other firms in the information and publishing fields. The Irving family owns most of New Brunswick, including large tracts of woodlands, pulp mills, all the English-language daily newspapers in the province, oil refineries, gas stations, shipbuilding companies, trucking firms, bus lines, railways, and potato operations.

The next tier of wealthy Canadian families includes the Montreal branch of the Bronfman family ($2.9 billion), the Eaton family ($1.7 billion), Ted Rogers ($1.4 billion), Galen Weston ($1.3 billion), the McCain family ($1.2 billion), and Paul Desmarais ($1 billion). Among the rest of the richest 30 Canadians are Jimmy Pattison, Izzy Asper, the Bombardier, Bata, Jodrey, and Richardson families, Hal Jackman, Ron Joyce, André Chagnon, Pierre Péladeau, Jean Coutu, the Ontario Bronfmans, and Conrad Black.

Another category of wealthy Canadians are the corporate chief executive officers who do not actually own their firms, as do those mentioned above. The annual remuneration packages of bank presidents and other top CEOs, including the value of salary, bonus, incentives, shares, and other benefits, now routinely exceed $1 million.[8]

The general lines of the public policy demands of the economic elite are easily drawn. Essentially, they want to be left alone: cut government spending on social programs so that their taxes can be minimized, and reduce the annual government deficit and the accumulated national debt. If taxes are necessary, avoid corporate and progressive individual taxes as much as possible, and provide generous loopholes, write-offs, and tax shelters. Minimize government regulation, labour legislation, and environmental protection, as well as anti-combines laws and other restrictions on corporate takeovers.

Governments have normally responded to such demands with alacrity. The Canadian state gives priority to big business demands in the first place because it depends on the private sector to create jobs. Second, corporate executives and the politicians often come from the same ranks, including prime ministers and ministers of Finance. Brian Mulroney and Paul Martin provide ideal examples. Third, companies have many avenues of influence available: making a direct, personal pitch, using professional lobby firms to help them make contact with public decision-makers for a fee, and taking advantage of their membership in pressure groups. Among the hundreds of business pressure groups in existence, the Business Council on National Issues is probably most powerful, representing as it does the chief executive officers of the 150 largest firms in the country. Finally, throughout their history both the Conservative and Liberal parties have been primarily financed by large corporate contributions. This has changed somewhat in recent years, but a link between corporate contributions and general public policy, if not to specific corporate favours, is not difficult to establish.

Thus, for example, a minimum tax on rich individuals and large corporations was established in the 1980s, but significant numbers continue to avoid it. The progressive nature of the personal income tax was reduced when 10 tax brackets were reduced to 3, and capital gains continue to be taxed at a lower rate than other forms of income. In her book *Behind Closed Doors*, Linda McQuaig shows how the rich use their political influence to obtain tax breaks that are paid for by those with lesser incomes.[9] Personal and corporate income taxes are riddled with loopholes, and Canada is one of the few countries in the world without a tax on wealth or inheritance.

Three principal exceptions to this corporate pressure to minimize the role of government must be noted. First, while the economic elite demands that government minimize spending on others, it often expects sizable chunks of public funds for itself, such as in government contracts. A second exception is the rare occasion on which the economic elite has actually favoured new social programs. Motives here include increasing the purchasing power of the poor and working class, reducing the amounts that companies themselves have to pay in employee benefits, and ensuring the basic stability of society so that upper classes do not have to worry about violent protests from the poor or unemployed. In the third place, business leaders expect government to provide basic utilities or infrastructure that will decrease their costs or increase their profits.

The Middle Class

While the middle class—divided between the "upper" and "new" components—is far from being a unified force, its members are normally well educated, and most are economically comfortable, since they receive above-average levels of income. They own their homes and cars and usually have assorted other material possessions. While they enjoy such tax shelters as RRSPs, members of the middle class pay a disproportionate amount of the taxes to finance government programs of all kinds. A study of federal tax changes between 1984 and 1988, for example, showed that while those earning under $13 000 and those over $117 000 gained, the hardest hit were middle-class families making between $29 000 and $43 000.[10] Thus it is on the "middle middle" and especially "lower middle" classes that the federal and provincial personal tax increases in recent years have fallen most heavily.

The Working Class

The working class is generally identified as doing manual or routine work. The typical member of the working class is engaged in resource exploitation, assembly line production, secretarial and clerical work, sales, and a variety of crafts and trades. Less affluent farmers could also be included. Normally lacking postsecondary education, members of the working class usually receive less income than those in the middle class.

Karl Marx's predictions of a violent proletarian revolt were dealt a blow when governments legalized trade unions and extended the franchise to the working class. Nevertheless, most governments and companies have been hostile toward the formation of unions, and Canada has experienced a large number of violent strikes, either over the formation of a union or over its subsequent demands. Among the key labour struggles in Canadian history were the 1919 Winnipeg General Strike, the 1937 General Motors Strike in Oshawa, the 1945 Ford Strike in Windsor, the 1949 Asbestos Strike in Quebec, and the wood-workers' strike in Newfoundland in 1959.[11] While legislation dealing with conciliation, mediation, arbitration, picketing, labour standards, occupational health and safety, and compensation for injury on the job is ostensibly passed to protect the working class, governments usually avoid offending their own corporate supporters in the design or implementation of labour laws.

Others things being equal, it is in the interests of members of the working class to belong to a union: unionized employees usually have higher wages, more adequate benefits, better working conditions, and more protection against dismissal than those who do not engage in collective bargaining. Nearly 80 percent of unionized workers have private pension coverage, for example, compared to only 30 percent of those who are not unionized.[12] In spite of these facts, the rate of unionization among "paid workers" in Canada is very low. Total union membership in January 1996 was 4 033 000 or 33.9 percent of the 11 900 000 potential members in the country.[13]

Moreover, the number of blue-collar jobs is declining in such areas as resource industries, construction, and manufacturing, where unionization used to be most common. New jobs in the "post-industrial" society are largely found in sales and services, especially in the private sector, where workers are traditionally part-time, poorly paid, and hard to organize. Lacking a union, and given the nature of their job, those in sales and service occupations are not as likely to be class-conscious or to develop social democratic values as those who produce goods.

The composition of the unionized workforce is also changing in another sense. Once made up primarily of private-sector, male, manual workers, it is increasingly composed of public-sector unions, and women now constitute over 41 percent of union members. In 1996, a higher proportion of employees were unionized in public administration than any other sector. Public-sector unions make up three of the seven largest unions in the country: the Canadian Union of Public Employees, 455 800 members; National Union of Public and General Employees, 310 600; National Automobile, Aerospace, Transportation and General Workers, 205 000; United Food and Commercial Workers, 185 000; United Steelworkers, 170 000; Public Service Alliance, 167 800; and the Communication, Energy, and Paperworkers, 165 200.

As far as labour legislation is concerned, the principal federal interest is in the Unemployment Insurance program, now called "Employment Insurance." This program was introduced in 1941 to tide workers over between jobs, but given the high national unemployment rates in many years since, and the even higher rates in certain regions in every year, it is relied upon much more heavily than was originally anticipated. With such large numbers of workers drawing on the fund, it has become both a vital source of individual and regional income and the subject of almost daily political controversy.

The Canadian Labour Congress is the main lobbying body for over 2.5 million workers. The CLC thus has the largest membership of any pressure group in the country and represents the greatest number of voters. Its influence is diminished, however, by its outsider status in Ottawa, as well as by the fact that not all unions belong to it. The historic factionalism within the Canadian union movement has not helped the cause of the working class.[14]

The Poor

The poor can be defined as those living below the poverty line. Different organizations use different definitions of poverty, and the lines vary according to location and size of family unit, but a wide consensus exists among them. The most common are those of Statistics Canada and the Canadian Council on Social Development.

Statistics Canada and the National Council of Welfare (NCW) use the bureaucratic term "low-income cut-off," calculated as follows: any individual or family that spends more than 56.2 percent of its income on food, clothing, and shelter is living in poverty (the average family spends 36.2 percent of its income on these three necessities). These Statistics Canada figures are rather conservative, so the Canadian Council on Social Development (CCSD) uses a different standard: anyone living on less than 50 percent of the average disposable income for a family unit of equivalent size. Table 2.5 shows the proportion of the population below the Statistics Canada/NCW and CCSD poverty lines in selected years.

TABLE 2.5 PERCENT OF POPULATION BELOW THE POVERTY LINE IN SELECTED YEARS

	Below the NCW Line				Below the CCSD Line			
	1969	1979	1986	1993	1973	1979	1986	1991
Families	20.8	13.1	12.3	14.8	17.4	21.6	21.2	21.1
Unattached individuals	42.8	40.3	34.2	37.1	39.7	41.3	36.7	37.1
Total households	23.1	15.7	14.9	17.4	23.3	27.4	25.9	26.3

Sources: *National Council of Welfare*, Poverty Profile 1993; *Canadian Council on Social Development*, The Canadian Fact Book on Poverty—1994. *Reproduced with permission.*

Depending on which poverty line is used, Canada had between 4 775 000 (NCW) and 6 054 000 (CCSD) people living in poverty in the 1991–93 period. The large group of near-poor that exists just above the arbitrary poverty line justifies using figures higher in this range, that is, over five million poor. Both organizations agree that the proportion of Canadians living in poverty has increased during the 1990s.

The aspect of poverty that is probably most heartbreaking and most intractable is that 30 percent of the poor people in Canada are children. While more than half of poor children live in two-parent families, over 40 percent of the children below the poverty line live with lone-parent mothers. Over 60 percent of such mothers exist in a state of poverty; moreover, they are further below the poverty line than other groups. In 1986, the high-school drop-out rate among children from poor families was 2.2 times the rate of others. This tie between low income and low education is self-perpetuating. *The Canadian Fact Book on Poverty* asserts that "the educational opportunities of children, whether at the primary, secondary or post-secondary level, must not be limited by the economic circumstances of their parents."[15] It also documents how children from low-income families stand out from their better-off peers:

> They are less healthy, have less access to skill-building activities, have more destructive habits and behaviours, live more stressful lives, and are subject to more humiliation. In short, they have less stable and less secure existences and as a result they are likely to be less secure as adults.[16]

Many poor people work full time, and others part time; the poor can be about equally divided between those who work and those who are unemployed or unemployable. The working poor try to scrape by on the minimum wage or on more than one low-paying job, and are sometimes better off if they go on social assistance. Rather than raising the minimum wage, however, some provincial governments actually reduced welfare benefits in the last half of the 1990s.

One of the great weaknesses of the poor in the political system is that they are generally unorganized and collectively inarticulate. They lack the skills to organize effectively as pressure groups, primarily because they are without the education, money, and time to develop such skills. Three main pressure groups exist to speak for the poor in the cacophony of the political process: the Canadian Council on Social Development, the National Council of Welfare, and the National Anti-Poverty Organization. Nevertheless, no one should expect any degree of equality in the struggle among interest groups representing different classes.

NOTES

1. For example, Pierre Berton, *The National Dream* and *The Last Spike* (Toronto: McClelland and Stewart, 1970 and 1971); Robert Chodos, *The CPR: A Century of Corporate Welfare* (Toronto: Lorimer, 1973).
2. Task Force on Canadian Unity, *A Future Together* (Ottawa: Supply and Services, 1979), 26–27.
3. Wallace Clement and Daniel Drache, *A Practical Guide to Canadian Political Economy* (Toronto: Lorimer, 1978), 9–14.

4. Rand Dyck, *Provincial Politics in Canada*, 3rd ed. (Scarborough: Prentice-Hall Canada, 1995).
5. David Kilgour, *Uneasy Patriots: Western Canadians in Confederation* (Edmonton: Lone Pine Publishers, 1988); *Inside Outer Canada* (Lone Pine, 1990); Don Braid and Sydney Sharpe, *Breakup: Why the West Feels Left Out of Canada* (Toronto: Key Porter Books, 1990).
6. Donald Smiley, *The Federal Condition in Canada* (Toronto: McGraw-Hill Ryerson, 1987), 159.
7. *The Financial Post Magazine*, January 1996.
8. *The Globe and Mail*, 10 April 1995; *Globe and Mail Report on Business*, July 1995; *The Toronto Star*, 19 June 1995.
9. Linda McQuaig, *Behind Closed Doors* (Toronto: Penguin, 1987).
10. Allan Maslove, *Tax Reform in Canada: The Process and Impact* (Halifax: Institute for Research on Public Policy, 1989).
11. Irving Abella, *On Strike* (Toronto: James Lewis & Samuel, 1974); Walter Stewart, *Strike!* (Toronto: McClelland and Stewart, 1977), ch. 4.
12. Economic Council of Canada, *Legacies, 1989 Annual Review* (Ottawa: Supply and Services, 1989), 45.
13. Statistics Canada, *CALURA, Part II—Labour Unions, 1992*, cat. no. 71-202, March 1994.
14. Gad Horowitz, *Canadian Labour in Politics* (Toronto: University of Toronto Press, 1968).
15. Canadian Council on Social Development, *The Canadian Fact Book on Poverty—1989*, 93.
16. Ibid., *1994*, 2.

FURTHER READING

Abella, Irving, ed. *On Strike*. Toronto: James Lewis & Samuel, 1974.
Braid, Don, and Sydney Sharpe. *Breakup: Why the West Feels Left Out of Canada*. Toronto: Key Porter Books, 1990.
Brooks, Stephen, and Andrew Stritch. *Business and Government in Canada*. Scarborough: Prentice-Hall Canada, 1991.
Clement, Wallace, ed. *Understanding Canada: Building on the New Canadian Political Economy*. Montreal: McGill–Queen's University Press, 1996.
Coleman, William. *Business and Politics: A Study of Collective Action*. Montreal: McGill–Queen's University Press, 1988.
Dyck, Rand. *Provincial Politics in Canada*. 3rd ed. Scarborough: Prentice-Hall Canada, 1995.
Gibbins, Roger. *Conflict and Unity*. 3rd ed. Scarborough: Nelson Canada, 1994.
Kilgour, David. *Inside Outer Canada*. Edmonton: Lone Pine Publishers, 1990.
Langdon, Steven, et al. *In the Public Interest: The Value of Public Services* (Prescott: Voyageur Publishing, 1995).
Lewis, David. *Louder Voices: The Corporate Welfare Bums*. Toronto: James Lewis & Samuel, 1972.
McQuaig, Linda. *Behind Closed Doors*. Toronto: Penguin, 1987.
Palmer, Bryan. *Working-Class Experience: The Rise and Reconstitution of Canadian Labour, 1800–1980*. Toronto: Butterworth, 1983.
Ross, David, and Richard Shillington. *The Canadian Fact Book on Poverty—1994*. Ottawa: Canadian Council on Social Development, 1994.
Savoie, Donald J. *Regional Economic Development: Canada's Search for Solutions*. 2nd ed. Toronto: University of Toronto Press, 1992.

Chapter 3

French Canada and the Quebec Question

Among all ethnic/cultural/linguistic issues in Canadian politics, it is the English–French cleavage that has always been of greatest significance. The prominence of the French question in Canada primarily reflects the large number of people involved, their historical rights, and the territorial base of Canada's francophones in Quebec. The French–English cleavage is at least as problematic as the regional–economic one in Canadian politics, and the two cleavages reinforce each other in the question of Quebec's place in Confederation.

This chapter begins by examining French–English relations up to 1960. It then discusses the Quiet Revolution in Quebec in the 1960s, and the Quebec and French–English issues up to 1982. The last sections deal with Quebec–Canada relations since 1982, including the Meech Lake and Charlottetown accords, and the future of French-English relations.

Historical Overview of French–English Relations
Pre-Confederation Developments

Almost every Canadian political decision for over 200 years has reflected the French–English division to some extent, and the tensions that currently threaten the continued existence of the country can probably best be understood in historical context. The French first colonized what is now the province of Quebec, and populated it with farmers, clergy, and seigneurs. But when the British defeated the French on the Plains of Abraham in 1759, the conquerors took control of the non-agricultural economy and the government.

The people, however, continued to speak French and attend the Roman Catholic Church, which became a highly influential and autonomous organization. It would probably have been impossible to make Quebec into an Anglo-Protestant colony; in any case, the British, after a brief attempt at assimilation, exhibited a policy of tolerance and accommodation, and in the 1774 Quebec Act they guaranteed the French their religious rights and their own system of civil law.

A large component of "English" immigrants—especially the United Empire Loyalists from the new United States—moved into what is now Ontario in the 1780s. The colony was thus divided into two: Lower Canada (Quebec) would be essentially French-Catholic, and Upper Canada (Ontario) would be Anglo-Protestant. In the 1830s conflict erupted in both colonies between the assembly and the executive, which in the case of Lower Canada translated into discord between French (assembly) and English (executive). After the colonies were reunited by the 1840 Act of Union, Lord Durham believed that the ethnic problem in Canada could only be solved by another attempt to assimilate the French. On the contrary, the French language came to be increasingly used along with English in the government in the pre-Confederation period. Cabinets were usually alliances between English and French leaders, and the legislature operated on the informal principle of the double majority—legislation had to have the approval of a majority of members from both sections of the colony.

Given this historical evolution, the cultural guarantees of section 133 of the Constitution Act, 1867, are perfectly understandable. Both French and English were given official status in all operations of the federal Parliament, and laws would be passed in both languages. Both languages could also be used in whatever federal courts were later established, as well as in the legislature and courts of Quebec. None of these constitutional provisions was particularly controversial in 1867.

Post-Confederation Conflicts

Although the two language groups have been regularly accommodated in government circles since 1867, a number of serious linguistic/ethnic conflicts erupted from the time of Confederation to the Second World War. The first was the Riel Rebellion, led by French-Catholic-Métis Louis Riel, precipitating the creation of the province of Manitoba in 1870. In 1885, he re-emerged in what is now Saskatchewan to lead the second Riel Rebellion on behalf of Western Natives and Métis who had been treated shamefully by the government. After quelling the rebellion, the federal government charged Riel with treason. This raised ethnic and religious tensions across the country to a fever pitch, for while Anglo-Protestants regarded Riel as a murderer, traitor, and madman, French-Catholics believed he was a patriot and a saint. Riel's hanging heightened the level of French-Catholic outrage across the country, especially in Quebec, and permanently damaged the close attachment of the people of that province to the Conservative Party.

The second linguistic conflict occurred in Manitoba. The small settlement was about equally divided between French and English, and at Riel's insistence, the 1870 Manitoba Act followed the Quebec precedent of giving the two languages official status in the new province's legislature and courts. After its creation, however, Manitoba attracted thousands of English-speaking immigrants and others who chose to identify with the anglophone community. Hence, in 1890, the anglophone majority passed the Official Language Act removing the official status of French in the province's legislature and courts.

The third linguistic conflict concerned minority French-language education rights in Ontario. In 1913 the Whitney government's Regulation 17 virtually abolished the use of French in the Ontario school system; English was to become the sole language of instruction after the third year, and the study of French as a subject was limited to one hour a day.

The conscription crisis of the First World War was the fourth major French–English confrontation. Having little in the way of standing armed forces, the Canadian military effort rested on appeals for volunteers. These appeals initially had promising results, but as reinforcements were needed later in the war, few recruits came forward. The government therefore decided to resort to conscription—compulsory military service—in 1917. Prime Minister Robert Borden knew that French Canada generally felt indifferent to the conflict and that conscription would divide the country along ethnic lines. The prime minister therefore appealed to Liberal leader Wilfrid Laurier to join him in a coalition government. Laurier refused the offer, although most of the English-speaking Liberal MPs did join in a Union Government. The subsequent enforcement of conscription entailed considerable violence, including a riot in Quebec City in the spring of 1918 that left four people dead and many others injured. This confrontation destroyed what little French-Canadian support for the Conservative Party was left after the execution of Louis Riel.

Ontario repealed Regulation 17 in 1927 and French–English tensions returned to their normal, controllable level until they were inflamed by the fifth ethnic conflict, another conscription crisis during the Second World War. But in 1939 Canada was led by Liberal Prime Minister Mackenzie King, with a strong contingent of ministers and MPs from Quebec. King knew that conscription would be resisted in French Canada, so on the basis of the slogan "conscription if necessary, but not necessarily conscription," he managed to postpone the adoption of compulsory military service until almost the end of the war.

....

The French–English Cleavage, 1960–1982
The Quiet Revolution: Quebec in the 1960s

Until 1960, Quebec was basically a traditional, conservative, rural, poorly educated, patronage-oriented society, heavily influenced by the Roman Catholic Church. Dominated by the authoritarian Premier Maurice Duplessis from 1935 onward, the inward-looking population was taught that only he could protect them from evil external influences, such as Ottawa. The Quebec of the past 40 years, however, is quite a different province and society. Since 1960, Quebec francophones have experienced a "Quiet Revolution," consisting of a dramatic change of values and attitudes—especially toward the state—a new collective self-confidence, and a new brand of nationalism. These features of the new Quebec had many implications for French–English relations in both the Quebec and Canadian political systems.

Quebec's Changes and Demands

The government of Jean Lesage (1960–66) took over many functions previously administered by the Church.[1] The most important of these, education, was radically modernized, but health and welfare programs were also made public rather than charitable responsibilities. With the nationalization of private power companies, Hydro-Québec became a huge Crown corporation supplying all the electricity in the province and serving as an engine of economic development. Lesage also reformed almost every piece of legislation on the books, especially labour and electoral laws, added reams of new ones, and created many government agencies. All these new and expanded public responsibilities required substantial additional revenues, and Lesage put immense pressure on Ottawa to increase federal–provincial grants, to allow Quebec to opt out of the conditions attached to them, and to give the province a greater share of joint taxation. In areas of provincial jurisdiction, Quebec began to move toward distinctive programs, designing its own pension plan, which was then used as a model for the Canada Pension Plan. As time went on, the province began to demand ever larger jurisdiction, leading to perpetual federal–provincial discord.

Federally oriented Quebec francophones such as future prime minister Pierre Trudeau began to demand that French be used as a language equal to English in the corridors of power in Ottawa. This group of Québécois was also concerned about the fate of francophone minorities in the other provinces. The new self-confidence of the Québécois inspired these dwindling minorities to greater self-assertiveness.

FEDERAL RESPONSES

During the 1960s, the federal government grappled somewhat haphazardly with these demands. The Diefenbaker government (1957–63) introduced simultaneous interpretation into Parliament, began printing federal government cheques in a bilingual format, and appointed a French-Canadian governor general. Immediately upon taking office, the Pearson government (1963–68) established the Royal Commission on Bilingualism and Biculturalism. Pearson also gave Quebec and the other provinces more federal funds and taxation power, removed conditions from many shared-cost programs, and permitted Quebec to make international arrangements with France and other francophone countries. Since the federal Parliament and courts were already theoretically bilingual, the main gap in official bilingualism at the national level was in the executive branch, where English was essentially the working language of the public service, at least at policymaking levels. Pearson therefore introduced the Official Languages Act to make the Canadian public service bilingual, and since its passage under Trudeau in 1969 Canada has become officially and effectively bilingual in its federal institutions. Ottawa also began to support French immersion educational programs as well as to assist francophone minorities in other provinces in order to try to stem their increasing assimilation into the anglophone majorities.

The question of French–English relations, or "national unity," was the principal political issue throughout the Trudeau era (1968–79, 1980–84). At that point it became clearer that two basic models existed to deal with the problem. The first was to recognize Quebec as the homeland of French Canada and to give that province powers and resources to protect and promote its linguistic and cultural distinctiveness. Quebec would be essentially "French" and the rest of Canada primarily "English." The second option was to treat Quebec as "une province comme les autres" and to promote bilingualism at the federal level and in the other provinces so that each Canadian could use either language anywhere in the country. English Canadians had difficulty accepting these demands that seemed excessive and contradictory: making Quebec more French and more autonomous at the same time as promoting French in Ottawa and the other provinces. Most English Canadians did not understand that the two demands came largely from two different groups of francophones, one that concentrated on Quebec and the other that wanted to expand French Canada beyond that province. Trudeau fought against recognizing Quebec as the homeland of French Canada and opposed giving that province any special status or power on the ground that this would be the first step toward separation. Part of Trudeau's popularity in English Canada stemmed from the perception that he was "anti-Quebec," but he was passionately "pro-French" in promoting French power and bilingualism in Ottawa and across the country.[2]

THE SEPARATIST OPTION

During the 1960s, advocates of a third option—Quebec separatism—began to emerge, most of them committed to democratic processes. One wing of the separatist movement, however, the Front de Libération du Québec (FLQ), believed that the normal political process was not responding quickly enough to the demands of the Quiet Revolution, and resorted to violence. Its periodic bombings killed several people and injured many others. In October 1970, two small cells of the FLQ kidnapped a British diplomat, James Cross, and abducted and murdered Quebec cabinet minister Pierre Laporte. Trudeau invoked the War Measures Act, giving the police and armed forces special powers to quell the violence, and arresting over 400 innocent, peaceful separatist supporters in the process. By crushing the FLQ, by giving French Canadians more clout in Ottawa, and by guaranteeing pan-Canadian bilingualism in the Constitution in 1982, Trudeau hoped to undercut any Quebec demand for special status or separatism in the defence of French Canada.[3]

Quebec–Canada Relations, 1970–1982

In the aftermath of the FLQ crisis, the first Robert Bourassa government in Quebec (1970–76) passed Bill 22 to give primacy to the French language in many spheres in the province, such as in the operations and documents of public authorities. As far as education was concerned, immigrant children had to show "sufficient knowledge" of English before being allowed to go to an English-language school. This was an attempt to have such children join the majority French linguistic group in the province rather than become "English," as so many previous immigrants had done. In fact, relying on immigration to bolster the francophone segment of the population became a vital point after the French-Canadian birthrate plummeted in the 1960s. Bill 22 also aimed at the francization of the private sector by pressuring companies to use French as the language of internal corporate operations. The more that Quebec moved in the direction of French unilingualism, of course, the greater was English Canada's resistance to Trudeau's policy of national bilingualism, and the greater the number of anglophones who left Quebec.

The Parti Québécois was elected to office in 1976 under René Lévesque with an even more nationalistic program.[4] Faced with a hostile Trudeau government in Ottawa, the PQ made few gains in provincial autonomy. But it did pass Bill 101, the Charter of the French Language, which considerably extended Bill 22 in making French the predominant language in the province. It generally turned the persuasive and optional aspects of Bill 22 into coercive and mandatory ones. It made French the only official language of the legislature (although laws continued to be translated unofficially into English); only individuals (not corporations) could use English in Quebec courts; essentially the only children who could go to English schools in the province were those whose parents had done so; and all commercial signs had to be in French only. All four of these clauses were subsequently ruled unconstitutional by the courts, but in other ways Bill 101 still stands, and French continues to be the official language of the province.

In 1980, the PQ government held a referendum on the question of pursuing a more independent relationship with Canada called "sovereignty-association." Many prominent politicians, including Trudeau, Justice Minister Jean Chrétien, and several provincial premiers, encouraged Quebeckers to defeat the PQ proposal, promising them "constitutional renewal" if they did so. When sovereignty-association was turned down by a vote of 60 percent to 40 percent, new federal–provincial constitutional negotiations began, culminating in the Constitution Act, 1982.[5] Ironically, even though the whole effort was supposed to appeal to the residents of Quebec, that province alone objected to the act as reflecting the Trudeau vision of a bilingual Canada rather than recognizing the distinctive francophone character of Quebec. Nevertheless, it became law in all parts of the country. As far as language was concerned, the act reinforced official bilingualism at the federal level and in New Brunswick, and guaranteed minority official language education in the provinces where numbers warranted. Many Quebeckers never forgave Trudeau and Chrétien for adopting such a significant constitutional document without Quebec's consent.

French–English Relations in the Other Provinces

The distribution of French and English communities in the various provinces is shown in Table 3.1. Defined by mother tongue, francophone minorities were located primarily in Ontario (484 265) and New Brunswick (237 570); as percentages they were largest in New Brunswick (34 percent), Ontario (5.3 percent), Manitoba (4.9 percent), Prince Edward Island (4.7 percent) and Nova Scotia (4.1 percent).

TABLE 3.1 MOTHER TONGUE AND HOME LANGUAGE BY PROVINCE, 1991 (PERCENTAGES)

	Mother Tongue		Home Language	
	English	French	English	French
Newfoundland	98.6	0.5	99.2	0.2
Prince Edward Island	94.2	4.5	97.3	2.3
Nova Scotia	93.6	4.1	96.3	2.5
New Brunswick	65.1	33.6	68.2	31.2
Quebec	9.7	82.2	11.2	83.0
Ontario	76.6	5.0	85.2	3.2
Manitoba	75.0	4.7	87.7	2.3
Saskatchewan	84.2	2.2	94.4	0.7
Alberta	82.5	2.3	91.5	0.8
British Columbia	80.5	1.6	89.6	0.4
North	66.1	2.7	76.5	1.3
Total	62.1	25.1	68.9	24.0

Source: Adapted from Statistics Canada, 1991 Census, Home Language and Mother Tongue, Cat. No. 93-317. Reproduced with permission of the Minister of Supply and Services Canada, 1997.

The Quebec government and most Quebeckers have been more concerned about internal linguistic matters than about what happened to French minorities in other provinces. Nevertheless, the Quiet Revolution led francophones outside Quebec to make a last-ditch attempt to preserve their language and culture. Often under pressure from Prime Minister Trudeau, some provincial premiers hoped that by extending rights or services to their francophone minority, they would help to forestall separatism in Quebec. Thus, many provinces have made considerable improvement in minority francophone rights since 1965. As mentioned, all were bound by the 1982 document to provide education in the minority official language where numbers warrant. All provinces were also committed to provide for criminal trials in French if demanded by the accused.

New Brunswick went farthest with its own Official Languages Act of 1969, which was constitutionalized at provincial request in 1982. New Brunswick also improved the Acadian educational system at all levels and the provision of provincial government services in both languages.

Even before Trudeau, Ontario began to provide for French-language secondary schools, and later established the right of every Franco-Ontarian to go to French-language school, whether or not numbers of francophones in the community warranted a school. Ontario then guaranteed French trials in the provincial courts and gradually extended French-language provincial services. Bill 8, becoming effective in 1989, provided for provincial government services in French in 22 designated regions of the province as well as for the translation of laws. Meanwhile, simultaneous interpretation in the legislature began in 1987, and Franco-Ontarians were granted the right to have French-language schools run by trustees elected by the francophone population.

Manitoba moved very slowly in this direction on its own, but was pushed by a series of Supreme Court of Canada decisions beginning in 1979. The 1890 Official Language Act was declared unconstitutional, and all laws had to be passed in both languages, trials had to be available in French, and most government documents had to be bilingual.

Quebec–Canada Relations since 1982

Three years after the controversial adoption of the Constitution Act, 1982, Quebeckers defeated the Parti Québécois and put Robert Bourassa's Liberals back in power. The second Bourassa government was first able to persuade the more receptive Mulroney government to allow Quebec to play a fuller part in the international French-speaking community, the Francophonie. Then, in 1988, the Supreme Court of Canada declared the sign provision of Bill 101 to be unconstitutional as a violation of freedom of expression, even "commercial expression." Bourassa responded by using the "notwithstanding clause" in the federal and Quebec charters of rights to pass Bill 178 providing for French-only outdoor signs but allowing some English signs indoors. Violating a constitutional right of anglophones in this way produced a vehement reaction among Anglo-Quebeckers and an anti-Quebec and anti-French response in the rest of the country. On the other hand, some aspects of Bill 101 were voluntarily relaxed in 1983, and in 1986 Quebec ensured the provision of social and health services in English to its anglophone minority. Moreover, when the five-year limit on Bill 178 ran out in 1993, Bourassa replaced it with Bill 86, which allowed bilingual signs outside as well as inside stores.

The Meech Lake Accord

The Constitution Act, 1982, including the Charter of Rights and Freedoms, was operative in Quebec even though the government of that province refused to endorse it. When he became prime minister, Brian Mulroney was determined that Quebec should symbolically rejoin the Canadian constitutional family "with honour and enthusiasm." In 1985, he asked Bourassa to outline his conditions for such a reunion. The Quebec government proceeded to make five demands:

1. constitutional recognition of Quebec as a "distinct society" within Canada

2. increased jurisdiction over immigration

3. participation in Supreme Court appointments

4. veto on constitutional amendments

5. opting out, with compensation, of national programs within provincial jurisdiction

Mulroney called the premiers together at Meech Lake in April 1987, where they unexpectedly agreed to a document that addressed Quebec's demands and became known as the Meech Lake Accord.[6] The prime minister secured unanimous provincial consent by extending to the other provinces the same rights as were demanded by Quebec, except for the distinct society clause. The document would also have constitutionalized the Supreme Court of Canada, provided for provincial participation in Senate appointments, and guaranteed annual first ministers' conferences on the constitution and the economy.

CRITICISM OF MEECH LAKE

Despite the relative ease with which it was drafted, the Meech Lake Accord generated much controversy. On the negative side, many critics did not approve of the designation of Quebec as a distinct society within Canada, and especially objected to the phrase that it was the role of the government and legislature of Quebec to "preserve and promote" that distinctiveness. No one was sure what implications the distinct society clause would have for the federal–provincial division of powers, leaving it for judicial clarification on an issue-by-issue basis. Some felt that in a federation all provinces had to have exactly equal status, and many argued that, armed with the distinct society clause, Quebec would immediately begin to challenge federal powers in a variety of fields. Others worried about the status of the English and Aboriginal minorities within Quebec, as well as the francophone minorities in other provinces.

A second objection to the Accord was that it enlarged the list of subjects that required unanimous provincial consent in the constitutional amending formula. Many critics felt that Senate reform and the transformation of the northern territories into provinces would be virtually impossible if they required agreement of all 10 provinces instead of only 7.

Much concern was expressed about the provision allowing provinces to opt out of national programs within provincial jurisdiction and be compensated by Ottawa. Fears were expressed that satisfactory new national social programs (such as daycare) would never materialize because provinces would be compensated for programs that merely met national *objectives*, not national *standards*.

Apart from criticizing what was in the Accord, many opponents faulted it for what was left out. The North was not allowed to nominate senators or Supreme Court judges; Aboriginal rights were not strengthened; and multiculturalism was ignored.

Others condemned the process through which the Accord had emerged—a behind-the-scenes gathering of (male) first ministers. In the post-Charter era, individual Canadians in all parts of the country insisted on being part of the constitutional amendment process; moreover, the primacy of Quebec's concerns was rejected by those given constitutional standing by the Charter—women, Aboriginals, and multicultural and other minorities.[7] The public now demanded more meaningful participation in the process of constitutional change.

IN DEFENCE OF MEECH LAKE

Those who defended Meech Lake argued that it would symbolically bring Quebec back into the constitutional fold and overcome the isolation and betrayal that many residents of that province felt after 1982. They called this the "Quebec round," and argued that Aboriginal, Northern, Western, and other concerns would be the next items on the constitutional agenda. Rather than promote incremental separatism, they felt that the Accord would give Quebec the flexibility to remain satisfied within Confederation. Supporters contended that in demographic, linguistic, and cultural terms, the distinctiveness of the Quebec society could not be denied. Those who felt that Trudeau's concept of official bilingualism was unrealistic for certain parts of the country thought that the Accord, in noting that French-speaking Canadians are centred in Quebec, might lessen linguistic tensions and the pressure for bilingualism.

Many political scientists and others had long argued that the provinces should have a say in the appointment of senators and Supreme Court judges. In the former case, this was because the Senate was intended to represent the provinces within Ottawa's decision-making structure; in the latter, because the Supreme Court rules on federal–provincial disputes. Many true federalists also contended that Ottawa should not be able to invade provincial jurisdiction with its spending power and set up national programs without provincial consent, as had often happened in the past.

According to the constitutional amending formula adopted in 1982, the Accord then had to be approved by the federal and all provincial legislatures within three years, that is, before June 1990. In most cases such legislative approval came rather easily, but new governments in Newfoundland, New Brunswick, and Manitoba had reservations about the Accord. Thus, with three provincial legislatures left to ratify it, Prime Minister Mulroney convened a first ministers' conference in Ottawa in May 1990. After a week of protracted, behind-the-scenes negotiations, the participants emerged with a modest companion resolution, adopted to the satisfaction of Manitoba and New Brunswick. Still with his substantive and procedural reservations, Clyde Wells would only agree to put it before the Newfoundland legislature, not to endorse it. Meanwhile, the Accord also ran into difficulty in the Manitoba legislature where Aboriginal MLA Elijah Harper delayed passage beyond the deadline because of the absence of any advance for Native peoples.

The Charlottetown Accord

With the death of the Meech Lake Accord, many Quebeckers felt betrayed again, and nationalist and separatist sentiment in Quebec mushroomed as the Quebec Liberals and Parti Québécois issued more nationalistic constitutional positions. Meanwhile, several Quebec members of Parliament quit the Conservative and

Liberal parties to sit as Quebec *indépendantistes* in the Bloc Québécois led by Lucien Bouchard, a former minister in the Mulroney cabinet.

The post-Meech position of the Quebec Liberal Party first appeared in the Allaire Report, calling for a highly decentralized federation in which Quebec and the other provinces would have almost all powers, a total of 22 more than they currently possessed. Then, the Bélanger–Campeau Committee Report, representing both major parties as well as other interests in the province, argued that Quebec should separate unless a satisfactory proposal for a new constitutional arrangement was forthcoming from the rest of Canada. It therefore recommended that a referendum on Quebec sovereignty be held in 1992.

The Mulroney government responded to these sentiments in November 1990 with the appointment of the Citizens' Forum on Canada's Future headed by CRTC Chair Keith Spicer. Reacting to the criticism that the public had been shut out of the Meech Lake negotiations, the Citizens' Forum encouraged ordinary Canadians to discuss constitutional issues and transmit their views to the committee.

The prime minister also appointed Joe Clark as the minister responsible for Constitutional Affairs and set up a special cabinet committee on Canadian Unity and Constitutional Negotiations. The committee agreed on a 28-point package of constitutional proposals in September 1991. Clark then tried to develop a collective federal–provincial–territorial–Aboriginal response to offer to Quebec before its constitutional referendum scheduled for the fall of 1992. After several rounds of negotiations, the nine premiers, territorial and Aboriginal leaders, and Clark all agreed on a comprehensive constitutional proposal in July 1992. Quebec Premier Bourassa considered it promising enough to return to the bargaining table for the first time since the demise of the Meech Lake Accord, and a full-fledged constitutional conference took place in Ottawa in mid-August. After nearly a week of hard bargaining, the leaders unanimously signed a new constitutional accord upon which they put the final touches in Charlottetown a week later.[8] The Charlottetown Accord had four main parts, two of primary concern to Quebec: the "Canada clause" and changes to the division of powers.

The Canada clause that began the Accord would recognize Quebec as a distinct society within Canada as well as enumerate the other fundamental values and characteristics of the country. These included democracy, the rule of law, a parliamentary and federal system, the Aboriginal peoples of Canada and their enhanced rights, official language minorities, cultural and racial diversity, individual and collective rights, gender equality, and the equality and diversity of the provinces.

The second main issue of interest to Quebec was the federal–provincial division of powers. As in the Meech Lake Accord, provinces could opt out of new national shared-cost programs set up within provincial jurisdiction and receive federal financial compensation if the programs met national objectives. In addition, Ottawa offered to withdraw from six fields at provincial request—forestry, mining, tourism, recreation, housing, and municipal and urban affairs—again with financial compensation. Culture and labour-market training would essentially become provincial powers, and the two levels would share jurisdiction in immigration, telecommunications, and regional development. Thus, beyond the immigration power in Meech Lake, provinces would now have full or partial power over 10 additional fields of public policy. In return for this increased decentralization of powers, Ottawa hoped to strengthen the economic union by eliminating interprovincial trade barriers, but had to settle for agreement in principle, with the issue to be negotiated later.

The other two major components of the Charlottetown Accord, Aboriginal self-government and the Triple-E Senate (equal provincial representation, elected, and effective), are dealt with elsewhere in this book, but it is appropriate to mention here some of the other ingredients in the Accord. Provisions of Meech Lake with respect to the Supreme Court of Canada were included, along with those concerning an annual meeting of first ministers, and changes in the constitutional amending formula, except that the creation of new provinces would no longer require unanimous consent. Ontario premier Bob Rae was successful in having a social charter added to the Constitution to guarantee rights to health care, social services, and education, along with workers' rights and protection for the environment. The guarantee of equalization payments was strengthened, and the federal reservation, disallowance, and declaratory powers were essentially removed.

THE 1992 REFERENDUM

The Accord would be of no effect until ratified by Parliament and the 10 provincial legislatures. Before ratification, however, the federal government announced that a national referendum would be held on the new constitutional deal on October 26, 1992—the same date selected by Quebec for its constitutional referendum, now on the Charlottetown Accord rather than sovereignty. The decision to hold such a nation-wide referendum was based on three main considerations: Alberta and B.C. laws required a referendum on constitutional amendments, so that three provinces would be voting on the Accord in any case; Meech Lake had been criticized for lack of public input; and public approval would lend legitimacy to the agreement and spur the 11 legislatures into speedy affirmative action.

On a national basis the referendum result was 55 percent no and 45 percent yes. Majorities voted no in Quebec, Nova Scotia, the four Western provinces, and the Yukon. Even though the referendum was not legally binding, there was no point in bringing the constitutional package before legislatures for ratification: the Charlottetown Accord was dead.

Public opinion polls showed that rather than basing their decision on the contents of the Accord as such, many of the people who voted no did so to vent their anger and frustration against Prime Minister Mulroney, the premiers, and politicians and governments in general. Voters were not in a generous frame of mind, and rather than seeing it as a multi-sided compromise, they generally felt that the Accord gave too much to others and not enough to themselves. Thus, the negative vote in Quebec was largely based on the view that the Accord did not give Quebec sufficient new powers, but many outside Quebec argued that that province got too much. Many Westerners did not see the proposed reforms to the Senate as sufficient protection of their interests in Ottawa, and many Aboriginal Canadians were dissatisfied with the provisions on Aboriginal self-government. Indeed, while the Accord was primarily designed to address the constitutional insecurity of Quebec, Aboriginal Canadians, and Western and smaller provinces, a majority in all three groups believed that their elites had not bargained hard enough.[9]

The Chrétien Government Record and the 1995 Referendum

After this disheartening if not traumatic experience, all federal parties decided to leave the constitutional issue alone, especially the Chrétien Liberals elected a year later on the promise that they would concentrate on improving the economy. In 1994, however, the Parti Québécois was returned to power in Quebec. With Ottawa largely ignoring the issue, the new Quebec premier, Jacques Parizeau, wanted a quick vote on a clear-cut separatist position. Others, however, including Bloc Québécois leader Lucien Bouchard, preferred a delayed vote on a scheme that retained significant ties to Canada. When the polls showed that Parizeau could not achieve the support of a majority of Quebec voters on the question of his choice, he succumbed to the pressure of public opinion (and of Bouchard), and provided for an extensive list of continuing links to Canada.[10]

This third Quebec referendum was held in October 1995. The proposal involved a convoluted question incorporating a kind of sovereignty that retained significant ties to the rest of Canada. In the final week of the campaign, Prime Minister Chrétien finally woke up to the possibility of a PQ victory, and made a vague promise of reform if the no vote prevailed.

The result of the referendum could not have been closer: 50.6 percent voted no, while 49.4 percent voted yes. Premier Parizeau promptly resigned the premiership in favour of Bloc leader Bouchard, who led observers to expect another referendum after the next provincial election. Fulfilling his last-minute promises, but not being able to persuade all provinces to make an actual amendment to the Constitution, Chrétien had Parliament pass a resolution recognizing Quebec as a distinct society within Canada. He also promised that regardless of the official constitutional amending formula, no constitutional amendments would be passed without the approval of each region of the country (including Quebec), and that labour-market training would be transferred from federal to provincial jurisdiction. The distinct society issue figured prominently in the 1997 election campaign that saw Chrétien's government returned to power. Chrétien then referred a hypothetical question to the Supreme Court of Canada, asking it to rule on the legality of a unilateral declaration of independence by Quebec.

The Future of French–English Relations

Given that francophones constitute about 25 percent of the Canadian electorate, given their historic constitutional rights, given their geographic concentration in Quebec and majority control of such a large province, and given their modern-day self-consciousness and self-confidence, the French fact in Canada cannot be ignored. If English Canada wants Quebec to remain part of the country, it cannot go back to the easy days of pre-1960 unilingualism and federal government domination.

Despite much confusion on the question, five alternatives can be identified:

- complete independence of Quebec (Parizeau)
- sovereignty of Quebec with links to Canada (Bouchard)
- Quebec as a distinct society within Canada (Bourassa, Mulroney, Chrétien, Charest, etc.)
- all provinces equal; strong central government; national bilingualism (Trudeau)
- all provinces equal; strong provinces; no bilingualism outside Quebec (Manning)

While Preston Manning's approach looks superficially acceptable to most sides of the conflict, many outside Quebec reject his idea of massive decentralization of federal powers. Moreover, his hostility toward bilingualism and refusal to see Quebec as distinct from other provinces makes his proposal a non-starter for most French Canadians. Trudeau wants to promote the bilingual character of the whole country and most or all of the provinces—a vision contending that French Canada extends from coast to coast to coast. Given the tiny proportion of residents who speak French in many provinces and in the North, however, and given the cool reception to the imposition of bilingualism in many parts of the country (as evidenced by the popularity of the Reform Party), it appears that the limits of national bilingualism have been reached. Meanwhile, Trudeau's opposition to the distinct society concept leads to rejection of his option in his home province. At least until the present time, the vast majority of Canadians outside Quebec would prefer a separate Quebec to one that was linked to Canada in the manner vaguely proposed by Lucien Bouchard.

If the other options are not realistic, it appears that the only way to accommodate the French presence within Canada is the "middle way."[11] Given that 85 percent of the French are located in Quebec and that 83 percent of Quebeckers are French-speaking, it is logical to recognize that Quebec is the heartland of French Canada. In the words of Brian Mulroney and Robert Bourassa, Quebec constitutes a distinct society within Canada. This approach would give that province special recognition and responsibility to protect itself in the North American English linguistic environment. Whether or not it is justified, Quebec has something of a "siege mentality" with respect to its language and culture, and language has replaced the Church as the focus of the French identity. The Quebec corporate elite is now a francophone group, and they, along with the new middle class in the Quebec public sector, see themselves benefiting from increased provincial autonomy.[12]

It may, however, be too late. In the early 1990s, especially in the wake of the Bill 178 controversy, many observers detected a visible decline in the will of both French and English to live together. Quebeckers felt increasingly self-confident about going it alone, and many English Canadians invited them to do so. The death of the Meech Lake Accord in 1990 caused many Quebeckers to feel rejected by English Canada, and support for the existing partnership fell to a new low on both sides. English-Canadian public opinion generally hoped that Quebec would remain in Canada, but it was neither prepared to grant that province much in the way of special powers nor to eviscerate the federal government in appeasement.

Between Pierre Trudeau and Preston Manning, English-Canadian opinion hardened toward the idea of recognizing Quebec as a distinct society within Canada.[13]

Nine provincial premiers (excluding Lucien Bouchard) gathered in Calgary in September 1997 to see if it would be productive to talk about the constitution again before Quebec's anticipated election in 1998 and referendum in 1999. The premiers' declaration tried to reconcile the "unique character of Quebec society" with the equality of all the provinces. While substituting "unique" for "distinct" and emphasizing provincial equality might attract some support in English Canada, however, it was less certain that it would appeal to most Quebeckers.

Points agreed to by provincial leaders from English Canada that could eventually lead to recognition of Quebec's "unique character":

1. All Canadians are equal and have rights protected by law.

2. All provinces, while diverse in their characteristics, have equality of status.

3. Canada is graced by a diversity, tolerance, compassion and an equality of opportunity that is without rival in the world.

4. Canada's gift of diversity includes Aboriginal peoples and cultures, the vitality of the English and French languages and a multicultural citizenry drawn from all parts of the world.

5. In Canada's federal system, where respect for diversity and equality underlies unity, the unique character of Quebec society, including its French-speaking majority, its culture and its tradition of civil law, is fundamental to the well being of Canada. Consequently, the legislature and government of Quebec have a role to protect and develop the unique character of Quebec society within Canada.

6. If any future constitutional amendment confers powers on one province, these powers must be available to all provinces.

7. Canada is a federal system where federal, provincial and territorial governments work in partnership while respecting each other's jurisdictions. Canadians want their governments to work co-operatively and with flexibility to ensure the efficiency ... of the federation. Canadians want their governments to work together particularly in

the delivery of their social programs. Provinces and territories renew their commitment to work in partnership with the government of Canada to best serve the needs of Canadians.

Notes

1. Dale Thomson, *Jean Lesage and the Quiet Revolution* (Toronto: Macmillan, 1984).
2. Kenneth McRoberts, *Misconceiving Canada: The Struggle for National Unity* (Toronto: Oxford University Press, 1997).
3. Ron Haggart and A.E. Golden, *Rumours of War* (Toronto: New Press, 1971); Denis Smith, *Bleeding Hearts … Bleeding Country: Canada and the Quebec Crisis* (Edmonton: Hurtig, 1971):
4. Graham Fraser, *René Lévesque and the Parti Québécois in Power* (Toronto: Macmillan, 1984).
5. Roy Romanow, J. Whyte, and H. Leeson, *Canada … Notwithstanding: The Making of the Constitution 1976–1982* (Toronto: Methuen, 1984); Edward McWhinney, *Canada and the Constitution 1979–82: Patriation and the Charter of Rights* (Toronto: University of Toronto Press, 1982).
6. Michael Behiels, ed., *The Meech Lake Primer: Conflicting Views of the 1987 Constitutional Accord* (Ottawa: University of Ottawa Press, 1989); Patrick J. Monahan, *Meech Lake: The Inside Story* (Toronto: University of Toronto Press, 1991).
7. Alan C. Cairns, *Constitution, Government, and Society in Canada* (Toronto: McClelland and Stewart, 1988); *Disruptions: Constitutional Struggles, from the Charter to Meech Lake* (Toronto: McClelland and Stewart, 1991).
8. Kenneth McRoberts and Patrick Monahan, eds., *The Charlottetown Accord, the Referendum and the Future of Canada* (Toronto: University of Toronto Press, 1993); Peter Russell, *Constitutional Odyssey: Can Canadians Become a Sovereign People?* 2nd ed. (Toronto: University of Toronto Press, 1993).
9. Richard Johnston, *The Challenge of Direct Democracy: The 1992 Canadian Referendum* (Kingston: McGill–Queen's University Press, 1996).
10. Curtis Cook, ed., *Constitutional Predicament: Canada after the Referendum of 1992* (Montreal: McGill–Queen's University Press, 1994); Parti Québécois, *Quebec in a New World* (Toronto: Lorimer, 1994); J.E. Trent, R.A. Young, and G. Lachapelle, eds., *Québec–Canada: What Is the Path Ahead? Nouveaux sentiers vers l'avenir* (Ottawa: University of Ottawa Press, 1996).
11. McRoberts, *Misconceiving Canada: The Struggle for National Unity.*
12. Thomas Courchene, "Market Nationalism," *Policy Options* (October 1968).
13. Alan Freeman and Patrick Grady, *Dividing the House: Planning for a Canada without Quebec* (Toronto: HarperCollins, 1995); Gordon Gibson, *Plan B: The Future of the Rest of Canada* (Vancouver: Fraser Institute, 1994); D.J. Bercuson and Barry Cooper, *Deconfederation: Canada without Quebec* (Toronto: Key Porter, 1991).

FURTHER READING

Behiels, Michael, ed. *The Meech Lake Primer: Conflicting Views of the 1987 Constitutional Accord.* Ottawa: University of Ottawa Press, 1989.

Cairns, Alan C. *Disruptions: Constitutional Struggles, from the Charter to Meech Lake*. Toronto: McClelland and Stewart, 1991.

Fraser, Graham. *René Lévesque and the Parti Québécois in Power*. Toronto: Macmillan, 1984.

Gibbins, Roger. *Conflict and Unity*. 3rd ed. Scarborough: Nelson Canada, 1994.

Johnston, Richard, et al. *The Challenge of Direct Democracy: The 1992 Canadian Referendum*. Kingston: McGill–Queen's University Press, 1996.

McRoberts, Kenneth. *Misconceiving Canada: The Struggle for National Unity*. Toronto: Oxford University Press, 1997.

McRoberts, Kenneth. *Quebec: Social Change and Political Crisis*. 3rd ed. Toronto: McClelland and Stewart, 1993.

McRoberts, Kenneth, ed. *Beyond Quebec: Taking Stock of Canada*. Montreal: McGill–Queen's University Press, 1995.

McRoberts, Kenneth, and Patrick Monahan, eds. *The Charlottetown Accord, the Referendum and the Future of Canada*. Toronto: University of Toronto Press, 1993.

McWhinney, Edward. *Canada and the Constitution 1979–82: Patriation and the Charter of Rights*. Toronto: University of Toronto Press, 1982.

Monahan, Patrick J. *Meech Lake: The Inside Story*. Toronto: University of Toronto Press, 1991.

Parti Québécois. *Quebec in a New World*. Toronto: Lorimer, 1994.

Romanow, Roy, J. Whyte, and H. Leeson. *Canada … Notwithstanding: The Making of the Constitution 1976–1982*. Toronto: Methuen, 1984.

Russell, Peter. *Constitutional Odyssey: Can Canadians Become a Sovereign People?* 2nd ed. Toronto: University of Toronto Press, 1993.

Thomson, Dale. *Jean Lesage and the Quiet Revolution*. Toronto: Macmillan, 1984.

Webber, Jeremy. *Reimagining Canada: Language, Culture, Community, and the Canadian Constitution*. Montreal: McGill–Queen's University Press, 1994.

Chapter 4

Aboriginal Peoples, Other Ethnic Groups, and Gender Issues

The French–English question has been a constant of Canadian politics since before Confederation, but until recently Aboriginal and other ethnic issues were largely ignored. Similarly, once women achieved the vote, the system paid little attention to them. About 1970, however, Aboriginal, other ethnic, and gender issues suddenly became prominent items on the political agenda.

This chapter is thus divided into three parts. The first examines Canada's Aboriginal peoples; the second part discusses other ethnic groups; and the last section of the chapter deals with the women's movement and other gender issues.

Canada's Aboriginal Peoples
History and Numbers

The Native or Aboriginal peoples who have inhabited Canada for perhaps as long as 40 000 years are an extremely varied group. They are officially categorized as North American Indians, Inuit, and Métis, but each of these groups contains variations in turn. Before Europeans came to the continent, the Indians and Inuit were self-sufficient and self-governing. They made decisions on the basis of consensus rather than by voting, and in many cases women (sometimes called clan mothers) played a significant role. In their close attachment to the land, they did not think in terms of private ownership; instead, they believed in the shared use of land and saw themselves as trustees of the land for future generations. The fur trade, which led to the invasion by Europeans, was devastating for the Aboriginal peoples, totally disrupting their way of life and introducing new diseases that severely reduced their population.

In the Royal Proclamation of 1763, which divided up the territory acquired by Britain, Indian rights were clearly defined, however much they have since been ignored. In a large area called Indian Territory, the purchase or settlement of land was forbidden without Crown approval, that is, without a treaty between the Crown and the Indian people concerned. The Crown later set aside reserves in exchange for the cession of Indian land, in addition to providing benefits such as the right to hunt and fish on unoccupied Crown land.

The 1867 Constitution Act gave jurisdiction over Indians and lands reserved for the Indians to the federal government. Parliament soon passed the Indian Act, providing for federal government control of almost every aspect of Indian life. One of its provisions allowed for "enfranchisement," which encouraged Indians to give up their Indian status. Thus began the distinction between *status Indians*, those registered with the federal government according to the terms of the Indian Act, and *nonstatus Indians*, those not so registered.

Meanwhile, the treaty-making process continued apace, covering most of northern Ontario and the Prairie provinces. These treaties were primarily designed to clear Aboriginal title so that the transcontinental railway could be built and Western immigrant settlement could begin. In return for surrendering title to the lands involved, Indians received tracts of land for reserves as well as other benefits such as small annuities, gratuities, schools, hunting and fishing rights, agricultural implements, cattle, and ammunition. In retrospect, almost everyone agrees that the Natives were taken advantage of in these negotiations; the land given them for reserves was usually small, remote, and lacking in resources.[1] Even worse off, however, were those Indians in much of British Columbia and the Arctic with whom no treaties were signed at all.

The Métis were the descendants of European fur traders and Indian women. Found largely on the Prairies, the Métis combined nomadic hunting with farming. Not covered by the Indian Act or by treaties, they were left to the mercy of new white settlers and provincial and territorial governments. It is not surprising that Louis Riel, leader of the rebellion that led to the creation of Manitoba in 1870, took up their cause in 1885 in the second Riel Rebellion in Saskatchewan. After having been crushed, they remained in an even weaker position to fend for themselves.

In the 1991 census, some 1 002 675 Canadians, or 3.7 percent of the total Canadian population, reported Aboriginal origins, but only 626 000 (2.3 percent of the total population) identified with an Aboriginal group. Moreover, of the slightly more than one million who reported Aboriginal origins, about half reported non-Aboriginal origins as well. Canada's Aboriginal population breaks down as follows: about three-quarters North American Indians, about 20 percent Métis, and about 5 percent Inuit.

The Department of Indian and Northern Affairs reported a slightly higher number of Aboriginal people in 1993: approximately 1.2 million, or 4.3 percent of the population. These were distributed as follows: status Indians on reserve, 326 444; status Indians off reserve, 226 872; nonstatus Indians, 405 000; Métis, 192 100; and Inuit, 50 800.[2] There were 2370 reserves in Canada in 1994, with an average size of about 1160 hectares. They are divided among some 600 bands, with an average band population of about 650 persons.

The Condition of Aboriginal Peoples

The above statistics present only part of the picture. At least of equal significance are the distressing statistics on Aboriginal poverty. Many reserve families have incomes *far* below the poverty line, and apart from a few urban professionals, the same is true for most of those who live off-reserve. Related to this level of poverty are alarming rates of Aboriginal alcoholism, violence, suicide, low educational attainment, and unemployment. The overall life expectancy of Aboriginal Canadians is almost 10 years shorter than of non-Natives, largely a result of poor health services and housing on reserves that is overcrowded and lacking in running water, indoor toilets, and central heating. The infant mortality rate among registered Indians is almost twice that of the Canadian population as a whole, and Natives suffer seven times as much from tuberculosis as non-Natives. The suicide rate and the rate of death due to injury and poisoning are both three times the national average.

In essence, the typical Native scenario runs as follows: having lost their land, original livelihood and culture, and being placed on unproductive reserves, many Indians find themselves with little to do. The resulting unemployment, idleness, and reliance on welfare often lead them to seek solace in substance abuse. In this intoxicated state, many Natives resort to family and other violence, which in turn brings them into trouble with the law. Not being able to pay their fines, and subject to discrimination at the hands of the police, the courts, and other aspects of the justice system, they then go to jail where they become even more alienated, depressed, and abused. Aboriginal Canadians have suffered from untold discrimination and indignity at every turn, and the Indian Act requires non-Native bureaucratic approval for almost any band decision. In the past, Indian babies were frequently removed from the reserves to be adopted by non-Native parents, and Indian children were forced to go to residential schools where they were punished, sometimes to the point of assault, for speaking their

Native language or engaging in Native customs. Native languages and cultures have been systematically discouraged, and traditional forms of government and medicine have been outlawed. Indians living on reserves did not even have the right to vote in federal elections until 1960.

Aboriginal Political Issues since 1970

Canadian Native peoples and their problems have been a major concern of Canadian politics since about 1970. They were greatly offended by the Trudeau–Chrétien White Paper on Indians of 1969 that called for their complete integration into the wider Canadian society. On the other hand, they were encouraged by the sympathetic Berger Inquiry into the proposed Mackenzie Valley gas pipeline in 1977. Moreover, their problems had become so serious that they simply could no longer be ignored, and the incidence of sit-ins, roadblocks, rallies, court cases, hunger strikes, and international protests increased. Post-1970 Aboriginal issues are primarily related to land and governance.

LAND ISSUES

In most of the country, as noted earlier, North American Indians signed treaties with the Crown under which they ceded the land to the government in return for protected reserves. But especially in British Columbia and the North, few such treaties were signed, leaving Indians and Inuit in these regions without a land base, along with the Métis who have never legally possessed any land. This gives rise to the issue of Aboriginal title, that is, a claim to land on the basis of traditional occupancy and use rather than treaty. The existence of such Aboriginal title was first recognized in the *Calder* case in 1973 in connection with the Nisga'a band in British Columbia, but the Supreme Court of Canada was split on the question of whether such title had been subsequently extinguished. In response, the government of Canada announced its intention to negotiate Aboriginal title. A great many Aboriginal land claims have therefore been launched in the past 25 years. They fall into two categories: comprehensive claims based on Aboriginal title (that is, traditional use and occupancy of land) that have not been dealt with by treaty or other legal means; and specific claims arising from alleged nonfulfilment of the terms of Indian treaties and other lawful obligations.

Such claims have moved relatively faster in the North than in the south, since north of the 60th parallel the federal government is in charge of the land as well as of Aboriginals. In fact, agreement in principle has been achieved in three comprehensive land claims in the North. Besides providing land and money, such comprehensive claims clarify Native hunting, fishing, and trapping rights, and clear obstacles to future economic development.

In the south, where Ottawa has responsibility for Indians and the lands reserved for the Indians but where the provinces have jurisdiction over public lands, such claims have moved more slowly. Aboriginals have generally found provincial governments even less sympathetic to Native issues than Ottawa, and conflict has often developed between Indian bands and large natural resource companies as well as other non-Aboriginals who now live on the land in question. Ottawa insists that provinces be party to such settlements and contribute to their costs. Thus far, relatively few comprehensive land claim successes can be reported below the 60th parallel.

The main provincial comprehensive land claim settlement was the 1975 James Bay and Northern Quebec Agreement between the Cree and Inuit and the government of Quebec. The James Bay Agreement gave the Natives exclusive use of 13 700 km^2 of land and an additional 450 000 km^2 of exclusive hunting, fishing, and trapping rights, along with $225 million in cash in return for allowing Quebec to construct a giant hydro development project in the area. One terrible side effect was the mercury poisoning of the fish, due to an unanticipated chemical reaction between water and rock in the flooded land, and of the Natives who ate them. This problem and the growing perception that the deal may otherwise have been less generous to the Native community than originally thought led the Cree of Quebec to reject the second, "Great Whale" phase of the James Bay project in the 1990s.

Since the province of British Columbia contains a large proportion of North American Indians, who have signed few treaties, the comprehensive land claims issue has been particularly significant there. The Nisga'a tribe in northwest B.C., which has been seeking recognition of their Aboriginal title for over 100 years, finally arrived at an agreement in principle in 1996.

Specific land claims resulting from dissatisfaction with treaties—especially the fact that bands did not receive the full amount of land that the treaties promised—have arisen in most other provinces, but until 1991 Ottawa did not want to hear them. By mid-1993, 584 specific claims had been filed, and by the end of 1994, 312 of these had been resolved, although not always to First Nations' satisfaction.

Another dimension of land issues concerns what treaties allow Aboriginals to do on public or Crown lands. Aboriginal treaty rights, especially hunting and fishing rights, frequently conflict with provincial law. After many court cases, some progress has been made on this front, including the issue of logging trees.

Yet another aspect of the land question arose in the conflict at Oka, Quebec, in the summer of 1990, the most serious Aboriginal–government conflict of modern times.[3] The municipal council's decision to expand a golf course on land claimed by resident Mohawks as sacred ground led to an armed standoff between Mohawk warriors and the Quebec Provincial Police, during which one police officer was killed. The Canadian Armed Forces were later brought in, and Aboriginal demonstrations took place across the country. Five years later, an Aboriginal was killed by police in a land claims demonstration at Ipperwash, Ontario.

GOVERNANCE ISSUES

Aboriginal Canadians have long demanded improvements in government health, social, and educational services, and some minor improvements have been made over the years. Natives began to feel, however, that they were too constrained by the Indian Act and that their problems required Native solutions. They were tired of living at the mercy of politicians and bureaucrats. Yet most Aboriginals did not want to gut the Indian Act and existing government programs until they had something better to put in their place.

Shortly after their rejection of the 1969 White Paper, Aboriginal Canadians began to argue that they should be able to choose their own decision-making processes, for they could hardly be expected to support the apparatus that created their current problems. Before the passage of the Indian Act, they had sophisticated and distinctive forms of government; many wanted to return to such traditional ways, feeling that the system of elected band councils was an alien imposition. But going well beyond such decision-making machinery, they also wanted Aboriginal self-government. Natives demand more control over their own affairs, but the specific structures of such proposed self-government are not clear-cut. Some advocates would accept a kind of super-municipality, but others have more ambitious plans that would be harder to fit into the Canadian constitutional framework. For the moment, the demand is for a "two-track" approach: constitutional recognition of the *inherent right of Aboriginal self-government* stemming from their unique history as Canada's original inhabitants, plus concurrent progress toward greater community-based control at the local level. In this way, an array of self-government arrangements and institutional models can be developed within the existing constitutional setup. Self-government would also help Natives take action to preserve Aboriginal languages that are in danger of becoming extinct.

The first improvement in the constitutional recognition of Aboriginal rights occurred in the Constitution Act, 1982. Section 25 guaranteed that Charter rights would not be construed so as to abrogate or derogate from any Aboriginal, treaty, or other rights or freedoms that pertained to the Aboriginal peoples of Canada, including any rights recognized by the Royal Proclamation of 1763, and any rights or freedoms "that now exist by way of land claims agreements or may be so acquired." Section 35 recognized and affirmed the existing Aboriginal and treaty rights of the Aboriginal peoples of Canada, including the Indian, Inuit, and Métis peoples. Inspired by the equality rights clause in the Charter, the Indian Act was amended to rescind the clause that had previously removed Indian status from Aboriginal women who married white men but granted such status to white women who married Indian men. Bill C-31 led to the reinstatement of nearly 100 000 Aboriginal women and their children, but since bands were allowed to control who could actually live on the reserve, many of those reinstated in status had difficulty in returning to the reserve.

Although mid-1980s constitutional talks on Aboriginal self-government broke down, two pieces of legislation were passed to provide for self-government in specific localities. The 1984 Cree-Naskapi (of Quebec) Act set in place self-government arrangements for the Indians of Quebec who were parties to the James Bay land claim agreement, and the 1986 Sechelt Indian Band Self-Government Act allowed the Sechelt band in British Columbia to assume control over their lands, resources, health and social services, education, and local taxation in what is usually called the "municipal model."

A special case in which land claims and self-government agreements were negotiated simultaneously should also be mentioned. In Nunavut in the eastern Arctic, the land claim was finalized in 1993; meanwhile, a plebiscite in 1992 had ratified the division of the Northwest Territories. In 1999 the territory of Nunavut will be separated from the NWT. It will have all the governmental institutions associated with a province or territory, but represents a kind of Aboriginal self-government in the sense that the population is almost completely composed of Inuit.

THE MEECH LAKE AND CHARLOTTETOWN ACCORDS

Canadian Natives were understandably opposed to the Meech Lake Accord, which addressed Quebec's constitutional demands but completely overlooked their own. Even supporters of the Accord found it hard to blame Elijah Harper for withholding unanimous consent when it came before the Manitoba legislature for approval in 1990. This action, together with the Oka affair, precipitated a dramatic breakthrough in constitutional concern with Aboriginal issues and in the participation of Native leaders in constitutional negotiations. Aboriginal leaders were given the same status as premiers in the talks leading up to the 1992 Charlottetown Accord, and that document actually addressed Aboriginal concerns in a more extensive and satisfactory way than it did the demands of Quebec.

The Charlottetown Accord recognized the inherent right of Aboriginal peoples to self-government within Canada, as well as agreeing that such First Nations governments would constitute a third order of government in Canada, analogous to provinces. The document provided for self-government agreements to be negotiated among the three levels of government. Federal and provincial laws would remain in place until superseded by Aboriginal laws, but the latter would have to be consistent with the preservation of peace, order, and good government in Canada.

POST-CHARLOTTETOWN DEVELOPMENTS

In the wake of the rejection of the Charlottetown Accord, activity in the area of Aboriginal governance has been limited to legislative and administrative changes, such as experiments in delegating federal or provincial government powers to First Nations bands. In 1995, the Chrétien government formally launched a negotiating process to implement the inherent right of self-government, with arrangements varying from one group to another. Some 80 First Nations are involved in such negotiations. Aboriginal people have thereby increased their control over how federal funding is spent and have assumed responsibility for delivering many educational, social, and health-care services.

Another interesting initiative is the experimental dismantling in Manitoba of the Department of Indian Affairs as it affects First Nations. A framework agreement to this effect was signed in December 1994 by the minister of Indian Affairs and the Grand Chief of the Assembly of Manitoba Chiefs. The

Department will essentially withdraw from exercising its functions at the request of local First Nations governments.

Much hope for the solution of Aboriginal problems was placed in the Royal Commission on Aboriginal Peoples, appointed in 1991 and reporting in 1996. It endorsed Aboriginal self-government in its widest sense and the basic separation of Aboriginal and non-Aboriginal societies. Among other things, it proposed an Aboriginal Parliament, dual Canadian-Aboriginal citizenship, an independent lands and treaties tribunal, an Aboriginal development bank, an action plan on health and social conditions, and an Aboriginal-controlled education system. Whether because of the magnitude or the direction of the recommendations, the Chrétien government seemed reluctant to rush into their implementation.

ABORIGINAL JUSTICE

Because of the high proportion of Natives in Canada's correctional system, one specific aspect of self-government raised is the concept of a parallel Aboriginal justice system. Native cases would be diverted from the regular judicial process to allow convictions and sentences based on Native values and community traditions. Support for this concept has come from many provincial inquiries into the treatment of Natives in the regular judicial system—especially the Donald Marshall Inquiry in Nova Scotia and the Aboriginal Justice Inquiry in Manitoba. Marshall was a Micmac imprisoned for over 10 years for a crime he did not commit. The Manitoba inquiry centred on the rape and murder of Helen Betty Osborne, an Indian girl in The Pas, by four white men who were protected from prosecution, and on the shooting of a Native leader by a Winnipeg police officer. These inquiries and others documented incidents of misunderstanding, prejudice, harassment, abuse, and brutality by police, courts, and jails. A precedent for the coexistence of two legal systems could perhaps be found in the distinctive civil law system in Quebec.

While governments have generally ruled out a wholesale parallel Aboriginal justice system, several provinces have allowed experimental judicial processes involving Aboriginal input. More Aboriginals have been hired as police officers; some reserves have their own Aboriginal police force; and a few even maintain their own correctional facilities.

Other Ethnic Groups and Multiculturalism

The third aspect of ethnic cleavage, involving other ethnic groups and multiculturalism, increasingly vies with the Aboriginal and French–English questions on the political agenda. The three principal issues that arise in this area are administering immigration, preserving and promoting the identity of ethnic groups (or multiculturalism), and ensuring that individuals belonging to such groups are treated equitably in law and society.

Canadian Immigration Patterns

Following the Aboriginals, the French, and the British, people from many other lands began to immigrate to Canada. The first dramatic surge of immigrants arrived during the 1880s, including Danes, Dutch, Icelanders, Poles, Ukrainians, Finns, Norwegians, and Swedes. In British Columbia, Asians were a leading group: between 1881 and 1884 nearly 16 000 Chinese were brought in as contract labourers to work on the CPR. Nova Scotia and Ontario also received a substantial number of Blacks escaping from slavery in the United States.

An even larger number and variety of immigrants arrived between 1903 and 1914, and the prosperous 1920s were another active decade on the immigration front. After the Second World War was over, another huge wave of immigrants came to Canada, largely from southern Europe. They were supplemented by postwar refugees from around the world. Table 4.1 indicates the fluctuation in numbers of immigrant arrivals in Canada by decade.

TABLE 4.1 IMMIGRANT ARRIVALS IN CANADA BY DECADE

1861–1871	183 000	1931–1941	150 000
1871–1881	353 000	1941–1951	548 000
1881–1891	824 000	1951–1961	1 543 000
1891–1901	828 000	1961–1971	1 429 000
1901–1911	1 759 000	1971–1981	1 447 000
1911–1921	1 612 000	1981–1991	1 374 000
1921–1931	1 203 000		

Source: Reproduced from Immigration Statistics 1992, published by Citizenship and Immigration Canada. Reproduced with the permission of the Minister of Public Works and Government Services Canada, 1997.

TABLE 4.2 PRINCIPAL SOURCES OF IMMIGRANTS TO CANADA IN SELECTED YEARS
(PERCENTAGE)

	Britain	Europe	Asia	Caribbean
1957	38.6	52.6	1.3	0.4
1967	28.0	43.8	9.3	3.9
1977	15.7	19.8	21.0	10.4
1987	5.6	19.1	44.3	7.4
1992	2.8	14.9	55.1	5.9

Source: Reproduced from Immigration Statistics 1992, *published by Citizenship and Immigration Canada. Reproduced with the permission of the Minister of Public Works and Government Services Canada, 1997.*

Overall, Britain was the leading source of immigrants between 1900 and 1965. Until 1967, immigration policy favoured British, American, and European newcomers, since they were considered well educated and skilled, and, being predominantly Caucasian, better able to assimilate.

After the Immigration Act was significantly amended in 1967, Canadian immigration patterns changed radically, as Table 4.2 shows. In 1957, over 90 percent of immigrants were from Britain or continental Europe, a figure that fell to 72 percent in 1967, 33 percent in 1977, 25 percent in 1987, and 17 percent in 1992. In contrast, Asian and Caribbean immigrants were less than 2 percent of the total in 1957, increasing to 13 percent in 1967, 30 percent in 1977, over 50 percent in 1987, and over 60 percent in 1992. The sources of such immigrants can be seen in Figure 4.1.

Such patterns point to the fact that immigrant groups can be subdivided between the generally more recent visible minorities, essentially those from Asia, Africa, the Caribbean, South America, and the Middle East, and those that mostly came earlier from southern or eastern Europe. Some public policies, such as multiculturalism, apply to both groups, while others, such as employment equity, apply only to visible minorities.

Multiculturalism and Related Policies

With the opening of the floodgates to visible minorities after 1967, the composition of the Canadian population changed significantly. Such an increase in the

Figure 4.1   Sources of 1992 Immigrants by Region

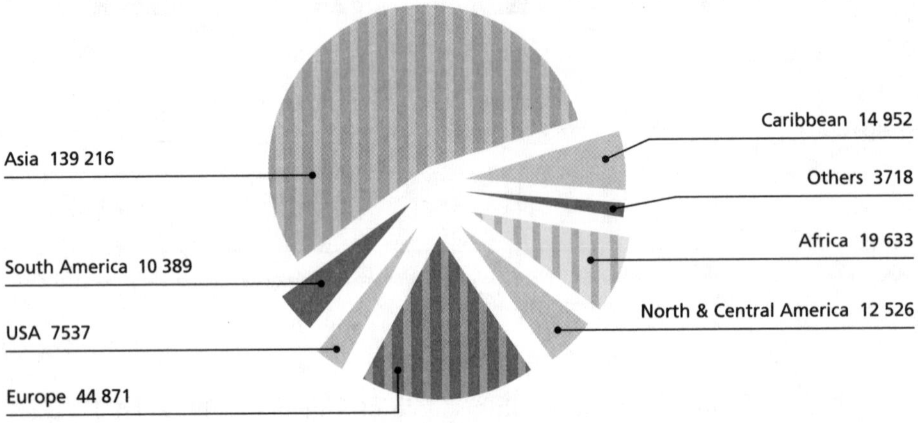

Asia 139 216

Caribbean 14 952

Others 3718

Africa 19 633

South America 10 389

North & Central America 12 526

USA 7537

Europe 44 871

Source: Reproduced from Immigration Statistics 1992, *published by Citizenship and Immigration Canada. Reproduced with the permission of the Minister of Public Works and Government Services Canada, 1997.*

numbers of people of "other" ethnic origin naturally gave them more leverage to push for changes in areas where they encountered indifference or discrimination.

Largely due to pressure from Ukrainian Canadians, the Royal Commission on Bilingualism and Biculturalism appointed in 1963 was ultimately also asked to examine "the contribution made by other ethnic groups to the cultural enrichment of Canada and the measures which should be taken to safeguard that contribution." While focusing primarily on English and French, the Commission recommended that increased government attention be given to other ethnic groups, including public funding in certain areas. With this encouragement, such groups began to demand public financial assistance in addition to verbal or moral support, and the term *multiculturalism* came into increasing currency about this time.

In 1971, because of the Royal Commission, group pressure, and politicians hoping to curry votes, the Trudeau government announced a new policy of multiculturalism within a bilingual framework. Multiculturalism is the official recognition of the diverse cultures in a plural society; it involves encouraging immigrants to retain their linguistic heritages and ethnic cultures instead of abandoning them. The government argued that the Canadian identity would not be undermined by multiculturalism; on the contrary, cultural pluralism was the very essence of the Canadian identity. Multiculturalism is based on the virtues of having a population of diverse origins who make Canada a more interesting place to live. In providing links to virtually every other country in the world, such a population also enhances Canada's international image and influence.

Once in place, the policy of multiculturalism legitimized demands for many other changes both in terms of promoting ethnic identities and removing barriers to equity. The next stage was the creation of the Canadian Human Rights Commission in 1978 to complement equivalent bodies at the provincial level. Another major advance for multiculturalism was the Charter of Rights and Freedoms in 1982, which provided constitutional protection against discrimination by federal and provincial governments in the equality rights clause, section 15. Moreover, the Charter endorsed affirmative action programs in order to overcome past discrimination. After intense pressure from various ethnic groups, another section was added to the Charter to the effect that it would be interpreted "in a manner consistent with the preservation and enhancement of the multicultural heritage of Canadians" (section 27). The Multiculturalism ministry that began to take form in the 1970s gradually increased in status, and 1988 saw the passage of a new Canadian Multiculturalism Act.

On a different front, the 1986 federal Employment Equity Act designated visible minorities along with women, the disabled, and Aboriginals as groups that could benefit from affirmative action programs with respect to hiring in the public service. While those not included complained about reverse discrimination, some ethnic leaders criticized the lack of specific goals and timetables in the legislation.

Two years later, the Mulroney government took action to compensate Japanese Canadians for their mistreatment during the Second World War. Unjustly suspected of being loyal to Japan, Canadian citizens of Japanese background were uprooted from the west coast, interned in "relocation centres," and had their property confiscated. The 1988 Japanese Redress Agreement provided $21 000 for each of the surviving internees. This led to demands from other ethnic groups that they be similarly compensated for wartime discrimination in Canada.

Reaction against Multiculturalism and Immigration

If the responses to demands from the multicultural community were largely positive in the 1970s and 1980s, such has not entirely been the case in the 1990s. Opposition has surfaced toward immigration in general and visible minority immigration in particular, multiculturalism, employment equity, and other policies and practices. Relatively few positive developments have occurred on the other side of the equation.[4]

This opposition was partly in response to the recession of the early 1990s and the continuing high unemployment rate afterward. Whatever the merits of immigration in economic terms, ordinary voters increasingly see recent immigrants in jobs that they feel would otherwise have gone to Canadian residents of longer duration. As for the source of immigrants, while the level of Canadian acceptance and tolerance of nontraditional immigrants is high, it is not unlimited. The Reform Party was the first to break ranks with an all-party consensus on this issue and call for a sizable cut in annual immigration levels, with a greater emphasis on skills. The Chrétien government reduced the level from about 250 000 to about 200 000 in 1994 and imposed a $975 right-of-landing fee. It also announced that "the balance between economic, family and other immigrant components would place greater emphasis on attracting those with the capacity to settle quickly and contribute to Canada's economy."

The policy of official multiculturalism has been criticized, especially in an era of government fiscal restraint. Even some members of the multicultural community have spoken out against the policy, especially MP John Nunziata and writer Neil Bissoondath. They maintain that official multiculturalism is divisive, ghettoizes visible minorities, fosters racial animosity, and detracts from national unity.[5] Critics argue that in the battle against the deficit, it seems hardly appropriate that the government is fostering the maintenance of foreign traditions while starving national cultural institutions. The money would be better spent teaching immigrants about basic Canadian values.

The Women's Movement and Other Gender Issues
Evolution of Women's Rights to 1970

Men and male-oriented issues virtually monopolized Canadian politics before 1900. In those early years, when all women were expected to marry and then became chattels of their husbands, they first had to fight for educational and occupational rights, such as admission to universities and to the medical and legal professions. Women demanded the right to make contracts and to own property, and increasingly began to work in factories and offices and to become teachers and nurses; others continued to make major contributions on the farm. At the turn of the century, farm women in particular became active in reform organizations of many kinds, including those that pressed for the prohibition of alcohol and the establishment of new public health facilities, better housing, and improved working conditions for women and children.

As influential as women were in promoting these causes, many began to feel that their impact would always be limited until they could vote. Thus, in what is sometimes called the "first wave" of the women's movement, women demanded the franchise. After the outbreak of the First World War, proponents of female suffrage had an additional argument: women should be rewarded for their contribution to the war effort. Thus Manitoba, Alberta, and Saskatchewan, containing some of the most articulate women of the day, pioneered the female franchise in 1916; Ontario and British Columbia joined them in 1917; and all the other provinces except Quebec followed shortly afterward.

At the federal level, the Borden government deliberately manipulated the franchise for the 1917 election, in part by giving the vote to women in the armed services (mostly nurses) and by allowing soldiers fighting abroad to appoint their nearest female relative at home—women who would likely support the war effort—to cast their vote by proxy. A year later the vote was extended to all women, and they had their first chance to exercise this new right in the 1921 election.

Many legislative reforms were achieved in the ensuing years in the virtual absence of women in the legislative bodies concerned. Two women were elected to the Alberta legislature in 1917. Agnes Macphail became the first woman elected to the House of Commons in 1921, serving alone until 1935, when a second woman was elected. Macphail stayed on until 1940 and then became the first woman elected to the Ontario legislature in 1943. Vigorous and articulate, Macphail promoted radical and progressive causes of many kinds, but she could only do so much by herself to advance women's issues in such an entrenched male bastion.

It was not until 1940 that Quebec women were enfranchised in provincial elections. Moreover, the legal status of a married woman under the Quebec Civil Code was such that until 1955 she could not seek a separation on grounds of adultery by her husband, and until 1964 she had no right to carry on a trade without her husband's consent.

The number of women who won seats in the House of Commons was minuscule before 1970, and many of those elected were the widows or daughters of male members of Parliament. Female political participation was inhibited by many factors. First, both sexes were traditionally socialized into the view that politics was a masculine pursuit and that women should remain in the home. Second, most women were constrained by the responsibilities of homemaking and child-rearing. Such roles had little prestige and prevented women from accumulating the money, contacts, and experience that political careers usually require. The long hours and unpredictable schedules of politicians conflicted with most women's family commitments, which prevented them from being away from home for any length of time. Third, political parties discouraged female candidacies, and when consciousness of the lack of female candidates increased, they were more frequently nominated as sacrificial lambs against a strong male incumbent.

Until the late 1920s, no women had been appointed to the other house of Parliament, the Senate. When an enterprising group of Western women took this issue to court, the Supreme Court of Canada ruled in 1928 that in terms of the law respecting Senate appointments, women were not persons. In 1929 this decision was appealed to the Judicial Committee of the Privy Council, which in the *Persons case* overruled the Supreme Court and declared women to be "qualified persons" within the meaning of s. 24 of the 1867 Constitution Act and eligible to sit in the Senate. The women's movement continues to celebrate this decision to this day in the form of the "Person's Day Breakfast." Prime Minister Mackenzie King immediately appointed Cairine Wilson to the Senate, but the second woman was not appointed until 1935, and 18 years would pass before three more received the call.

It was not until 1957 that the first woman, Ellen Fairclough, was appointed to the federal cabinet; she was followed by Judy LaMarsh in 1963. The advance of women to the cabinet at the provincial level was generally even slower. Nevertheless, gradual improvements continued to be made in federal and provincial legislation and programs of benefit to women. The federal Family Allowances Act of 1944, for example, provided a small monthly payment to each Canadian mother to help care for her children, and often represented the only independent income the woman possessed. In 1952 Ontario passed the first equal pay legislation, to be followed by federal legislation two years later. Amendments to the Criminal Code in 1969 made it legal to advertise birth-control devices in Canada, and a new Divorce Act made it easier to get out of an unfulfilling marriage.

The Women's Movement since 1970

By 1970 attitudes had changed sufficiently that it was possible to speak of a *women's movement*, and the word *feminist* became common. In their most general sense, such terms are used to apply to those who seek to establish complete gender equality, to free men and women from restrictive gender roles, and to end any semblance of the subordination of women.

This "second wave" of the women's movement coincided with the Royal Commission on the Status of Women, appointed in 1967 and reporting in 1970. That report "provided a solid statistical base and a framework for most of the feminist action that followed during the 1970s"[6] and made 167 recommendations, not all of which have been implemented. Since that time gender issues have become an important, daily factor in Canadian politics, and most governments now designate a minister to be responsible for women's issues. At the federal level, a general plan for gender equality was issued in 1995.

The number of women's groups has increased remarkably in recent years, the foremost pressure group being the National Action Committee on the Status of Women (NAC). NAC was established in 1972, largely because of government inaction on the Status of Women report, and functions as an umbrella lobbying group for over 250 local and national member groups representing over three million women.

POLITICAL REPRESENTATION

In the post-1970 era, women's participation in politics and government increased substantially and, for the first time, regularly. Table 4.3 indicates this progress. Many of the factors mentioned above that inhibited women from becoming

TABLE 4.3 REPRESENTATION OF WOMEN IN THE HOUSE OF COMMONS, 1921–1997

Election	Number Elected	Election	Number Elected	Election	Number Elected
1921	1	1953	4	1974	9
1925	1	1957	2	1979	11
1926	1	1958	2	1980	14
1930	1	1962	4	1984	27
1935	2	1963	4	1988	39
1940	1	1965	3	1993	53
1945	1	1968	1	1997	62
1949	0	1972	4		

Source: Status of Women Canada, "A Canadian Chronology," 1994, supplemented by 1997 election results. Reproduced with the permission of the Minister of Public Works and Government Services Canada, 1997.

politicians before 1970 are still present, although in recent years most parties have created special funds to support female candidates.

At the cabinet level, a few more women were appointed during the 1970s, but by the 1980s, one or two token female ministers were clearly considered to be insufficient. Brian Mulroney appointed six women to his 1984 cabinet, for example, while the provinces eventually appointed women ministers, too. Bob Rae came close to gender equality in his Ontario NDP cabinet in 1990.

It was also in the post-1970 period that Canada finally saw women elected as political party leaders. Alexa McDonough (NDP, Nova Scotia) led the way in 1980, to be followed by Sharon Carstairs, Elizabeth Weir, Barbara Baird-Filliter, Lynda Haverstock, Lyn McLeod, Rita Johnston, and Catherine Callbeck. After Rosemary Brown made a serious stab at the NDP national leadership in 1975 and Flora Macdonald for the PCs in 1976, it remained for Audrey McLaughlin to make history when she was elected leader of the federal New Democratic Party in 1989, the first woman to lead a major national party. Alexa McDonough succeeded her in 1995.

Three women have become first ministers: Rita Johnson (B.C.), Catherine Callbeck (P.E.I.), and Prime Minister Kim Campbell. Jeanne Sauvé was the first woman Speaker of the House of Commons and first woman governor general; Bertha Wilson became the first woman to sit on the Supreme Court of Canada (1982). At one point three women sat on the Supreme Court (out of nine), but the number fell back to two after 1990. Nevertheless, woman judges have been appointed at an ever-increasing rate in other courts, and in 1993, 123 or about 15 percent of federally appointed judges were women.

Within the federal bureaucracy, the first women joined the RCMP in 1974, and the first woman deputy minister (Sylvia Ostry) was appointed in 1975; women gradually became eligible for full combat roles in the armed forces, and the first woman general was named in 1988. In 1993, Jocelyne Bourgon became the first woman to hold the top public service position in Ottawa, Secretary to the Cabinet and Clerk of the Privy Council.

EMPLOYMENT ISSUES

Since about two-thirds of women of working age are now in the labour force, and since women constitute about 45 percent of the labour force, one major feminist concern is employment. Women have traditionally been discriminated against in pay, underrepresented in managerial positions, and discouraged from undertaking nontraditional occupations. In 1985, full-time female workers earned on average 65.5 percent of what men earned, leading women to demand "equal pay for work of equal value" or "pay equity." Most Canadian governments now have pay equity legislation, and by 1995, women's earnings had risen to an average of 73.1 percent of men's.[7]

Beyond pay equity is the broader subject of employment equity, that is, the elimination of discrimination in hiring and promoting women, which is sometimes combined with affirmative action programs to give women preference in order to make up for past inequities. In 1983, affirmative action with respect to the hiring of women was made mandatory in all federal government departments, and the 1984 Royal Commission Report, *Equality in Employment,* became the foundation of the 1986 Employment Equity Act. It extended employment equity requirements to all Crown corporations, all federally regulated companies with over 100 employees, and other large companies in receipt of major government contracts. Nevertheless, while women constituted 48 percent of the federal government workforce in 1996, they occupied only 21 percent of managerial jobs. Ontario passed an even more extensive Employment Equity Act in 1993, but it was quickly repealed by the new Conservative government of Mike Harris.

The area in which women are most severely underrepresented is at the top of private corporations. In a 1993 survey of over 500 companies, *The Financial Post* found only seven women who held the position of chair, chief executive officer, or president, and only 1.6 percent of corporate vice-presidents were women. By 1997, the two most notable examples were Maureen Kempston Darkes at General Motors and Bobbie Gaunt at Ford.

LEGAL ISSUES

A third category of post-1970 women's issues is related to the law. The first such major issue was the question of equality rights in the 1982 Charter of Rights and Freedoms. As the Charter emerged from federal–provincial negotiation, gender equality was to be lumped into section 15 with such other factors as race, religion, and age, which governments would be allowed to override with the notwithstanding clause. Such treatment at the hands of 11 male first ministers galvanized the women's movement as never before; as a result of its tremendous pressure, section 28 was added to the final document to give gender equality a place of its own, protected from the notwithstanding clause.[8]

There followed a series of feminist challenges to laws that women believed discriminated against them. The government itself encouraged such legal activity with the Court Challenges Program under which it subsidized the Legal Education and Action Fund (LEAF) in making such challenges. When the Mulroney government cancelled the Court Challenges Program in 1992, women protested, and it was reinstated by the Chrétien government.

REPRODUCTIVE, SEXUAL, AND VIOLENCE ISSUES

One of the main feminist rallying cries of the post-1970 period is that women must be able to control what happens to their own bodies. Many women's organizations supported Dr. Henry Morgentaler in his long fight to reform the Criminal Code's provisions on abortion.[9] Although amendments were made in 1968, feminists did not regard these as sufficient, and the Supreme Court of Canada threw out the abortion law in the famous 1988 *Morgentaler* case. In 1990, the Mulroney government introduced a compromise abortion law, but it was defeated in the Senate, leaving Canada with no federal law restricting abortion. That government also appointed a Royal Commission on New Reproductive Technologies, whose 1993 report generally endorsed a cautious approach to this controversial subject. Prostitution, pornography, sexual stereotyping, sexual harassment, and physical and sexual assault are other major issues of concern to women.

THE FEMINIZATION OF POVERTY

Chapter 2 revealed the large extent to which Canada has experienced the feminization of poverty. As pointed out there, more than 60 percent of sole-support mothers raise their children below the poverty line. With or without a male partner, large numbers of women with pre-school children find it necessary to work outside the home to support themselves and their families.[10] This has continued even after the Child Tax Credit was added to the income tax system in 1978 to supplement and eventually replace the Family Allowance for low-income families. To decrease the incidence of women living in poverty, measures such as pay equity, employment equity, higher minimum wages, increased unionization, and improved job training and literacy programs will be required.

One of the major unresolved women's issues today is that of daycare for children. In 1991, there were 350 680 licensed full-time childcare spaces available, but some 2.2 million children 12 years of age or younger required such care. Of course, in some cases, parents were happy to rely on relatives, friends, or other unlicensed facilities, but it is clear that a serious shortage of childcare spaces exists. The Mulroney government introduced legislation for a national program in this field, but when the bill failed to pass before the 1988 election, it fell victim to the budgetary restraints of 1989–92.

Gay and Lesbian Issues

A variety of political issues related to homosexuality have arisen in recent years, and these also figure prominently on the agenda of the 1990s. In most cases, politicians are reluctant to deal with demands coming from the gay, lesbian, and bisexual communities, often leaving such groups to take their concerns directly to the courts.

One of their first demands was protection from discrimination in human rights codes. Somewhat surprisingly, the breakthrough in this connection came in Quebec, but by the mid-1990s, it had been followed by all provinces except Alberta, Newfoundland, and P.E.I. Even stranger, perhaps, is that the federal government was among the laggards in adding such a clause to the federal Human Rights Act, not doing so until 1996. The federal and provincial legislation protects homosexuals from discrimination in the private sector.

When the Charter of Rights was adopted in 1982, section 15 prohibited discrimination by government or in law on the basis of sex. Sexual orientation was not explicitly included, but in 1995 the Supreme Court of Canada ruled unanimously that the clause did indeed include sexual orientation. In the very case where it made this declaration, however, the Court split on whether such discrimination was involved in denying the spouses' pension to same-sex couples. The deciding judge in the case ruled that denial of pension rights constituted a reasonable limit on such discrimination, so that the specific claimants actually lost. Justice Minister Allan Rock even ran into considerable difficulty with his attempts to increase the sentences for those who committed violent acts that involved hatred, with the inclusion of hatred toward homosexuals being particularly controversial.

Regardless of the Constitution and the law, many employers in both the public and private sectors have extended employee benefits (health, dental, and retirement plans) to same-sex couples. No government has yet made this practice mandatory by law, and an attempt to do so was defeated in the Ontario legislature in 1994.

NOTES

1. Thomas R. Berger, *A Long and Terrible Shadow: White Values, Native Rights in the Americas* (Vancouver: Douglas and McIntyre, 1991).
2. "Building a New Partnership" (March 1995); *Basic Departmental Data, 1994* (January 1995).
3. Geoffrey York and Loreen Pindera, *People of the Pines: The Warriors and the Legacy of Oka* (Toronto: Little Brown, 1991); Craig MacLaine and Michael Baxendale, *This Land Is Our Land* (Toronto: Optimum, 1990).
4. Jean Leonard Elliott and Augie Fleras, *Multiculturalism in Canada: The Challenge of Diversity* (Scarborough: Nelson Canada, 1991); Elliott and Fleras, *Unequal Relations: An Introduction to Race and Ethnic Dynamics in Canada* (Scarborough: Prentice-Hall Canada, 1991).
5. Neil Bissoondath, *Selling Illusions: The Cult of Multiculturalism in Canada* (Toronto: Penguin, 1994); John Nunziata, "Multiculturalism Policy Feeds Discrimination," *The Toronto Star*, 31 October 1989.
6. Penney Kome, *Women of Influence* (Toronto: University of Toronto Press, 1985), 86.
7. Statistics Canada, *Earnings of Men and Women, 1995*, cat. no. 13-217-XPB (January 1997).
8. Penney Kome, *The Taking of Twenty-Eight* (Toronto: Women's Educational Press, 1983); *Women of Influence*, ch. 10.
9. Janine Brodie et al., *The Politics of Abortion* (Toronto: Oxford University Press, 1992).
10. National Council of Welfare, *Poverty Profile 1994*; David Ross and Richard Shillington, *The Canadian Fact Book on Poverty—1994* (Ottawa: Canadian Council on Social Development, 1994).

FURTHER READING

Aboriginals

Berger, Thomas. *A Long and Terrible Shadow: White Values, Native Rights in the Americas.* Vancouver: Douglas and McIntyre, 1991.

Boldt, Menno. *Surviving as Indians: The Challenge of Self-Government.* Toronto: University of Toronto Press, 1993.

Canada. *Report of the Royal Commission on Aboriginal Peoples.* 5 vols. Ottawa: Minister of Supply and Services Canada, 1996.

Dickerson. Mark O. *Whose North? Political Change, Political Development and Self-Government in the Northwest Territories.* Vancouver: UBC Press, 1992.

Frideres, James S. *Native People in Canada: Contemporary Conflicts.* 4th ed., Scarborough: Prentice-Hall Canada, 1993.

Mercredi, Ovid. *In the Rapids: Navigating the Future of First Nations.* Toronto: Viking, 1993.

Purich, Donald J. *The Inuit and Their Law: The Story of Nunavut.* Toronto: Lorimer, 1992.

York, Geoffrey, and Loreen Pindera. *People of the Pines: The Warriors and the Legacy of Oka.* Toronto: Little, Brown, 1991.

Other Ethnic Groups

Bissoondath, Neil. *Selling Illusions: The Cult of Multiculturalism in Canada.* Toronto: Penguin, 1994.

Elliott, Jean Leonard, and Augie Fleras. *Multiculturalism in Canada: The Challenge of Diversity.* Scarborough: Nelson Canada, 1991.

————. *Unequal Relations: An Introduction to Race and Ethnic Dynamics in Canada.* Scarborough: Prentice-Hall Canada, 1991.

Gender

Bashevkin, Sylvia. *Toeing the Lines.* Toronto: University of Toronto Press, 1985; 2nd ed., 1992.

Canada. *Report of the Royal Commission on the Status of Women.* Ottawa: Information Canada, 1970.

Herman, Didi. *Rights of Passage: Struggles for Lesbian and Gay Legal Equality.* Toronto: University of Toronto Press, 1994.

MacIvor, H. *Women and Politics in Canada.* Peterborough, Ont.: Broadview, 1994.

Sharpe, Sydney. *The Gilded Ghetto: Women and Political Power in Canada.* Toronto: HarperCollins, 1994.

Chapter 5

The American Presence and Other External Forces

Canada does not exist in a vacuum; instead, it is linked to the rest of the world by all sorts of political, economic, defensive, cultural, demographic, and individual ties. These links have an ever-increasing impact upon the Canadian political system, complicating the efforts of governments to pursue their own policy preferences.

In colonial times, all basic governmental decisions for the country were made abroad. As Canada emerged into a sovereign state, however, the world was becoming increasingly interdependent, so that even though it gained the legal powers to make decisions for itself, it faced a multitude of external influences. Given its location next to the most powerful country on earth, Canada has been particularly susceptible to influence from the United States in the second half of the twentieth century.

This chapter details Canada's road to sovereignty from Britain and its slow but steady absorption into the U.S. sphere of influence. The United States serves as a model for many Canadians. Its influence can be seen most clearly in the areas of defence and foreign policy, economics, culture, and the free trade agreements. The chapter discusses the demands and pressures that the United States makes upon the Canadian political system, the effects of the U.S. presence on Canadian values and opinions, and the policies that have been adopted both to foster and to resist such absorption. Finally, the variety of other international, multinational, and supranational pressures to which the Canadian political system is subject will also be addressed.

The Road to Canadian Sovereignty from Britain

The British North American colonies were largely self-governing in internal affairs even before 1867. Contrary to popular belief, the British North America Act of 1867 (that is, the Constitution Act, 1867) did not directly advance the cause of Canadian independence. That act simply divided the powers that were already being exercised in Canada between a new central government and the provincial governments. The act of confederation made Canada a more respectable and viable entity and ultimately strengthened its case for greater autonomy, but 1867, as such, did not alter the British–Canadian relationship.

Canada had succeeded in claiming the right to control its own tariffs even before Confederation, and between 1867 and 1914 it became increasingly autonomous in making commercial treaties with other countries. The same was true in terms of political treaties, although progress in this area came more slowly.

By the turn of the century Canadian autonomy had progressed to the point that when Canada sent an official contingent to the South African (Boer) War, it was done more in response to Canadian public opinion than to British pressure. In the Alaska Boundary dispute of 1903, however, the British representative on the Anglo-Canadian half of the judicial tribunal voted with the three American representatives to award the United States a long strip of the northern British Columbia coastline.

The ultimate independence of Canada and several other British colonies is usually attributed to developments connected to the First World War. Although Canada was automatically at war in 1914 as a result of British action, the Canadian government determined the extent of its own commitments. A series of conferences of Dominion prime ministers called the Imperial War Cabinet began in 1917 as Canada and the other Dominions demanded a policymaking role in return for their wartime contributions. Prime Minister Robert Borden and his counterparts took part in the Paris Peace Conference and signed the peace treaties, and the Dominions became individual members of the League of Nations. Thus, by 1919, Canada had gained new international status as a result of accomplishments on the battlefield and subsequent demands for recognition at the conference table.

Postwar attempts to forge a unified Empire foreign policy broke down as various Dominions sought to flex their fledgling muscles, and Canada insisted on being the sole signatory of the 1923 Halibut Treaty with the United States. The Imperial Conference of 1926 ended with a proclamation of the complete equality of the United Kingdom and the Dominions in internal, international, and imperial affairs. They were proclaimed

> autonomous Communities within the British Empire, equal in
> status, in no way subordinate one to another in any aspect of
> their domestic or external affairs, though united by a common

allegiance to the Crown, and freely associated as members of the British Commonwealth of Nations.[1]

Besides giving Canada complete autonomy in all policy fields, the developments of 1926 had implications for the position of governor general. This official would no longer be an agent of the British government, but rather only a representative of the Crown. These arrangements were refined at another conference in 1930 and then constitutionalized in the Statute of Westminster of 1931.

After 1931, therefore, Canada was completely independent of Britain, but a number of anomalies continued to disguise this fact. First, Canada continued to share a head of state with Britain, although from the Canadian perspective, that person was King or Queen of Canada. Of more importance, since Canada had not been able to decide how to amend the B.N.A. Act within Canada, such amendments still had to be passed by the British Parliament, albeit only at Canadian request. In 1949 a procedure was developed to make constitutional amendments in Canada if they affected only the federal government, but it was not until 1982 that a comprehensive domestic formula for making constitutional amendments was agreed to. Also of great significance, the Judicial Committee of the Privy Council remained Canada's final court of appeal in criminal cases until 1933 and in all other cases, notably constitutional, until 1949. Other British legacies included the fact that until 1965 the Union Jack and the Red Ensign continued to serve as Canadian flags, and only in 1967 did the government recognize "O Canada" rather than "God Save the Queen" as the Canadian national anthem.

Once Canada made an autonomous decision to take part, the Second World War saw its armed forces integrated with the allied powers. Afterward, however, British–Canadian ties declined as Canada's population became more diversified in its ethnic origins, as Britain occupied a diminished role in world affairs, and as Canada drew closer to the United States.[2] The 1982 Constitution Act provided a made-in-Canada amending formula, representing a final break with Britain.

In the 1990s, Canada is part of the Commonwealth and continues to share the Queen with Britain and several other countries; nationals of both Canada and Britain have invested in each other's economies; the Canadian parliamentary and legal systems are based on those of Britain; a majority of Canadians speak a variant of the English language; and many are still linked to Britain by family ties. Otherwise, however, both Canada and Britain see each other as just another friendly, foreign country, with minimal influence and no control.

....

American Influence in Defence and Foreign Policy

Canada's first military engagement after achieving full autonomy was the Second World War, but in the early 1940s, Canada signed two defence pacts with the United States. After the war, the United States became increasingly obsessed with containing Soviet communism, and in 1949 persuaded Canada and most west European countries to form a new military alliance, the North Atlantic Treaty Organization (NATO). Commitments to NATO required a great increase in the size of the Canadian armed forces. U.S. attention was then drawn to the confrontation between North and South Korea, and the United Nations military intervention in the Korean War was effectively a U.S. effort to which Canada made a significant military contribution, losing 1550 lives.

The next phase of the North Americanization of Canadian defence was a series of radar screens built across the United States and Canada during the 1950s to intercept anticipated Soviet bombers. These arrangements logically led to the North American Aerospace Defence Command (NORAD) of 1958. The agreement provided for a joint Canada–U.S. air defence system with headquarters in Colorado; an American was commander-in-chief and a Canadian was second in command. A Defence Production Sharing Program was established in 1959.

Prime Minister John Diefenbaker encountered two serious missile crises with the United States in the 1957–63 period. When U.S. President John Kennedy used the establishment of Soviet missile bases in Cuba as an excuse to announce a naval blockade of that country, the Canadian cabinet waited three days before putting its armed forces in a state of highest alert. Since the Americans expected this would be done automatically, the Cuban missile crisis soured relations between the two leaders. The problem was compounded by American annoyance at Canada's stand with respect to BOMARC missiles. These had been established by the United States at two bases in Canada as part of the NORAD Agreement and were intended to be armed with nuclear warheads. Some cabinet ministers wished to take possession of the warheads as planned, but others argued that to place the warheads on Canadian soil would appear to proliferate the nuclear arms race. The Canadian–American defence relationship thus became a prominent issue in the 1962 and 1963 election campaigns. The Diefenbaker government fell apart over the issue in 1963 and was defeated on a nonconfidence motion; the Liberals won the resulting election under Lester Pearson. The new prime minister had the warheads installed as part of Canada's international commitments, but they were ultimately removed in 1971.

Pearson's successor, Pierre Trudeau, cut military spending and, in a new emphasis on protecting domestic sovereignty, halved Canada's NATO contingent in 1969. Nevertheless, the NORAD Agreement was repeatedly renewed. The most prominent new issue had to do with allowing the United States to test yet another new weapon, the Cruise missile, over Canadian territory because of the resemblance of its terrain to that of the Soviet Union. In spite of considerable popular protest, the Trudeau government allowed the tests to take place starting in 1983, as did successor governments.

The Mulroney government promised to make defence a much higher priority than during the Trudeau years and published a hawkish White Paper on the subject in 1987. Public opposition and budgetary considerations prevented the paper's implementation, a decision that appeared to have been far-sighted when the Cold War effectively ended a year or so later.

Thus it is clear that from 1945 to 1991 the United States exerted significant pressure on Canadian defence policy. Even though Canada did not always respond as energetically as the United States wished, such external demands influenced Canadian political outcomes. Some Canadians were satisfied with the arrangement because the country was essentially protected by the U.S. military arsenal and had to pay relatively little for its own defence. Others did not like the U.S. pressure and the loss of control of a vital aspect of public policy.

To the extent that foreign policy can be distinguished from defence policy, the degree of U.S. influence in this field has also been a controversial question. Canada sees itself as a "middle power" that has staked out an independent position on recognizing and/or trading with countries such as China, Cuba, and the Soviet Union. On the other hand, the United States tends to view Canadian support of its initiatives as automatic. The Canadian government was quick to respond to U.S. demands to contribute to its military efforts in Kuwait and its peacekeeping mission in Somalia, both ostensibly in the name of the United Nations. In the mid-1990s, long after the demise of the Soviet Union, the United States continued to retaliate against Canadian companies that did business in Cuba.

More independently, Canada responded to international pressure and made a major humanitarian contribution in the Bosnian civil war, as well as in Rwanda. Until Somalia, Canada had an impressive record as an international peacekeeper, but the outrageous behaviour of some members of the Airborne Regiment somewhat sullied this reputation.

....

American Economic Influence on Canada

The economic influence of the United States on Canada is even more pervasive than its impact on defence and foreign policy. This influence is felt in almost every aspect of Canadian life, including investment, trade, environment, energy, and labour unions. In many ways, Canada constitutes a zone within the American economy rather than a distinctive national economy.

Foreign Investment

A new country is not likely to produce enough domestic capital to finance all the development projects that appear desirable. Therefore, in the early years, a great deal of investment in Canada came from Britain. Some of this foreign capital was in the form of British companies operating in Canada, such as the Hudson's Bay Company, but to a large extent it took the form of Canadian borrowing in the London bond market. Interest had to be paid on such loans, but ownership remained largely in Canadian hands.

Later, the source of foreign investment largely shifted from Britain to the United States. Moreover, the form of investment switched from loans to "direct" or "equity" investment, that is, control through the ownership of shares. Table 5.1 indicates the shift from British to U.S. investment in Canada between 1900 and 1967. Thus, to a large extent the Canadian economy has come to consist of branch plants of U.S. parent corporations. These companies typically operate in many other countries, too, and therefore gain the label of *multinational* or *transnational corporations*.

This pattern of economic development was fostered in the first instance by the National Policy of 1879, which put a tariff on imported manufactured goods. Rather than export to Canada from the United States and pay the tariff, U.S. companies set up branch plants within Canada behind the tariff wall. This was advantageous for the creation of employment in Canada and contributed to the general prosperity of the country, especially Ontario. As time went on, however, considerable capital was generated within Canada, but the degree of foreign ownership continued to increase.

TABLE 5.1 PERCENTAGE OF BRITISH, U.S., AND OTHER FOREIGN INVESTMENT IN
CANADA, 1900–1967

	1900	1914	1930	1939	1946	1950	1960	1967
U.S.	13.6	23.0	61.2	60.0	71.8	75.5	75.2	80.7
U.K.	85.2	72.4	36.3	35.8	23.2	20.1	15.1	10.3
Other	1.1	4.6	2.4	4.1	4.9	4.2	9.6	8.9

Source: Privy Council Office, Foreign Direct Investment in Canada (the Gray Report, 1972), 15. Reproduced with the permission of the Minister of Public Works and Government Services Canada, 1997.

It was not only U.S. manufacturers that moved into Canada; so too did foreign companies that sought to exploit Canadian natural resources. "A large proportion of the investment in resource exploitation reflected the needs of the United States investors for raw materials for their processing and manufacturing plants in the United States." This integration often had the practical impact "of reducing the likelihood of further processing activity of Canadian natural resources in Canada."[3] Thus, along with many aspects of manufacturing, the mining, forestry, and petroleum industries came to be characterized by a high degree of foreign, mostly American, ownership. In fact, Canada has more foreign ownership than any other advanced industrial country.

The 10 largest multinationals operating in Canada in 1997 are identified in Table 5.2. Other familiar foreign-owned corporate names include Mitsui, Honda, Cargill, A & P, Mobil Oil, Price Costco, Weyerhaeuser, Ultramar, DuPont, Fletcher Challenge, General Electric, McDonald's, Toyota, Digital Equipment, and Pratt & Whitney. In total, 30 of the top 100 companies in Canada in terms of 1996 sales were foreign owned.

Most advocates of the capitalist system such as "free-market" economists are enthusiastic boosters of unlimited foreign investment. They claim that maximum efficiency results from capital being able to flow to wherever it will yield the greatest returns. In this case, defenders of foreign investment argue that Canada still needs foreign capital and that such investment creates jobs, which in turn raise the Canadian standard of living. They also say that efficiency is enhanced when multinationals transfer "state-of-the-art" technology as well as well-trained managers and management techniques to their branch plants.

Others take the view that these advantages are short-term or short-sighted.[4] In the first place, multinationals are likely to purchase supplies and component

TABLE 5.2 TEN LARGEST MULTINATIONAL COMPANIES IN CANADA, 1996 SALES

Company	Home Country	National Ranking
General Motors of Canada	U.S.	2
Ford Motor Co. of Canada	U.S.	3
Chrysler Canada	U.S.	4
IBM Canada	U.S.	11
Imperial Oil	U.S.	13
Amoco Canada Petroleum	U.S.	20
Shell Canada	Netherlands	26
Canada Safeway	U.S.	30
Sears Canada	U.S.	36
Total Petroleum (North America)	France	38

Source: The Financial Post 500, *Summer 1997. Reproduced with the permission of* The Financial Post.

parts from the parent company or parent country, rather than buying them and creating employment in Canada. Second, their plants usually remain small and inefficient because they are designed to serve only the Canadian market rather than being encouraged to compete in export markets with the parent plant or with branches set up in other countries. Critics also claim that a branch-plant economy suffers because most of its research and development (R & D) is done in the parent plant. This limits the number of interesting and challenging jobs in science, engineering, and technology located in Canada. As convenient as it is to import such technology, this process hinders Canadian innovative efforts to develop distinctive export products, for almost all studies indicate that R & D is the secret of future economic success.

Critics of the situation also worry that if layoffs or shutdowns are necessary, these are usually slated for branch plants first. Such a high degree of U.S. ownership perpetuates the resource-export orientation of the Canadian economy and discourages Canadians from becoming more than "hewers of wood and drawers of water." The ultimate symbolic disadvantage of foreign-owned companies is that they may occasionally choose or be required to conform to the laws of the country in which their parent is located rather than those of Canada. The extension of U.S. laws to branch plants located in Canada is called *extraterritoriality*, and has regularly occurred, especially in the case of the Trading With the Enemy Act and the Helms-Burton Act. When branch plants in Canada have tried to do business with countries on the U.S. "enemy list," they have been told that they must follow U.S. law, thus reducing production and job opportunities in Canada.

The policies that Canadian governments have adopted to counter this threat of U.S. or other foreign ownership of the Canadian economy can be divided into four main categories. First, Crown corporations—government-owned enterprises—have been established to ensure that the company involved remains in Canadian hands. The Bank of Canada, Atomic Energy of Canada Ltd., and Petro-Canada were federal outputs in response to demands that a Canadian presence in strategic industries be retained.

Second, while leaving other corporations to function privately, the federal government has often created regulatory agencies. The main such agency was the Foreign Investment Review Agency (FIRA), established in the early 1970s. FIRA screened foreign takeovers of larger Canadian companies and new ventures by foreign firms in Canada, approving the deal if it involved "significant benefit to Canada." In fact, FIRA and the cabinet rarely disallowed any such initiatives and imposed minimal conditions, but FIRA became a major irritant to the United States, and the Mulroney government replaced it with Investment Canada. In its recast form, the agency had the opposite objective of attracting increased foreign investment to Canada. Other regulatory agencies include the National Energy Board and the Atomic Energy Control Board, both of which were designed to protect the Canadian national interest in certain important respects.

In the third place, ownership restrictions and tax incentives have been introduced. Maximum foreign ownership limits exist in certain fields such as broadcasting, financial institutions, newspapers and publishing, and (before the Free Trade Agreement) banking. Incentives to Canadian ownership were exemplified by the National Energy Program of 1980, under which, largely via tax write-offs, the Reichmann brothers bought Gulf Canada from its American owners. Finally, the government has established funding agencies such as the Business Development Bank of Canada, whose mandate is to encourage Canadian entrepreneurship when the commercial banks are not interested.

Many of these policies were half-hearted and others were later diluted under U.S. pressure. Many were weakened or withdrawn by the Mulroney government, both to increase foreign investment and to remove irritants in the Canada–U.S. relationship. Thus, economic nationalists regard the situation as more critical than ever, especially in the light of the free trade agreements. Others remain indifferent or take the opposite side of this issue, seeing foreign investment as the source of badly needed jobs.

Other Economic Influences

TRADE

Because of geographic proximity, it is only logical that Canada and the United States be closely linked by trade. It is even more likely because of their complementary resources and industries—the abundance of primary resources in Canada and the extent of manufacturing in the United States. Thus, Canadian dependence on the United States as a market for its exports and as a source of its imports has gradually increased over time. Indeed, most provinces trade more with neighbouring states than with each other, although much of this trade is of an intrafirm character rather than truly international.

Canadian exports to the United States exceeded those to the United Kingdom after 1921 and edged up to over 82 percent of all exports by 1994. Imports from the United States constituted nearly 50 percent of the Canadian total from the start and rose to 75 percent in 1994.

Given the degree to which Canadian prosperity depends on export trade, it is advantageous to have ready access to the U.S. market; it is also convenient to have such a close supply of goods that are not produced in Canada. On the other hand, to have put so many eggs in one basket means that in times of U.S. recession, demand for Canadian goods falls off and the Canadian economy declines, whereas in prosperous periods, U.S. inflation also tends to increase prices in Canada. Furthermore, protectionist pressure in the United States for new or increased tariffs or quotas against Canadian exports can have a devastating effect on certain industries. This problem could be dealt with by diversifying the Canadian export effort or by negotiating sectoral or comprehensive free trade agreements with the United States. While the Pearson government signed the sectoral Auto Pact with the United States to guarantee a balanced exchange of automobiles and parts, the Mulroney government chose to sign a comprehensive free trade deal and then to extend it to Mexico. Canada often has a positive balance with the United States in merchandise trade, but this is somewhat artificial, given the extent of imported parts within the exported goods; moreover, the non-merchandise sector, including travel, services, and outflowing profits and dividends, usually results in an overall Canadian deficit in the total trade between the two countries.

THE ENVIRONMENT

Canadians have seriously damaged their own environment over the years, but the situation has been aggravated by proximity to the United States and by some of its even less restrictive anti-pollution laws. The largest transboundary environmental issue is that of acid rain. Canadian research generally shows that about 50 percent of the acid rain falling north of the Canada–U.S. border is caused by U.S. sources. These emissions fall into Canadian lakes and rivers, killing plant and animal life, as well as damaging trees, cars, and buildings. Thus, after pressing the issue for many years, Canada warmly welcomed the U.S. Clean Air Act of 1990 as a major forward step in controlling North American air pollution.

The pollution of the Great Lakes is the other serious bilateral environmental problem. Here again, each side is to blame, but most of the responsibility rests with the chemicals discharged from the larger number of factories and waste dumps situated on the U.S. shores of the lakes. Phosphorous levels were reduced in the 1970s, but the Great Lakes are still in a critical state because of toxic pollution. Indeed, recent government cutbacks in environmental protection on both sides of the border have made the problem worse.

Canada has been involved in many offshore fishing disputes, especially on the Atlantic coast, and often not involving Americans. But in the late 1990s, the major confrontation in this field was the "salmon war" with the United States on the Pacific coast.

ENERGY

In the energy sector, the voracious U.S. industrial complex usually wants to import Canadian electric power and petroleum. Governments in Quebec, New Brunswick, Manitoba, and B.C. have been eager to export electricity, and those of Alberta, Saskatchewan, and B.C., to supply oil and natural gas. The federal government has normally approved these sales with little hesitation, although the National Energy Board is charged to ensure that long-term Canadian needs will not be compromised in the process. Native and environmental groups in some provinces have not been so favourably disposed to the hydro or nuclear plants necessary to produce the electricity, however, and Canadian nationalists worry about the future supply of petroleum for domestic purposes.

The degree of U.S. ownership of the Canadian petroleum industry has also caused considerable conflict between the two countries. The National Energy Program (NEP) of 1980 set a target of 50 percent Canadian ownership of the oil and gas industry by 1990 and gave certain preferences to Petro-Canada and private Canadian firms. U.S. petroleum companies in Canada protested, and their government pressured Canada to remove these incentives to Canadianization. The Mulroney cabinet dismantled the NEP and began to privatize Petro-Canada.

TRADE UNIONS

Historically, Canadian trade unions have been just as closely allied with those in the United States as was the case with the corporations for which their members worked. Many unions in Canada, such as the United Steelworkers of America and the United Food and Commercial Workers, are part of "international unions" with their headquarters in the United States. The Canadian union movement justified the relationship by arguing that as long as it had to bargain with multinational corporations it needed the support of international unions, especially their larger strike funds. Membership in international unions peaked in 1965 at 67 percent of all union members in Canada. In recent years, however, a nationalist trend has been apparent in the Canadian labour movement, and several unions have cut their ties with the international headquarters. Bob White's creation of an autonomous Canadian Auto Workers union is the most striking example. Thus, in 1996, 1 188 000 Canadians belonged to international unions out of a total union membership of 4 033 000, or 29.4 percent.[5]

The Free Trade Agreements

Canada is one of the leading trading countries of the world on a per capita basis and was seventh in absolute terms in 1989. Trade constitutes over 30 percent of its national income, and provides about three million jobs. At the same time as they try to maximize their exports, however, all countries seek to protect their domestic industry from foreign competition through the imposition of tariffs, quotas, and customs duties.

In 1947, Canada was among the signatories of the General Agreement on Tariffs and Trade (GATT) under which countries pledged to remove such trade restrictions on a multinational basis. GATT allows its members to go even further with bilateral agreements, as Canada and the United States did in defence production arrangements and the 1965 Auto Pact. One way or another, close to 80 percent of Canada–U.S. trade was tariff-free even before 1985.

Canadian policymakers had been concerned for some time that the country was left out of the regional trading blocks being formed, especially the European

Union. Then, in the early 1980s, a protectionist mood descended upon the U.S. Congress, and new barriers to many Canadian exports were imposed: on shakes and shingles, softwood lumber, potash, potatoes, fish, and specialty steel.

THE CANADA–U.S. FREE TRADE AGREEMENT

Such protectionist measures combined with the recommendation of the Macdonald Royal Commission on the Economic Union and Development Prospects for Canada that the country take such a "leap of faith" apparently converted Brian Mulroney to the concept of free trade. Mulroney found another advocate of free trade in the White House, so he and Ronald Reagan set the negotiations in motion. The Canada–U.S. Free Trade Agreement (FTA) was finalized in October 1987, given congressional and parliamentary approval in 1988, and took effect on January 1, 1989. It was a wide-ranging pact covering almost every aspect of the relationship between the two countries.[6]

The agreement removed almost all barriers to the flow of goods and services between the two countries over a 10-year period. Each country could henceforth send its products to the other without tariffs, quotas, or other impediments, extending the "national treatment" principle to each other, but each continued to apply its own tariffs to imports from other countries. Most services were also included.

In the area of financial services, a significant change was the elimination for U.S. investors of the 25 percent ceiling on foreign ownership of Canadian banks. As for other investment, U.S. businesses would now be able to start new operations in Canada without restriction (and vice versa); Investment Canada could only screen acquisitions of firms with a value over $150 million and could not impose any performance requirements. Thus, the investment situation essentially returned to the pre-FIRA era.

Energy, agriculture, the Auto Pact, and cultural industries were four of the most controversial sections of the agreement. A North American energy pool was created in which prices could not be discriminatory (that is, Canada had to sell oil, gas, or electricity to the United States at the Canadian domestic price), and if cutbacks were ever necessary, domestic sales had to be reduced by the same proportion as exports. In agriculture, Canada had to remove import restrictions on chickens, turkeys, and eggs, as well as tariffs on processed food, and the agreement enunciated the goal of ultimately eliminating all subsidies that distort agricultural trade. The Auto Pact was also changed to some extent (to Ontario's chagrin) in order to incorporate U.S. concerns. In theory, the agreement did not affect existing cultural programs; however, any new support of cultural industries could be met by retaliation of equivalent value by the other country.

For any future conflicts in trade between the two countries, a complex dispute-settlement mechanism was set up that involved binational panels and binding arbitration. If either country refused to abide by the final decision of the arbitrators, however, the other could retaliate ("countervail"), as before.

ADVANTAGES AND DISADVANTAGES OF THE FTA

Those Canadians who favoured the agreement argued that in the absence of the deal the United States would have continued to apply a series of protectionist measures, threatening more jobs. Canadian firms would now have access to the huge unprotected U.S. market, allowing them to expand and create employment. Supporters of the FTA admitted that many Canadian firms would go under and thousands of Canadian jobs would be lost because of the competition from larger American companies, but they claimed that such competition would force Canadian corporations to become stronger, more efficient, and more capable of functioning in the global economy. Defenders also hailed the likelihood of increased U.S. investment in Canada, as well as higher levels of investment from other countries wishing to take advantage of Canadian access to the U.S. market. The deal was clearly designed to enshrine neoconservative values and prevent the recurrence of such economic nationalistic measures as FIRA and NEP.[7]

While the Conservative government found supporters among big business, Western resource industries, and the province of Quebec, the federal Liberal and New Democratic parties opposed the FTA, along with the province of Ontario, organized labour, and nationalist groups.[8] Opponents argued that the deal would lead to a loss of jobs rather than an increase because the Canadian market would be inundated by U.S. exports and small Canadian firms would not be able to compete. Massive layoffs and shutdowns were predicted, particularly in such industries as processed food, electrical goods, textiles, clothing, and footwear, where the labour force was largely female. Jobs would also be lost because U.S. branch plants would close, the Canadian market being supplied instead from the parent plant south of the border, and some Canadian firms would move to the United States to take advantage of backward labour and environmental laws in certain states.

The actual results have been mixed, but more significantly, the number of conflicts under the agreement has been large. Some of the same issues that precipitated the Free Trade Agreement have continued to be problems, especially

Canadian exports of softwood lumber. Other areas of dispute include uranium, beer, government procurement, magnesium, steel, swine, wheat, sugar, peanut butter, tobacco, milk, meat, paper, salmon and herring, poultry products, magazine publishing, and country-music television.

THE NORTH AMERICAN FREE TRADE AGREEMENT

The ink was hardly dry on the Canada–U.S. Free Trade Agreement when the Mulroney government entered talks with the United States and Mexico that produced the North American Free Trade Agreement (NAFTA). It essentially extended FTA to Mexico: most provisions in the two agreements were identical. This initiative was not so much of Canada's choice; Canada mainly entered it to preclude the other partners from endangering its position, although some corporations saw it as a means of enhancing the efficiency of their operations. Opponents feared that companies would move from Canada to Mexico because of the low wages and environmental standards in that country; they also complained that Mexico was able to negotiate a stronger energy clause with the United States than Canada had been able to under the FTA. Despite pre-election fanfare, the new Chrétien government was content with minor changes in the pact once in office.

In the wake of these agreements, Canada signed the "Open Skies" agreement with the United States in 1995. It deregulated the cross-border airline industry, giving U.S. and Canadian companies equal access to routes between the two countries. Shortly afterward, Canada participated in negotiating the Multilateral Agreement on Investment, agreeing to treat foreign companies the same as domestic ones.

American Influence on Canadian Culture

People around the world enjoy U.S. popular culture. Canadians are a particularly captive market, given their geographical proximity, their linguistic similarity, their small domestic market, their chronic feeling of dependence and inferiority, and the degree of economic integration between the two countries. The general public has little consciousness of the origin of most pop culture fare, and even less concern that so much of it comes from the United States. But many nationalists among the intellectual elite are disturbed by the high proportion of television, magazines, movies, books, and music in Canada that emanates from the United

States. They are concerned that this cultural invasion stifles the development of a distinctive Canadian national identity, worry about its influence on Canadian attitudes and values, and wonder how long a separate political system can be maintained in these circumstances.

Television, Magazines, Motion Pictures, Books, and Sound Recordings

Television was the most significant cultural institution of the second half of the twentieth century. The average Canadian watches about 22.8 hours of television per week, and 63.5 percent of that is foreign (mostly American) programming.[9] Broken down by language group, anglophones watch 74.5 percent foreign programs, while francophones watch only 35.1 percent. Some Canadians live close enough to the U.S. border to receive U.S. channels through the air; failing that, Canadian stations broadcast a large proportion of U.S. programming. Then, almost 75 percent of Canadian households have purchased cable television that normally offers them all the U.S. networks as well as additional Canadian channels. Beyond cable, many Canadians have pay television, which extends the U.S. content. Finally, satellite dishes can pick up even more U.S. channels, and by 1997 pizza-sized dishes allowed direct-to-home satellite transmission.

There are two main reasons why Canadian television networks broadcast so much U.S. programming. First, it is much cheaper to buy a U.S. show or series than to produce a Canadian one. Second, while Canadians watch their own news, public affairs, and sports programs quite conscientiously, U.S. programs otherwise attract a larger audience. They therefore command higher advertising rates than do Canadian programs. (CTV contends, for example, that each hour of Canadian television represents over $5 million in lost annual profit margin.) Nevertheless, Canadian television has a higher reputation abroad than it does at home, and those few Canadian series that are produced are readily sold to foreign networks.

Magazines are perhaps the second most important vehicle of popular culture, and this Canadian industry is also permeated by U.S. content. While Canadian magazines lead foreign magazines in subscriptions in Canada, foreign magazines account for 81 percent of English-language newsstand sales. Overall, Canadian magazines have increased from 23.3 percent in 1959 to 67.6 percent of the total circulation in 1992, but as with television, the picture is much more positive on the French side (95 percent) than the English (60 percent).

The Canadian motion picture industry is even weaker than television or magazines, and the average Canadian moviegoer has rarely if ever seen a Canadian feature film. Less than 5 percent of the screen time in Canadian movie theatres was devoted to Canadian films in 1992, and most of that is in the large, sophisticated Toronto and Montreal markets. U.S. movie producers make many feature films in Canada every year, taking advantage of its prices, scenic locations, and technical expertise, but these are almost always disguised as U.S. movies. The problem has many causes, including the fact that the film distribution system is U.S.-controlled, the undeniable Canadian fascination with Hollywood, the small Canadian market, and a shortage of funds. Canadian productions do slightly better in the home video market, where Canadian-content films rose to 23 percent in 1992.

When it comes to books, the Canadian market is again dominated by U.S. content. Sales of Canadian-authored books by Canadian-owned publishers totalled $331 million out of total book sales in Canada of $1286 million in 1992–93.[10] Both Canadian-owned companies and foreign-owned publishers operating in Canada sell foreign as well as Canadian titles, for books are like television shows: they are cheaper to import than to make domestically. Most Canadian bookstores make little effort to sell Canadian books, and paperback books at newspaper stands, drug stores, supermarkets, and cigar stores come almost entirely from the United States because the publisher-distributors who control the supply are U.S.-owned companies.

As for sound recording, some 15 foreign-controlled companies had 84.6 percent of sales in Canada, even though 172 Canadian-controlled companies were also in business. More significantly, sales with Canadian content constituted only about 12 percent of total sales, and among new releases, 673 contained Canadian content compared to 5602 that did not.

In short, in the five cultural industries of television, magazines, movies, books, and sound recordings, Canadian-owned companies produce virtually all of the Canadian output. But these companies are marginal players in a Canadian market dominated by subsidiaries of large, mainly U.S., multinationals. That there is a Canadian presence at all in such industries is largely the result of demands made by the nationalist minority for protection from U.S. domination and for promotion of Canadian content.

Countering the U.S. Influence

The Crown corporation is a nationalistic instrument in the cultural field, as it is in economic matters. The Canadian Broadcasting Corporation (CBC), in its radio and television networks, and Radio-Canada, its French-language equivalent, is perhaps the most crucial agent of Canadian cultural expression. Today, CBC radio has virtually 100 percent Canadian content, and can be heard in almost every part of the country. Its programs are widely regarded as crucial links in keeping the country together. CBC television is less successful, mainly because the television medium is so expensive. The Mulroney government slashed millions of dollars from the CBC budget after 1984, making the corporation's task even harder. Every study of the problem has said that the CBC should receive stable, multiyear public funding to enable it to fulfil its mandate, but the Chrétien government cut its budget even further.[11]

Another Crown corporation, the National Film Board, has also had an illustrious existence, making impressive Canadian films and winning many international awards. It has two serious disadvantages, however: insufficient funding to make feature films, so that it has specialized instead in documentaries and shorts; and no effective mechanism for making its films available to the general public.

A second policy instrument to protect and promote Canadian culture is a regulatory agency, the Canadian Radio-television and Telecommunications Commission (CRTC). This agency issues broadcasting licences and Canadian-content regulations, the latter being more stringent for the CBC than for private stations and networks. CBC television has recently aired all-Canadian programs in prime time, whereas news, public affairs, and sports take up most of the required Canadian time on the private television networks, which produce very little Canadian drama. The CRTC also requires that radio stations play 30 percent Canadian music, a regulation that is generally seen as the catalyst for the explosion of the Canadian musical industry over the past 25 years.

The CRTC has been under strong industry and popular pressure to allow more U.S. outlets in Canada, so it permitted cable and pay television that diluted the audiences of Canadian channels. In 1995, the CRTC authorized direct-to-home (DTH) satellite services, the so-called "death-stars." Many nationalists fear for the fate of Canadian content in the not-too-distant future when the largely American 500-channel universe is beamed directly into Canadian homes.

A third policy instrument consists of Canadian ownership restrictions and financial incentives. Ownership restrictions in the cultural field apply to radio, television, and newspaper companies in Canada. Canadian firms can deduct magazine or television advertising expenses from their income tax only if those advertisements are placed in Canadian magazines or on Canadian TV channels. Moreover, tariff rules prohibit the entry into Canada of split-run editions of foreign magazines containing advertisements directed at Canadians. A major controversy occurred when these measures were introduced in 1965 against the Canadian edition of *Time* magazine, which was masquerading as a Canadian magazine. In the 1990s, *Sports Illustrated* started to produce a Canadian split-run edition that challenged the law because such editions could now be physically printed in Canada via satellite.

A fourth device to promote Canadian culture is the funding agency. The Canada Council, set up in 1957, gives life-saving grants to hundreds of individual writers, artists, musicians, and playwrights, as well as to almost every orchestra, theatre centre, art gallery, ballet and opera company in the country, while Telefilm Canada subsidizes the production of feature films.

Other External Influences

Besides its membership in NATO and NORAD, Canada is also part of the British Commonwealth and the French equivalent, the Francophonie. These organizations provide some distinctive touches to Canadian foreign policy. So, too, does membership in the United Nations, where Canada has often played a distinguished part. Canada's admission to the Organization of American States and NAFTA will provide a new Latin American dimension to Canadian foreign policy in the future.

As in foreign policy, Canadian economic and social policies are also subject to many contemporary supranational influences beyond those of the United States.[12] The United Nations has had reason to criticize several domestic Canadian policies, including Quebec language legislation, and federal or provincial laws on labour, Aboriginals, women, and other subjects. The International Monetary Fund puts pressure on member countries to limit national deficits, and the leaders of the G7 (the Group of Seven leading Western industrialized countries) or the Summit of Eight (the G7 plus Russia) meet annually to try to come to a consensus on economic and other matters. The General Agreement on Tariffs and Trade, now renamed the World Trade Organization (WTO), actually orders its members to change their trading practices. In the Uruguay Round of GATT talks that concluded in 1993, Canada agreed to abandon its historic use of agricultural marketing boards, for example; in 1997, the WTO ordered Canada to allow split-run magazines and to discontinue postal subsidies to domestic magazines.

In addition to supranational organizations deliberately influencing Canadian public policies, Canada must increasingly respond to all sorts of other global forces. Money and investment flow between countries almost at will, and the government must cope with questions of international exchange rates and the balance of payments. When Canadian governments borrow money in foreign markets, bond-rating agencies and lending institutions influence government policies. It is widely acknowledged that national governments anywhere in the world have difficulty in regulating or taxing transnational corporations. Indeed, the "globalization" that has characterized corporate behaviour in recent years has meant that more companies are outgrowing their domestic state, that they are introducing new forms of technology at an incredible rate, and that they are opening or closing operations strictly on the basis of economic efficiency. Such globalization has had many implications for the economy, mostly in the form of transnational corporations closing their manufacturing plants in Canada. It is increasingly difficult for national or provincial governments to maintain distinctive labour, tax, or environmental laws because such companies regularly threaten to move to jurisdictions that they find more congenial.

Ironically, despite all this transnationalism, Canada's response is increasingly determined by its own domestic economic interests. A case in point is assistance to Third World countries that Canada provides regardless of human rights records, as long as it benefits Canada economically. The Chrétien government also announced that Canada would keep "trade before aid" in dealing with the Third World, as external policy was influenced by the government's internal budgetary situation.

....

NOTES

1. R. McGregor Dawson, *The Government of Canada*, 5th ed., rev. Norman Ward (Toronto: University of Toronto Press, 1970), 54.
2. Donald Creighton, *Canada's First Century* (Toronto: Macmillan, 1970); George Grant, *Lament for a Nation: The Defeat of Canadian Nationalism* (Toronto: McClelland and Stewart, 1965); J.L. Granatstein, *How Britain's Weakness Forced Canada into the Arms of the United States* (Toronto: University of Toronto Press, 1989).
3. Canada, *Foreign Direct Investment in Canada* (Ottawa: Supply and Services, 1972), 14. See also Stephen Brooks and Andrew Stritch, *Business and Government in Canada* (Scarborough:

Prentice-Hall Canada, 1991).

4. The pioneer of this theme was Kari Levitt, *Silent Surrender: The Multinational Corporation in Canada* (Toronto: Macmillan, 1970).

5. *Directory of Labour Organizations in Canada 1996*, Canada Communication Group, cat. no. L2-2/1996.

6. Bruce Doern and Brian Tomlin, *Faith and Fear: The Free Trade Story* (Toronto: Stoddart, 1991); Brooks and Stritch, *Business and Government in Canada*, ch. 13.

7. Glen Williams, "Regions within Region: Continentalism Ascendant," in Whittington and Williams, eds., *Canadian Politics in the 1990s*, 4th ed. (Scarborough: Nelson Canada, 1995).

8. Duncan Cameron, *The Free Trade Deal* (Toronto: Lorimer, 1988); Marjory Bowker, *On Guard for Thee* (Hull: Voyageur, 1988); John Warnock, *Free Trade and the New Right Agenda* (Vancouver: New Star Books, 1988); Maude Barlow, *Parcel of Rogues* (Toronto: Key Porter Books, 1991); Mel Hurtig, *The Betrayal of Canada* (Toronto: Stoddart, 1991).

9. Statistics Canada, *Television Viewing 1993*, cat. no. 87-208 (December 1994).

10. Statistics Canada, *Book Publishing 1992–93*, cat. no. 87-210 (February 1995).

11. Department of Communications, *Report of the Task Force on the Economic Status of Canadian Television* (Ottawa: 1991), 9.

12. G. Bruce Doern et al., eds., *Border Crossings: The Internationalization of Canadian Public Policy* (Toronto: Oxford University Press, 1996).

....

FURTHER READING

Barlow, Maude, and Bruce Campbell. *Take Back the Nation*. Toronto: Key Porter Books, 1991.

Cameron, Duncan, ed. *The Free Trade Deal*. Toronto: Lorimer, 1988.

Canada. *Foreign Direct Investment in Canada* [the Gray Report]. Ottawa: Supply and Services, 1972.

Canada Among Nations. Toronto: Lorimer, annual.

Dewitt, David, and John Kirton. *Canada as a Principal Power*. Toronto: Wiley, 1983.

Doern, G. Bruce et al., eds. *Border Crossings: The Internationalization of Canadian Public Policy* (Toronto: Oxford University Press, 1996).

Doern, Bruce, and Brian Tomlin. *Faith and Fear: The Free Trade Story*. Toronto: Stoddart, 1991.

Dorland, Michael, ed. *The Cultural Industries in Canada: Problems, Policies and Prospects*. Halifax: Lorimer, 1996.

Drache, Daniel, and Meric Gertler, eds. *The New Era of Global Competition: State Policy and Market Power*. Montreal: McGill–Queen's University Press, 1991.

Granatstein, J.L., and Norman Hillmer. *For Better or Worse: Canada and the United States in the 1990s*. Mississauga: Copp Clark Pitman, 1991.

Raboy, Marc. *Missed Opportunities: The Story of Canada's Broadcasting Policy*. Montreal: McGill–Queen's University Press, 1990.

PART 2

Linking People to Government

Having outlined the societal context in which Canadian politics operates, we are now ready to examine how the people are linked to the government—the study of Canadian politics as such. The three traditional elements of Canadian politics are the electoral system, political parties, and pressure groups, each of which is discussed in its own chapter in the following section. But the context of values, attitudes, opinions (and how they are acquired), and patterns of political participation must also be examined. Moreover, no one can deny the importance of the mass media and public opinion polls in linking people to government. Thus we begin with chapters on the Canadian political culture, socialization and participation, and the media and public opinion polls.

Chapter 6

Political Culture, Socialization, and Participation

Understanding how Canadians feel about politics and government, how they develop such feelings, and how they participate politically provides a useful context in which to study elections, political parties, and pressure groups. This chapter therefore examines Canadian political values and attitudes—the Canadian political culture; how these values and attitudes are acquired—political socialization; and the related subject of patterns of Canadian political participation.

Political Culture

Political culture can be defined as the sum total of the political values, beliefs, attitudes, and orientations in a society. Vague and elusive as these values and attitudes may be, most political scientists think they are worthy of analysis because they influence what is done within a political system.

Political culture includes feelings people have toward the overall political community of Canada, such as their reaction to national symbols—flag, anthem, Constitution—and feelings of patriotism, nationalism, and pride, including the question of how people feel toward their province as opposed to the whole country. A second aspect of political culture involves beliefs regarding the role of the state—how large a part Canadians want it to play in their lives. Another variable consists of orientations to the decision-making apparatus. Are people aware of it, and to what extent do they want to control it? How do Canadians feel, in general, about the police, the bureaucracy, the courts, and the politicians? Do citizens *trust* them? Alternatively, do people feel that their participation in the political system can make any difference? When such values and attitudes are widely shared, they can be said to constitute the collective political culture. While political culture is usually considered to be fairly stable, it will also be necessary to sketch how in the Canadian case it seems to be changing.

Democracy

The first conclusion that emerges from a quest for Canadian political values is that almost all Canadians believe in democracy. The preamble to the Canadian Charter of Rights and Freedoms acknowledges democracy to be a foremost value in the country when it speaks of Canada as a "free and democratic society," but the Charter is not very specific about what this means. Definitions of democracy in the modern Western world usually include the following elements:[1]

- popular sovereignty
- political equality
- political freedom
- majority rule

POPULAR SOVEREIGNTY

Popular sovereignty means that the people have the final say, which in large, modern political systems usually takes the form of elections at certain specified intervals. For most Canadians, this is a sufficient opportunity for the exercise of popular sovereignty, although few would be content with anything less. Some states use plebiscites or referendums on a regular basis, but these devices have largely been foreign to the Canadian mentality. Only three national referendums have occurred since 1867, although the incidence is slightly higher at the provincial and municipal levels. Popular sovereignty is thus normally exercised in periodic elections that are essentially opportunities to select those who will make the big political decisions over the next four years or so. At least in the past, Canadians cherished representative democracy in which such elected and appointed authorities made decisions on their behalf.

POLITICAL EQUALITY

Given the significance of elections as the means of implementing the principle of popular sovereignty, a second aspect of the Canadian conception of democracy is political equality—that is, everyone is equal on election day. In essence, this means that every person has one vote and no more than one vote. It is only in relatively recent times, however, that Canada has met this ideal, and at one time or another in the past several groups were excluded.

POLITICAL FREEDOM

The 1982 Charter of Rights and Freedoms provided an explicit constitutional statement of political freedom in Canada. It says: "Everyone has the following fundamental freedoms: freedom of conscience and religion; freedom of thought, belief, opinion and expression, including freedom of the press and other media of communication; freedom of peaceful assembly; and freedom of association." The Charter did not create these political freedoms, however; it enumerated them and provided a new means of protecting them—using the courts to invalidate legislation that infringed them rather than having to persuade politicians to do so.

MAJORITY RULE

The Canadian conception of democracy also incorporates the notion of majority rule—that is, in case of dispute, the larger number takes precedence over the smaller number. This principle is generally accepted in elections and in the legislatures that result from elections. On the other hand, it is sometimes felt necessary to protect certain minorities from the actions of the majority, so that specific minority rights are given constitutional protection. The Constitution Act, 1867, recognized certain religious and linguistic minority rights, while the Charter of Rights and Freedoms extended constitutional minority rights to a considerable degree.

Distinguishing between Canadian and American Values

Once we get beyond the consensus on democracy, it is difficult to find widespread agreement on other Canadian political values. One approach that bears promise, however, is to contrast widely held Canadian values with those of the United States. Canadian and American values are, of course, very much alike. But some analysts have found subtle differences that have their foundation in the revolutionary origins of the United States and in the Canadian reaction against that revolution.

Many have made the point that while the American Declaration of Independence lists the objectives of "life, liberty and the pursuit of happiness," Canada's 1867 Constitution Act talks about "peace, order and good government." Seymour Martin Lipset goes on from this point to outline a basic distinction: "Canada has been and is a more class-aware, elitist, law-abiding, statist, collectivity-oriented, and particularistic [group-oriented] society than the United

States."[2] Pierre Berton has similarly noted that Canadians are law-abiding, peaceful, orderly, deferential toward authority, cautious, elitist, moralistic, tolerant, diffident, and unemotional.[3] The results of a 1995 Allan Gregg survey of what ordinary Canadians thought was distinctive about Canada included non-violence, tolerance of minorities, humane treatment of the poor and disadvantaged, official bilingualism, and reluctance to boast.[4] When U.S. President George Bush spoke of wanting to make the United States into a "kinder, gentler" society, many observers thought of Canada. This approach leads us to identify five basic Canadian values that can be distinguished from those in the United States:

- Canadians prefer a closer balance between individualism and collectivism.
- Canadians are more tolerant and value particularisms.
- Canadians are more deferential toward authority.
- Canadians have a stronger belief in egalitarianism.
- Canadians are more cautious, less confident, and less violent.

BALANCE BETWEEN INDIVIDUALISM AND COLLECTIVISM

If there is one value other than democracy to which most Canadians adhere, it is probably that of individualism, liberalism, or capitalism, often expressed as the sanctity of private enterprise or individual economic freedom. Canadians generally believe that those with the greatest talent or those who work hardest should reap the benefits of their abilities and/or labour. The extent of such commitment can be best gauged, however, in comparison to the United States.

While both countries have "mixed economies" today—that is, a combination of private enterprise and government involvement—the United States remains the world's last stronghold of individualism, with a relatively smaller public sector than other modern states. Canada, on the other hand, has been less hostile toward public intervention and more inclined to rely on government. This is partly because of the distinctive geographic environment of the Canadian political system and the desire to protect Canada from various U.S. influences, but it also stems from the basic Canadian value of *collectivism,* or community, derived in large part from the United Empire Loyalists who opposed the American Revolution. They saw society, not as a mass of grasping, ambitious, "free" individuals, but as an organic community in which all people had their place and did their respective part to contribute to the welfare of the whole.

Canada is generally less collectivist than western Europe, and the difference between the two North American countries should not be overstated, but much concrete evidence of a significant variation exists. The extent of federal and provincial Crown corporations is unheard of south of the border; the Canadian public health-insurance system stands out in great contrast to that of the United States; the Canadian social security system is considered more adequate; and taxes are generally higher in order to finance such collective activity. In just about every policy field, in fact, the extent of government intervention is greater in Canada than in the United States.

TOLERANCE AND PARTICULARISM

A second difference between the basic values of the two countries is commonly expressed in terms of the melting pot and the mosaic: immigrants to the United States are urged to become "unhyphenated" Americans, whereas Canada encourages the retention of cultural particularities. Sometimes this Canadian heterogeneity is simply called tolerance. The distinctiveness of the French-Canadian Roman Catholic community based in Quebec was the original basis of this value, but it has now spread to policies of multiculturalism and recognition of other group rights, even in the Constitution. This official policy is seen as a means of enriching and enlivening the country, encouraging new Canadians to feel at home, promoting tolerance and minimizing discrimination, and perhaps enhancing Canada's contribution to world harmony. Particularism also has a territorial dimension—the fact that Canadian provinces are much stronger than the American states relative to the central government. Decentralization in Canada is accompanied by stronger regional or provincial loyalties and identities, due again to the example set by Quebec.

Table 6.1 indicates the federal and provincial orientations of Canadians by province and shows that Ontarians are most federally oriented, while Quebec and Newfoundland residents identify most with their province.

DEFERENCE TO AUTHORITY

Another fundamental difference between Canadian and American values is the greater deference to authority in Canadian society. Canadians demonstrate more respect toward the law, judges, police, religious leaders, and many others with "legitimate power." Peace, order, and good government rather than individual liberty is the Canadian ideal, and many observers have noted that Canada is

TABLE 6.1 FEDERAL AND PROVINCIAL ORIENTATIONS OF CANADIANS: "DO YOU THINK OF
YOURSELF AS A CANADIAN FIRST OR AS A CITIZEN OF YOUR PROVINCE?"

	Canadian	Provincial
Newfoundland	39%	57%
Prince Edward Island	50%	44%
Nova Scotia	69%	27%
New Brunswick	64%	26%
Quebec	45%	49%
Ontario	90%	9%
Manitoba	77%	11%
Saskatchewan	82%	7%
Alberta	74%	16%
British Columbia	76%	17%
All Canada	72%	22%

Source: Maclean's *(3 January 1994). Used with permission.*

probably the only country where a police officer is a national symbol. It is not
part of the Canadian psyche to be instinctively suspicious of the state; indeed,
Canadians have not seen the government in terms of an alien imposition, but as
the authorized agent to respond to their individual and collective demands. Less
obsessed with material success than Americans, Canadians are more likely to
obey a law even if they do not like it. Crime rates are considerably lower in
Canada, gun control laws are stronger, and the drug problem is less severe.

EGALITARIANISM

In the fourth place, Canada is in many ways more egalitarian than the United
States. One striking example is in the constitutional equality of women. Canada
adopted a strong guarantee of gender equality (including affirmative action) in
the 1982 Canadian Charter of Rights and Freedoms at the very time that a similar proposal failed in the United States. The health and welfare programs that
flow from Canadian collectivism similarly ensure a greater degree of equality for
the poor and working classes. Canada extends this redistributive egalitarianism
to have-not provinces through equalization payments. Even in the realm of

Figure 6.1   Ten OECD Countries with the Highest Percentage of Young Adults Enrolled[1] in University, 1988

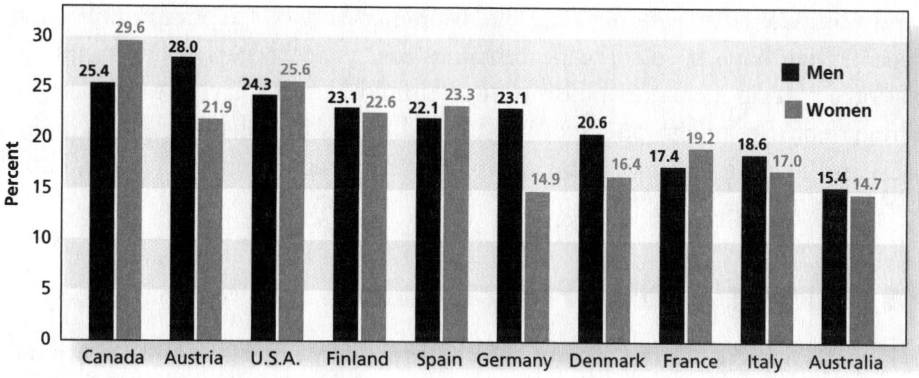

[1] Full-time and part-time enrollment converted to full-time equivalents. Population is those of theoretical university enrollment age (18–25 in Canada).

Source: Adapted from Statistics Canada, Canadian Social Trends *(Autumn 1993), Catalogue No. 11-008. Reproduced with the permission of the Minister of Supply and Services Canada, 1997.*

higher education, Canada now appears to be more egalitarian than the United States, as seen in Figure 6.1.

CAUTION, DEPENDENCE, NONVIOLENCE

A final value difference to emerge from this analysis relates to Canadian diffidence, sometimes called a national inferiority complex. It includes a historical dependence on other countries and the absence of a spirit of innovation and risk taking. Canadians delight in the security of savings and understatement. Of course, there have been many Canadian "winners" in all walks of life, in whose accomplishments Canadians vicariously share: Donovan Bailey, Margaret Atwood, Céline Dion, Glenn Gould, Anne Murray, Wayne Gretzky, Karen Kain, Michael J. Fox, Bryan Adams, Nobel Prize winners Frederick Banting, Lester Pearson, John Polanyi, and others. But Canadians are obsessed with "survival" rather than success; they are especially good at deprecating themselves, and almost always think things American are superior. They are prudent and cautious, sober and solemn, introverted, uncertain, and always questioning themselves. Most

Canadians take quiet satisfaction in their achievements—the 1995 survey showed that 89 percent of Canadians felt proud when they saw the Canadian flag or heard the national anthem—but they rarely proclaim it aloud.

Along similar lines, although Canada made major contributions to two world wars, Canadians are not a warlike people and abhor violence at home and abroad. They have tried to be peacemakers and peacekeepers in international relations, putting special emphasis on the United Nations, trying to reduce the militancy of the foreign policy of the United States in quiet, backroom diplomacy, and helping to remove the causes of war through assistance to the Third World.

The Changing Canadian Political Culture

As Canada approaches the turn of the century, many aspects of this traditional value structure seem to be changing. Different concepts of democracy are emerging, and the distinction between Canadian and American values appears to be in decline. Much of this transformation can be attributed to the presence of the United States, directly or indirectly, while some of it is part of a worldwide change in political values.

As far as democracy is concerned, the 1990s saw an upsurge in interest in the means of more direct popular participation. The most common prescription in this regard is the referendum, in which legislators would be guided or bound by the frequent referral of policy questions to the electorate as a whole. Quebec has used this device repeatedly on the question of sovereignty; certain other provinces now require it for approval of constitutional amendments; and some have prescribed its use for other issues such as significant tax increases.

As for the distinctions between Canadian and American values, these are threatened in at least three ways. First, given the extent of U.S. control over Canada and Canadian exposure to the United States, values implicit in that country's popular culture, as transmitted by television, movies, books, magazines, and music, are likely to have considerable impact on those north of the border. It is debatable whether distinctive Canadian values can withstand the homogenizing force of modern technology, especially that emanating from the south. Second, Canadian nationalists see all these influences increasing under the free trade agreements. Third, some observers feel that the adoption of a U.S.-style Charter of Rights and Freedoms will further diminish distinctive Canadian values.

In a country that articulates its basic values so diffidently to start with, these powerful threats are not to be taken lightly. There are several recent indications that support for collectivism and feelings of deference in Canada are already on the decline.[5] Although it cannot be blamed entirely on Americans, the new obsession with government debts and deficits at both federal and provincial levels has seriously eroded social programs, and shifted the basis of pensions and child benefits from universality to selectivity. Privatization of Crown corporations and deregulation have also become rampant. Moreover, Canadians seem increasingly concerned with the *legal* equality of all citizens, rather than with their socioeconomic equality or well-being.

Political Socialization

Political socialization is the process through which individuals acquire their political values, attitudes, information, and opinions. The process consists in part of direct, individual observation of political phenomena, but is mostly performed by intermediaries or agents of socialization. It is relatively easy to identify the main agents of political socialization in Canada, but much more difficult to evaluate their relative impact. We begin with the four traditional agents—family, school, peers, and the media—and then examine other such influences.

Agents of Socialization

THE FAMILY

Despite many modern pressures that have transformed the role of the family, including the increasing incidence of mothers working outside the home and the high divorce rate, it remains the basic cell of Canadian society. Parents, stepparents, or sometimes grandparents are the first major influence on a child's attitudes and values. Most children absorb attitudes and values, some of which are of political significance, in a kind of osmosis from their family's talk and behaviour. Parents' casual comments about politics, politicians, parties, and police are good examples. Some parents also deliberately try to indoctrinate their children with certain political values, such as supporting a particular political party. It seems, however, that what children pick up unconsciously and unintentionally is just as significant as what parents try to teach. For example, if parents talk about politics in the home, with or without attempting to guide their children's orientations, their children will usually become more politically interested later in life. Nevertheless, the political impact of the family should not be overemphasized, for political socialization is a process that continues throughout one's life.

THE SCHOOL

The school is the second main agent of political socialization. All school systems in Canada and elsewhere deliberately attempt to inculcate certain basic values and attitudes, including some of a political nature, such as a feeling of affection or support for the country, the governmental apparatus, the head of state, the police, the flag, and the national anthem. Moreover, with the decline of the family's influence, the school has probably increased in importance, and like the family it is an early enough influence that it may shape basic lifelong values.

Given the diversity of Canadian society, many questions arise about the role of the school in the political socialization process. Since the provinces have jurisdiction over education, for example, do they deliberately contribute to distinctive provincial political cultures at the expense of the overall country? The radically different accounts of certain historical events found in French and English textbooks are often cited as an example of the biased role of formal education in this process.[6] One point is clear: the forces of dualism, regionalism, and continentalism in Canadian society make it difficult for the school system to develop any pan-Canadian sense of national identity.[7]

Just as happens in the family setting, the school also contributes to the development of attitudes and values informally and unintentionally. Such unconscious transmissions occur in teachers' remarks beyond the formal curriculum, in class discussions and excursions, and in extracurricular activities. Moreover, different attitudes toward participation and dissent would likely result from exposure to an authoritarian teacher or principal than in a more democratic setting.

PEERS

Peers are the third main agent of political socialization. Peers are simply friends, acquaintances, and associates. The concept of "peer pressure" is probably most familiar at the adolescent level and is not usually concerned with political values, attitudes, and opinions; but we are all susceptible to peer influence at any stage of our lives. In any group setting, including peer-group discussions that turn to politics, one person often becomes dominant, whether because of knowledge, position, or strength of character. At this stage, given the likelihood that basic values have already been established, it is attitudes and opinions that are most open to persuasion.

THE MASS MEDIA

The mass media are the fourth main agent of socialization. They are more often instruments of entertainment than enlightenment, however, and personal interaction with family members, teachers, or peers normally carries greater impact than passive, impersonal exposure to the media. Moreover, the media are less likely to influence lifelong values and attitudes, primarily transmitting opinions on topical issues and personalities. Nevertheless, "there is evidence that Canadians do learn from this coverage, even though the average citizen has a limited grasp of the details of the political system or of the major issues of the day."[8] Moreover, such short-term stimuli are becoming more important in determining how people vote.

Once again, media influence can be divided between the unconscious and the deliberate. In their editorials, newspapers explicitly attempt to influence opinions, while on the other pages of the paper, Canadians generally expect news coverage to be as unbiased and factual as possible. Whether newspapers can keep such a fine line between subjective editorials and objective reporting is an interesting question, and some have detected bias in the headlines, positioning, pictures, and selection of items to be included or excluded. Television does not usually have editorials as such, but it actually has much greater scope for presenting biased news coverage than do newspapers, as noted in Chapter 7.

OTHER AGENTS OF POLITICAL SOCIALIZATION

The family, school, peers, and media are probably the main agents of political socialization in Canada, but certainly not the only ones. Political parties, churches, groups of various kinds, corporations, and the government itself are secondary influences on political attitudes, values, information, and opinions.

Political parties practise the art of persuasion and seek to influence opinions and party preferences on a daily basis. Those who already identify with a particular party find that the simplest means of forming an opinion on any issue is to take their cue from the party leader. The classic case of religion influencing political values, attitudes, and opinions was the Roman Catholic Church in Quebec prior to 1960. It had a close relationship with political authorities and did not hesitate to tell its members how to behave politically. The influence of religion in Canadian society may be on the decline, but its political role remains significant.

Over half the population belongs to a group of some kind, and although the orientation of such groups is primarily nonpolitical, all have the potential to influence their members' political views. Some, such as the Catholic Women's League, the Canadian Medical Association, and the Canadian Labour Congress, are quite determined to do so. As with parties and churches, taking one's opinions from the urging of a group leader obviates the need to make further individual effort to understand the issue. Other groups such as the Boy Scouts or Girl Guides try to instill in children an informed affection for the country.

Like political parties, individual corporations are in the business of persuasion, trying to sell their own goods and services. Sometimes, however, companies also try to influence political attitudes and opinions, an effort that is called *advocacy advertising*. Many corporations were involved in the free trade debate, especially during the 1988 election campaign, expressing their support through "speeches, debates, letters, advertisements, information sessions with employees, and inserts in newspapers."[9] Employers also try to influence the voting preferences of their own employees with internal memos about how different parties or policies would affect the firm.

Finally, the government itself is often engaged in efforts to influence public views and behaviour. Sometimes this is widely recognized as legitimate, such as encouraging physical fitness, and discouraging smoking, impaired driving, racial discrimination, wife battery, and the use of drugs. Sometimes it is done for broadly acceptable political purposes, such as promoting vacations in Canada, the purchase of Canadian-made goods, or national unity. Governments are also expected to inform the public about new laws, regulations, and programs, but it is a fine line between providing simple information and extolling the virtues of such initiatives for partisan purposes. The Mulroney government, for example, spent large sums of public funds promoting the merits of the Free Trade Agreement and the Goods and Services Tax in advertising campaigns that most observers felt were excessive and self-serving. In the latter case, the Speaker declared such advertising to be an affront to the House of Commons, as it took place even before debate there had concluded.

How Canadians individually and collectively acquire their political values, attitudes, and opinions is a complicated question. The whole process is so haphazard and complex and the stimuli in each person's own environment are so diverse that no deliberate effort is guaranteed to be successful. Instead, Canadians acquire many of their political values, attitudes, and opinions in a totally unconscious way. Moreover, many Canadians are only semi-socialized: they simply do not have many political values, attitudes, and opinions or much political information. The general level of political awareness is not high, which in turn is reflected in patterns of political participation.

Political Participation

Political participation consists "of those voluntary activities by citizens that are intended to influence the selection of government leaders or the decisions they make."[10] Numerous avenues of political participation exist, but actual participation takes effort, which not everyone is willing to exert. Participation is also related to the possession of political efficacy—a sense of political competence and a feeling that one can have some impact on the system. In a 1993 survey, for example, two-thirds of respondents complained that politics was too complicated for them to understand, that people like themselves had no say about what government did, and that government did not care about their opinions.[11] Participation also depends on the possession of such resources as time, money, and information. Regrettably, the opportunities for participation in Canada far exceed actual levels of involvement.

Electoral Participation

Voting on election day is a crucial aspect of democracy and is the most common form of political participation in Canada. The voter turnout rate is also one of the few forms of participation that can be regularly and reliably measured. The overall average national turnout rate since 1900 has been about 73 percent, or nearly three-quarters of those eligible to vote. The rate for each federal election between 1974 and 1997 is provided in Table 6.2.[12]

The figures in Table 6.2 disguise the fact that the turnout rate varies considerably from one province to another. Prince Edward Island, for example, stands out with an average turnout in recent federal elections of about 81 percent, while Saskatchewan, Ontario, and B.C. are in the 74–75 percent range. Quebec, Nova Scotia, New Brunswick, and Manitoba are slightly lower, at

TABLE 6.2 PERCENTAGE VOTER TURNOUT IN FEDERAL ELECTIONS, 1974–1997

Year	Total
1974	71
1979	76
1980	69
1984	75
1988	75
1993	70
1997	67
Average	72

Source: Data compiled from Chief Electoral Officer of Canada, Reports of the Chief Electoral Officer. Material reproduced with permission of the Chief Electoral Officer of Canada, 1997. Full responsibility for calculations and for conclusions drawn rests with the author.

72–73 percent. Alberta, at 68 percent, the North at 62 percent, and Newfoundland, at 61 percent are substantially less participative. These figures reflect varying levels of interest in federal politics, the degree of federal party competition within the province, and other factors.

The roughly 25 percent who do not vote have consistently been shown to be alienated from or uninformed about the political system, and primarily belong to the poor and working classes. Canada's 75 percent figure falls between the extremes of other countries; as revealed in Table 6.3, Canada is well above the United States in voter turnout, about the same as Britain, and behind many other states.

Within the 75 percent who do vote, we can distinguish other degrees of electoral involvement. For one thing, the level of information of the typical voter should not be overestimated. Even if around 80 percent claim to have exposed themselves to television or newspaper coverage of the election campaign, only about 20 percent follow politics closely on a daily basis between elections.[13]

A study of the 1984 election found that as a national average, voters could name 3.3 provincial premiers and 36 percent could define the concepts of *left* and *right* and place the NDP as the farthest left of the three main parties. The level of factual and conceptual knowledge increased with level of education and reading about politics in newspapers and magazines, but viewing political programs on television was of negligible impact.[14]

Beyond those who cast an "informed vote," a smaller proportion of the electorate actually becomes actively involved in the election campaign: attending

TABLE 6.3 PERCENTAGE VOTER TURNOUT RATES IN EIGHTEEN COUNTRIES, 1980s

Australia	94.3	Greece	82.0
Belgium	93.8	Ireland	74.2
Austria	91.5	United Kingdom	74.0
New Zealand	90.5	Spain	73.4
Italy	89.8	**Canada**	**73.3**
Sweden	89.1	Japan	71.4
France	86.2	India	62.0
Denmark	86.1	United States	54.3
Netherlands	83.4	Switzerland	47.5

Source: Privy Council Officer, Royal Commission on Electoral Reform and Party Financing, Vol. I (Ottawa: Minister of Supply and Services Canada, 1991), 52–53. Reproduced with permission of the Minister of Public Works and Government Services Canada, 1997.

all-candidates meetings; joining a political party; voting at the party's local nom-ination meeting; contributing money to political parties; or helping a local can-didate to do mailing, telephoning, door-to-door canvassing, and election-day work. A small number in each constituency become totally preoccupied with the local campaign; these people, including candidates themselves, are sometimes called "gladiators" as distinct from the great bulk of the population who are pri-marily "spectators."

Table 6.4 indicates the number of individuals who contributed money to national parties and local candidates in 1993. Since some made contributions to both parties and candidates, a total of those who made financial contributions is between 200 000 and 300 000 out of an electorate of 19 million, or between 1 and 2 percent.

Nonelectoral Participation

The political participation of most Canadians peaks at election time, but many avenues are open between elections in which to make demands or otherwise become involved in the political process. One would be to join a political party. Most Canadian political parties do not maintain reliable lists of party members, but Ken Carty estimates that about 2.7 percent of the population belong to a party.[15] It is known, however, that many people sign up before or during the

TABLE **6.4** NUMBERS OF INDIVIDUALS MAKING FINANCIAL CONTRIBUTIONS TO NATIONAL
PARTIES AND LOCAL CANDIDATES, 1993

	To Parties	To Candidates
PC	44 728	25 460
Liberal	41 058	32 907
NDP	65 301	12 367
Reform	49 488	25 211
BQ	29 084[1]	26 337
Total	229 659	122 282

[1] BQ figures include nonelection year 1994.

Sources: Data compiled from Chief Electoral Officer of Canada, Report of the Chief Electoral Officer Respecting Election Expenses, 1993, and party returns. Material reproduced with permission of the Chief Electoral Officer of Canada, 1997. Full responsibility for calculations and for conclusions drawn rests with the author.

campaign, often to participate in the nomination of candidates, and then let their membership lapse.

Another means of political participation is to join a voluntary group, an action that some 60 percent of Canadians claim to do. As seen in Chapter 10, any group, whatever its primary orientation, can become a pressure group, so that membership in any group is potentially political. Even if the group itself takes a political turn, however, passive members rarely do more than send the occasional preprinted postcard to their MP or the prime minister. On the other hand, active executive and staff members of such groups may become highly involved in political campaigns and the pressure-group politics that goes on in Canada every day. Even more initiative is required to form such a group, usually to protest against some political decision or lack of action at the municipal, provincial, or federal level.

Such group participation usually involves communicating with the authorities in routine ways, but occasionally it takes the form of peaceful demonstrations (locally or on Parliament Hill), sit-ins and other types of civil disobedience, and the rare case of violent protest. As noted above, Canadians are generally a peaceful lot, and political violence is uncommon. The main historical incidents were the Riel Rebellions of 1870 and 1885, the conscription riots in Quebec City in 1918, the Winnipeg General Strike of 1919, the Regina Riot of 1935, the various FLQ incidents of the 1960s culminating in the FLQ crisis of 1970, and the Mohawks' armed standoff at Oka in 1990.[16]

Canadians can also participate politically between elections as individuals—writing, faxing, or e-mailing letters to MPs or the prime minister, writing letters to the editors of newspapers, calling radio or television phone-in shows, signing petitions, or telephoning or meeting an MP. As with so many other aspects of political participation, however, it is difficult to obtain solid data on the degree of individual involvement in these activities. In general, few people take the initiative to do any of these things, one survey reporting about 20 percent.[17]

One interesting question in this connection is the relationship between degree of participation and social status. Table 6.5 indicates five forms of participation broken down by level of income, education, and occupational status. In almost any measure of participation, whether discussing politics, working for a

TABLE 6.5 PERCENTAGE LEVEL OF PARTICIPATION IN SELECTED POLITICAL ACTIVITIES, 1993, BY OCCUPATION, INCOME, AND EDUCATION

	Discuss Politics	Party Work	Sign Petition	March/ Rally	Sit-in
Occupation					
Blue Collar	75	4	71	26	9
White Collar	89	6	76	26	7
Professional/Managerial	86	9	78	37	10
Income					
Under $20 000	70	5	54	21	7
$20 000–39 999	80	5	69	24	8
$40 000–59 999	82	7	77	30	9
$60 000–69 999	87	9	76	27	10
$70 000 & over	87	12	79	30	7
Education					
Elementary or less	68	9	34	14	5
Some secondary	75	4	57	18	6
Complete secondary	82	8	69	19	6
Some university	82	7	78	32	10
University degree	86	7	86	45	13

Source: Mishler and Clarke, "Political Participation in Canada," 137. Used with permission.

party, signing a petition, or engaging in marches, rallies, or sit-ins, the degree of involvement increases with level of income and education and from blue-collar to white-collar to professional and managerial occupations. Possession of money often provides such resources as leisure time, political information, and contacts that facilitate such high levels of participation. Such a pattern even exists for political protests.

....

Notes

1. Henry B. Mayo, *An Introduction to Democratic Theory* (New York: Oxford University Press, 1960), ch. 4.
2. Seymour Martin Lipset, *Continental Divide* (New York: Routledge, 1990), 8.
3. Pierre Berton, *Why We Act Like Canadians* (Toronto: McClelland and Stewart, 1982).
4. *Maclean's* (1 July 1995): 15.
5. Neil Nevitte, *The Decline of Deference* (Peterborough, Ont.: Broadview Press, 1996).
6. Marcel Trudel and Genevieve Jain, *Canadian History Textbooks: A Comparative Study* (Ottawa: Royal Commission on Bilingualism and Biculturalism, 1970).
7. Ronald Landes, "Political Education and Political Socialization," in Jon Pammett and Jean-Luc Pépin, eds., *Political Education in Canada* (Halifax: Institute for Research on Public Policy, 1988), 17.
8. Frederick Fletcher, "The Mass Media and Political Education," in Pammett and Pépin, 92.
9. Alan Frizzell et al., *The Canadian General Election of 1988* (Ottawa: Carleton University Press), 69.
10. William Mishler and Harold D. Clarke, "Political Participation in Canada," in Michael Whittington and Glen Williams, eds., *Canadian Politics in the 1990s*, 4th ed. (Scarborough: Nelson Canada, 1995), 130.
11. Ibid., 134.
12. The 1993 rate appears to be lower than normal, but it is possible that this is because a year-old voters' list was used (from the 1992 referendum). The number who voted is accurate, but the list of eligible voters was inflated because an estimated 205 000 people on the 1992 list had died and an estimated 1 617 384 people on the 1992 list had moved without asking to be deleted, but had their names added under their new address. Thus if these 1 822 384 people are subtracted from the 19 906 796 names of eligible voters in 1993, the real number would be 18 984 412, and the real turnout rate would be 73.0 percent.
13. Mishler and Clarke, "Political Participation," 134, 143.
14. Ronald D. Lambert et al., "The Social Sources of Political Knowledge," *Canadian Journal of Political Science* (June 1988): 359–74.
15. R. Kenneth Carty, *Canadian Political Parties in the Constituencies*. Royal Commission on Electoral Reform and Party Financing Research Studies, Vol. 23, cat. no. 21-1989/2-41-23E.
16. Judy Torrance, *Public Violence in Canada* (Montreal: McGill–Queen's University Press, 1986).
17. Mishler and Clarke, "Political Participation," 134.

FURTHER READING

Bashevkin, Sylvia. *True Patriot Love: The Politics of Canadian Nationalism*. Don Mills, Ont.: Oxford University Press, 1991.

Bell, David. *The Roots of Disunity: A Look at Canadian Political Culture*. Rev. ed. Oxford University Press, 1992.

Berton, Pierre. *Why We Act Like Canadians*. Toronto: McClelland and Stewart, 1982.

Friedenberg, Edgar J. *Deference to Authority*. White Plains, N.Y.: M.E. Sharpe, 1980.

Lipset, Seymour Martin. *Continental Divide*. New York: Routledge, 1990.

Mishler, William. *Political Participation in Canada: Prospects for Democratic Citizenship*. Toronto: Macmillan, 1979.

Mishler, William, and Harold Clarke. "Political Participation in Canada." In Michael Whittington and Glen Williams, eds. *Canadian Politics in the 1990s*. 4th ed. Scarborough: Nelson Canada, 1995.

Nevitte, Neil. *The Decline of Deference*. Peterborough: Broadview Press, 1996.

Ostry, Sylvia. "Government Intervention: Canada and the United States Compared." *Policy Options* (March 1980): 26–31.

Pammett, Jon, and Jean-Luc Pépin, eds. *Political Education in Canada*. Halifax: Institute for Research on Public Policy, 1988.

Chapter 7

The Mass Media and Public Opinion Polls

The mass media, principally television, radio, and newspapers, are the primary source of most Canadians' knowledge and opinions about topical political issues and current political personalities. But also being important to public policy-makers, the media provide an important two-way communications link between the governors and the governed. Another link between people and government of central importance in all aspects of Canadian politics today is the public opinion poll. Parties rely heavily on such polls immediately before and during election campaigns, but the media report the results of such polls almost daily, as governments and the media themselves seek to discover Canadians' opinions on every conceivable matter. This chapter examines these two important features of the political system.

··

The Mass Media
The State of the Media

In surveying the state of the newspaper, radio, and television industries today, it should first be noted that the privately owned media exist primarily to make a profit, and that whatever political functions they serve are incidental to that purpose.

NEWSPAPERS

In 1997, 104 daily newspapers were published in Canada, 93 in English and 11 in French.[1] Conrad Black effectively owned 58 of these papers under such names as Hollinger and Southam. The largest Black dailies were the Vancouver *Province* and *Sun*, the Montreal *Gazette*, *Calgary Herald*, *Edmonton Journal*, *Hamilton Spectator*, *Ottawa Citizen*, and *Le Soleil* in Quebec. Black's papers totalled 41.5 percent of the overall daily circulation in the country (just over 5 million copies). The Sun and Thomson chains were the next largest, with

11 and 9 papers respectively, each representing 12–13 percent of the total daily circulation. *The Toronto Sun* is the flagship of the Sun chain, just as the Toronto *Globe and Mail* is the leading Thomson product. *The Globe and Mail* calls itself "Canada's National Newspaper" and publishes a national edition transmitted by satellite to several printing locations so that it is available every morning in all major centres across the country. The *Winnipeg Free Press* is Thomson's second-largest paper. Pierre Péladeau's Québecor four-paper chain contains two of the largest dailies in Quebec: *Le Journal de Montréal* and *Le Journal de Québec*, while the Desmarais family's four Quebec papers are led by *La Presse* of Montreal. The Irving family owns all four English dailies in New Brunswick, and the Newfoundland Capital Corporation is a small three-paper chain. If a "chain" is defined as a minimum of three papers, then 93 dailies out of 104 belonged to chains, leaving only 11 daily newspapers in Canada to be independently owned and operated. Of these, *The Toronto Star*, the largest single newspaper in the country, could also be regarded as a chain because it publishes many suburban Toronto community weeklies.

Thus, some of the wealthiest men in Canada—Black, Thomson, Irving, Desmarais, and Péladeau—control most of the country's newspaper industry. Moreover, one chain or another often has an overwhelming dominance in a single province, such as Irving in New Brunswick and Black in Saskatchewan, Newfoundland, and Prince Edward Island. Meanwhile, Péladeau, Desmarais, and Black collectively control 96 percent of the daily French newspaper circulation in Quebec. Most of these newspaper-owning families have substantial holdings beyond newspapers, and especially in the small confines of New Brunswick, it has been charged that Irving newspapers refrain from critical comment on the family's ubiquitous other operations in the province.

Concentrated ownership of Canadian newspapers has always caused considerable concern. Many fear that the owner of several papers will gain an unhealthy degree of influence over public opinion by establishing a common point of view for all papers in the chain. This anxiety deepened when there appeared to be collusion between the Southam and Thomson chains, prompting the Trudeau government to appoint the Kent Royal Commission on Newspapers. The Commission did not find much evidence that any central owner had imposed a common editorial policy or standardized news coverage on all the newspapers; the most undesirable result was a reduction in the diversity of perspectives on national politics.[2] While chain ownership even has some advantages, Kent emphasized the possibility of owners intervening in undesirable ways.

Responding to strong corporate pressure, however, the government abandoned a bill aimed to implement some of Kent's recommendations to restrict concentrated media ownership.

Since the Kent Report was published, two principal developments in the Canadian newspaper industry have occurred. The first is the expansion of populist morning tabloids, many belonging to the Sun chain. These tend to be ideological and sensational, aiming for a less sophisticated audience more vulnerable to its right-wing and visceral approach. The second development is the dramatic expansion of Conrad Black's holdings; Black has bought much of the Thomson chain and now controls the entire Southam operation. Black's extensive ownership concerns many observers for two main reasons: the massive layoffs that occurred upon his purchase of certain papers, and his inclination to provide more editorial direction than previous owners.

RADIO AND TELEVISION

The radio and television industries are distinct from newspapers in two respects: the degree of government regulation involved and public ownership of English CBC and French Radio-Canada networks. There are some 29 CBC AM and 35 CBC FM originating stations (English or French), and through transmitter stations, coverage is almost nationwide. In addition, 20 private radio stations are affiliated with the CBC. CBC radio has a relatively large and sophisticated audience, and plays a major role in transmitting information and opinion.

Apart from CBC/Radio-Canada, the Canadian radio industry consists of nearly 500 local AM and FM stations. These stations used to be independently owned, but are increasingly characterized by chain ownership, just as in the newspaper industry. Ownership changes quite frequently, but in 1990, fully half of the radio market in Canada was controlled by the 10 leading firms. Like newspapers, radio stations must be Canadian-owned, but the limited Canadian content on private radio stations has become a problem. Since private radio mainly transmits music, the CRTC has issued Canadian content rules, as noted in Chapter 5.

Requiring Canadian television stations to be domestically owned or to telecast 50 percent or more Canadian content is virtually meaningless when almost all residents are within reach, directly or via cable, of a large assortment of U.S. television channels. On this point, Fred Fletcher talks of "American images crowding out Canadian ones,"[3] and Ed Black writes of the problem of trying to serve a small population in two language groups "who live in tempting, embarrassing, and almost smothering proximity to [10 times as many] Americans who

speak the language of Canada's majority.... They also have the world's most pen-
etrating and effective system for transmitting ideas en masse."[4] Peter Trueman
adds: "Think of the overwhelming preponderance of American programming,
which in an unobtrusive way pumps us full of American values, American hopes,
American history, even American patterns of speech."[5]

The publicly owned CBC/Radio-Canada television network has about 20
stations across the country. English production is centred in Toronto and French
production in Montreal. These are supplemented by agreements with 26 privately owned affiliated stations, which agree to telecast a certain amount of CBC
programming.

Twenty-eight privately owned stations comprise the CTV network, centred
on CFTO in Toronto. The network is basically owned by the Eaton family under
the Baton name and run by Ivan Fecan. The Toronto-based Canwest Global system is owned by Izzy Asper of Winnipeg; its transmitters serve most of Ontario.
Asper also owns stations in other provinces and is trying to cobble together a
third national English-language network. Several major cities also have an unaf-
filiated, independent private English station. On the French side, the equivalent
of CTV is TVA, centred on Télé-Métropole in Montreal and comprising nine
other private stations; a second private French network is the seven-station
Quatre Saisons.

CBC television has a strong commitment to Canadian programming, but
suffers from a chronic shortage of funds. After severe bloodletting under the
Mulroney government, the CBC had reason to expect better treatment under the
Chrétien regime. Instead, that government slashed the CBC budget even further,
precipitating the resignation of the Corporation's president.

The private stations and networks realize that profits can be maximized by
telecasting as much U.S. programming as the CRTC will allow. Nevertheless, the
importance and popularity of CBC and CTV national newscasts, CBC's "The
Morning News," "The Fifth Estate," and "Marketplace," Radio-Canada's
"Téléjournal" and "Le Point," and CTV's "Canada AM" and "W5" should not be
underestimated. Table 7.1 indicates that 24 percent of Canadian television viewing consists of news and public affairs, and that most of this is Canadian in origin. In 1993, the average Canadian watched 22.8 hours of television per week,
higher in Atlantic Canada and French Quebec, and lower in Alberta and British
Columbia.

TABLE 7.1 PERCENTAGE DISTRIBUTION OF VIEWING BY PROGRAM TYPE AND CANADIAN
vs. FOREIGN ORIGIN

Program Type	English-language Canadian	Foreign	French-language Canadian	Foreign	Total Canadian	Foreign
News & public affairs	15.0	7.9	25.0	1.4	17.9	6.1
Documentary	0.5	1.5	1.4	0.4	0.8	1.2
Instructional	0.9	1.8	2.7	0.3	1.4	1.4
Religion	0.2	0.1	0.3	0	0.2	0.1
Sports	5.2	2.7	5.7	0.7	5.4	2.1
Variety & games	0.7	6.2	15.7	1.9	4.8	5.0
Music & dance	0.4	1.0	1.0	0.2	0.6	0.7
Comedy	0.4	16.2	2.7	8.0	1.0	13.8
Drama	2.3	29.5	10.4	18.1	4.5	26.3
Other	0	7.7	0	4.2	0	6.9
Total	25.5	74.5	64.9	35.1	36.5	63.5

Source: Adapted from Statistics Canada, "Television Viewing 1993," cat. no. 87–208 (December 1994). Reproduced with permission of the Minister of Supply and Services Canada, 1997.

Another effort to strengthen Canadian television content was the establishment of CBC Newsworld in 1989. This all-news channel covers many political events live and more extensively than regular CBC, with which it works closely, and provides much regional coverage, documentaries, and in-depth interview programming. While its audience is small, most members of the political elite tune in regularly. The national parliamentary channel on cable is now called CPAC; in some provinces another channel carries provincial legislative proceedings; and several provinces have educational television channels.

About 75 percent of Canadian homes are hooked up to (and hooked on) cable television, more than in any other country. Cable stations receive television signals from the air via large dishes and transmit them by means of cables to individual subscribers. The CRTC regulates which channels they carry, but cable television brings the major U.S. networks into almost every Canadian home and permits subscribers to watch U.S. news, public affairs, and sports programs. The Canadian cable industry is essentially dominated by the giants of Canadian television and radio: Rogers Communications, Shaw, Vidéotron, CFCF, and Moffat

Communications. The variety of other channels on cable television, some of them of Canadian origin, is constantly increasing, but for some channels (including movie channels) the subscriber must pay an additional fee. CRTC approval of new "specialty services," Canadian or American, including "pay-per-view," and direct-to-home (DTH) satellite services, has further served to dilute the audience of the conventional Canadian television stations.

The Media and the Public

PUBLIC PERCEPTIONS OF THE MEDIA

The influence of the mass media on the political system is profound and appears to be constantly increasing.[6] Most of the information Canadians receive about the political process comes from newspapers, radio, or television rather than from direct observation or other sources such as books or magazines, except perhaps for *Maclean's*. Some recipients may be able to separate this information from whatever commentary or biases accompany it, but many are swayed by the particular perspective that the media give to the data they present.

The current consensus on the role of the media is that they set the political agenda for the country.[7] In other words, the media tell people what to think about, what the important issues are, and which political personalities are significant. *They help to define what is political.*[8] This is a function that the media share with political parties, and while parties may be more important as initiators of issues, these will not likely remain on the agenda without media attention.

The parliamentary press gallery, containing about 400 members, seems to have a "herd instinct" or to engage in "pack journalism" in developing a consensus about what these significant issues are.[9] In part, this reflects the influence of the daily oral Question Period in the House of Commons, which provides them with short, superficial, and controversial issues well suited to television coverage.

When asked about the political role of the three media, people invariably prefer television in almost every respect and newspapers second. Research done for the Royal Commission on Newspapers found that television was preferred as the medium that best kept people up to date, was fairest, most influential, most believable, and best for both Canadian and international news. More recent polls indicate that Canadians prefer television over newspapers even for coverage of local news.[10]

THE REALITY OF DIFFERENT MODES OF MEDIA COVERAGE

These results are somewhat distressing to those who know the real advantages and disadvantages of the three media in question. Because of cost and time constraints, television must present a shorter and more superficial account of political events than either radio or newspapers. Coverage of any item rarely exceeds a 90-second "news clip" with a 10-second "sound bite" of the voice of political leaders, in which how something is said is usually more important than what is said. The transcript of a 30-minute newscast would make up about one-third of a single newspaper page.[11] Moreover, because it is a visual medium, television must seek out colourful, dramatic, emotional, conflictual, or entertaining pictures. Riots, demonstrations, and political conventions usually make good television, but the daily routine of politics does not lend itself so well to compelling visual coverage. Witness the efforts taken by politicians and the media to find contrived and engaging settings in which to stage political happenings, make announcements, or tape interviews.

Television portrays images and impressions, and is therefore much better at dealing with political leaders and personalities than with issues. When John Turner issued a 40-point policy manifesto just before the 1988 election, for example, "the electronic media, which have trouble transmitting more than a single idea in a 30-second clip, could not cope with such a cornucopia of ideas that had not been pre-digested into a simple theme wrapped around a few easily grasped issues."[12] These characteristics make television the most open of the three media to distortion and exploitation, so that it is actually the least believable and—however unintentionally—the most biased.[13] Television meets the needs of the average citizen with a short attention span who is looking for visual stimulation and does not wish to invest much effort in understanding the political system.

This situation is exacerbated by the increasing tendency of political parties and politicians to gear their activities to the demands of television rather than the other media or the public. Press conferences are now dominated by television lights and cameras; leaders' tours during election campaigns are "photo opportunities"; and party conventions and leaders' debates are scheduled when the television networks have spare time. In preparing for elections, parties put greater effort into designing television commercials and trying them out before focus groups than in devising solutions to the country's problems. The leaders' debate has become the single most important event in an election campaign because elections usually turn more on leader images than issues, policies, local candidates, or other leading figures in the party. The appearance, style, and general image of the party leader, including the ability to perform on television, has become of crucial importance. This increasing emphasis on appearance is often said to trivialize politics. In this respect, it is encouraging to note that the PC effort to mock Jean Chrétien's partially paralyzed face in the 1993 election campaign backfired in a demonstration of the traditional decency of the Canadian public.

It would be too soon, however, to write off the political importance of newspapers. Daily newspapers generally offer more comprehensive coverage of political events and they excel at covering issues, which they can do at length, in depth, and in detail, presenting both greater factual information and a wider range of interpretation. While the "average" Canadian relies on television for political information, those with political influence, whether in government, parties, pressure groups, or peer-group situations, depend on newspapers. Those who prefer newspapers over television have higher educations, higher incomes, are better informed, and tend to be middle-aged and live in urban areas. Furthermore, even though print journalists must often defer to the paraphernalia of their television colleagues, the broadcast media and opposition parties tend to take their cues from newspapers.

It should be added that the degree of political participation increases sharply with a person's level of newspaper consumption. In other words, those who make the effort to increase their political information by reading a newspaper (as opposed to sitting passively in front of a TV set) are not only better informed, but are also most likely to go on to engage in some form of political participation.

The Globe and Mail is read by nearly three-quarters of top-level decision-makers across the country and more than 90 percent of media executives; it thus tends to set the agenda for other news organizations. The independent but financially troubled *Le Devoir* occupies a somewhat similar position in French Canada.

The Media and the Politicians

Politicians and their bureaucratic advisers need publicity and therefore have a great interest in how the media cover their behaviour. Even though they have their own direct sources, they also depend on the media to provide information they need about what is happening at home and abroad. The media in turn rely on the authorities for most of their information, and much media reporting of politics is of the "government handout" variety. Several issues arise in this mutually dependent relationship.

POLITICIANS AND JOURNALISTS

In principle, reporters should remain far enough away from politicians so that they can cover them objectively; on the other hand, it is often necessary to cultivate close relations in order to get the kind of information the media seek. Allan Fotheringham writes that "the narrowest line in journalism is the line between exploiting your sources (without ever destroying them) and being captured by them."[14] Furthermore, since politicians often confidentially seek out the opinions of working reporters, the latter sometimes have to agonize over whether to reveal information that was given to them "off the record," that is, in the expectation that it would not be used.

Another problem the media have to face is how much privacy to leave politicians. When do drinking too much, sexual infidelity, or family and financial problems begin to interfere with a politician's public functions, and when should they be revealed? Beyond personal privacy is the question of whether the media should transmit information they are not supposed to have, such as when Global Television came into advance possession of a summary of the 1988 budget.

NEWS MANAGEMENT

"News leaks" are another issue in the relations between media and politicians. When governments do not know what course to follow, they sometimes leak a proposal to the media as a "trial balloon," hoping for guidance from the public reaction received. Ed Black points out that this practice is helpful in these days when politicians usually have little time to respond to problems or give them comprehensive consideration.[15]

Leaks are a part of a broader and increasingly common problem of "news management" and manipulation. This relates especially to the timing and selective distribution of information; exaggerating the positive while keeping secret or past deadline time that which is negative; giving preference to friendly reporters over others; making prime ministerial requests for network television time for less than important announcements; or outright lying. News management also involves putting the best face on a deficient government action or politician's performance by having a partisan official tell the media how successful it actually was, in the hope that the media will transmit this evaluation to their audience.

Those involved in such efforts are often called "media handlers" or "spin doctors," because they try to put the best face, or "spin," on any event.

The ultimate problem in media–government relations is political interference with the "freedom of the press," one of the sacred principles of democracy as discussed in Chapter 6. The most blatant examples of such political interference have occurred at the provincial level. In Quebec, Premier Maurice Duplessis kept the press under control by means of awarding advertising and printing contracts to newspaper owners and financial gifts to members of the press gallery. In Alberta, Social Credit in the 1930s tried to force newspapers to retract any criticisms of the government. Occasional attempts have apparently been made by the Prime Minister's Office over the years to have the CBC take a certain perspective on a vital national issue. The most celebrated case in English Canada was the cancellation in 1966 of the highly popular but critical CBC public affairs program, "This Hour Has Seven Days."[16] On the French side, the Trudeau government accused the Radio-Canada network of being riddled with separatists who gave a biased interpretation of federal–provincial relations. Although there was probably some truth to the charge, it smacked of political interference.

The most serious aspect of political interference, although one that is sometimes justified, is censorship via the War Measures Act, the Emergencies Act, or the Official Secrets Act. In 1970, for example, the media were prohibited from carrying anything that supported the FLQ. Short of actual censorship is the highly secretive tradition of Canadian governments. In 1982, however, the Access to Information Act made it somewhat easier for the media as well as other interested parties to obtain access to government information.

Public Opinion Polls

The phrase *public opinion* sometimes implies that a unanimous, informed view on a particular issue is held by all members of the public. In actuality, many opinions are held on any issue, and each issue interests only a certain segment of the population. Furthermore, most political opinions are not well informed. They are based on little information, they are simplifications of complex issues, and they are often internally contradictory. Indeed, people often form their opinions first and then look for information to confirm them; at the very least, they "seek out information that conforms to their predispositions ... and avoid or reinterpret any contrary and non-supportive messages."[17] Nevertheless, public opinions about topical issues frequently influence the actions of government.

Measuring Public Opinion

Given this great conglomeration of viewpoints, public opinion is very difficult to gauge. Haphazard methods such as reading editorials or letters to the editor or listening to open-line programs are obviously unreliable, but so are many amateur public opinion surveys. On the other hand, professional polling agencies claim to be able to select a small representative sample of people, ask carefully worded questions, and report with a high degree of accuracy the opinions of the whole population. Such polls have assumed an immense importance in contemporary Canadian politics: "no political party plans campaign strategy without them, no government is prepared to risk major policy initiatives without gauging public opinion, and for major news organizations they are an indispensable reporting tool, both between and during elections."[18]

Beyond the now common procedure for conducting a public opinion poll, two special techniques deserve mention. The first is "tracking," which entails telephoning samples of 100 to 500 people nightly during an election campaign in order to see how day-to-day developments are affecting them. The second is the "focus group," in which a small number of people are gathered together behind a one-way mirror with a group leader who encourages them to voice their "gut" reaction to various leaders, issues, and slogans.

Who are these professional pollsters? The Canadian Institute for Public Opinion (CIPO) is the Canadian branch of the Gallup organization in the United States, the pioneer of public opinion measurement. It has operated in Canada since 1941 and is financed primarily by the newspapers in which its results appear. Gallup regularly asks the question "If an election were held today, which party's candidate do you think you would vote for?" Both the politicians and media anxiously await its monthly appearance.

Many other pollsters have links to a particular media outlet or political party, although these alliances may change over time. The Environics Research Group is a well-respected polling firm headed by Michael Adams and Donna Dasko. Michael Marzolini has replaced Martin Goldfarb as the official Liberal Party pollster, while for many years Allan Gregg and his Decima Research was the official Conservative Party pollster. Angus Reid is another well-known national polling firm.

Exactly how accurate are the polls? The only way a survey's accuracy can really be tested is through a comparison of its results immediately prior to an election with the electoral outcome itself. The immediate pre-election findings of most professional agencies have usually been within the range of accuracy claimed—typically plus or minus 4 percent 19 times out of 20. The way a question is worded, the optional responses available, the sequence of the questions, the degree to which respondents are telling the truth, and many other variables can influence the results.

Impact of Polls on the Public

Perhaps the main issue that arises in the discussion of polls and pollsters is whether their pre-election predictions influence the actual election results. This question cannot be answered categorically, but it is unlikely that their direct effect is that great. First, most voters do not pay much attention to poll results; second, not everyone believes them; and third, it is not important to everyone to vote for the winning side even if this is clear in advance. While some voters may want to jump on the victorious bandwagon—the "bandwagon effect"—at least a few are likely to switch to the predicted loser—"the underdog effect"—either out of sympathy or to try to prevent an overwhelming victory for the prospective winner.[19]

On the other hand, the polls probably have a significant indirect effect on the election results. The media are just as obsessed with the polls as the politicians are, and survey results may well lead the media to concentrate on those parties and politicians who are in the lead or to ignore those who are trailing. Furthermore, polls have a considerable impact on party morale. A positive poll usually generates greater enthusiasm and effort, better candidates, and larger financial contributions, while a negative poll saps the spirit of leaders, candidates, and footsoldiers alike. Both of these results undoubtedly affect the subtle "momentum" of the campaign.

Another issue can be addressed more categorically: polls definitely detract from the discussion of real issues in the election campaign.[20] The media are fascinated by polls primarily because they are good for business, and given the media's ability to influence the political agenda even during election campaigns, they emphasize the "horse-race effect" of the contest. They tend to spend more time on who is ahead than on comparative analysis of party platforms, asking leaders to comment on the latest poll results, for example, rather than how the party would deal with a particular public problem. Now that the media actually hire or own polling firms, survey results are becoming major news items themselves.

Many political losers have blamed their fate on negative public opinion polls, and some have called for the prohibition of polls during part or all of the campaign. Such bans do exist in many countries. Whatever their faults, however, polls enliven the campaign and increase the information available, and many argue that to prohibit their publication in the media would not prevent parties, candidates, and others from conducting their own surveys. The main effect of a publication ban would be to give certain crucial information to those who could afford a survey and to deny it to the general public, a rather undemocratic suggestion.

One of the amendments to the Canada Elections Act made in the wake of the Royal Commission on Electoral Reform was to prohibit, in the final three days of the campaign, the broadcast, publication, or dissemination of the results of new scientifically conducted opinion surveys that would identify a political party or candidate. This restriction was soon challenged by the Thomson and Southam newspaper chains as a violation of freedom of the press, but so far unsuccessfully.

Impact of Polls on the Authorities

The other main question in the study of public opinion is the relationship between it and the response of the authorities. For nearly 100 years after Confederation, governments had to act in the absence of a reliable survey, but it now sometimes seems that they are reluctant to make any decision until it can be based on a poll. Even with such a poll, however, opinion is likely to be considerably divided, so that clear-cut guidance cannot always be found.

Sometimes, even when public opinion is clearly in favour of a certain course of government action, the authorities may decide otherwise. This may be the consequence of the politicians' own convictions, the recommendations of the public service, the pressure of interest groups, or the rigidity of party discipline. Indeed, some hold the view that even in a democracy, politicians are not obliged to follow public opinion; they may also lead it. This is especially so, now that we realize how uninformed, superficial, and changeable most public opinions really are. While politicians and bureaucrats may be accused of acting in their own self-interest if they do not follow a clear preference among the public, they may actually be relying on a deeper understanding of the issue, the greater information at their disposal, a more sophisticated analysis of its implications, or a concern for minority rights. For example, capital punishment has been an issue on which public opinion overwhelmingly supported one side but on which the authorities repeatedly went their own way. Should Parliament reinstate capital punishment in response to popular opinion based on a mistaken impression about rising crime rates, a desire for retribution, and a questionable assumption of deterrence? Most political issues are even more complicated than capital punishment, and on most, public opinion is much more divided; thus the correlation between public opinion and public policy is not as strong as might be expected.

In his book *Margin of Error*, Claire Hoy reveals just how many public policies were adopted over the years and how many election dates were set on the basis of public opinion polls. He also shows how important polls were in the 1988 election campaign. First, the Conservatives used many publicly funded polls to determine their election platform. Second, the Liberals surveyed public opinion in Quebec to see if a Senate veto of the Free Trade Agreement would detract from their support in that province. Third, the NDP avoided the Free Trade issue (and left the Liberals to capitalize on it) because party polling indicated that the NDP lacked public credibility on economic issues.[21] Indeed, the NDP used focus groups as early as 1984 to find that the phrase "ordinary Canadians" was preferable to "working Canadians" to use as its slogan.[22] When even the NDP starts to base its slogan and strategy on focus groups and public opinion polls, it is hard to overstate their significance.

....

NOTES

1. I am indebted to the Canadian Newspaper Association for providing the raw figures on which this account is based.
2. Frederick J. Fletcher, *The Newspaper and Public Affairs* (Ottawa: Royal Commission on Newspapers, 1981), 29, 35, 87. The main exception was Paul Desmarais, who insisted that his newspapers in Quebec not support the "oui" position in the 1980 Quebec referendum. See also the Royal Commission Report, 163–67, and David Taras, *The Newsmakers* (Scarborough: Nelson Canada, 1990), 8–17.
3. Frederick J. Fletcher and Daphne Gottlieb Taras, "Images and Issues: The Mass Media and Politics in Canada," in Michael Whittington and Glen Williams, eds., *Canadian Politics in the 1990s*, 3rd ed. (Scarborough: Nelson Canada, 1990), 229.
4. Edwin R. Black, *Politics and the News: The Political Functions of the Mass Media* (Toronto: Butterworths, 1982), 80.
5. Peter Trueman, *Smoke and Mirrors: The Inside Story of Television News in Canada* (Toronto: McClelland and Stewart, 1980), 161.
6. The general thrust of David Taras in *The Newsmakers* (Scarborough: Nelson Canada, 1990).
7. Ibid., 30–31.

8. Fletcher, *The Newspaper and Public Affairs*, 16; Fletcher and Taras, "Images and Issues," 222; Black, *Politics and the News*, 183; Peter Desbarats, *Guide to Canadian News Media* (Toronto: Harcourt Brace Jovanovich, 1990), 149; Arthur Siegel, *Politics and the Media in Canada* (Toronto: McGraw-Hill Ryerson, 1983), 14.

9. Taras, *The Newsmakers*, ch. 3; Allan Levine, *Scrum Wars: The Prime Ministers and the Media* (Toronto: Dundurn Press, 1993).

10. Environics Media Study (Environics Research Group, December 1986), cited by Desbarats, *Guide to Canadian News Media*, 28; and its *1991 Media Study*.

11. Taras, *The Newsmakers*, 102.

12. Alan Frizzell et al., *The Canadian General Election of 1988* (Ottawa: Carleton University Press, 1989), 33.

13. Taras, *The Newsmakers*, ch. 4.

14. Allan Fotheringham, *Birds of a Feather: The Press and the Politicians* (Toronto: Key Porter Books, 1989), 139.

15. Black, *Politics and the News*, 12; Taras, *The Newsmakers*, 234.

16. Desbarats, *Guide to Canadian News Media*, 41.

17. Black, *Politics and the News*, 168.

18. Frizzell, *1988*, 91.

19. John Turner's election in Vancouver Quadra in 1984 is often cited as an example of the underdog effect, given that all polls in the constituency indicated that he would lose.

20. Taras, *The Newsmakers*, 187, 192–94; Desbarats, *Guide*, 138.

21. Claire Hoy, *Margin of Error* (Toronto: Key Porter Books, 1989), 1–5.

22. Howard R. Penniman, ed., *Canada at the Polls, 1984* (Durham, N.C.: Duke University Press, 1988), 131.

FURTHER READING

Canada. Royal Commission on Newspapers. Ottawa: Supply and Services, 1981. See also its background research studies.

Desbarats, Peter. *Guide to Canadian News Media*. Toronto: Harcourt Brace Jovanovich, 1990.

Fletcher, Frederick J. *The Newspaper and Public Affairs*. Ottawa: Royal Commission on Newspapers, 1981.

Fotheringham, Allan. *Birds of a Feather: The Press and the Politicians*. Toronto: Key Porter Books, 1990.

Frizzell, Alan, et al. *The Canadian General Election of 1988*. Ottawa: Carleton University Press, 1989.

Hoy, Claire. *Margin of Error*. Toronto: Key Porter Books, 1989.

Levine, Allan. *Scrum Wars: The Prime Ministers and the Media*. Toronto: Dundurn Press, 1993.

Seigel, Arthur. *Politics and the Media in Canada*, 2nd ed. Toronto: McGraw-Hill Ryerson, 1996.

Taras, David. *The Newsmakers*. Scarborough: Nelson Canada, 1990.

Chapter 8

Elections and the Electoral System

Elections are one of the most important features of a democratic political system, and are usually one of the most exciting. This chapter examines the formal, legal aspects of the electoral system, as well as the unofficial campaign organization at both the national and local levels. It also contains an evaluation of the electoral system and suggestions for reform; a discussion of party and election finance; and an assessment of electoral behaviour and party support.

....

The Redistribution Process

Redistribution is the process of dividing the country into electoral districts or constituencies. It involves two stages: first, deciding how many seats in the House of Commons to allot to each province and territory, and second, actually drawing constituency boundaries within them.

The Constitution Act, 1867, requires that the readjustment process be repeated after each decennial census, such as after 1981, 1991, and 2001. Given the federal character of Canada with its strong provincial loyalties, the search for a reasonably fair means of distributing seats in the House of Commons among the provinces has been a long and unsatisfactory one. The formula used following the 1991 census and the one that resulted in the current 301 seats in the House of Commons for the 1997 election involved the four following steps.

1. Starting with 282 seats, 2 seats are allocated to the Northwest Territories and 1 to the Yukon, leaving 279 seats.

2. The total population of the 10 provinces is divided by 279 to obtain the electoral quota or quotient.

3. This electoral quota is divided into the population of each province to obtain the number of seats each is entitled to.

4. Additional seats are awarded where necessary, so that each province has as many House of Commons seats as it has senators, and as many seats as it had in 1985.

Thus, for the 1997 election, the House of Commons seats were distributed as follows: Ontario, 103; Quebec, 75; British Columbia, 34; Alberta, 26; Manitoba and Saskatchewan, 14 each; Nova Scotia, 11; New Brunswick, 10; Newfoundland, 7; Prince Edward Island, 4; Northwest Territories, 2; and Yukon, 1.

The second phase of the redistribution process, drawing constituency boundaries within each province, was historically the prerogative of the politicians. They regularly engaged in the process of "gerrymandering," that is, manipulating constituency boundaries so as to ensure as far as possible the re-election of the members of the government party. In the absence of any written rules, some constituencies had huge populations while others were extremely small. A new system was adopted in the Electoral Boundaries Readjustment Act of 1964, however, so that this task is now performed by independent commissions. An electoral boundaries commission is appointed for each province and the Northwest Territories, chaired by a judge designated by the chief justice of the province. The other two members of each commission are appointed by the Speaker of the House of Commons. All commissions draw extensively on the support staff of Elections Canada.

The commissions swing into action as soon as the provincial population figures are available from the census. Theirs is a very delicate task of trying to arrive at a design that will provide constituencies of approximately equal population size throughout the province at the same time as accounting for geographic characteristics, communities of interest, and other peculiarities. The most difficult problem is in dealing with sparsely populated rural or northern regions at the same time as concentrated urban centres. In recognition of this problem, the commissions in the 1960s and 1970s were allowed to deviate from the average population figure in any province to a maximum tolerance of plus or minus 25 percent, but in the 1980s and 1990s they were allowed to exceed this limit in extraordinary circumstances. Thus, rural and northern constituencies tend to be below the provincial quotient and southern, urban ones slightly above it. The Royal Commission on Electoral Reform and Party Financing recommended a tolerance of 15 percent.

The publication of the map of proposed electoral boundaries is followed by a period of public hearings, normally held at several different locations in the province. Interested individuals, municipalities, groups, and MPs appear to express their views on the proposals. Then, within a year of the population data becoming available, the commissions must complete their reports. They are sent to the House of Commons for committee deliberation and then back to the electoral boundaries commissions, who have the authority to alter the reports or leave them as is. Thus, it is the independent commissions and not the politicians who have the final say.

In general, since it takes fewer votes in smaller provinces and in rural parts of all provinces to elect a member of Parliament, such votes are worth more than those in large provinces or in urban areas. Whether out of charity, ignorance, or recognition of the fact that the population is peculiarly distributed, Canadians seem unconcerned about this deviation from the principle of representation by population or political equality.

The Election Organization
The Official Electoral Machinery

SETTING THE DATE

The prime minister normally has the prerogative to call the election within five years of the previous one. Largely based on the government party's standings in the public opinion polls, the election is typically called about four years after the previous campaign. Going into the fifth year, especially to the five-year limit, is seen as a sign of political weakness, and most governments waiting that long have been defeated. Public opinion polls can be wrong, of course, or public opinion can change between the calling of the election and the actual voting day, since Canadian party preferences are highly volatile. The apparent advantage for the party in power in choosing the date is therefore not absolute, as several prime ministers and premiers have discovered to their chagrin.

The governor general must approve the prime minister's request to dissolve Parliament in order to call an election, but this is normally automatic. Only once in Canadian history (1926), in rather peculiar circumstances, did a governor general refuse such a request. The defeat of a government in a nonconfidence vote in the House of Commons is the alternative method of precipitating an election, in which case the prime minister's leeway is limited to choosing the exact date.

ELECTION OFFICIALS

The Chief Electoral Officer is responsible for the overall administration of the election and must act with absolute impartiality. On the other hand, the *returning officers*, who organize the election in each of the 301 electoral districts (also called constituencies or ridings), are chosen by the cabinet on a partisan basis. Once appointed, however, they are expected to function in a nonpartisan fashion.

THE VOTERS LIST

In Canadian federal elections, the voters list has historically been compiled from scratch after the election writ is issued. This was done by means of a door-to-door enumeration, and it was largely because of this lengthy process that Canadian election campaigns used to be at least 47 days long.

Reforms introduced in 1996 provided for a Register of Electors, the base of which was compiled in one last door-to-door enumeration in April 1997. Henceforth it will be automatically updated from such sources as tax files, citizenship and immigration files, and driver's licence and vital statistics files. With such a permanent voters list, it was possible to reduce the length of the 1997 election period to 36 days.

NOMINATION

Most candidates are nominated by a political party, but they must submit formal nomination papers endorsed by 100 people on the local voters list accompanied by a $1000 deposit. Candidates receive one-half of this amount back if and when they file their financial statement, and those who receive at least 15 percent of the vote are also reimbursed the other $500. Official candidates of registered parties must obtain the party leader's endorsement in order to use the party name on the ballot. This requirement was mainly adopted to pre-empt the possibility of local conflicts over who was the legitimate standard-bearer of the party, but it effectively gives the leader a veto over nominations.

ELECTION DAY

After nomination day, the returning officer arranges for the ballots to be printed and allows people to vote in advance polls or by special ballot. Recent reforms have made voting much more convenient for those not at home on election day, including those outside the country. The returning officer also hires and trains deputy returning officers and poll clerks to look after each polling station on election day and finds appropriate polling station locations.

Canadian federal elections are held on Mondays, and the polls used to be open from 9 a.m. to 8 p.m. local time. Because voters in the western part of the country complained that the winner was often decided even before their votes had been counted, a system of staggered hours for different time zones was implemented for the 1997 election. This meant that the polls would close at approximately the same time all across the country, and ballots could be counted and the results announced more or less simultaneously. As before, however, broadcasters are not allowed to report results from other regions until the polls close in their own time zone. Voters are entitled to three consecutive hours off work in which to cast their ballot, and since 1993, the sale of liquor is no longer prohibited during polling hours.

Voters mark their X in private on the ballots provided, and when the polls close, the deputy returning officer and poll clerk count them, usually in the company of scrutineers from the various candidates who are allowed to challenge unorthodox markings on ballots and generally keep the whole process honest. Results are announced an hour or two after the polls close and the candidate with the most votes, the *first-past-the-post*, is declared elected. This means that the winner usually does not actually have a majority of the votes cast, only a plurality.

THE BALLOT

The secret ballot was introduced into federal elections in 1874. The candidates are listed in alphabetical order, and since 1970 the ballot has contained their party affiliation, if any. The Chief Electoral Officer keeps a registry of political parties; only registered parties (those that run at least 50 candidates) are allowed to use the party label on the ballot. Such parties must also register their national and constituency official agents and auditors for the purposes of keeping track of the party's and candidates' finances. Twelve parties were registered for the 1988 election, 14 for 1993, and 10 for 1997.

THE FRANCHISE

The extension of the franchise beyond males with substantial property was mentioned in passing in earlier chapters. This evolution in Canada was complicated by the use of different provincial franchises in federal elections between 1867 and

1917. Moreover, the franchise was manipulated in 1917 so as to maximize support for the incumbent government. The vote was extended to women serving in the war as well as to female relatives of men overseas, but denied to Canadian citizens who had come from "enemy alien" countries. In 1918 all women were granted the vote, and since 1920 a uniform federal franchise has existed. Most Canadians of Asian ancestry (especially those from Japan, China, and India) were denied the right to vote in federal elections because the federal law disqualified anyone who for reasons of race was denied the vote under provincial electoral statutes. All such restrictions were removed by 1948. The vote was extended to the Inuit in 1953 and to Indians living on reserves in 1960. The voting age was reduced from 21 to 18 in 1970, and British subjects who were not Canadian citizens lost their vote in 1975.

By that time, the Canada Elections Act disqualified only the following individuals from voting: the Chief and Assistant Chief Electoral Officers, returning officers (except in the case of a tie), federally appointed judges, prison inmates, those deprived of their liberty by reason of mental disease, and those convicted of corrupt or illegal electoral practices. In the course of the 1988 campaign, however, three of these disqualifications were challenged in the courts in terms of the Canadian Charter of Rights and Freedoms, which guarantees the vote to every Canadian citizen. In the case of judges and those in mental institutions, the provisions of the act were declared unconstitutional and the disqualifications removed. The courts made a number of contradictory decisions on whether prison inmates should be able to vote, and the 1993 amendments gave the vote (in federal elections, at least) to inmates serving sentences of less than two years. Just prior to the 1997 vote, however, long-term prisoners were successful in persuading the courts to remove the two-year restriction.

The National Party Campaign

At the national level, political parties usually set up a campaign committee about two years before they expect the election to be called. It starts to think about strategy, policy, image, and budget, as party headquarters conducts public opinion polls to see how the voters perceive the various leaders, parties, and issues.[1] For the party in power, such polls are central to deciding when to call the election in the first place, and for all major parties, polls serve to guide general strategy, media advertising, and the selection of priority ridings once the campaign begins.

Another national activity that begins before the calling of the election is the search for good candidates. While party headquarters rarely impose a candidate on an unwilling constituency association, they may try to guide the local decision or even to parachute a few "star" candidates into safe seats. The Liberals, Conservatives, and NDP all run a full slate of candidates, so where local organizations are weak, the national level of the party sometimes has to take the initiative to find a candidate for them. Because Liberal nominations were dominated by men and coveted by anti-abortionists and myriad ethnic groups, and to ensure a minimum number of candidates of cabinet calibre, in 1993 Chrétien had the party give him the power to appoint candidates in certain cases.

The NDP hoped to achieve gender parity in its candidates, but later was content with nearly 50 percent being either women or visible minorities. Meanwhile, because of the Reform Party's tendency to attract a certain number of racists and other extremists, it made prospective candidates complete a form detailing their background. If an "undesirable" person still manages to get nominated, the party leadership may have to expel a candidate, as it did in one case in 1993.

Party headquarters organize training sessions for campaign managers and candidates (right down to personal deportment), and produce mounds of election material for local candidates. One of the Liberals' great assets in the 1993 campaign was their election platform, commonly called the "Red Book." It provided a tremendous prop for a leader who was otherwise not overly policy-oriented in his public appearances.[2] "Red Book II," used in 1997, was less effective.

THE LEADER'S TOUR AND ITS MEDIA COVERAGE

Once the campaign begins, party headquarters organize each leader's tour and the national media campaign, and gear up for the televised leaders' debate. Each party leader criss-crosses the country over the campaign period in an effort not only to give a boost to promising local candidates, but also to generate stories for the national media. Such "free" coverage is eagerly sought, and parties spare no trouble or expense to obtain it.

The leader is accompanied by a horde of strategists and support staff, as well as by reporters who pay to travel aboard the party-chartered plane or bus. In general, national television newscasts contain one item per leader per day, and have provided almost equal time to the main parties.

NATIONAL MEDIA ADVERTISING

Each party also buys media advertising during (and sometimes immediately before) the campaign, and most parties spend huge amounts of money on the production of television commercials alone. The purchase of broadcast time is regulated by the Elections Act, requiring each broadcaster to make available, for purchase by registered political parties, six and one-half hours of prime time during the 27 days before the last 48 hours of the campaign. The broadcasting arbitrator allocates time among the parties primarily based on the number of seats held in the House of Commons and on popular vote received in the previous election, but no party can receive more than one-half of the total time. As a result of a Reform Party court challenge, parties can now purchase more than these allotments, subject to their overall expense ceiling, so that the significance of the allocation of time has diminished. In addition to purchasable time, parties are awarded free radio and television time in the same proportions.

THE LEADERS' DEBATE

The other main aspect of the national campaign is the televised leaders' debate. These have been held in all recent elections and are probably here to stay. The debates have become crucial aspects of the campaign because of the combined importance of leaders and television.

The debates are not mentioned in the law, so the consortium of television stations that carry them essentially set the rules. The debates have to fit into the television networks' schedule and are held when least advertising revenue would be lost. In 1993, with a large number of parties in the race, the consortium agreed that only five parties would take part—that is, those represented in Parliament and having had a consistent impact in public debates and public opinion. Mel Hurtig, leader of the new National Party of Canada, went to court to try to force his way into the debate, but did not succeed. The leaders of the same five parties participated in 1997.

After the debate, each party sends forth its "spin doctors" to persuade reporters that its leader won, but whether the public makes up its own mind on the winner or awaits the verdict of media commentators is not entirely certain. About two-thirds of the electorate watched at least one debate in both 1984 and 1988, and nearly 60 percent in 1993.[3] While 45 percent of respondents told a *Maclean's* poll that the 1988 debate, which ended with John Turner as "victor," had helped them decide how to vote,[4] much of this advantage had worn off by election day. The Conservatives had strategically insisted on having the debate early in the campaign in case they needed time to recover from just such an inferior performance. The 1997 debates were of little significance in the overall result.

The Local Candidate Campaign

NOMINATION

At the local level, each party's first priority is to nominate its candidate. Holding the nomination meeting even before the election is called allows many preparations to be made ahead of time, so the campaign can get off to a strong and early start.

THE LOCAL CAMPAIGN

Once the nomination has taken place, each party sets up a campaign committee under a campaign manager (see Figure 8.1). The Official Agent is responsible for ensuring that the candidate complies with the *Elections Act*. In most campaigns the other key official is the canvass organizer, who organizes the door-to-door "foot canvass" to distribute literature and/or a telephone canvass. Whether canvassers contact voters on the doorstep or on the phone, the object is both to spread the party's message and to seek out its own supporters. Armed with a voters list, canvassers put a positive, negative, or other distinguishing mark beside the name of all voters contacted. To cover an entire constituency in this fashion requires a veritable army of volunteers and an elaborate hierarchical organization. If money is more plentiful than volunteers, the local campaign may rely instead on media advertising. In recent elections, parties in targeted constituencies engaged in local polling and computer-assisted mail and telephone campaigning directed to members of key groups. In the past, much of this work was voluntary, but parties increasingly engage paid staff, sometimes consisting of "volunteers" paid by a business or union. The local campaign is a complex operation requiring ever more sophistication, staffing, and funding.

All this activity culminates on election day, when the organization tries to have a party scrutineer placed in each of the polls. Ideally, an inside scrutineer keeps track of which people on the list have cast their ballot, while an outside scrutineer periodically collects this information and heads out to round up all those previously identified as party supporters.

Figure 8.1   Structure of a Typical Local Campaign Committee

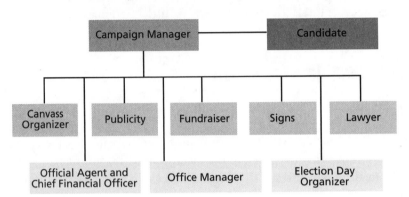

Evaluating the Electoral System

In each constituency, the candidate with the most votes wins, even if this is less than 50 percent. Among the advantages of this electoral system are its simplicity, its quick calculation of results, and its provision for each constituency of a clear-cut representative. When all the local results are cumulated nationally, however, the proportion of seats a party wins does not necessarily bear much relationship to its overall share of the popular vote. Take as an extreme, hypothetical example a two-person race in each constituency in which the Liberal candidate beat the Conservative candidate by one vote in every case: the Liberal Party would then win 100 percent of the seats from just over 50 percent of the vote, and the Conservative Party would have 0 percent of the seats from just under 50 percent of the vote. In fact, this example is not so hypothetical: in the New Brunswick election of 1987, the Liberals won 100 percent of the seats with about 60 percent of the popular vote. Many political scientists and other observers are therefore concerned that such overall disparities can occur between percent of seats won and percent of popular vote.

The actual disparities can be analyzed for both the national and provincial levels.[5] Overall, in 23 elections starting in 1921, the party with the largest popular vote won more seats than it deserved on 22 occasions. The system also typically favoured third parties with concentrated regional support, but those with broad national support usually lost out, and the CCF/NDP, for example, regularly received only about half as many seats as its popular vote merited.

Some observers tolerate these disparities because this first-past-the-post electoral system usually produces a majority government—the leading party obtaining more than 50 percent of the seats—even though a party rarely wins over 50 percent of the popular vote. Table 8.1 indicates that on 3 occasions (1940, 1958, and 1984) the winning party obtained at least 50 percent of the vote, and this automatically produced a majority government. On 12 other occasions out of 23, this electoral system manufactured a majority government in terms of seats, even though the leading party did not win a majority of the vote. This left only 8 occasions when a minority government resulted. While applauding the system for its tendency to produce majority governments, however, we should note that it weakens the opposition. Moreover, on three occasions (1957, 1962, and 1979) the party with the second-largest popular vote ended up with more seats than the party that came first, and therefore went on to form the government.

In the 1993 context, it is worth noting that the PCs and NDP deserved more seats in terms of their popular vote, enough in fact to be recognized as official parties, and the Reform Party deserved to be the Official Opposition in the sense that it received more votes than the Bloc. The 1997 election rectified these points, but continued to underrepresent the PCs and NDP.

Another set of disparities between popular vote and seat figures exists on a province-by-province basis. In this case, Alan Cairns was particularly struck by the disparity between the Conservative vote and seats in Quebec (1896–1984) and the disparity between the Liberal vote and seats in Western Canada (since 1957). Tables 8.2 and 8.3 provide the figures for 1997.

Cairns observed that such disparities affect parties in three principal ways: image, strategy, and policy. When the Conservatives had virtually no members from Quebec prior to 1984, they gained an anti-French image, even though they usually obtained at least 13 percent of the popular vote in that province. Similarly, after 1957, the Liberals acquired the image of an anti-Western party because they rarely elected members west of Ontario, even though they normally received over 20 percent of the Western vote.

As far as strategy is concerned, when Conservatives despaired of electing members from Quebec and felt they could form a government without much representation from that province, they ignored it. The Liberals have often similarly felt that campaigning in the West was a waste of time and money, and concentrated

TABLE 8.1 COMPARISON OF PERCENTAGE OF POPULAR VOTE AND PERCENTAGE OF SEATS
BY PARTY FOR FEDERAL ELECTIONS 1921–1997

	Liberals		Conservatives		CCF/NDP	
	% Vote	% Seats	% Vote	% Seats	% Vote	% Seats
1921	41	49	30	21	—	—
1925	40	40	46	47	—	—
1926	46	52	45	37	—	—
1930	45	37	49	56	—	—
1935	45	71	30	16	9	3
1940	52	74	31	16	9	3
1945	41	51	27	27	16	11
1949	49	74	30	16	13	5
1953	49	64	31	19	11	9
1957	41	40	39	42	11	9
1958	34	18	54	79	10	3
1962	37	38	37	44	14	7
1963	42	49	33	36	13	6
1965	40	49	33	36	18	8
1968	45	58	31	27	17	8
1972	38	41	35	40	18	12
1974	43	53	36	36	16	6
1979	40	40	36	48	18	9
1980	44	52	33	37	20	11
1984	28	14	50	75	19	11
1988	32	28	43	57	20	15

		Liberal	PC	NDP	Reform	BQ
1993	% Vote	41.3	16.0	6.9	18.7	13.5
	% Seats	60.0	0.7	3.1	17.6	18.3
1997	% Vote	38.4	18.9	11.1	19.4	10.7
	% Seats	51.4	6.6	7.0	19.9	14.6

Source: Data compiled from Chief Electoral Officer of Canada, Reports of the Chief Electoral Officer. Material reproduced with permission of the Chief Electoral Officer of Canada, 1997. Full responsibility for calculations and for conclusions drawn rests with the author.

TABLE 8.2 RESULTS OF 1997 ELECTION—SEATS WON BY PARTY BY PROVINCE

	Liberal	Reform	BQ	PC	NDP	Ind.	Total
Newfoundland	4	0	0	3	0	0	7
P.E.I.	4	0	0	0	0	0	4
Nova Scotia	0	0	0	5	6	0	11
New Brunswick	3	0	0	5	2	0	10
Quebec	26	0	44	5	0	0	75
Ontario	101	0	0	1	0	1	103
Manitoba	6	3	0	1	4	0	14
Saskatchewan	1	8	0	0	5	0	14
Alberta	2	24	0	0	0	0	26
B.C.	6	25	0	0	3	0	34
N.W.T.	2	0	0	0	0	0	2
Yukon	0	0	0	0	1	0	1
Total	155	60	44	20	21	1	301

Source: Data compiled from Chief Electoral Officer of Canada, Reports of the Chief Electoral Officer. Material reproduced with permission of the Chief Electoral Officer of Canada, 1997. Full responsibility for calculations and for conclusions drawn rests with the author.

their effort elsewhere. These strategies are not good for keeping the country together, one of the functions that political parties and elections are supposed to perform.

Finally, since the elected members of the party have a major role to play in the development of party policy, Conservative policy did not reflect the concerns of French Canada when the party lacked francophone and Quebec MPs, just as Liberal policy tended to ignore Western concerns. This is especially serious for the party that forms the government, for it has few or no MPs from a province or region to put into the cabinet. Because of such regionalized party standings between 1962 and 1984, either Quebec or the West was effectively left out of national decision-making at the cabinet level. Residents of those neglected regions understandably feel that national policy does not reflect their interests and turn to provincial governments to defend these interests or start to think in separatist terms.

Since Cairns first brought these problems to scholarly attention, reform of the electoral system has been frequently discussed. Many observers would like to

TABLE 8.3 COMPARISON OF PERCENTAGE OF SEATS WON AND VOTES IN 1997 ELECTION BY PROVINCE

	Liberals		Reform		BQ		PC		NDP	
	%V	%S	%V	%S	%V	%S	%V	%S	%V	%S
Newfoundland	38	57	3	0	0	0	37	43	22	0
P.E.I.	45	100	1	0	0	0	38	0	15	0
Nova Scotia	28	0	10	0	0	0	31	45	30	55
New Brunswick	33	30	13	0	0	0	35	50	18	20
Quebec	37	35	0	0	38	59	22	7	2	0
Ontario	50	98	19	0	0	0	19	1	11	0
Manitoba	34	43	24	21	0	0	18	7	23	29
Saskatchewan	25	7	36	57	0	0	8	0	31	38
Alberta	23	8	55	92	0	0	15	0	6	0
B.C.	29	18	43	74	0	0	6	0	18	9
N.W.T.	43	100	12	0	0	0	17	0	21	0
Yukon	22	0	25	0	0	0	14	0	29	100
Total	38.4	51.4	19.4	19.9	10.7	14.6	18.9	6.6	11.1	7.0

Source: Data compiled from Chief Electoral Officer of Canada, Reports of the Chief Electoral Officer. Material reproduced with permission of the Chief Electoral Officer of Canada, 1997. Full responsibility for calculations and for conclusions drawn rests with the author.

overcome the lack of representation of important segments of opinion in party caucuses and the cabinet, as well as to avoid the sense of regional–ethnic alienation that stems from this situation. A full-scale system of proportional representation is probably too extreme a reform in the circumstances, but a hybrid scheme combining constituency MPs with "supplementary MPs" has much merit.

Several authorities have suggested the addition of 50 or 60 supplementary "provincial MPs," who would overcome the worst problems of the existing system but still make majority government possible. This system would start with the regularly elected constituency MPs who are necessary to ensure the representation of all parts of Canada. But the supplementary MPs would be added, to be distributed on the basis of popular vote by party by province. They would correct the greatest discrepancies between the proportion of seats and votes. For the party in power, such supplementary MPs could provide provincial representation in the cabinet.[6]

Financing Elections

Prior to 1974 Canada essentially had no laws with respect to party and election finance. The Liberal and Conservative parties relied almost completely on contributions from big business at the national level, which usually produced a surplus to be distributed to candidates' campaigns as well. Candidates were otherwise dependent on donations from local small firms. Both parties had fundraisers or "bagmen"—often senators who could exploit their corporate connections and make use of their abundant spare time—assisted by corporate volunteers. Business also made contributions in kind, such as skilled personnel. The CCF/NDP depended primarily on individual membership fees supplemented by union contributions, but in this case the flow of funds was reversed and the local candidates had to help finance the central campaign. Overall, the Liberals and Conservatives raised and spent far more than the CCF/NDP, both at the national and local levels.

The secrecy surrounding party and election finance before 1974 makes it difficult to know exactly how many irregularities and scandals actually took place, but they were probably numerous. Small-scale scandals in the 1960s, together with increasing public expectations of political morality, caused the Pearson government to appoint a commission on the subject of party and election finance in 1964. Opposition pressure in the minority government period of 1972–74 finally forced reform more or less as that commission recommended. Amendments to the Canada Elections Act were passed in 1974 but did not take effect until the election of 1979. The legislation had six basic provisions:

- ceiling on candidate spending
- ceiling on party spending
- disclosure of contributions over $100
- tax credit for contributions
- public subsidy for candidates winning at least 15% of vote
- public subsidy for major parties

While no limit was placed on the size of contributions, a ceiling was imposed on national party spending; a ceiling was also placed on candidate expenditures. A disclosure provision required that the names of those contributing over $100 be filed with the Chief Electoral Officer and such records be open to public inspection. A tax credit provision was added so that contributors with taxable incomes would receive a 75 percent income tax refund for contributions up to $100, a 50 percent tax credit for contributions between $100 and $550, and a 33 percent credit for contributions over $550 to a maximum tax credit of $500. Candidates who received at least 15 percent of the vote would have a portion of their expenses subsidized by the public purse, the original formula being replaced by a flat 50 percent rate in amendments made in 1983. Finally, under the same amendments, instead of receiving subsidies for 50 percent of their broadcasting costs, parties would henceforth pay full price for such commercials and be subsidized for 22.5 percent of their total national expenditures if they spent at least 10 percent of their maximum. This provision was further amended in 1996 so that any party that won at least 2 percent of the popular vote was eligible for this subsidy, regardless of how much it spent.

The objectives of the legislation were thus to increase the equity, openness, and participatory nature of the electoral system. Equity was enhanced in limiting candidate and national party spending, as well as by the public subsidy provision; the disclosure clause would make it difficult for large secret contributions to be made in return for some favourable government decision, policy, or grant; and the tax credit would encourage individual contributions, reducing Liberal and Conservative dependence on corporations. For all the difficulties and loopholes remaining in the act, it has produced a more honest and equitable system of election finance.

Third-Party Advertising

Another major problem in the realm of election finance is third-party advertising. The 1983 amendments prohibited all advocacy-group spending during an election campaign that was not channelled through a party or candidate campaign. It was argued that the only way party and candidate spending ceilings could be effective was if any spending on their behalf was included in the parties' budgets. But in the 1980s more and more groups began to advertise on their own, for or against various parties or candidates. While such advertising was clearly a violation of the spirit of the law as well as its specific terms, the National Citizens' Coalition (NCC) challenged these sections in the Alberta Court of Queen's Bench in 1984. The court ruled the clauses unconstitutional as a violation of the freedom of expression provisions of the Charter of Rights and Freedoms.

Third-party advertising increased enormously in the 1988 election campaign, especially in the case of the pro–free trade group, the Canadian Alliance for Trade and Job Opportunities. With only the Conservative Party in favour of free trade, any advertising that promoted the Free Trade Agreement also promoted the Conservative Party. Thus the Conservatives benefited from some $5 million in advertising by advocacy groups on top of its own national budget of nearly $8 million. Such third-party advertising made a mockery of party spending ceilings and is widely thought to have helped the Conservatives achieve re-election by turning the momentum of the campaign back in their favour.

In response to widespread public criticism of this problem and to address other electoral issues, the Mulroney government appointed a Royal Commission on Electoral Reform and Party Financing shortly after the 1988 election, headed by Pierre Lortie. On this issue, the Royal Commission recommended that spending by individuals or organizations other than candidates and political parties be restricted to $1000 during the election period. The Commission argued that given the significance of the issue, to limit paid advertising of such advocacy groups during 36 days every four years was a "reasonable limit" on freedom of expression and would stand up to judicial scrutiny. The law was so amended just prior to the 1993 election, but successfully challenged by the NCC again. In 1997 the Supreme Court of Canada hinted that it would uphold the law if it were appealed to that level.

Electoral Behaviour and Party Support
Electoral Behaviour

Given the fact that the Liberals were so regularly victorious in Canadian federal elections between 1935 and 1984 and again in the 1990s, it is tempting to believe that a large proportion of voters have a strong Liberal Party identification and that any result other than a Liberal triumph is unlikely. Research shows, however, that more and more voters have no enduring party identification. A majority of voters constitute a large pool ready to be moved by the particular issues, candidates, and leaders in the campaign.[7] The overall aggregate stability, therefore, masked "the potential for significant variation in electoral outcomes,"[8] as became evident in the 1984 Conservative landslide. Other factors that add flexibility to the system are the group that votes in one election but not the next, as well as the newly eligible voters in each election. Table 8.4 summarizes the lack of durability among the electorate between the 1988 and 1993 elections. Only 31 percent of 1993 voters were consistent with 1988, while 41 percent switched parties.

TABLE **8.4** 1993 VOTER PREFERENCE COMPARED WITH 1988 (PERCENTAGE)

Voted same party	30.9
Switched parties	40.6
Previous voters not voting	7.6
Previous non-voters voting	4.4
Not voting either time	5.1
New voters	10.7

Source: Jon H. Pammett, "Tracking the Votes," in Alan Frizzell et al., The Canadian General Election of 1993 *(Toronto: Dundurn Press). Used with permission.*

In most other Western democracies the degree of voter identification with a specific party is much higher: the flexibility of the Canadian electorate demands explanation. Jon Pammett accounts for this phenomenon as follows:

> The most basic [factor] is that Canadian political culture is relatively apolitical. While Canadians are moderately interested in politics, this interest does not translate for most into substantial political involvement. The amount of detailed political information possessed by the average Canadian is low. Studies of children's political learning, or socialization, show a relatively weak transference of preference for a political party from parent to child ... because these feelings may not be strongly or persistently held in the adult "socializer."[9]

Another factor is that a large proportion of voters feel negatively about almost everything associated with the political system, and switch from party to party for negative rather than positive reasons.

The voting decision is an extremely complex and subtle one that is not easily explained. Nevertheless, voters are often asked what factor was most influential in helping them make up their mind—party, leader, issues, or local candidate. For all but those with the strongest party identification, it is usually the leader or issues that are most important. The local candidate is not normally a crucial factor. Voters will often say that they were moved by the issues, but many have trouble identifying the issues that supposedly influenced them. The relative importance of issues and leaders also varies from one election to another. In short, as Lawrence LeDuc writes, "the Canadian electorate continues to be one with relatively weak long-term attachments to political parties, low ideological commitment, and high responsiveness to short-term forces such as leaders, issues, or political events."[10] Such flexibility means that over half of the electorate makes up its mind during the course of the campaign, and that elections remain highly unpredictable.

These revelations also cast doubt on the question of whether elections provide a policy mandate for the successful party. First, Canadian parties rarely present a comprehensive election platform. Next, victorious parties do not seem to feel bound by the specific policies they proposed in the campaign. In the third place, the limited extent to which issues play a part in the campaign seriously detracts from the claim of any government that it has a mandate to pursue a particular policy. Finally, even on the rare occasion that a single issue figures prominently, the winning party almost never obtains a majority of the total votes cast, and certainly not a majority in all regions of the country. The free trade issue in 1988 provided the closest thing to a policy mandate for any Canadian government in recent times, yet the Conservatives received only 43 percent of the overall popular vote and less than 40 percent in six provinces and territories. The Liberals made much of their Red Book during the 1993 campaign, but even though a large part of it was unfulfilled, the electorate returned them to office in 1997.

Party Support

The other aspect of electoral behaviour that has attracted much attention from political scientists is the relationship between voters' regional, cultural, and socioeconomic background and their party preference. This relates to the cleavages encountered in earlier chapters. At least until the 1984 federal election, certain fairly clear-cut patterns of socioeconomic support for the three main parties could be identified.

First, there were wide variations in regional support. The Liberals dominated Quebec and the Conservatives excelled in the West, especially Alberta. While these respective patterns were not quite as dramatic in terms of popular vote as in the proportion of seats won, they were still significant. Liberal support in Quebec had been virtually unchanged since 1900, but the Conservative popularity in the West was primarily a legacy of John Diefenbaker in the 1950s and 1960s. Such party strongholds resulted in the situation that election campaigns were most heatedly contested in Ontario, which could swing either way.

A second marked pattern in Canadian voting behaviour was religion.

Roman Catholics have been strongly inclined to vote Liberal, whether they were French, English, or of other ethnic background, and regardless of where they lived in the country. This situation is especially striking when one considers that no serious religious issues divided the parties in Canadian federal politics for generations.

Ethnicity was another significant factor in Canadian electoral behaviour. The French-Canadian preference for the Liberal Party is well known and exists outside as well as within Quebec. Among those of non-British and non-French origins, the Liberals also did best, especially among post–Second World War immigrants (largely of Mediterranean and Indian subcontinental origins), who apparently reacted with gratitude to the fact that the Liberal Party was in office when they arrived.

A final demographic factor is social class, the expectation being that upper-class citizens would vote Conservative, the middle class would support the Liberals, and the working and poorer classes would vote NDP. In most Western democracies such a pattern is quite significant, but it is not borne out well in Canada.[11] The Liberal Party has usually attracted nearly the same degree of support from all classes except farmers. Only a small proportion of the working class actually votes for working-class parties. The NDP, for example, normally gets relatively more support from skilled and unskilled labour than from other groups, but not as much as does each of the other parties. The low level of class-consciousness and class-based voting in Canada is quite striking, and many explanations have been offered.[12]

The 1984 and 1988 elections ran counter to generations of traditional voting patterns, especially with Quebec French-Canadian Roman Catholics preferring the Conservatives over the Liberals. The 1993 election then saw the West abandon the Conservatives for Reform, and Quebec switch to the Bloc Québécois. Thus, such socioeconomic patterns of party support as were once evident seem to have vanished. But this new pattern of regional party support was reinforced in 1997, especially in terms of elected MPs, with Reform dominating the West, the Liberals overwhelming Ontario, the Bloc doing well in Quebec, and the NDP and PCs reviving in Atlantic Canada.

....

NOTES

1. Alan Frizzell, Jon Pammett, and Anthony Westell, *The Canadian General Election of 1988* (Ottawa: Carleton University Press, 1989), 16–17, 45–46.

2. Stephen Clarkson, "Yesterday's Man and His Blue Grits: Backward into the Future," in Frizzell, *The Canadian General Election of 1993* (Ottawa: Carleton University Press, 1994), 33.

3. Lawrence LeDuc and Richard Price, "Great Debates: The Televised Leadership Debates of 1979," *Canadian Journal of Political Science* (March 1985).

4. Ibid.; Frederick Fletcher, "The Media and the 1984 Landslide," in Howard Penniman, ed., *Canada at the Polls, 1984* (Durham, N.C.: Duke University Press, 1988), 181; *Maclean's* (5 December 1988).

5. Alan C. Cairns, "The Electoral System and the Party System in Canada," *Canadian Journal of Political Science* (March 1968): 55–80.

6. William Irvine, *Does Canada Need a New Electoral System?* (Kingston: Institute of Intergovernmental Relations, Queen's University, 1979) proposes a more extreme reform.

7. Lawrence LeDuc, "The Flexible Canadian Electorate," in Penniman, *Canada at the Polls, 1984*, 40.

8. Frizzell, *The Canadian General Election of 1988*, 109.

9. Jon H. Pammett, "Elections," in M. Whittington and G. Williams, eds., *Canadian Politics in the 1990s*, 4th ed. (Scarborough: Nelson Canada, 1995), 242.

10. LeDuc, "The Flexible Canadian Electorate," 51.

11. Jon Pammett, "Class Voting and Class Consciousness in Canada," *Canadian Review of Sociology and Anthropology* 24, no. 2 (1987): 269–90; Keith Archer, "The Failure of the New Democratic Party: Unions, Unionists, and Politics in Canada," *Canadian Journal of Political Science* (June 1985): 353–66.

12. See the section on class-based parties in Chapter 9; Janine Brodie and Jane Jenson, *Crisis, Challenge and Change: Party and Class in Canada Revisited* (Ottawa: Carleton University Press, 1988); Pammett, "Class Voting;" and Archer, "The Failure."

. . . .

FURTHER READING

Brodie, Janine, and Jane Jenson. *Crisis, Challenge and Change: Party and Class in Canada Revisited.* Ottawa: Carleton University Press, 1988.

Cairns, Alan C. "The Electoral System and the Party System in Canada." *Canadian Journal of Political Science* (March 1968): 55–80.

Canada. Royal Commission on Electoral Reform and Party Financing. *Reforming Electoral Democracy.* Ottawa: Supply and Services, 1992.

Clarke, Harold D., et al. *Absent Mandate: Interpreting Change in Canadian Elections.* Toronto: Gage, 1991.

Courtney, John C., et al., eds. *Drawing Boundaries: Legislatures, Courts, and Electoral Values.* Saskatoon: Fifth House Publishers, 1992.

Elections Canada. *Reports of the Chief Electoral Officer of Canada; Representation in the Federal Parliament, 1993;* and *Report of the Chief Electoral Officer Respecting Election Expenses.*

Frizzell, Alan, and Anthony Westell. *The Canadian General Election of 1984.* Ottawa: Carleton University Press, 1985.

Frizzell, Alan, Jon H. Pammett, and Anthony Westell. *The Canadian General Election of 1988.* Ottawa: Carleton University Press, 1989.

———. *The Canadian General Election of 1993.* Ottawa: Carleton University Press, 1994.

Gidengil, Elizabeth. "Canada Votes: A Quarter Century of Canadian Election Studies." *Canadian Journal of Political Science* (June 1992).

Pammett, Jon. "Class Voting and Class Consciousness in Canada." *Canadian Review of Sociology and Anthropology* 24, no. 2 (1987): 269–90.

Chapter 9

Political Parties

Political parties are integral to the operation of almost every aspect of a modern political system, and are mentioned in almost every chapter of this book. This chapter discusses them in four main sections: the historical evolution of Canadian political parties; interpretations of the Canadian party system; party organization; and party ideology. Party and electoral finance and the role of parties in the electoral campaign, including electoral behaviour and party support, were discussed in Chapter 8.

Political parties can be defined as organized groups that nominate candidates and contest elections in order to influence the personnel and policy of government. Compared to other groups in society such as interest groups that possess a fairly narrow focus and *articulate* a single interest, political parties are usually broader in scope and seek to *aggregate*, combine, consolidate, or appeal to many different interests or demands. In the process, parties reduce interests and demands to a manageable quantity called "issues."

Historical Evolution of Canadian Parties

A brief outline of the historical evolution of Canadian political parties can be structured around Table 9.1, which lists the prime ministers of Canada, their parties, and their dates of office. This evolution is often divided into three periods.

1867–1921

The Conservative Party is usually said to have had its beginnings in 1854 when John A. Macdonald formed a coalition of four pre-Confederation groupings: Tories and Moderates from Upper Canada (Ontario), along with English businessmen and French Conservatives from Lower Canada (Quebec). Party lines for individual politicians were quite flexible in those days, and alliances among groups were also unstable, but Macdonald's coalition gradually melded into an organized political party. The two main groups left out of this coalition—the French radicals in Quebec and the Clear Grits from Upper Canada—periodically joined forces in the pre-Confederation era, but it was not until much later that

TABLE 9.1 PRIME MINISTERS OF CANADA

John A. Macdonald	Conservative	1867–1873
Alexander Mackenzie	Liberal	1873–1878
John A. Macdonald	Conservative	1878–1891
John Abbott	Conservative	1891–1892
John Thompson	Conservative	1892–1894
Mackenzie Bowell	Conservative	1894–1896
Charles Tupper	Conservative	1896
Wilfrid Laurier	Liberal	1896–1911
Robert Borden	Conservative	1911–1920
Arthur Meighen	Conservative	1920–1921
Mackenzie King	Liberal	1921–1926
Arthur Meighen	Conservative	1926
Mackenzie King	Liberal	1926–1930
R.B. Bennett	Conservative	1930–1935
Mackenzie King	Liberal	1935–1948
Louis St. Laurent	Liberal	1948–1957
John Diefenbaker	Progressive Conservative	1957–1963
Lester Pearson	Liberal	1963–1968
Pierre Elliott Trudeau	Liberal	1968–1979
Joe Clark	Progressive Conservative	1979–1980
Pierre Elliott Trudeau	Liberal	1980–1984
John Turner	Liberal	1984
Brian Mulroney	Progressive Conservative	1984–1993
Kim Campbell	Progressive Conservative	1993
Jean Chrétien	Liberal	1993–

they became the nucleus of the Liberal Party. After Macdonald was disgraced in the Pacific scandal over fundraising practices, the Liberals took office between 1873 and 1878 under Alexander Mackenzie, but his government reflected this early lack of party cohesion. Macdonald returned to power in 1878, and the Conservatives demonstrated increasing unity as time went on. After the execution of Louis Riel, however, French-Canadian support started to fall away from the Conservative Party, helped by the fact that an attractive French Canadian, Wilfrid Laurier, became leader of the Liberal Party shortly afterwards. Macdonald died in 1891, and his party experienced a period of great instability in the subsequent five years. Thus, with the government party in decline and the Liberals finally showing the marks of a well-organized national party, it is not surprising that Laurier won the watershed election of 1896. At that time Canada moved from a Conservative *one-party dominant* system to a classic *two-party system* in which Liberals and Conservatives competed on equal terms.

Laurier governed quite successfully until he was beaten in 1911 when the two main issues were reciprocity (free trade with the United States) and the naval question (whether Canada should establish its own navy or contribute to that of Britain). Robert Borden's Conservatives took over and were soon confronted with the monumental task of managing Canada's war effort. After three years of war, Borden concluded that conscription would have to be adopted. Most English-speaking MPs agreed to join the Conservatives in a Union Government in 1917, but Laurier and the French-Canadian Liberals remained aloof, leaving that party badly split. With conscription, the Conservatives almost totally alienated French Canada, at the same time as the policies of both Conservative and Liberal parties upset the farming community in English Canada, notably the West. Thus, while Mackenzie King succeeded Laurier as Liberal leader in 1919 and skillfully pursued party reconciliation, Arthur Meighen inherited an unpopular Conservative Party in 1920 when he took over from Borden.

1921–1957

The 1921 election marked the end of the two-party system in Canada. On that occasion, farmers entered the contest with their own Progressive candidates and elected more members than the Conservatives, while two Labour members were also successful. Farmers were particularly unhappy with conscription, tariff, agricultural, and transportation policies, as well as prevailing political practices such as party patronage and rigid party discipline in the House of Commons. Nevertheless, Mackenzie King led his Liberals to victory in 1921, in 1925, and again in 1926 (after a brief Conservative interruption caused by the King–Byng dispute discussed in Chapter 13), and by the late 1920s most of the Progressive MPs had either become Liberals or been defeated. The Liberals themselves were defeated in 1930, however, primarily because of the onset of the Depression.

By this time the Conservatives were led by R.B. Bennett. Although he exercised vigorous leadership and even departed from orthodox Conservative policy to some extent, Bennett could not cope with the unemployment, poverty, and general devastation wrought by the Depression. Along with almost every other government in office during this period, Bennett's Conservatives were defeated in 1935, and Mackenzie King's Liberals returned to power.

Besides contributing to this change of government, the Depression was the catalyst for the creation of several new political parties. The Co-operative Commonwealth Federation (CCF) was formed in 1932, an amalgam of farmer and Labour MPs, eastern intellectuals, and various farmer, labour, and socialist groups and parties, primarily from the West. In 1933 the party adopted its radical platform, the Regina Manifesto, and chose Labour MP J.S. Woodsworth as its leader. The party elected several MPs in 1935 and took office in Saskatchewan in 1944 under T.C. Douglas.

The Social Credit Party was born in Alberta in 1935 around charismatic evangelist William Aberhart. The party was originally concerned with the reform of the banking system as a means of dealing with the Depression, but abandoned this platform when it proved to be both unworkable and unconstitutional. After Alberta became prosperous with the discovery of oil in the 1940s, Social Credit transformed itself into an orthodox conservative party under E.C. Manning. The party remained in power in Alberta for 36 years, came to power in British Columbia in 1952, and also elected several Western MPs.

In Quebec, a group of disgruntled progressive Liberals defected from their provincial party in 1935 to join forces with the chronically unsuccessful provincial Conservative Party to form the Union Nationale. The leader, Maurice Duplessis, quickly discarded the comprehensive reform program on which the party was elected a year later and became ultra-conservative. Despite this shift in emphasis, the Union Nationale remained in power in Quebec until 1960 with only a four-year interruption.

None of these developments impeded the Liberal Party at the federal level; it continued to elect majority governments from 1935 to 1948 under Mackenzie King and then until 1957 under his successor, Louis St. Laurent. King's conciliatory skills were severely tested during the Second World War (1939–45), but his government avoided a serious second conscription crisis. He also presided over the initiation of the Canadian welfare state. The St. Laurent period was one of great prosperity, largely financed by a tremendous inflow of American investment.

1957–Present

The Conservative Party floundered for 20 years after 1935, having previously alienated French Canada, and having been blamed, however unfairly, for the Depression. It changed leaders repeatedly, changed party policy to some extent, and changed the party name to Progressive Conservative in 1942, all to no avail. The political climate was suddenly transformed in 1956 with the choice as party leader of John Diefenbaker, who benefited from the public's increasing resentment of Liberal arrogance (as demonstrated in the pipeline debate) and complacency. Diefenbaker led the Conservatives to a surprising minority government victory in 1957 and then to a record majority in 1958. His decline was almost as rapid as his ascent, however, as his government fell apart over defence policy. The party was defeated in 1963, after which it engaged in a long period of bitter infighting over the leadership question.

During the Diefenbaker period, significant developments in two minor parties took place. The CCF, which had seen its federal fortunes decline throughout the 1950s, decided to combine its efforts with those of the new national labour organization, the Canadian Labour Congress. The result was the creation of the New Democratic Party (NDP) in 1961. T.C. Douglas was persuaded to leave the premiership of Saskatchewan to become the first national NDP leader. Then, out of the blue, a group of Social Credit, or Créditiste, MPs was elected from Quebec in 1962, just when the Western wing of the party was starting to decline.

Lester Pearson's Liberals were elected in 1963 and re-elected in 1965, but were always denied a majority of seats. Nonetheless, Pearson tackled many controversial issues, particularly the new nationalism in Quebec, the Canada Pension Plan, medicare, and a new flag. One opposition party or another supported each of Pearson's measures, so that he was able to continue in office until he retired in 1968.

The Liberals then gained a majority government under their new leader Pierre Elliott Trudeau, but just narrowly defeated Robert Stanfield's Conservatives in 1972. In the resulting minority government, the Liberals worked closely with the NDP for two years. With Trudeau ridiculing Stanfield's proposal for wage and price controls, the Liberals were returned with a majority in 1974, only to turn around and implement such a policy themselves. In 1979 the Liberals were defeated by the Conservatives, now led by Joe Clark. Nine months later, the Clark government fell with parliamentary rejection of its budget, and Trudeau led his party back to power in early 1980.

The separatist Parti Québécois formed the provincial government in Quebec in 1976 under René Lévesque. Then, after helping to defeat the PQ's 1980 referendum proposal, Trudeau patriated the Constitution, together with a Charter of Rights and Freedoms, but against the will of most Quebeckers. Trudeau also alienated the West with his controversial National Energy Program. He resigned in 1984, turning the reins over to John Turner who was pitted against the new Conservative leader, Brian Mulroney. In the September 1984 election, the Conservatives won a landslide victory, including a startling majority of the seats in Quebec. After the negotiation of the Canada–U.S. Free Trade Agreement and the Meech Lake Accord, Mulroney led his party to a second successive majority in 1988, only to see Meech Lake fail to acquire the unanimous approval of new provincial governments.

Because various minor parties made their presence felt but did not seriously challenge the dominance of the Liberals and Conservatives between 1921 and 1980, the Canadian party system during that period can be called a "two-plus" or "two-and-one-half" party system. The 1980s, on the other hand, might better be termed a "three-party" decade. While both western and eastern wings of Social Credit disappeared, the NDP became entrenched as the third major national party under Ed Broadbent's leadership between 1975 and 1989.

The Liberal Party's obsession with Quebec was the main reason that the West preferred the Conservatives after 1957. When the Mulroney Conservatives proved to be primarily concerned to hold on to their unprecedented Quebec support after 1984, however, many Westerners turned to the Reform Party, headed by Preston Manning, son of the former Social Credit premier of Alberta. Besides being an expression of Western alienation, Reform was a manifestation of right-wing populism in its opposition to big government, its desire for lower taxes, and its concern with law and order. Then, with the collapse of the Meech Lake Accord, sovereignist sentiment increased in Quebec, giving rise to a new federal separatist party, the Bloc Québécois. Thus, five parties of considerable strength contested the 1993 federal election, and produced a highly unusual result: the Liberals did well across the country, the Bloc Québécois displaced the Conservatives in Quebec, and the Reform Party usurped the Conservatives in the West. The PCs held on to 16 percent of the popular vote but retained only 2 seats, and the NDP did badly everywhere. Given that a minimum of 12 seats is required for official party standing in the House of Commons, only three parties came back as recognized parties, two of them new, and it seemed that a regionalized multiparty system had developed. The 1997 election returned five official but highly regionalized parties, at least in terms of seats won.

....

Interpretations of the Canadian Party System

Faced with the rather unusual party system—or succession of party systems—just outlined, several political scientists have proposed theories or interpretations in order to explain it.

The Broker System

The most traditional interpretation is the *broker* or *brokerage* theory.[1] The essence of this interpretation is that, given the multiple cleavages in Canadian society and the function of parties to aggregate interests, political parties in Canada should be conciliators, mediators, or brokers among such cleavages as regions, ethnic and linguistic groups, classes, and genders. The theory suggests that maximizing their appeal to all such groups is not only the best way for parties to gain power, but in the fragmented Canadian society, this approach is also necessary in order to keep the country together. Thus, in their search for power, parties should act as agents of national integration and attempt to reconcile as many divergent interests as possible.

Throughout most of Canadian history, the two overriding cleavages that have concerned people as well as parties have been region and culture. While the class cleavage is the central focus of politics in most countries, it has usually attracted least attention in Canada; the broker theory thus emphasizes the middle-class consciousness of most Canadians. The broker theory can thus be seen to argue that the Liberal and Conservative parties have no central ideological interests and merely promise to satisfy the most important interests held by the voters at any point in time. Alternatively, they disguise their real ideological interest—protecting the capitalist system—by emphasizing ethnic and regional concerns instead of class interests. In any case, ideological differences between the two main parties are not profound. Defenders of the broker system argue that parties should not foment artificial class conflicts and ideological differences in a country that is already seriously divided; they should bring people together rather than drive them apart.

However appealing the broker system, its implications should not be overlooked. By concentrating on regional and ethnic cleavages, parties minimize the role of ideology in Canadian politics. Parties are opportunistic and pragmatic rather than offering the electorate a choice of principles and distinctive programs. They do not generate innovative policy approaches, but are content instead to respond to public opinion polls and interest group demands. What parties offer to the electorate in the place of alternative solutions to national problems are alternative leaders and slogans. Especially in a television age, leader images have become the focus of election campaigns.

Class-Based Parties

A second perspective on the Canadian party system, and a reaction to the broker approach, is the concept of a *class-based* party system.[2] Like the broker model, the class-based theory is partly an explanation of the existing system; however, it rejects the status quo. Class-based analysts expect that in the pre-democratic period two parties will develop, both of which defend the capitalist system. When the vote is extended to the working class, however, a new working-class party will emerge, generally forcing politics to take on an ideological and class-based character. This evolution clearly occurred in Britain.

In late nineteenth-century Canada, the Liberal and Conservative parties both defended capitalism, differentiating themselves on ethnic and religious grounds as well as on minor policy differences such as the tariff. When the vote was extended to the working class at the turn of the century, some isolated labour, socialist, and communist political activity occurred, and by 1920 new class-based farmer and labour parties existed. But the newly enfranchised working class did not manage to create a successful class-based party, as the Liberals and Conservatives did everything in their power to discourage such a development, using both seductive and coercive techniques. Eventually, the farmers' intense interest in politics declined, and the working class continued to support the two old-line parties on ethnic/religious and regional grounds, rendered content by the occasional piece of social legislation.

The Depression represented the collapse of the capitalist system and might have been expected to give rise to new class-based parties. The CCF did emerge to become the most sustained working-class party to that point, but most members of the working class continued to support the two traditional parties. Unionization expanded significantly in the 1940s, and the CCF achieved its highest popular standing in the 1943–45 period, after which Liberal welfare initiatives helped to draw off working-class support. This decline led to the creation of the NDP in 1961, but even with the NDP's organic link to the labour movement, most working-class Canadians continued to vote Liberal or PC.

Analysts have proposed many reasons for the lack of class-consciousness among the Canadian working class.[3] Those who defend the lack of such consciousness argue that other divisions take precedence in Canada, that the system permits social mobility, that most people feel themselves to be middle class, that material benefits are widely shared, and that the Liberal and Conservative parties have accommodated working-class interests along with ethnic, religious, and regional interests in the broker system. Those who decry the lack of working-class consciousness contend that the Liberals and Conservatives were firmly entrenched when the franchise was extended to the working class and had already defined politics around social differences other than class. These two parties either appealed to one or more ethnic/religious and regional groups or else developed pan-Canadian appeals that diverted attention from class-based issues. These parties deluded most voters into the belief that they belonged to the middle class and gave them the false impression of inclusion and social mobility. Janine Brodie and Jane Jenson make the additional point that class-consciousness requires prior ideological and organizational activity by groups such as unions, farmers, and cooperatives. They demonstrate that classes as active and self-conscious social actors have to be created, and that class-based organizations must precede the expectation of class-based voting.

Advocates of a class-based party system thus point out that the existing system is partially class-based—the upper and upper middle classes are conscious of their class position and vote accordingly; it is just that the working class does not vote appropriately. They claim that a class-based system would provide ideological alternatives in elections, making them more meaningful and more likely to offer innovative solutions to national problems. Moreover, the broker system, with its emphasis on multiple cleavages, is dangerously destabilizing, for if the Liberals and Conservatives are unsuccessful as brokers, the separation of one or more ethnic–regional units is possible. In such circumstances, class could be the integrating ingredient: "a nation like Canada, which is in danger of falling apart on ethnic–regional lines, may be held together by a politics which unites the people of various regions and ethnic groups around the two poles of left and right."[4] Canadians would ideally be united by their common class position into two or three national class-based parties. Finally, class-based politics and parties are already apparent in certain Canadian provinces, so that this theory is quite a realistic proposition after all.

One-Party Dominance

The *one-party dominant* thesis is a third general theory regarding Canadian parties. H.G. Thorburn, for example, maintains that the Canadian party system has really been dominated not by two major parties but by one—the Liberals—since about 1900.[5] The Liberals are the *government party*, power-oriented rather than issue-oriented, attracting "winners" and "successes" as supporters and candidates, and maintaining themselves in office with the help of public service expertise, public opinion polls, and the chance to choose election day. The Conservatives can be seen as the *opposition party*, ordinarily having to settle for the role of critics and being elected to office only on those rare occasions when the people get thoroughly fed up with the Liberals. However, with their divisiveness, "opposition mentality," and lack of preparedness to govern, the Conservatives do not remain in power very long. Finally, the NDP can be termed the *innovative party*, never really having a chance to govern nationally, but being responsible for introducing new ideas from beyond the range of current ideological conformity.

The Decline of Parties

A final interpretation, coming from John Meisel, emphasizes the decline of political parties.[6] He suggests a number of reasons why this is the case and why traditional party functions have been taken over by other institutions. A decline in ideological differences among the parties has resulted in their being less capable of offering innovative solutions to national problems. People prefer to participate directly in specialized voluntary associations rather than take their concerns to an omnibus political party, with the result that interest groups have greatly increased in number and strength. The quantity and complexity of information with which governments have to deal has come to mean that generalist politicians can no longer cope with it, leaving them increasingly dependent upon the bureaucracy. This culminates in a situation in which interest groups confer with bureaucrats to work out policies that the politicians can neither understand nor alter, further reducing the role of political parties in the policymaking process. Federal–provincial conferences and committees have become the forum in which many public policies are ironed out, and once certain political and bureaucratic compromises have been made, there is little that other politicians or parties can do about them.

Meisel also notes that parties now gear most of their activity to the demands of the media, and to the extent that elections are dominated by leader images and leader debates, the need for traditional party organizations diminishes. Similarly, public opinion polls provide better feedback to politicians than their traditional discussions with party activists. Investigative journalism has reduced the role of the opposition in Parliament; direct-mail appeals have replaced traditional forms of party fundraising; and modern transnational corporations are beyond the control of any party or government. Other recent developments that have contributed to the decline of parties are the increasing power of the prime minister, the influence of election strategists and other specialist advisers, and the new role of the courts and the Charter of Rights and Freedoms.

Minor Parties

Because Canada has had more minor (or "third") parties than other similar political systems, political scientists have developed several theories to account for them. Essentially, these parties can all be explained by the fact that at one time or another, ethnic, regional, or class grievances have gone unsatisfied by the broker parties. Moreover, new minor parties are only to be expected when party identification is weak, and in the context of the ideological stagnation and opportunism of the broker system. In particular, if the working class never managed to establish a major party in Canada, it is not surprising that minor working-class parties would be created. The principal factors responsible for the rise of the various minor parties in Canada involve region, ethnicity, class or ideology, the poor economy, and charismatic leadership, as seen in Table 9.2.

Party Organization

A political party has been defined as an organized group, but the structure of such a group requires clarification. Several different components of each party can be identified: the *parliamentary party* or caucus, that is, the party's elected representatives in Parliament; the *extra-parliamentary party* organization made up of party activists and executive members; the party headquarters, bureaucracy, or staff; and ordinary party members. These structural features can be useful in distinguishing the various political parties in Canada.

TABLE 9.2 FACTORS INVOLVED IN THE RISE OF MINOR PARTIES

	Region	Ethnicity	Class/Ideology	Economy	Leader
Progressives	*		*	*	
CCF			*	*	
Social Credit	*		*	*	*
Reconstruction			*	*	
Bloc Populaire	*	*			
NDP			*		
Créditistes	*	*	*	*	*
Libertarian			*		
Christian Heritage			*		
Green			*		
Confederation of Regions	*	*			
Reform	*	*	*		*
Bloc Québécois	*	*			*

Party Membership

The most active local organizations of the NDP operate an annual, year-round membership drive. New members must take an oath that they support the party's principles, and only those who have been members for at least 30 days and who live in the constituency are allowed to vote at nomination meetings. Constituency association representation at party conventions is based on the size of the local membership, and the party is unique in also having affiliated members, that is, members of unions that have voted to affiliate with the party. Like the NDP, the Reform Party has a 30-day membership qualification period, and convention representation is based on the number of local members.

Although they may conduct membership drives for a few weeks a year, the Liberals and Conservatives are normally more casual about the annual renewal of party memberships. For the most part, their members sign up in connection with a meeting to nominate a candidate for the next election or to choose delegates to a national convention. Although the Liberals are usually more restrictive than the Conservatives, it is typical for aspiring Liberal candidates or delegates to recruit large numbers of new members (often from ethnic groups in large urban centres) just prior to the deadline.

All parties have difficulty maintaining complete and current lists of their members, especially at provincial or national headquarters. But the NDP, Reform, and Bloc Québécois usually have a better grasp of their actual membership than the others and use their list repeatedly during the year for fundraising purposes.

Party Leadership

The Liberals relied on the parliamentary party to select their leaders before 1919, and the Conservatives did so until 1927, but federal parties currently choose their leaders at national delegate conventions.[7] While leadership conventions are a more democratic means of choosing the party leader, the preference of party delegates does not always correspond to that of the parliamentary party, sometimes leading to considerable friction between the new leader and the caucus. Nevertheless, conventions attract much free media attention, they usually raise the morale of party members, and they can have a unifying effect on the party.

An even more democratic procedure than the leadership convention has been proposed in recent years, that is, to allow every card-carrying member of the party to cast a vote for the leadership. Such a procedure avoids much of the cost of holding a national convention; it eliminates the unholy fight among various candidates for delegates at the constituency level; and it ensures that the decision is not left to the more affluent members of the party who can afford the travel costs. The Parti Québécois was the first party to move to a "one member–one vote" leadership selection process, and many provincial party leaders have now been elected on this basis. It has become popular to issue party members a personal identification number and have them telephone in their choice. Such procedures have potential problems of their own, however, including technological breakdowns, an unrepresentative electorate, and the involvement of voters who have no knowledge of the candidates or who actually support other parties. Many partisans also feel that the loss of the publicity value of a nationally televised convention is too high a cost, and suggest that by imposing spending limits on candidates and subsidizing delegates' expenses, some of the worst features of conventions can be avoided.

Some parties try to combine the best of both worlds: giving every member a vote, but also having a leadership convention. After choosing Jean Chrétien in the traditional way in 1990, the Liberals adopted a new system in 1992 modelled on their provincial counterparts in Ontario. Every party member votes at the local level on the leadership candidates, as well as for delegates, and the latter are elected in proportion to the popular vote received by each leadership candidate. Similarly, when the NDP replaced Audrey McLaughlin in 1995, it wished to give the grassroots of the party a direct vote but still retain the drama of a convention. It sought to do so by providing for regional "primaries" in which all members could vote and which would determine the candidates who would appear on the ballot at the actual convention.

Most parties also have leadership review mechanisms in their constitutions, although these vary in detail. The NDP opens nominations for the position of leader at their national convention every two years, so that an unsatisfactory leader can be immediately replaced. However, in the absence of a concrete challenger, no vote is needed. Leadership review provisions were not added to the other parties' constitutions until after the Conservative civil war over John Diefenbaker's leadership between 1962 and 1967. The Conservatives put the question "Are you in favour of having a leadership convention?" only at the first convention following an election that the party loses. The Liberals added a leadership review clause in 1966 to the effect that at the first convention after each election (win or lose) delegates vote on whether they want a leadership convention to be called. The Reform party asks the question at every biennial national party assembly.

Party Policymaking

All political parties have difficulty designing their policymaking process. On the one hand, they want to give ordinary party members an opportunity to contribute to party policy, but at the same time, no party establishment wants to be saddled with unrealistic policy commitments. Thus, they all struggle to combine these two forces in the most appropriate way.

Liberal and Conservative national conventions or general meetings usually include a policy session and sometimes focus primarily on policy. But even if specific resolutions are debated and passed, party leaders or cabinets retain the right to determine official party policy. The Liberals' Red Book, used as the party platform in the 1993 election, drew substantially from party policy meetings over the previous two years without being bound by them. As part of its rebuilding process after 1993, the PC Party designed a new policymaking process combining greater membership input with expert advice. The party moved from "principles to policy to platform" with a major policy convention in August 1996 that determined the main lines of its 1997 election platform.

The NDP always claimed to be particularly distinctive in the realm of party policymaking. It has regular policy sessions every two years, which are the predominant item on the convention agenda. Constituency associations are invited to submit resolutions in advance, and resolutions passed by the convention are considered to be official and binding on the leader and the parliamentary party. The reduced post-1993 NDP was not so sure that its traditional policymaking system was adequate, however, and revamped it in 1995. Instead of passing random policy resolutions at whim, ridings would be expected to do more research in the first place, and such resolutions would then be vetted by the policy committee with its considerable resources before being transmitted to the party's federal council and on to the convention.

A certain tension exists in the Reform Party between its populist intentions and the dominance of Preston Manning. The party adopted a full-scale platform at its founding convention but also established an elaborate policymaking process in which resolutions can originate at the constituency level, from caucus, from party task forces, and from the executive council. At its national assembly, changes to party policy must be approved by a majority of votes cast as well as a majority of votes in a majority of provinces. In keeping with its populist approach, the executive council of the party can conduct an informal poll of the membership on an issue as well as hold a formal referendum.

General Structures and Operations

CONVENTIONS

All parties have constitutions that outline their objectives, structures, and procedures. In theory, at least, the ultimate power in each party is held by the convention that all parties now hold at regular two-year intervals. The convention agenda normally includes the election of the party executive, constitutional amendments, and policy discussions, but such conventions also serve important social and morale-building purposes. In the Liberal and Conservative parties each constituency association is entitled to an equal number of delegates, while in the NDP and Reform, representation is based on the size of the local membership. All parties include certain ex-officio delegates such as MPs, while in the NDP, affiliated labour unions also send delegates. The array of women's, youth, campus, Native, and ethnic groups is extremely complicated.

PARTY EXECUTIVE

Each party has a national executive of some kind, including such officers as a president, vice-presidents, and treasurer, and each establishes a number of executive committees. These officials usually perform their duties on a part-time basis, although it is helpful for the president to be close to Ottawa and readily available for meetings, campaign organization, and other functions. Liberals and Conservatives have sometimes elected a senator as party president since such a person has considerable free time and is on the public payroll, saving the party the cost of a presidential salary.

PARTY HEADQUARTERS

Three parties maintain a headquarters in Ottawa staffed by permanent party employees. This office is headed by the national director in the Liberal and Conservative cases, and the federal secretary in the NDP's. The size of the party staff varies considerably, depending on party finances and the imminence of an election. The PC and NDP offices were dramatically scaled down after the 1993 election, the latter party having to sell its building and move into smaller rented space. In 1995, the Liberals maintained a staff of about 20, some of whom worked in the Federal Liberal Agency, the fundraising branch of the office. The PCs, including the PC Fund, employed 14 people, with 3 additional organizers in the field, while the NDP was slashed to a complement of 6. Between elections, headquarters performs a variety of functions such as collecting money, ensuring local organizations are alive and well, arranging for speakers to local annual meetings, publishing newsletters, planning conventions, conducting surveys, and researching policy.

The Reform Party maintains a research and communications office in Ottawa that deals largely with parliamentary work, while the official national office of the party is in Calgary with a staff of about 20. This separation of the parliamentary and extra-parliamentary offices is consistent with its populist intentions and image, but creates certain difficulties in coordination and communication.

FEDERAL–PROVINCIAL PARTY LINKS

The federal nature of Canada and the existence of two levels of government at which political parties seek to influence policy and personnel raises the question of the relationship between national and provincial party organizations.[8] To oversimwhat the situation somewhat, the Conservative Party could be said to have a "confederal" character—that is, the federal and provincial PC parties are essentially independent. There is virtually no formal organizational or financial link between the two wings of the party, while there is no provincial Conservative Party at all in Quebec. Thus, federal and provincial party memberships are usually separate, and a complete set of federal riding associations and executives coexists with provincial party organizations at the grassroots level.

By contrast, the NDP could be called an "integrated" party because, with the exception of Quebec, one joins the NDP at the provincial level and automatically becomes a member of the national party. Only in areas of its strongest support does the party maintain full-fledged separate federal and provincial constituency associations, while provincial offices of the party serve the needs of both federal and provincial parties. The two levels of the party are integrated financially, such that the provincial parties must contribute 15 percent of their annual revenues to the federal party. In Quebec, however, federal and provincial wings of the party are quite separate. The 1995 Renewal Convention sought to liberate the federal party by severing many of the formal links with its provincial branches.

The Liberal Party is characterized by two different federal–provincial relationships. In Quebec, Ontario, Alberta, and British Columbia, the party is split into federal and provincial wings, each of which has separate finances, memberships, constituency associations, executives, conventions, and offices. In the other provinces and territories, the party is more "unitary." As in the case of the NDP, however, such an integrated relationship gives the party a provincial orientation. It is possible to join the federal party directly, but more common to join the provincial party and become an automatic member of the federal organization. The unitary relationship involves a complicated and troublesome financial connection.

Preston Manning wanted to concentrate all of Reform's attention at the national level, and persuaded his members to back his objection to provincial party branches. Nevertheless, a provincial party in British Columbia had previously adopted the "Reform Party" label and continued to operate with a similar platform, but without organic links to the federal party.

Party Ideology

Three different perspectives exist within the literature of Canadian political science with respect to party ideology. The first view is that there are no basic ideological differences between the Liberal and Conservative parties.[9] They are either both pure broker parties with no ideology, responding pragmatically and opportunistically to public opinion polls in the pursuit of power, or else they are equally committed to the capitalist system, but prepared to remedy its worst faults in order to maintain popular support.

The second interpretation of Canadian party ideology is that while no fundamental ideological differences exist between the Liberals and Conservatives, they have maintained certain consistent historic policy differences.[10] Failing that, they at least offer marginal policy differences at any point in time.

The third and most theoretical perspective is that genuine ideological differences do exist in Canada, and that such ideologies as liberalism, conservatism, and democratic socialism can be found to differentiate the three traditional parties to some extent.[11] The ideological continuum can be sketched in diagrammatic form as in Figure 9.1.

This perspective suggests that the overwhelming ideology in Canada is *liberalism*, but that traces of *socialism* and *conservatism* also exist and that each of the ideologies is represented by a corresponding party. Liberalism seeks to liberate the individual and maximize each individual's freedom and potential, something that

Figure 9.1   The Ideological Continuum in Canada

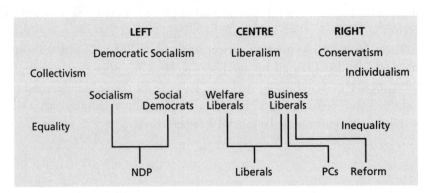

almost all Canadians would support. The differences that emerge essentially centre on the role of the state.

Democratic socialism seeks to liberate the individual from the inequalities and exploitation of the capitalist system; it believes in equality of condition, not merely equality of opportunity; and it prescribes a large element of state action or collectivism in order to achieve such liberation and equality.

In discussions of political ideology these views are generally referred to as being on the "left." In particular, democratic socialism emphasizes government planning, regulation, ownership of some of the major industries of the country, progressive taxation, and redistribution of income via social programs. Democratic socialists are sometimes subdivided between "socialists" and "social democrats," depending on the extent to which they wish the state to intervene and the extent of equality they wish to effect. The CCF/NDP take credit for introducing public hospital and medical insurance when they formed the government of Saskatchewan, pressing for other social programs, advocating a more progressive taxation system, creating a variety of Crown corporations in the provinces where they held power, and supporting the establishment of new government bodies in Ottawa.

Liberalism, too, has a dual personality and can be subdivided into welfare and business variants. Business liberals believe that the state inhibits individual self-fulfilment and that its role should therefore be minimized so that individualism can prevail. Welfare liberals, on the other hand, take the view that the state can be a positive agent in liberating individuals from the constraints of other forces including the private-enterprise economy. Welfare liberals therefore stand for a combination of individualism and collectivism and a combination of equality and inequality that they usually label "equality of opportunity." In terms of the diagram, then, the Liberal Party is composed of business and welfare liberals, leaving it in the centre of the Canadian ideological continuum. While Liberals obviously hold the private enterprise system in greater esteem than does the NDP, Liberal governments introduced old age pensions, family allowances, and many other social welfare programs over the years, although many observers see a rightward shift after 1993.

Conservatism also has two variants. On the one hand, conservatives seek to liberate the individual from the restrictions of the state. Reducing the role of the state to a minimum and allowing capitalistic market forces to determine the distribution of power and wealth is often labelled "individualism." If this results in inequalities or elitism, conservatives are generally unconcerned; inequalities are both natural and deserved—some people are more talented and work harder than others. These attitudes are labelled as being on the "right," and these conservatives can be called "business liberals" in terms of the diagram. The second wing of the Canadian Progressive Conservative Party is the progressive element, people who are sometimes called *red tories*. These Conservatives combine beliefs in privilege and collectivism, seeing society as an organic whole, emphasizing community values as well as individualism, and standing for order, tradition, and stability. They believe in hierarchy—that everyone should occupy his or her place—but they also have a paternalistic concern for the condition of all the people. This aspect of conservatism is not unique to Canada, being found quite commonly in Britain and the rest of Europe; it stands out only in contrast to a lack of such sentiment within American conservatism.

Thus, the ideology of the Canadian Conservative party is not as clear-cut as the diagram indicates and is as divided as in the other two parties. Furthermore, the red tory element overlaps to some extent with welfare liberalism and even social democracy. While the Mulroney government and Charest party pursued a fairly consistent business-liberal agenda—privatization, deregulation, deficit reduction, and cutting of social programs—their Conservative predecessors sometimes exhibited a strong red tory touch, such as in the creation of the RCMP, CBC, CNR, and the National Energy Board, the Bennett New Deal, and the Stanfield proposal for wage and price controls. An alternative diagram, Figure 9.2, clarifies the position of the red tory influence in the Conservative Party.

Figure 9.2   Canadian Party Ideology

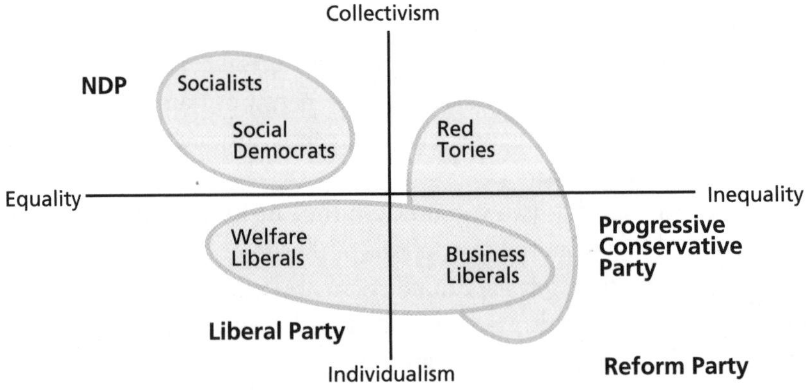

If liberalism in the United States lacks the collectivist touch, how does one explain its presence in all three of the traditional Canadian party ideologies? One explanation focuses on the United Empire Loyalists, who removed most of the collectivist tendencies from the U.S. political culture when they migrated to Canada, and left behind undiluted business liberalism in that country. The United Empire Loyalists rendered ideological diversity legitimate in Canada and because of their early predominance, made collectivism a respectable and important element in the Canadian political culture. In fact, they added to the collectivist approach already found in the feudal background of French Canada, that is, the ideas of hierarchy, order, stability, and community. Collectivism was reinforced by subsequent waves of British immigration whose intellectual baggage included both red tory and socialist views, along with the influence of the Social Gospel movement. Such collectivist tendencies were discussed in Chapter 6.

There is so much overlap in the ideological orientation of the Liberal and Conservative parties in particular that it is often difficult to detect the distinctions made above, and political scientists often ask the question: "Does party matter?" Indeed, from about 1945 to 1980 the Liberal and Conservative parties shared a basic ideological approach that emphasized economic growth based on foreign investment, expanding the welfare state, and engaging in a certain amount of macroeconomic government regulation called "Keynesian economics."[12] As time went on, however, this consensus broke down. The Liberals started to become concerned about the dangers of so much foreign investment, the Conservatives began to feel that the economy could not support any further social programs, and Keynesian economics did not seem to prevent the simultaneous occurrence of unemployment and inflation. Thus, especially after the Conservatives took office in 1984, policy and ideological differences between the two parties were much more obvious, with the Mulroney government pursuing a business-liberal or "neoconservative" agenda in which renewed reliance was placed on market forces and the extent of government intervention was reduced.

Indeed, over the past decade, the whole ideological spectrum has shifted to the right. For the first time in Canadian history, social programs are being cut back rather than expanded; Crown corporations are being privatized rather than created; regulations are being repealed rather than promulgated; public debts and deficits are being reduced rather than increased; and public servants are being fired rather than being hired. The phenomenon goes beyond one or two parties; it has affected governing parties of all ideological persuasions: PCs, Liberals, the Parti Québécois, and even the NDP in Saskatchewan.

The Reform Party is very much part of this shift to the right, and has exerted great influence at both federal and provincial levels even though it has not formed the government. The other leaders of this right-wing crusade, Ralph Klein in Alberta and Mike Harris in Ontario, are following the Reform program to a tee. Reform believes in reducing the role of government, reducing taxes, reducing regulation, privatizing Crown corporations, laying off public servants, reducing the debt and the deficit, and cutting back on social programs. This is all consistent with a belief in individualism, which is unconcerned about whether it leads to socioeconomic inequalities. (Ironically, the Reform Party is a strong believer in treating everyone, including provinces, equally in *law*.) The Reform Party also embraces social conservatism, such as in its opposition to multiculturalism and gay rights. The only respect in which Reform is not completely right-wing is in its populist streak: it is against elitism and professes to value the wisdom of ordinary people. But even this is an Americanism as opposed to the traditional Canadian belief in British parliamentary democracy. It should be added that the other main concern of the Reform Party is a territorial rather than ideological issue—that the West was getting shortchanged within Confederation. What distinguishes Reform from other Canadian parties is a complete absence of the collectivist value. In this respect, it is a clone of the U.S. Republican Party, with which it maintains contact.

The other new party, the Bloc Québécois, has one main objective: Quebec sovereignty. The question of nationalism generally overwhelms the left–right ideological approach in Quebec, but the BQ and PQ have usually been placed on the left side of the continuum, somewhere between the Liberals and the NDP.

To return to the shift to the right, the NDP is generally occupying the previous position of the Liberal Party. The Chrétien government is pursuing the same kind of leaner government that it previously condemned under Mulroney, and Finance Minister Paul Martin is forced to rationalize his dismemberment of the welfare state that was largely the creation of his father, a long-time Liberal cabinet minister. As a result, a crush is occurring on the right-wing side of the spectrum. The Conservative Party is finding it difficult to identify its own ideological space between the Chrétien Liberals and Manning's Reform Party. The PCs claim to be more understanding of Quebec than Reform, of course, and therefore to be a "national" party; but it is hard to carve out a niche just slightly to the left of Reform, especially when so many provincial Conservatives are voting for that other federal party.

NOTES

1. H.G. Thorburn, "Interpretations of the Canadian Party System," in H.G. Thorburn, ed., *Party Politics in Canada*, 6th ed. (Scarborough: Prentice-Hall Canada, 1991).
2. Janine Brodie and Jane Jenson, *Crisis, Challenge and Change: Party and Class in Canada Revisited* (Ottawa: Carleton University Press, 1988); Charles Taylor, *The Pattern of Politics* (Toronto: McClelland and Stewart, 1970); Gad Horowitz, "Toward the Democratic Class Struggle," in Trevor Lloyd and Jack McLeod, eds., *Agenda 1970* (Toronto: University of Toronto Press, 1968).
3. Jon Pammett, "Class Voting and Class Consciousness in Canada," *Canadian Review of Sociology and Anthropology* 24, no.2 (1987): 269–90; Keith Archer, "The Failure of the New Democratic Party: Unions, Unionists, and Politics in Canada," *Canadian Journal of Political Science* (June 1985): 353–66.
4. Horowitz, "Towards the Democratic Class Struggle," 254.
5. Thorburn, "Interpretations of the Canadian Party System"; Reginald Whitaker, *The Government Party: Organizing and Financing the Liberal Party of Canada 1930–58* (Toronto: University of Toronto Press, 1977); George Perlin, *The Tory Syndrome: Leadership Politics in the Progressive Conservative Party* (Montreal: McGill–Queen's University Press, 1980).
6. John Meisel, "Decline of Party in Canada," in H.G. Thorburn, ed., *Party Politics in Canada*, 5th ed.; John Meisel, "The Dysfunctions of Canadian Parties: An Exploratory Mapping," in Thorburn, 6th ed.
7. John C. Courtney, *Do Conventions Matter? Choosing National Party Leaders in Canada* (Montreal: McGill–Queen's University Press, 1995); Maureen Mancuso et al., eds., *Leaders and Leadership in Canada* (Toronto: Oxford University Press, 1994).
8. Rand Dyck, "Relations Between Federal and Provincial Parties," in A.B. Tanguay and A.G. Gagnon, eds., *Canadian Parties in Transition*, 2nd ed. (Scarborough: Nelson Canada, 1996).
9. Conrad Winn and John McMenemy, *Political Parties in Canada* (Toronto: McGraw-Hill Ryerson, 1976), 4–5.
10. R.M. Dawson, *The Government of Canada*, 4th ed. (Toronto: University of Toronto Press, 1963), 466–72; James R. Mallory, *The Structure of Canadian Government* (Toronto: Macmillan, 1971), 197.
11. Louis Hartz, *The Founding of New Societies* (New York: Harcourt, Brace and World, 1964); Gad Horowitz, "Conservatism, Liberalism and Socialism in Canada: An Interpretation," *Canadian Journal of Economics and Political Science* (May 1966): 143–71; Colin Campbell and William Christian, *Parties, Leaders, and Ideologies in Canada* (Toronto: McGraw-Hill Ryerson, 1996).
12. Duncan Cameron, "Political Discourse in the Eighties," in Tanguay and Gagnon, *Canadian Parties in Transition*.

FURTHER READING

Brodie, Janine, and Jane Jenson. *Crisis, Challenge and Change: Party and Class in Canada Revisited*. Ottawa: Carleton University Press, 1988.
Campbell, Colin, and William Christian. *Parties, Leaders, and Ideologies in Canada*. Toronto: McGraw-Hill Ryerson, 1996.

Flanagan, Tom. *Waiting for the Wave: The Reform Party and Preston Manning.* Toronto: Stoddart, 1995.

Gagnon, Alain, and Brian Tanguay, eds. *Canadian Parties in Transition*, 2nd ed. Scarborough: Nelson Canada, 1995.

Sharpe, Sydney, and Donald Braid. *Storming Babylon: Preston Manning and the Rise of the Reform Party.* Toronto: Key Porter Books, 1992.

Thorburn, H.G. *Party Politics in Canada.* Scarborough: Prentice-Hall Canada, 7 editions, incl. 1994.

Wearing, Joseph. *Strained Relations: Canadian Parties and Voters.* Toronto: McClelland and Stewart, 1988.

Whitehorn, Alan. *Canadian Socialism: Essays on the CCF and the NDP.* Toronto: Oxford University Press, 1992.

Chapter 10

Pressure Groups and Lobbying

Pressure groups or interest groups develop in almost every political system when individuals with common concerns band together in order to strengthen their cause. This chapter will proceed to identify some of the leading Canadian pressure groups, outline their targets and methods, assess their resources, and give an account of the activity of new lobbying firms.

A *pressure group* or *interest group* (terms used interchangeably here) can be defined as any group that seeks to influence government policy without contesting elections, that is, without putting forward its own candidates. Alternatively, they have been defined as "organizations whose members act together to influence public policy in order to promote their common interest."[1] The term *lobbying* is generally used to refer to any organized attempt to influence the authorities, an activity that is most commonly undertaken by pressure groups but could of course be done by individuals, companies, or other political actors. Increasingly, however, pressure groups have been joined by professional lobbying firms in this activity.

Pressure groups are primarily involved in the function of interest articulation; they normally have a narrow focus and are organized around a single interest that they try to impress upon those in authority. As society becomes more complex, Canadians increasingly demonstrate a preference to form or join such specialized, functional groups in order to transmit their demands to government, rather than rely exclusively on the territorial representation of parties and elections. Thus, in the promotion of interests, pressure groups provide a supplementary kind of functional representation, especially between elections.[2]

The Array of Canadian Interest Groups

The number of interest groups operating in Canada is in the thousands. Only some of the largest and most influential are listed in Table 10.1.

TABLE 10.1 LEADING NATIONAL CANADIAN PRESSURE GROUPS

Business	Canadian Manufacturers' Association
	Canadian Chamber of Commerce
	Business Council on National Issues
	Canadian Federation of Independent Business
	Canadian Bankers' Association
	Canadian Association of Broadcasters
	Pharmaceutical Manufacturers Association of Canada
Agriculture	Canadian Federation of Agriculture
	National Farmers Union
Labour	Canadian Labour Congress
Professions	Canadian Bar Association
	Canadian Medical Association
	Canadian Federation of Students
Ethnic	Fédération des francophones hors Québec
	Assembly of First Nations
	Canadian Ethnocultural Council
	National Congress of Italian Canadians
Religious	Canadian Council of Churches
	Canadian Conference of Catholic Bishops
	Canadian Jewish Congress
Causes	John Howard Society
	Canadian Civil Liberties Association
	National Action Committee on the Status of Women
	Pollution Probe
	Mothers Against Drunk Driving
	Non-Smokers' Rights Association

Business Groups[3]

In the case of business, nothing prevents individual companies from lobbying on their own behalf for grants, subsidies, tariff protection, loan guarantees, tax write-offs, government contracts, or policy changes, and many firms do so on a regular basis. In addition, the firms within almost every industry have organized a common pressure group to promote the interests of the industry as a whole. William

Coleman calculates that over 600 business groups are active in Canadian politics.[4] Superimposed upon these industrial groupings are such "peak" organizations as the Canadian Manufacturers' Association, the Canadian Chamber of Commerce, the Business Council on National Issues, and the Canadian Federation of Independent Business. On the agricultural side of business, Coleman found 95 active associations in 1980. The Canadian Federation of Agriculture tends to represent the more affluent farmers, while the National Farmers Union speaks for the others.

Nonbusiness Groups

The Canadian Labour Congress functions as a common voice for organized labour, but only about 34 percent of paid workers in Canada belong to unions, and of those, only 63 percent belong to unions affiliated with the CLC. Another 10 percent either belong to the breakaway Canadian Federation of Labour or the Quebec-based Conseil des syndicats nationaux, while most of the rest have not joined any central labour organization. The CLC maintains a link to the New Democratic Party, as do many of its individual unions, a unique relationship among Canadian pressure groups.

Many of the ethnic groups in Canada have their own organized associations, such as the National Congress of Italian Canadians. Most of these have been brought together, with government support, in the peak organization, the Canadian Ethnocultural Council. The largest of several Aboriginal groups is the Assembly of First Nations. The English and French, on the other hand, are only organized where they are minorities—the anglophone Alliance-Quebec and the Fédération des francophones hors Québec, incorporating provincial units such as the Association canadienne-française de l'Ontario (ACFO). Religious denominations in Canada also function as pressure groups from time to time, with the Canadian Conference of Catholic Bishops, the United Church of Canada, and the Canadian Jewish Congress probably being most influential. In recent years the Roman Catholic Church has joined the umbrella Christian group, the Canadian Council of Churches. Most professions have organizations that speak for their members on relevant issues, the Canadian Medical Association and Canadian Bar Association being two of the oldest and most important.

Other Categorizations of Pressure Groups

However much any of the above-mentioned groups claim to be pursuing the public interest, they can be generally categorized as "self-interested" groups because their principal concern is to improve their own economic position. The true "public-interest" group exists to promote causes that it sees as beneficial to society as a whole and that do not directly benefit its own members, such as the John Howard Society (improving prison conditions and the lot of ex-inmates), the Canadian Council on Social Development (promoting better social policy), the Canadian Civil Liberties Association (protecting civil liberties from government infringement), and a variety of environmental groups.

With the exception of some of the public interest and ethnic groups, those named above and many others are called *institutionalized* groups because they are permanent, well-established, formal organizations. Almost all maintain a head office in Ottawa with a full-time staff, a sizable budget, and a reasonably stable membership. Most have developed continuous links with the authorities, and represent their members' interests on a daily basis, year after year.

In contrast, some groups spring up spontaneously around a specific issue, and once the issue is resolved, they fade away. Such *issue-oriented* groups lack the institutionalized groups' permanence, office, staff, budget, membership, and access to the authorities. Instead, they more likely resort to attracting public attention to their cause through media coverage of such actions as demonstrations. Examples of issue-oriented groups include the Stop Spadina group that opposed extension of the Spadina Expressway in Toronto in the early 1970s and "Bread Not Circuses," which objected to Toronto's bid to host the 1996 Olympic Games. In the 1980s, when Finance Minister Michael Wilson attempted to de-index the old age pension, an ad hoc group of seniors organized across the country and forced him to back down. If their issue is not resolved, or if they anticipate further challenges, such groups may become a more permanent fixture.[5]

Political scientists often find it useful to distinguish between pressure groups and social movements. Many of the issue-oriented groups referred to are, in fact, part of larger unstructured social movements, of which the environmental, women's, and peace movements have been most prominent. Other examples include the Aboriginal, gay, and animal rights movements. Social movements begin at the margins of the political system, possessing an alternative vision of "the good life," and usually consist of coalitions of small local groups that have not yet hardened into a cohesive national group.[6] The National Action Committee on the Status of Women is a coalition of some 580 member groups, while the Canadian Environmental Network contains nearly 2000 groups. Such movements run into much bureaucratic and political party resistance, and often do not achieve immediate success. In the long run, however, they widen the scope of public discourse, and parties and other mainstream political institutions eventually respond. Take recent improvements in legislation with respect to women and the environment, for example, and changes in public attitudes toward war, Aboriginals, homosexuals, and the treatment of animals.

Other categorizations are also sometimes useful in discussing pressure groups. Most groups are "autonomous" in the sense that they develop without government initiative, although they may later seek government financial support. But politicians or bureaucrats are sometimes involved in the creation of interest groups, whether for personal gain or in the hope of promoting a certain public policy objective. In the late 1960s, for example, the federal government began to fund anti-poverty, women's, minority official language, Aboriginal, and other ethnic groups to ensure that these interests would be involved in the marketplace of ideas.[7] The Mulroney government cut back on grants to Native, women's, poor, and disabled people's groups, however, both for fiscal and ideological reasons, something the Trudeau government had also done on occasion when a particular group became too critical of the hand that fed it. Canada has been something of a world leader in government support of critical interest groups, but such grant reductions reveal the dangers involved in a group's becoming too critical and too dependent.

Pressure Group Structures

As far as the structure of pressure groups is concerned, issue-oriented groups can burst forth anywhere an issue arises—at the federal, provincial, or municipal level. Institutionalized groups, on the other hand, tend to be organized wherever government decisions regularly affect them. The federal nature of the country means that authoritative decisions are made at two (or even three) levels of government, and most institutionalized groups parallel the federal structure of government. They find it advantageous to be organized at both levels because the division of powers between the federal and provincial governments is so blurred. The Canadian Medical Association is composed of 10 autonomous provincial divisions (such as the Ontario Medical Association), the Canadian Chamber of

Commerce has strong provincial branches (such as the Alberta Chamber of Commerce), and so does the Canadian Labour Congress (the Nova Scotia Federation of Labour). These latter two groups in particular also maintain municipal organizations—some 500 community chambers of commerce or boards of trade and 123 local labour councils across the country.

Many pressure groups, including teachers, nurses, and students, are actually more strongly organized at the provincial level than in Ottawa. This is because they are more affected by decisions of provincial governments than by federal ones. Some, such as the medical and legal professions, are even delegated powers by provincial governments to regulate themselves.

Targets and Methods of Pressure Group Activity

Besides being affected by the federal system, Canadian interest groups are very much influenced in their operations by the fact that they exist in a parliamentary system. This system, despite its name, places most of the decision-making power in the hands of the bureaucracy and the cabinet. Pressure groups that understand this basic truth direct most of their attention to these two branches of government.

In this connection Paul Pross's conception of *policy communities* should be mentioned.[8] This concept is based on the premise that each field of public policy is discrete and specialized, with its own constellation of participants. Each policy community consists of a grouping of government agencies, pressure groups, corporations, institutions, media people, and individuals who have an interest in that particular policy field and attempt to influence it. These actors initially attempt to establish their legitimacy with the lead government agency, and if they achieve such recognition and status, they may be made part of the agency's information flow. Pross cites the examples of the Canadian Bankers' Association and the Canadian Tax Foundation as groups that have achieved such legitimacy, as opposed to the National Farmers Union, which has not. Once such groups are given the privilege of consultation and access to strategic information, they normally behave quite cooperatively, and the whole policy community becomes cohesive and mutually supportive. All the actors involved, including the lead agency, prefer to keep the issues that concern them within the "community" and have a strong incentive to resolve any problems there rather than open the issues up to cabinet discussion or, even worse, public debate and confrontation.

The Bureaucracy

As discussed in Chapter 14, the bureaucracy advises the cabinet on almost all of its decisions. It drafts legislation and regulations according to the cabinet's general instructions; it proposes budgets and spends government money; and it implements policies and programs once they have been given cabinet and/or legislative approval. All of these areas hold considerable scope for bureaucratic discretion. It is for this reason that institutionalized groups in particular direct their messages at the bureaucratic target more than at any other institution of government. Many pressure group demands involve technical matters that only the bureaucracy understands and may be able to satisfy without reference to the politicians.

Such groups try to cultivate close relationships with senior public servants, hoping to be able to contact these officials on an informal, direct, day-to-day basis via telephone calls, faxes, meetings, letters, and business lunches. Although bureaucrats may be suspicious of their motives and consider that meeting pressure groups is a waste of precious time, the relationship between a pressure group and its most relevant government department may ultimately become a reciprocal one, as desirable for the public service as it is for the group.

Thus, what is called a *clientele relationship* often develops between such groups as the Canadian Federation of Agriculture and the Department of Agriculture, the Canadian Medical Association and the Department of Health, the petroleum and mining associations and the Department of Natural Resources, and business organizations and the Department of Finance. The relations between such an agency or department and its allied pressure groups may become so close that it is difficult to tell them apart. The agency or department almost becomes an extension of the pressure group, making policy in the interest of the group and promoting the interest they both represent within the higher councils of government. The minister, deputy minister, and Department of Finance speak for the business community, while the minister, deputy minister, and Department of Agriculture speak for the farming community, and so on.

In return for the various ways in which the bureaucracy responds to group demands, the group may pass on information that the department needs or desires in order to do its work. As issues become too complex for politicians—

ministers or MPs—to understand, and larger numbers of issues, constituents, and obligations eat up their time, legislation is increasingly drafted in skeletal form with the specifics delegated to the bureaucracy to be added later in the form of regulations or "delegated legislation." Bureaucrats regularly consult pressure groups as they draft legislation, design programs, and draw up regulations. The group may also be a valuable ally in persuading other bureaucratic agencies or ministers to do what the department wants.

Although pressure groups are usually seen in terms of their "input" function of making demands, they also perform various "output" functions. A group may be better equipped to inform its specialized membership about new laws, regulations, or programs than a department that is restricted to the media or other regular channels of communication. In addition, the cooperation of the group might be indispensable to the successful execution of a program. In some cases, as noted, certain groups are even delegated powers of self-regulation.

When public servants themselves are members of interest groups, it naturally assists the group in maximizing its influence. For example, bureaucrats in welfare departments often belong to the Canadian Council on Social Development, medical bureaucrats to the Canadian Medical Association, and legal bureaucrats to the Canadian Bar Association. In fact, considerable movement of personnel takes place between interest groups and the higher levels of the public service; officials often move from pressure group jobs to the bureaucracy or vice versa.

The Cabinet

The cabinet is the second-most frequently targeted branch of government because it makes the major governmental decisions in a parliamentary system. Since many decisions are now made by individual ministers or cabinet committees, groups often find it productive to submit single-issue representations to individual ministers, who spend much of their time in meetings with such groups. If a minister stays in one position long enough, a pressure group may be able to construct a more personal, informal relationship, as did the Canadian Federation of Agriculture with Jimmy Gardiner, who served as minister of Agriculture from 1935 to 1957. The social scene in Ottawa should also be mentioned, for parties and receptions provide excellent opportunities for cabinet ministers, deputy ministers, and established pressure-group representatives (especially corporate) to meet and mingle.

The Trudeau government established the precedent of encouraging various groups to meet with the minister of Finance prior to the preparation of the annual budget, a practice that was even more widespread under Mulroney's first Finance minister, Michael Wilson. But in 1990 Wilson evoked considerable protest when he told business, labour, and social groups that he was too busy to meet with them before the budget, inviting them to submit written advice instead.

The concept of *elite accommodation*[9] is particularly relevant to this process. It claims that most public decisions in Canada emerge from the interaction of three agents: the cabinet, the senior public service, and pressure groups, especially in the business field. The individuals who occupy the top positions in these sectors are elites both in the sense of being small numbers of people with disproportionate amounts of power (compared to ordinary citizens) and in the sense of their exclusive socioeconomic backgrounds, coming from families of higher social class, higher incomes, and higher educations. Robert Presthus thus postulates that the common backgrounds and values of political, bureaucratic, and corporate leaders help to facilitate agreement among them. Commanding the heights of these sectors of society, they easily accommodate each other in the working out of public policies. Lobbyists from professional lobbying firms also fit perfectly into this arrangement.

Parliament

The third main branch of the government is the legislature or Parliament, but as discussed in Chapter 15, it largely legitimizes decisions previously taken by the executive. That being the case, the House of Commons is not as often the target of interest group activity, but it does remain the object of considerable attention. One of the main reasons that a bill is usually sent to a legislative committee during its passage is to allow interest groups to make representations on it. The Standing Committee on Finance, with its pre-budget hearings, is now integrated into the expenditure management system, and provides an excellent opportunity for pressure groups to make their case.

Especially in a majority government situation, however, ministers have traditionally been reluctant to accept amendments proposed at the legislative stage, so that groups are better advised to make their case at the executive level before the bill is made public. It has even been said that the sight of a pressure group at the legislative level in Canada is a sign that the group already failed at the level of the bureaucracy and the cabinet. Nevertheless, groups converge on MPs in their offices or inundate them with letters, telegrams, or postcards. For example, while not ignoring the cabinet and bureaucracy, the Canadian Chamber of Commerce is particularly adept at applying pressure on MPs through its base in almost every constituency across the country. Pressure groups also meet with individual party caucuses, and certain MPs may already belong to a group, in which case they can be expected to speak on its behalf.

The upper chamber of Parliament, the Senate, is probably even more involved in the lobbying process. Because so many senators have close corporate connections and function regularly as lobbyists for big business, the Senate has been called "a lobby from within."[10] During passage in that chamber, much legislation is considered by the Senate Committee on Banking, Trade and Commerce, most of whose members hold directorships in Canadian banks and other large corporations. Such holdings have not deterred Committee members from active consideration of questions relating to financial institutions in what many observers see as a classic case of conflict of interest.

Other Targets

Interest groups have many targets beyond these three main branches of government. If they can find a legal or constitutional angle to their demand, for example, such groups may take cases to the courts. Corporations have sometimes challenged federal or provincial legislation in the courts as a violation of the division of powers; francophone groups have used the courts to uphold constitutionally guaranteed minority language rights; and Aboriginal groups are increasingly using the courts to uphold or broaden the meaning of treaty and Aboriginal rights. The Charter of Rights and Freedoms provides added potential for targeting the courts by actually inviting individuals and groups to challenge federal or provincial legislation that they consider to be discriminatory.

As mentioned, only the Canadian Labour Congress has seen fit to attach itself formally to a political party. This strategy may have reduced the group's impact on Liberal and Conservative governments as it awaited an NDP victory, however; other groups remain scrupulously nonpartisan so that they can exert equal influence on whichever party is in power. Another target of pressure group activity is the royal commission. These elaborate investigations of public problems normally invite pressure groups and experts to submit briefs in public hearings, supplementing whatever original research the commission itself undertakes.

Besides their direct representations to government, pressure groups and corporations increasingly try to influence public opinion in what is called "advocacy advertising" in the hope that the authorities will respond to a clear message from the public.[11] In 1991, for example, both the Pharmaceutical Manufacturers Association and the rival Canadian Drug Manufacturers' Association took out media advertisements to make their case on the question of patent protection for new drugs.

Many pressure groups increase their public profile once an election has been called. This phenomenon, discussed in Chapter 8, is usually called "third-party" advertising. Pressure groups often seek the response of parties and candidates to questions of concern to the group and then indicate their support or opposition in media advertising. The National Citizens' Coalition regularly does so, contrary to the spirit of expenditure ceilings in the Canada Elections Act, while the Canadian Alliance for Jobs and Trade Prospects and its anti–free trade counterpart, the Pro-Canada Network, were particularly visible in 1988. National or local pressure groups sometimes target particular politicians or ministers for defeat.

If all else fails, a group may resort to demonstrations, protest marches, tractor parades, sit-ins, and road and bridge blockades. Some of these are peaceful and legal, such as the orderly demonstrations that are an almost daily occurrence on Parliament Hill and frequently greet prime ministers on their travels. But the frustration of Aboriginal, environmentalist, and other radical or issue-oriented groups increasingly takes the form of civil disobedience. The armed stand-off at Oka, Quebec, in 1990 was one of the rare occasions in which a group resorted to violence.

Group Resources and Determinants of Success

Why are groups sometimes successful and sometimes not? A variety of factors is involved in accounting for such success and failure, including the following:

- members
- cohesion
- money
- information
- leadership and prestige

- tenor of message
- financial position of government
- absence of opposition

The size of the group is probably most important, considering that numbers represent votes. The authorities feel comfortable ignoring very small groups, for example, because the electoral consequences would be minimal. In this respect, the Canadian Labour Congress should be regularly successful in having the authorities respond to its demands because, with 2.5 million members, it is the largest pressure group in Canada.

The fact that the CLC is not usually very influential points to the importance of the cohesiveness of the organization. First of all, as mentioned, the labour movement as a whole is not very cohesive. But even among those who are members of the CLC, unity, commitment, and militancy are notoriously lacking. In addition to the weak sense of class-consciousness in Canada, there is a lack of union-consciousness, an unwillingness of one union to support another. Even on those occasions when the CLC "declared war" on the government, the bulk of its members continued to vote for the old-line parties instead of the NDP. Liberal and Conservative governments apparently feel that the CLC is so incapable of mobilizing its members behind the demands issued by its leadership that it can often be ignored. In contrast, the Royal Canadian Legion and the Canadian Chamber of Commerce are able to mobilize their members to inundate the authorities with demands for concerted action.

As in other aspects of politics, money is an important resource. In the case of pressure groups, money can buy staff, offices, organization, expertise, publicity, and other useful weapons with which to get the group's message across. The Canadian Medical Association has a staff of about 100 and an annual budget of about $27 million, for example; the Canadian Bar Association, a staff of 44 and a budget of about $9 million; and the Canadian Manufacturers' Association, a staff of 85 and a budget of about $5 million. The Business Council on National Issues and the Canadian Chamber of Commerce are also very well endowed financially, giving them the capacity both to generate information to strengthen their case and to transmit it to relevant targets. Except for those representing big business or highly paid professions, however, most groups have financial problems. The Canadian Federation of Agriculture is typical of many groups in trying to scrape by on less than $1 million annually.

Information is a fourth crucial resource in pressure group politics. Especially at the bureaucratic level, where much of this politics takes place, any vital information that is lacking as the public service drafts technical laws and regulations will be eagerly accepted. Even at the political level, the group may be able to present data and alternative analyses of policy that will lead ministers to rethink their proposals. Closely associated with information is the professional expertise of the pressure group's staff, and in this connection, the large business groups are able to produce mounds of well-researched and glossy documents. The Canadian Bar Association makes frequent representations to parliamentary committees, royal commissions, and government departments, and because of its expertise both in the substance of many issues and in the drafting of legislation, it is often asked for advice. The CBA and Canadian Chamber of Commerce are among many groups that monitor federal political issues and the passage of legislation and keep their members informed via monthly newsletters.

The quality of group leadership and the prestige of the group are other important factors. In recent years, for example, even the Canadian Labour Congress has quite deliberately sought to choose "smooth," articulate, attractive leaders to make its case. When dealing with a Liberal or Conservative government, however, organized labour probably does not rival doctors, lawyers, or businesspeople as far as prestige is concerned.

The tenor of the group's message is also important. If a basic correspondence exists between the demands of the group and the government's stated objectives or the prevailing values of society in general, the pressure group will have greater success than if there is a vast gap in ideological perspective. It is not surprising, for example, that the CLC would be virtually ignored by the business-oriented Mulroney government. Similarly, the minister responsible for the Status of Women in that cabinet repeatedly refused to meet the National Action Committee on the Status of Women because of the group's intense criticism. The government even cut NAC's annual grant and gave the first federal grant to its rival, REAL Women (Realistic, Equal, Active for Life). Related to ideology is the sharing of a professional orientation between group leaders and authorities, especially in the bureaucracy. Many examples could be given of the success of a group because its officials shared the professional norms of the relevant public servants in their reciprocal relationship.

Since many pressure group demands relate to the spending of public money, the financial position of the government will often influence a group's success. In the prosperous and free-spending 1960s and 1970s, for example, requests for funds were more likely to be fulfilled than in the 1980s and 1990s, an era of government restraint.

Finally, a group will be more influential if it has no organized opposition. One of the reasons for the success of the Canadian Medical Association over the years, for example, was that it had medical politics almost all to itself.[12] Contrast that situation with the evenly divided forces on either side of the abortion debate.

Lobbying in Canada

The tendency of the rich and powerful, including big business, to benefit from pressure group politics and elite accommodation can only be enhanced by recent developments in the practice of lobbying in Canada. If lobbying is the activity of trying to influence the authorities, it is, of course, a perfectly legitimate activity for anyone to undertake in a democracy. Traditionally, individuals, companies, unions, and pressure groups of all kinds have done their own lobbying, but in recent years Canada has seen the mushrooming of professional lobbying—consultant or government relations firms that lobby on behalf of an individual, company, or pressure group in return for a fee.

Those engaged in the new lobbying industry justify their existence largely in terms of the increasing size and complexity of government. The federal government grew enormously in the 1960s and 1970s and the policymaking process was restructured such that corporations and interest groups could no longer find their way around Ottawa.

The early 1980s constituted a period in which new means of influence were being sought, and an expansion of such firms appeared to take place about the time the Mulroney government was elected in 1984. Many of the leading figures in the early establishment of professional lobby firms were old cronies of the prime minister.

Given that the bureaucracy can satisfy many of the corporations' needs, ex-bureaucrats have also joined or formed lobbying firms in order to capitalize on their inside knowledge and connections. Federal conflict-of-interest guidelines preclude senior government employees from dealing with their former departments for one year after their departure from public employment, but these rules are sometimes broken, and in any case, many critics doubt that it is sufficient time in which to be away.

The largest consultant lobbying firms in 1997 are presented in Table 10.2; a sample of the clients of some of the principal lobbying firms in 1995 is given in Table 10.3.

TABLE 10.2 LARGEST CONSULTANT LOBBYING FIRMS, 1997

	Registrations
Capital Hill Group	87
Government Policy Consultants	68
SAMCI (S.A. Murray)	55
Hill & Knowlton	49
Global Public Affairs Inc.	47
Earnscliffe Strategy Group	31

Source: John A. Chenier, ed., The Federal Lobbyists 1997 (Ottawa: ARC Publications, 1997). Used with permission.

TABLE 10.3 A SAMPLE OF CLIENTS OF PRINCIPAL LOBBYING FIRMS

Capital Hill Group	SAMCI	Hill & Knowlton
Canadian Tire	CTV Television	Amex Canada Ltd.
Cineplex Odeon	Eli Lilly Canada	British Aerospace
Coopers & Lybrand	Hudson's Bay Co.	CP Rail System
Spar Aerospace	Labatt Breweries	INCO Ltd.
Stentor	Macmillan Bloedel	Pepsi-Cola Ltd.
Unitel	Noranda Inc.	Shell Canada Ltd.

Source: Chenier, The Federal Lobbyists 1995. Used with permission.

After the emergence of such professional lobbying firms, a consensus developed among politicians that legislation, registration, and regulation were necessary. The registration idea was part of the Mulroney government's ethics package unveiled after its early troubled record of cabinet resignations due to conflicts of interest and numerous legal charges against Tory backbenchers.[13]

According to the 1989 Lobbyists Registration Act, a lobbyist is an individual

> who, for payment, on behalf of any person or organization … undertakes to arrange a meeting with a public office holder or to communicate with a public office holder in an attempt to influence
>
> (a) the development of a legislative proposal …
>
> (b) the introduction, passage, defeat or amendment of any bill or resolution …

(c) the making or amending of any regulation ...

(d) the development or amendment of any policy or program ...

(e) the awarding of any monetary grant or contribution or other financial benefit ... or

(f) the awarding of any contract.

The law divided lobbyists into two categories: those who work for any client for a fee are classified as "Tier I" lobbyists, while "Tier II" lobbyists include those who engage in traditional pressure group or corporate lobbying—that is, in-house employees of an organization whose duties involve communicating with public officeholders on behalf of that organization. Both types of lobbyists had to register their activities in the Registry of Lobbyists.

The legislation acknowledged that lobbying public officeholders is a legitimate activity, but required lobbyists to register because it is desirable that officials and the public know who is attempting to influence government and because paid lobbyists should not impede free and open access to government. With certain exceptions, lobbyists had to file a return including the name and address of the lobbyist and the lobbying firm, the name and address of the client, and the subject matter of the solicitation.

Many critics felt that the 1989 legislation was very weak and contrasted it with the U.S. law on this subject adopted in 1946.[14] Some lobbyists did not register, and even when they did, the disclosure provisions in the Canadian law were minimal. The law did not even require revelation of the specific object of the representations. Furthermore, the act was almost totally lacking in an effective enforcement mechanism.

The whole procedure provided a lucrative living to those who claimed to be intimates of ministers or ministries, and favoured those who could afford to hire such professional lobbyists. In what John Sawatski calls "one of the most odious lobby campaigns in the history of Canada," the fight of the Pharmaceutical Manufacturers Association to extend drug patent protection, "Gerry Doucet handled the PMAC file in GCI's [Government Consultants International's] office; his brother Fred handled the issue in the Prime Minister's Office."[15]

A Parliamentary committee reviewed the Lobbyists Registration Act in 1993 and made many recommendations to strengthen the act. These recommendations were not implemented before the PCs were defeated, but the Liberal Party promised in the 1993 Red Book to take such action. Not surprisingly, the lobbyists lobbied ferociously against greater transparency in their operations, and the amendments that were finally adopted in 1995 were a pale imitation of what had been recommended by the committee and promised during the election campaign. Rather than doing away with the distinction between Tier I and Tier II lobbyists, the new act recognized three categories: Tier I (consultant lobbyists who lobby for clients) and two types of Tier II lobbyists, in-house lobbyists (corporate), and in-house lobbyists (organization)—that is, employees of corporations or interest group organizations for whom lobbying was a significant part of their duties. Otherwise, the new legislation required coalitions and grassroots lobbying to be registered, and was slightly more rigorous in what else must be reported. Rather than just the general object of lobbying, the specific legislative proposal, bill, resolution, regulation, policy, program, or contract in question had to be identified, along with the name of each department or other governmental institution lobbied. Contingency fees were not outlawed, but any contingency fees must be disclosed, as must the source and amount of any government funding of the client. As for enforcement, the registrar may audit information contained in any return or other document submitted and issue interpretation bulletins and advisory opinions. The six-month limitation of proceedings on contraventions was extended to two years. The ethics counsellor previously appointed by the Liberal government to administer the Conflict of Interest Code for ministers, parliamentary secretaries, and senior government officials was required to work with interested parties to develop a code of conduct for lobbyists. Lobbyists had a legal obligation to comply with the code. The ethics counsellor had to investigate and publicly report on breaches of the code, and could report publicly the fees, disbursements, and expenses paid to a lobbyist relating to any lobbying activity.

While this revised law was an improvement on the original, it remained highly defective. "By leaving vague the definitions of lobbying, and by excluding any lobbying associated with a consultative exercise, the government ... left much room for those sincerely wishing to avoid disclosing their activities or their aims to do so."[16] In other words, much lobbying is simply not recorded. The law did not require lobbyists to disclose positions currently or recently held in national political parties, ministers' offices, or the federal public service; it did not actually prohibit the use of contingency fees; and it did not require disclosure of the global cost of each lobbying campaign. At the same time, the industry was invaded by associates of the Liberal Party, such as defeated cabinet minister Douglas Young.

Since the reports of the Lobbyists Registration Branch are not particularly revealing, it is fortunate that a private company, Advocacy Research Centre (ARC), fills the gap with a bi-weekly edition of the *Lobby Monitor*. This publication reveals the major lobbying efforts currently in progress, the techniques being used, and the people involved. The same company publishes a monthly Policy Advocate's Report and an annual edition of *The Federal Lobbyists*, giving a complete listing of lobbyist registrations for the year. Armed with these sources, the public can obtain a better understanding of the lobbying process, since the *Lobby Monitor* in particular is an investigative effort that reveals much more than is required under the law.

....

NOTES

1. Paul Pross, *Group Politics and Public Policy* (Toronto: Oxford University Press, 1986).
2. Ibid., esp. ch. 11.
3. William D. Coleman, *Business and Politics: A Study of Collective Action* (Montreal: McGill–Queen's University Press, 1988); Stephen Brooks and Andrew Stritch, *Business and Government in Canada* (Scarborough: Prentice-Hall Canada, 1991), ch. 7; W.T. Stanbury, *Business–Government Relations in Canada* (Toronto: Methuen, 1986), esp. ch. 7.
4. William D. Coleman, "One Step Ahead: Business in the Policy Process in Canada," in Mark Charlton and Paul Barker, eds., *Crosscurrents: Contemporary Political Issues*, 2nd ed. (Scarborough: Nelson Canada, 1994).
5. Paul Pross, *Group Politics and Public Policy*, ch. 5.
6. Susan Phillips, "Competing, Connecting, and Complementing: Parties, Interest Groups, and New Social Movements," in A. Brian Tanguay and Alain-G. Gagnon, eds., *Canadian Parties in Transition*, 2nd ed. (Scarborough: Nelson Canada, 1996).
7. Leslie Pal, *Interests of State: The Politics of Language, Multiculturalism, and Feminism in Canada* (Montreal: McGill–Queen's University Press, 1993).
8. Pross, *Group Politics and Public Policy*, ch. 6.
9. Robert Presthus, *Elite Accommodation in Canada* (Toronto: Macmillan, 1973).
10. Colin Campbell, *The Canadian Senate: A Lobby from Within* (Toronto: Methuen, 1983); John McMenemy, "The Senate as an Instrument of Business and Party," in Paul Fox and Graham White, eds., *Politics: Canada*, 7th ed. (Toronto: McGraw-Hill Ryerson, 1991).
11. Brooks and Stritch, *Business and Government in Canada*, 260–64; Stanbury, *Business–Government Relations in Canada*, ch. 12.
12. Malcolm Taylor, "The Role of the Medical Profession in the Formulation of Public Policy," *Canadian Journal of Economics and Political Science* (February 1960): 108–27.
13. Ian Greene, "Conflict of Interest and the Canadian Constitution: An Analysis of Conflict of Interest Rules for Canadian Cabinet Ministers," *Canadian Journal of Political Science* (June 1990): 233–56.
14. Brooks and Stritch, *Business and Government in Canada*, 240; John Sawatsky, *The Insiders: Government, Business, and the Lobbyists* (Toronto: McClelland and Stewart, 1987), Epilogue.
15. Sawatsky, *The Insiders*, 315–16.

16. John A. Chenier, ed., *The Federal Lobbyists 1995* (Ottawa: ARC Publications, 1995), ii.

....

FURTHER READING

Chenier, John A., ed. *The Federal Lobbyists*. Ottawa: ARC Publications, annual.

Coleman, William. *Business and Politics*. Montreal: McGill–Queen's University Press, 1988.

Coleman, William, and Grace Skogstad. *Policy Communities and Public Policy in Canada*. Mississauga: Copp Clark Pitman, 1990.

Pal, Leslie. *Interests of State: The Politics of Language, Multiculturalism, and Feminism in Canada*. Montreal: McGill–Queen's University Press, 1993.

Phillips, Susan. "Competing, Connecting, and Complementing: Parties, Interest Groups, and New Social Movements." In A. Brian Tanguay and Alain-G. Gagnon, eds. *Canadian Parties in Transition*. 2nd ed. Scarborough: Nelson Canada, 1996.

Pross, Paul. *Group Politics and Public Policy*, 2nd ed. Toronto: Oxford University Press, 1992.

Sawatsky, John. *The Insiders: Government, Business, and the Lobbyists*. Toronto: McClelland and Stewart, 1987.

Stanbury, W.T. *Business–Government Relations in Canada*. Toronto: Methuen, 1986.

The Lobby Monitor. Ottawa: ARC Publications, bi-weekly.

PART 3

The Constitutional Context

If "politics" and "government" can be separated, the first half of this text dealt with politics and the second half considers government. The second part is itself divided between the constitutional context and the process of governing. The Constitution forms the framework of the whole political system, and is analyzed in the following two chapters. Chapter 11 outlines the historical development of the Canadian Constitution, its ingredients and principles, and the addition of the Charter of Rights and Freedoms in 1982. Since one of the most important aspects of the Constitution is the relationship between the federal and provincial governments, Chapter 12 examines all aspects of Canadian federalism.

The Canadian Constitution and the Charter of Rights and Freedoms

This chapter begins with an overview of Canadian constitutional history; its second section deals with the road to Canadian Confederation. The chapter then proceeds to examine the basic ingredients and principles of the Canadian Constitution. The final section provides a more detailed treatment of the Charter of Rights and Freedoms, which was added to the Constitution in 1982.

Early Political Institutions

The territory that is now called Canada was first occupied by Aboriginal peoples. France and Britain colonized parts of this territory in the 1500s and 1600s, and periodically fought over them and others for nearly 200 years. The British Hudson's Bay Company took possession early on of Rupert's Land around Hudson Bay; Nova Scotia and Newfoundland came under permanent British control by the 1713 Treaty of Utrecht. Then, after the 1759 Battle of the Plains of Abraham, part of the Seven Years' War between these traditional European rivals, the 1763 Treaty of Paris transferred Quebec, Prince Edward Island, Cape Breton, and New Brunswick to British control. Interaction between the new British power and the Aboriginal peoples is discussed in Chapter 4.

The Royal Proclamation of 1763, the first distinctively Canadian constitutional document, created the colony of Quebec.[1] As far as ex-Europeans were concerned, Quebec at the time was largely made up of French-speaking farmers, clergy, and seigneurs. The British-appointed government was English-speaking, and the nonagricultural economy increasingly came under British control. On the other hand, British governors resisted the idea of imposing the English language and Protestant religion on such a homogeneous French-Catholic population.

In 1774, the Quebec Act provided for a new set of government institutions. It established a council in the colony, but no assembly. Roman Catholics were allowed freedom of religion and could be appointed to the council, and the colony combined British criminal law with French civil law. Meanwhile, the first elected assembly in the "Canadian" part of British North America had been summoned in Nova Scotia in 1758, followed by Prince Edward Island in 1773.

When the residents of the thirteen "American" colonies revolted against British rule, French Canadians essentially remained neutral. Thousands of ex-Americans loyal to Britain—the United Empire Loyalists—migrated to "Canada." This influx led to the severing of New Brunswick from Nova Scotia in 1784, together with the creation of its own assembly, since the Loyalists were accustomed to operating with such elected offices. Then, in response to pressure from those Loyalists who migrated to Quebec, as well as to reward the loyalty of the French, Britain passed the Constitutional Act of 1791. It divided the colony into two—Upper and Lower Canada—each with a governor, an appointed executive council, an appointed legislative council, and a locally elected assembly. In Upper Canada, almost exclusively English, the Constitutional Act provided for British civil law. The executive council gradually evolved into the cabinet, while the legislative council was the forerunner of the Senate. Thus, by 1791, all the colonies had achieved *representative government*, that is, a set of political institutions including an elected legislative assembly.

Subsequently, discord developed between the Canadian colonies and Britain as well as between the local assembly and the executive, composed of the governor and his appointed executive council. The elected assembly represented the people and could articulate their views, but had no real power over the appointed councils. This situation was complicated by the cultural division in Lower Canada—a French assembly and an English executive—with "two nations warring in the bosom of a single state."[2] Reformers demanded *responsible government*, in which the members of the executive council would come from and reflect the views of the elected assembly. This presented a problem in the colonies, however, because on many subjects Britain wanted the governor to do *its* will, not that of the local assembly. This problem eventually erupted into the Rebellions of 1837 in both Upper and Lower Canada, led by William Lyon Mackenzie and Louis-Joseph Papineau respectively. The British government was forced to appoint Lord Durham to investigate the situation. The 1839 Durham Report provided a blueprint for solving the problems of assembly–executive relations, recommending that the principle of responsible government be imple-

Figure 11.1   Evolution of Canadian Pre-Confederation Political Institutions

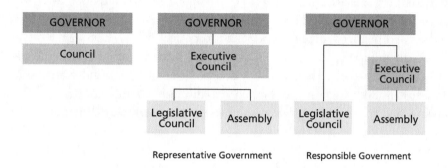

mented with respect to local affairs, so that the executive branch would govern only as long as it retained the confidence of the assembly. Durham outlined a division of powers between local and imperial authorities such that in local matters the governor would follow the advice of colonial authorities, but in matters of imperial concern he would act as an agent of the British government. Responsible government came to Nova Scotia, New Brunswick, and the colony of Canada in 1848, and three years later to Prince Edward Island. Thus, by 1851, all the pre-Confederation colonies operated on the basis that the cabinet or executive council had to resign if it lost the confidence of the elected legislative assembly.

Durham also recommended that Upper and Lower Canada be united into a single colony of Canada, partly as one last attempt to submerge and assimilate the French. The colonies were amalgamated by the 1840 Act of Union, but when it became clear that this assimilation would not be achieved, French was recognized as an official language of the legislature. Moreover, most governments of the period had one English and one French leader.

The Road to Confederation

Economic, political, and military factors drove the British North American colonies to consider uniting.[3] Because the British had discontinued colonial trading preferences, and because a reciprocity treaty with the United States had expired, the colonies hoped to establish a new, large tariff-free trading area among themselves. This large internal market would be enhanced by a railway link between the Maritimes and central Canada, also providing the latter with a winter Atlantic port. The future prospect of annexing and developing the West was seen as a further source of economic prosperity.

Meanwhile, the colony of Canada had experienced political deadlock between its two parts, then called Canada East (Quebec) and Canada West (Ontario), as well as between French and English component groups. Public decisions had to be made in one combined set of governmental institutions, yet the needs and demands of the two parts were often quite different. This led to the practice of requiring a "double majority" (a majority of members from each part of the colony) for the passage of bills. Confederation would allow greater autonomy to the two parts because it would entail a central government to deal with common problems, but would also provide for provincial governments to handle distinctive internal matters on their own. Such a two-tier structure also appealed to the Maritime provinces, which did not wish to turn all decisions over to a distant central government.

The individual colonies also felt vulnerable in a military sense. The United States had a powerful army on their doorstep, and prominent Americans could be heard advocating the takeover the existing colonies and/or the vast territories to the west. Since the British government no longer seemed interested in providing military protection, the colonies would make American aggression more difficult by joining together.

Confederation was thus precipitated by economic, political, and military problems, and seemed to most colonial leaders to be a means of solving them. But it also held out the hope that the new country would one day become a prosperous, transcontinental nation similar to its southern neighbour.

In the 1860s, Nova Scotia, New Brunswick, and Prince Edward Island began to consider forming a Maritime union, and called the Charlottetown Conference of 1864 for this purpose. When delegates from the colony of Canada arrived, however, the idea of a larger union was put up for debate. The essentials of the Confederation scheme were agreed upon at the Quebec Conference later that year, and the London Conference of 1866 fine-tuned the agreement, leaving Prince Edward Island temporarily on the sidelines. Thus, the four provinces of Nova Scotia, New Brunswick, Quebec, and Ontario were officially united on July 1, 1867, by the British North America Act, later renamed the Constitution Act, 1867.

Components and Principles of the Canadian Constitution

The Canadian Constitution would be easier to comprehend if it consisted of a single piece of paper by that name. In the absence of such a document, we can define a *constitution* as the whole body of fundamental rules and principles according to which a state is governed. Canada's Constitution provides for the basic institutions of government and relations between them, relations between national and provincial governments, and relations between governments and citizens.[4] Such a comprehensive definition suggests that the final product may not be neat and tidy, and that some of it may not be written down at all.

In the search for the components that fit the definition of a constitution provided above, it will be seen that the Canadian Constitution is a great hodge-podge. It essentially consists of the following:

- Constitution Act, 1867, and its amendments
- British and Canadian statutes
- Constitution Act, 1982, principally the Charter of Rights
- judicial decisions
- constitutional conventions

The Constitution Act, 1867, and Its Amendments

We turn first to the formal, legal documents, the most important of which is the Constitution Act, 1867, as mentioned above. The act provided much of the basic machinery and institutions of government and established a federal system.

Its Part III deals with the executive power, and section 9 declares that the executive authority over Canada is vested in the Queen. Subsequent clauses refer to the governor general and to the Canadian Privy Council, which is "to aid and advise in the Government of Canada." Section 13 observes that the *governor general in council* refers to the governor general acting by and with the advice of the Canadian Privy Council. Note that the prime minister and cabinet are not explicitly mentioned.

Part IV establishes the legislative power—the Senate and House of Commons. The act requires that money bills originate in the House of Commons, and within it, from members of the executive branch.

Part V concerns provincial constitutions, including the position of lieutenant governor. Since the 1867 act created the provinces of Ontario and Quebec, it had to establish their legislatures, whereas the legislatures of Nova Scotia and New Brunswick continued in their pre-Confederation form.

Part VI, the "Distribution of Legislative Powers" between the central and provincial governments, is probably the most important part of the document. This includes section 91, the federal powers; section 92, provincial powers; section 93, education; and section 95, concurrent powers.

Part VII is concerned with the judiciary. It is a short section that gives the governor general the power to appoint superior, district, and county judges. It also provides for judges' retirement and removal, and allows Parliament to set up a general court of appeal. Note that the 1867 act does not explicitly establish the Supreme Court of Canada.

Part VIII deals with the division of provincial revenues, debts, and assets at the time of Confederation. It makes clear that the provinces have possession of their own lands, mines, and minerals. Part IX is a miscellaneous collection, including section 132, the treaty power, and section 133, regarding the English and French languages. The final section provides for the admission of other colonies.

The Constitution Act, 1867, was thus very brief on the executive and judicial branches of government. It included virtually nothing about limiting the powers of government in relation to the people. The act also lacked any mention of the means to amend it; since it was a statute of the British Parliament, most formal changes to the act have been made by the British Parliament at Canadian request.

Such formal amendments to the 1867 act are also part of the Canadian Constitution, some of them more important than others. They were often termed "British North America Acts," of whatever year in which they were passed, but in 1982, they were mostly renamed "Constitution Acts" of the appropriate year. For example, the Constitution Act, 1940, transferred jurisdiction over unemployment insurance from the provincial to the federal level of government.

British and Canadian Statutes

The second major component of the Canadian Constitution is a collection of British statutes and orders-in-council, and Canadian statutes. Chief among the British statutes is the Statute of Westminster, 1931, which declared Canada to be totally independent of Britain. The Northwest Territories, British Columbia, and Prince Edward Island were British colonies added to Canada by means of British orders-in-council, that is, decisions of the British cabinet. Therefore, these orders-in-council must also be considered part of the Canadian Constitution.

The Canadian statutes that carved provinces out of the Northwest Territories, the Manitoba Act of 1870 and the Saskatchewan and Alberta Acts of 1905, must also be considered part of the Canadian Constitution. Other Canadian statutes of constitutional significance include the Supreme Court Act, an ordinary law that fleshes out the provisions of the 1867 act with respect to the judicial branch of government, the Federal Court Act, the Parliament of Canada Act, the Bill of Rights, the Canada Elections Act, the Citizenship Act, the Emergencies Act, the Canadian Human Rights Act, the Yukon Act, and the Nunavut Act.

The Constitution Act, 1982

Although the Constitution Act, 1982, was in a sense the last amendment to the Constitution Act, 1867, to be passed by the British Parliament, it is worthy of separate mention. While Canada was completely self-governing after 1931, most amendments to the 1867 act still had to be made by the British Parliament, because no formula had been developed to do so in Canada. The Constitution Act, 1982, contained such a domestic constitution-amending formula, and the Canada Act passed by the British Parliament at the same time finally terminated all British authority over Canada. Part V of the act actually provided for five different formulas, depending on the subject matter of the amendment:

- unanimous consent of federal and provincial legislatures
- consent of Parliament and seven provincial legislatures representing 50 percent of the population
- consent of Parliament and one or more provinces affected
- consent of Parliament alone
- consent of a provincial legislature alone

The second main aspect of the Constitution Act, 1982, was the Charter of Rights and Freedoms, discussed in detail later in the chapter. The 1982 act also contained statements on Aboriginal rights and equalization payments to have-not provinces. As far as the division of powers was concerned, a new section 92A was added to clarify and extend provincial powers over natural resources. The

1982 documents did not alter the position of the monarchy in Canada, however; Elizabeth II continues to be recognized as Queen of Canada.

Judicial Decisions

The fourth ingredient of the Canadian Constitution consists of judicial decisions that have clarified or altered provisions of the 1867 act or other parts of the Constitution. The largest body of such decisions are the judgments of the British Judicial Committee of the Privy Council, Canada's final court of appeal until 1949. It was John A. Macdonald's intention to create a strong central government, but the Judicial Committee interpreted the 1867 act in such a way as to minimize federal powers and maximize those of the provinces. The court decisions that effected such a wholesale transformation of the federal nature of the country must be considered a part of the Constitution alongside the actual provisions of the original act. The very power of the courts to invalidate legislation in this manner—judicial review—is a basic principle of the Constitution.

Constitutional Conventions

Thus far, all the ingredients listed can actually be found in written form, however difficult it would be to collect them all together. The final component of the Constitution, on the other hand, has never been committed to paper. It consists of *constitutional conventions*, that is, unwritten rules of constitutional behaviour that are considered to be binding by and upon those who operate the Constitution, but are not enforceable by the courts.[5] Conventions develop from traditions, and through constant recognition and observance become as established, rigid, and sacrosanct as if they were written down. Many of these informal rules have been inherited from Britain, some have been modified in the Canadian environment, and others are unique to Canada. Many of them relate to the executive branch of government, given such slight attention in the 1867 act. The dominant position of the prime minister and cabinet, the subordinate place of the governor general, and the principle of responsible government are three of many conventions that are part of the Constitution.

Principles of the Constitution

The preceding discussion has identified three basic principles of the Canadian Constitution: responsible government, federalism, and judicial review. At least three other fundamental principles are also embedded in the Canadian Constitution, however, these being constitutional monarchy, the rule of law, and democracy.[6]

In terms of its head of state, Canada is a *constitutional monarchy*. This is not a principle that attracts much attention, largely because the monarch herself lives in another country and because her actual power, as well as that of her Canadian representative, the governor general, is not extensive. Nevertheless, the monarchical system underlies a great deal of the operation of government in Canada, largely in the form of the Crown, as discussed in Chapter 13.

The *rule of law* is another constitutional principle inherited from Great Britain that rests largely on convention and judicial precedent. In essence, it means that all government action must be based on law and that governments and government officials must obey the law. In other words, the law is supreme, and no one, including the lawmakers, is above it. Courts in Canada as well as Britain have had occasion to overturn government decisions and actions that were not based on law. As for *democracy*, this term was analyzed fully in Chapter 6.

The Charter of Rights and Freedoms

In the eyes of some observers, the pre-1982 Canadian Constitution was deficient in lacking a statement of civil liberties, that is, of the rights and freedoms that individuals enjoy beyond the reach of the government or the state. Such rights and freedoms are an integral part of a democratic political system and represent territory into which the government is not allowed to enter. In typical British manner, however, the fact that they were not written down did not mean that they did not exist.

Political systems that value civil liberties have adopted two principal methods to protect them. The British approach is to make Parliament supreme, but on the presumption that neither the legislature nor the executive would infringe rights and freedoms because both branches of government are held in check by public opinion, tradition, the political culture, and self-restraint. Civil liberties are so deeply ingrained in the values of the people and politicians alike that they do not need to be written down and the authorities would never think of infringing them—even though, in theory, Parliament could do so. While the courts cannot overturn legislation in Britain—that is, they do not have the power of *judicial review*—they have wide *judicial discretion* in the interpretation of laws, and many civil libertarian values have been introduced into the law as canons of interpretation. Thus, even in the British system, judicial precedents accumulated into the *common law* offer some protection against arbitrary government action. So does the basic constitutional principle, the rule of law.

The American approach, derived in reaction to an imperial government that *did* encroach upon colonial liberties, is to provide for a written statement of civil rights in the constitutional Bill of Rights. Then, if legislation is passed or the executive takes action that is felt to violate a person's rights, such acts can be challenged in the courts. It is up to the courts to determine whether the government has infringed rights and freedoms as defined in the Constitution. The courts thus have the power of judicial review, and can overturn offensive legislation or executive acts.

The fact that federal and provincial politicians occasionally violated civil liberties persuaded Prime Minister John Diefenbaker to enact the Canadian Bill of Rights in 1960. The bill's apparent aim was to allow the courts to invalidate legislation that they found to conflict with the Bill of Rights, but this aim was not clearly articulated. Other serious gaps in the bill were that it applied only to the federal government, not to the provinces; that it allowed legislation to be passed that overrode the bill, as long as this was acknowledged (that is, a notwithstanding clause); that as an ordinary piece of legislation, the bill could be amended in the routine way; and that it was superseded by the War Measures Act, at the very time when it might be needed most.

Not surprisingly, the courts made very limited use of the Bill of Rights. In only one case, the *Drybones* case of 1970, did they decide that a clause of an act violated the Bill of Rights and was therefore inoperative. The bill was more useful in clarifying legal rights and was referred to in several cases to fill in gaps in such definitions as what was meant by the "right to counsel," the "right to an interpreter," and the "right to a fair hearing."

Pierre Trudeau recognized the limitations and ambiguities of the Canadian Bill of Rights and wanted to incorporate new kinds of rights into the Constitution. Finally, in 1982, with the adoption of the Canadian Charter of Rights and Freedoms, he accomplished his objective. The Charter was entrenched in the Constitution, and it is increasingly the task of the judiciary to determine if and when governments have encroached upon the following rights and freedoms:

- fundamental freedoms
- democratic rights
- mobility rights
- legal rights
- equality rights
- language rights
- Aboriginal rights

Trudeau not only wanted to remedy the deficiencies in the Bill of Rights; he was also determined to protect official minority language rights across the country in an effort to undercut Quebec's claim that it represented French Canada. Moreover, Trudeau hoped to counter centrifugal forces throughout the land and pressures for decentralization to the provinces by creating an instrument that the courts could use to cut down self-serving provincial laws. As a new national symbol, the Charter would also serve to increase the allegiance of all citizens to the national government.

The Charter is generally a much stronger document than its predecessor. Besides being broader in scope, the Charter applies equally to both federal and provincial governments, and being entrenched into the Constitution, it is difficult to amend. It also states very clearly that the courts are to invalidate any legislation that they find to conflict with the provisions of the Charter. Let us briefly examine the provisions of the Charter and note a few of the prominent court decisions it inspired.

Guaranteed Rights and Freedoms

FUNDAMENTAL FREEDOMS

At least from a political point of view, section 2 of the Charter is probably most important. It lists the following fundamental freedoms: freedom of conscience and religion; freedom of thought, belief, opinion and expression, including freedom of the press and other media of communication; freedom of peaceful assembly; and freedom of association.

With respect to freedom of religion, the Supreme Court threw out the Lord's Day Act as an infringement of freedom of religion because its restrictions on Sunday activities were clearly related to the Christian sabbath and discriminated against other religions. On the other hand, the Court upheld Ontario's Retail Business Holidays Act, an act designed to limit Sunday shopping and preserve Sunday as a day of rest on a secular rather than a religious foundation. The Court also decided that public schools may no longer hold a compulsory and exclusively Christian school prayer or religious studies classes.

Freedom of expression has brought a wide range of issues before the courts. Perhaps most controversial was the Supreme Court's rejection of the French-only sign provision of Quebec's Bill 101, which also violated Quebec's own Charter of Rights. The Court decided that freedom of expression not only included the freedom to express ideas, but also the freedom to choose the language in which to express them. Moreover, the concept of freedom of expression incorporated "commercial expression." A majority of the Court later concluded that prohibiting the dissemination of hate literature was acceptable as a reasonable limit on freedom of expression.

Obscenity also falls into this category, where one main case stands out, *R. v. Butler*. The Court divided pornography into different categories, saying that portrayal of sex with violence and sex that is degrading or dehumanizing can be restricted by the authorities, but that portrayals of explicit sex that is neither violent nor degrading is generally acceptable unless children are depicted. In a later case, an artist's depiction of children in various sexual activities was deemed to be art rather than pornography. As for prostitution, the Court upheld the prohibition on communicating for the purposes of sidewalk solicitation, feeling that this was a reasonable limit on freedom of expression.

In another controversial decision, the Court ruled that freedom of association does not guarantee the right of trade unions to strike. It therefore does not prevent federal or provincial legislatures from passing back-to-work legislation or otherwise interfering in the collective bargaining process.

DEMOCRATIC AND MOBILITY RIGHTS

Under democratic rights in sections 3 to 5, the Charter guarantees that every citizen of Canada has the right to vote in federal and provincial elections; that no Parliament can continue for more than five years, except in time of real or apprehended war, invasion, or insurrection; and that Parliament must sit at least once every year. Section 3 has been used in several cases dealing with federal and provincial electoral laws that deny the vote to certain categories of people.

Rather unexpectedly, this section has also been used to assess the validity of electoral maps that determine the size of constituencies.

Under section 6, mobility rights, every citizen of Canada has the right to enter, remain in, and leave Canada, and every citizen or permanent resident has the right to take up residence and pursue a livelihood in any province. On the other hand, laws establishing reasonable residency requirements for receiving public services are acceptable, as is giving preference to local residents if the unemployment rate in that province is higher than the national rate. Trudeau included mobility rights because of his concern that some provinces were restricting the entry of residents of other provinces, as in the case of cross-border employment, but they have not featured frequently in judicial interpretation.

LEGAL RIGHTS

Legal rights are contained in sections 7 to 14. In section 7, everyone has the right to life, liberty, and security of the person and the right not to be deprived thereof except in accordance with the principles of fundamental justice. "Security of the person" was used to throw out the abortion provision of the Criminal Code in the famous *Morgentaler* case in 1988. A majority of the Court ruled that the law, with all its arbitrary and bureaucratic procedures, violated the security of the person of the woman concerned and constituted a "profound interference with a woman's body." Sue Rodriguez was not so fortunate in arguing that security of the person provided her with the right to assisted suicide—only a minority of judges agreed with her.

In the *Singh* case, "security of the person" required that the Immigration Department provide an oral hearing for refugee claimants when their lives could be in danger if deported. "Fundamental justice" also necessitated giving such claimants an opportunity to state their case and to know the case against them.

Section 8 establishes the right to be secure against unreasonable search and seizure. In dismissing the charge of collusion between the Southam and Thomson newspaper chains, the Court extended this right to corporations and decided that the search of their offices by anti-combines officials had indeed been unreasonable.

Section 9 grants the right not to be arbitrarily detained or imprisoned, and section 10 reads that on arrest or detention, everyone has the right to be informed promptly of the reasons, and the right to contact a lawyer without delay and to be informed of that right. The Court has ruled that random police spot checks are a reasonable limit on the right not to be arbitrarily detained, and that roadside breath tests do not include the right to retain counsel. However, a person who fails that test and is asked to accompany the police officer to a police station has a right to retain counsel before the breathalyzer test is conducted there. Moreover, the Court has ruled that a person has the right to be told of his or her right not only to a lawyer but also to legal aid, and must have a reasonable opportunity to exercise these rights.

Section 11 includes a variety of rights available to a person charged with an offence. "To be tried within a reasonable time" has been extremely controversial after the *Askov* decision found that a delay of almost two years between a pre-liminary hearing and a trial had been excessive. The lower courts took this to mean that everyone had a right to a trial within six to eight months of being charged, and some 34 500 cases were thrown out in Ontario alone.

Persons charged cannot be compelled to testify against themselves, cannot be denied reasonable bail without just cause, and are presumed innocent until proven guilty according to law in a fair and public hearing by an independent and impartial tribunal. The presumption of innocence was addressed in the *Oakes* case. Under the "reverse onus" clause of the Narcotics Control Act, a person proven to be in possession of a narcotic was also presumed to be guilty of traf-ficking, and it was up to the person charged with possession to prove his or her innocence on the trafficking charge. Although many observers find this to be a perfectly acceptable requirement, the *Oakes* case invalidated this clause as an unreasonable limit on the presumption of innocence. Persons charged with an offence are guaranteed a trial by jury where the maximum punishment for the offence is imprisonment for five years or more, and, whether finally acquitted or found guilty and punished, they cannot be tried for the offence again.

Everyone has the right not to be subjected to any cruel and unusual treat-ment or punishment. Moreover, a party or witness in any proceedings who does not understand or speak the language in which the proceedings are conducted or who is deaf has the right to the assistance of an interpreter.

EQUALITY RIGHTS

Equality rights are contained in section 15, which reads as follows:

> Every individual is equal before and under the law and has the right to the equal protection and equal benefit of the law with-out discrimination and, in particular, without discrimination based on race, national or ethnic origin, colour, religion, sex, age or mental or physical disability.

In the *Andrews* case, the Supreme Court laid down a two-step process for interpreting equality rights. The Court first determines if there has been a violation of the equality rights listed in section 15 (or of others analogous to them), and then whether there has been a harmful or prejudicial effect. In other words, inequalities and distinctions are permitted if no negative discrimination is involved. According to Ian Greene, the Court made it clear that "it intends to interpret section 15 to help clearly disadvantaged groups in society."[7] Moreover, the second part of the section permits affirmative action programs that give preference to those who have been discriminated against in the past.

The concept of reasonable limits has also been used to justify certain other kinds of discrimination. In the case of mandatory retirement, for example, the Court ruled that while such a policy was a violation of equality rights and did involve discrimination, it was reasonable for laws to require retirement at age 65. In 1995, the Supreme Court ruled unanimously that the Charter prohibited discrimination on the basis of sexual orientation, even though this was not explicitly listed in section 15. However, a majority immediately found that the case in question (old age spousal benefits for a same-sex couple) was subject to reasonable limits.

LANGUAGE RIGHTS

Sections 16 to 22 of the Charter constitutionalize the federal and New Brunswick Official Languages acts. These sections guarantee that certain government agencies will operate on a bilingual basis, as discussed in Chapter 3. Section 23 constitutionalizes minority language education rights, and some would argue that this was the only part of the Charter with which Pierre Trudeau was truly concerned. The clause guarantees such access in all provinces in areas "where numbers warrant." The Supreme Court thus decides when the number of francophone students warrants a French-language school, but has also ruled that such a school must have a "distinct physical setting" and that French-language parents must have a say in the "management and control" of it. The Supreme Court struck down the provision in Quebec's Bill 101 that limited access to the English school system in Quebec to the children of parents who were themselves products of that system (the "Quebec clause"). Indeed, section 23 (the "Canada clause") was deliberately drafted so that it would conflict with Bill 101, in order that Canadian citizens who moved to Quebec could also send their children to the English schools.

OTHER PROVISIONS

Section 24 makes clear, where the Bill of Rights did not, that the courts have the power to interpret the Charter and to invalidate laws that conflict with it. The Charter does not actually bar illegally obtained evidence, as in the United States; the admission of such evidence is acceptable as long as it does not bring the administration of justice into disrepute.

Sections 25 through 30 relate to specific groups in society. Section 25 reads that the rights and freedoms in the Charter shall not be construed so as to abrogate or derogate from any Aboriginal, treaty, or other rights or freedoms that pertain to the Aboriginal peoples of Canada, including any rights or freedoms that have been recognized by the Royal Proclamation of 1763 and any others that may be acquired by the Aboriginal peoples of Canada by way of land claims settlements.

Section 27 asserts that the Charter shall be interpreted in a manner consistent with the preservation and enhancement of the multicultural heritage of Canadians, and section 28 ensures that notwithstanding anything in the Charter, the rights and freedoms referred to in it are guaranteed equally to male and female persons. The women's movement considered the addition of section 28 to be essential in order that governments would not be able to use the notwithstanding clause (section 33) to override the gender-equality provision of section 15. According to section 29, nothing in the Charter abrogates or derogates from any rights or privileges guaranteed by or under the Constitution of Canada in respect of denominational, separate, or dissentient schools. This section thus protects section 93 of the 1867 Constitution Act, which guaranteed existing Protestant and Roman Catholic separate schools.

Section 32 clarifies that the Charter applies to the Parliament and government of Canada, including the Yukon and Northwest Territories, and to the legislature and government of each province. By implication, it also applies to the municipal level of government. Thus all legislation in Canada must be consistent with the Charter, as must all actions of government executives, including ministers, public servants, and police officers. It is not intended to apply to the private sector, but certain institutions occupy an ambiguous position. The Charter has been applied to community colleges, for example, but more autonomous semi-public institutions such as hospitals and universities are exempt. Federal and provincial human rights codes rather than the Charter regulate certain aspects of the private sector, but since such codes take the form of laws, they must also remain consistent with the Charter.

Limitations on Rights and Freedoms

The rights articulated in the Charter are not absolute. In the first place, section 1 indicates that such rights are subject to "such reasonable limits, defined by law, as can be demonstrably justified in a free and democratic society." The courts are thus allowed to find that, while a piece of legislation does violate certain rights, it is still acceptable according to their definition of *reasonable limits*. In fact, the Supreme Court has made extensive use of section 1, upholding many laws that it considered to be in violation of Charter rights but that were saved by being reasonable limits upon them. As far as restrictions that can be "demonstrably justified in a free and democratic society" are concerned, the Court developed guidelines in the *Oakes* case that have come to be called the "Oakes test": The objective of the government in limiting a right must be pressing and substantial, and the means adopted proportional to that objective and rationally connected to the objective. Finally, the limit must impair the right as little as possible.

The second limitation on Charter rights revolves around the notwithstanding clause in section 33. In the areas of fundamental freedoms, legal rights, and equality rights, either level of government is allowed to pass legislation contrary to the Charter. The legislation cannot be used to circumvent democratic rights, mobility rights, or linguistic rights. The notwithstanding clause would normally come into play when legislation was introduced to override a judicial decision regarding a Charter right. Such a bill can be exempted from the provisions of the Charter only for a five-year period, however, after which it becomes inoperative if not passed once again for another five years.

Despite the number of times the Supreme Court has thrown out federal or provincial legislation since 1982, governments have rarely re-enacted such provisions under section 33. Over the first 15 years, it was used only in Saskatchewan and Quebec. The government of Grant Devine used section 33 even before a court interpretation of its back-to-work legislation to settle a public-service strike in 1986. The first Parti Québécois government in Quebec (1976–85) routinely applied the notwithstanding clause, as a matter of principle, to all new legislation. The next Liberal government discontinued that practice, but when the Supreme Court ruled that French-only store signs violated their owners' freedom of expression, Bourassa invoked section 33 (and the equivalent clause in the Quebec Charter of Rights) and then passed what he considered to be a compromise law that allowed certain English signs inside the store. While this incident in particular gave the notwithstanding clause a negative reception in most of English Canada, section 33 is often defended as a general principle. It allows democratically elected legislators to have the final say in many areas.

Implications of the Charter for the Political System

The Charter of Rights and Freedoms has attracted both passionate support and opposition. Supporters and opponents alike agree, however, that the adoption of the Charter has significantly changed the operation of the Canadian political system. The courts have become involved in almost all of the most difficult political issues that have arisen over the past 15 years: Aboriginal rights, abortion, assisted suicide, French-only signs, gender equality, impaired driving, mandatory retirement, minority language schools, official bilingualism, political rights of public servants, pornography, prostitution, redistribution of constituency boundaries, the right to strike, same-sex spousal benefits, separate schools, Sunday shopping, and testing the cruise missile. Such cases have enmeshed the courts in considerable political controversy and, as Peter Russell says, the Charter has "judicialized politics and politicized the judiciary."[8]

While many observers are pleased with this development, the most scathing attack on the "legalization of politics" in Canada has been made by law professor Michael Mandel.[9] His first point is that an enormous leeway exists within which the courts make highly political decisions, but judges disguise this fact through legal interpretations and abstract principles that are unintelligible to the general public. Mandel challenges the generally accepted view that while politicians make decisions that are popular, political, and self-serving, judges' decisions are impartial, objective, technical, rational, and in the public interest. Their invocation of the reasonable limits clause, for example, has been highly discretionary.

Mandel's second argument is that while the Charter has been sold as enhancing democracy and the power of the people, it has really reduced the degree of popular control over government by transferring power from representative, accountable legislatures and politicians to unrepresentative, unaccountable, and unrestrained judges, courts, and an elitist legal profession.

In the third place, legalized politics enhances individual and corporate rights against the collective welfare of the community. The adoption of individualistic American values in the Charter, as opposed to traditional Canadian collectivism, is strengthened by the tendency of the courts to cite American precedents when making their decisions.

Mandel's fourth point is that legalized politics is conservative, class-based politics that defends existing social arrangements and undermines popular movements. For a variety of reasons—including the cost of litigation, the background and attitudes of judges, and the biases in the law and the Charter—the socially disadvantaged and labour unions were better off without it.

In making these points, Mandel at least offers a salutary reminder to question the face value of court decisions, to refrain from glorifying the Charter, judges, lawyers, and courts, and to remember traditional ways of making public decisions and of protecting rights and freedoms.

Another implication of adopting the Charter is that minority groups increasingly ignore the usual political processes—legislatures, cabinets, and bureaucracies—and take their demands to the courts instead.[10] To some extent this has happened when such groups were unable to accomplish their goals through traditional political activity, in which case this alternative avenue is probably advantageous. However, groups may simply believe it is less trouble to go to court than to engage in the struggle of mobilizing popular support for their cause. Few observers would welcome a general transformation of political activity into legal activity with the attendant loss of political skills and organization that traditionally characterize a democracy. Seymour Martin Lipset fears that the Charter will remove one of the last traits that distinguish Canadians from Americans by increasing the litigious character of citizen–state relations, and bring about a "rights-centred" political culture.[11]

While reflecting the fact that it was born of political compromise, the Charter nonetheless retains one main limitation on judicial interpretation, the notwithstanding clause. As long as they say so explicitly, legislatures may pass an act violating certain aspects of the Charter. Canadians are left with a strange system under which the courts can overrule the legislatures but the legislatures can overrule the courts. Rank Canadian political compromise that it is, this system of protecting rights and freedoms may turn out to be superior to either total legislative supremacy or exclusive judicial review. Some observers advocate the abolition of the notwithstanding clause, but others (including the author), not wanting to entrust their fate entirely either to legislatures or to courts, prefer the check and balance that they provide on each other.

NOTES

1. Some of the key sources on Canada's constitutional evolution are W.P.M. Kennedy, ed., *Documents of the Canadian Constitution, 1759–1915* (Toronto: Oxford University Press, 1918); R. MacGregor Dawson, *The Government of Canada*, 5th ed., rev. Norman Ward (Toronto: University of Toronto Press, 1970); Bayard Reesor, *The Canadian Constitution in Historical Perspective* (Scarborough: Prentice-Hall Canada, 1992).
2. Lord Durham, *Report of the Affairs of British North America*, ed. Gerald M. Craig (Toronto: McClelland and Stewart, 1963).
3. P.B. Waite, *The Confederation Debates in the Province of Canada/1865* (Toronto: McClelland and Stewart, 1963); Donald Creighton, *The Road to Confederation* (Toronto: Macmillan, 1964).
4. See also Alan C. Cairns, *Constitution, Government, and Society in Canada* (Toronto: McClelland and Stewart, 1988), 31.
5. Andrew Heard, *Canadian Constitutional Conventions* (Toronto: Oxford University Press, 1991). My definition is an amalgam of those he cites.
6. Reesor, *The Canadian Constitution in Historical Perspective*, ch. 4.
7. Ian Greene, *The Charter of Rights* (Toronto: Lorimer, 1989), 172.
8. Peter Russell, "The Political Purposes of the Canadian Charter of Rights and Freedoms," *Canadian Bar Review* (March 1983).
9. Michael Mandel, *The Charter of Rights and the Legalization of Politics in Canada* (Toronto: Wall and Thompson, 1989; rev. ed., 1994).
10. Russell, "The Political Purposes of the Canadian Charter."
11. Seymour Martin Lipset, *Continental Divide* (New York: Routledge, 1990).

FURTHER READING

Berger, Thomas. *Fragile Freedoms*. Toronto: Clarke Irwin, rev. and updated, 1982.

Borovoy, Alan. *When Freedoms Collide: The Case for Our Civil Liberties*. Toronto: Lester & Orpen Dennys, 1988.

Favreau, Guy. *The Amendment of the Constitution of Canada*. Ottawa: Queen's Printer, 1965.

Greene, Ian. *The Charter of Rights*. Toronto: Lorimer, 1989.

Heard, Andrew. *Canadian Constitutional Conventions*. Toronto: Oxford University Press, 1991.

Hogg, Peter. *Canada Act Annotated*. Toronto: Carswell, 1982.

Knopff, Rainer, and F.L. Morton. *Charter Politics*. Scarborough: Nelson Canada, 1992.

Mandel, Michael. *The Charter of Rights and the Legalization of Politics in Canada*. Toronto: Wall and Thompson, 1989; rev. ed., 1994.

Reesor, Bayard. *The Canadian Constitution in Historical Perspective*. Scarborough: Prentice-Hall Canada, 1992.

Romanow, Roy, J. Whyte, and H. Leeson. *Canada … Notwithstanding: The Making of the Constitution 1976–1982*. Toronto: Methuen, 1984.

Russell, Peter. *Constitutional Odyssey*. 2nd ed. Toronto: University of Toronto Press, 1993.

Russell, Peter, Rainer Knopff, and Ted Morton, eds. *Federalism and the Charter*. Ottawa: Carleton University Press, 1989.

Chapter 12

The Federal System

The adoption of a federal system was one of the crucial decisions in the creation of Canada, and the shape of the federal–provincial relationship remains at the heart of contemporary Canadian politics. This chapter begins by outlining the federal system in Canada at its creation and then traces the evolution of that system, especially through changes in the division of powers and federal–provincial financial relationships. The chapter concludes with a discussion of Canadian federalism today.

In a formal sense, *federalism* can be defined as a division of powers between central and regional governments such that neither is subordinate to the other. This definition distinguishes the relationship between provincial and national governments from that between municipal and provincial governments, for in the latter case the municipalities are clearly subordinate entities. This federal–provincial equality of status is provided for in the constitutional division of powers between the two levels of government that is found primarily in sections 91 and 92 of the Constitution Act, 1867. Other aspects of federalism are also important, however, such as federal–provincial financial relations and joint policy-making mechanisms. The increasing tendency of federal and provincial governments to download their responsibilities illustrates both the subordinate and the significant role of municipalities.

The Confederation Settlement

The fundamentals of Canadian federalism, often called the *Confederation Settlement*,[1] were incorporated into the Constitution Act, 1867. As noted earlier, the principal architect of Confederation was Sir John A. Macdonald, who intended the new country to be a highly centralized federation. In fact, the Confederation Settlement was not consistent with the modern definition of federalism because in certain respects the provinces were made subordinate to the central government.

The Confederation Settlement consisted of five principal components:

- division of powers between federal and provincial governments

- division of financial resources
- federal controls over the provinces
- provincial representation in central institutions
- cultural guarantees

As far as the division of powers between the central and provincial governments was concerned, the Fathers of Confederation gave the provinces 16 specific *enumerated powers* in section 92 (e.g., hospitals and municipal institutions) and then left everything else—the *residual powers*—to Ottawa in section 91. For greater certainty, however, they also included 29 enumerations of federal powers such as trade and commerce and national defence. Two *concurrent powers*—agriculture and immigration—were listed in section 95, and the treaty power in section 132 gave the federal government the power to implement Empire treaties, regardless of their subject matter.

In the division of financial resources, federal dominance was even more apparent. The settlement gave Ottawa the power to levy any mode or system of taxation, including both direct and indirect taxes. Since the only tax widely used at the time was the customs duty, an indirect tax, provincial power over direct taxation was not considered to be significant. Instead, the provinces were expected to raise their revenues from the sale of shop, saloon, tavern, and auctioneer licences, as well as to rely on federal subsidies. The federal government was to pay each province an annual per capita grant of 80 cents plus a small subsidy to support its government and legislature. The act also stated that the federal government would assist the provinces by assuming their pre-Confederation debts. It should be added that the provinces were authorized to raise revenues from their natural resources, but this source was not taken seriously at the time because few such resources had yet been discovered.

In the third place, in a clear departure from what is now regarded as the federal principle, Ottawa was given several means of controlling the provinces. The lieutenant governor, a federal appointee, was permitted to reserve provincial legislation for the consideration of the federal cabinet, which could then approve or reject it. Even if the lieutenant governor gave assent to a piece of provincial legislation, however, the federal cabinet could subsequently disallow it. Then, the federal government could declare any local work or undertaking to be for the general advantage of Canada and unilaterally place it within federal jurisdiction. These three controls are respectively referred to as *reservation, disallowance,* and the *declaratory power.*

Given the highly centralized nature of the division of powers, the limited financial resources of the provinces, and the federal controls, it is clear that the Confederation Settlement of 1867 placed the provinces in a subordinate position, somewhat akin to municipalities, rather than giving them the equal or coordinate status provided for in the modern definition of federalism.

In the light of the federal government's dominant position, it is not surprising that the smaller provinces were concerned with their representation in Ottawa. The fourth aspect of the Settlement, therefore, was agreement on provincial representation in the House of Commons and the Senate, a question of much more concern at the time than the division of powers. The great compromise that allowed Confederation to go forward was that the provinces would be represented according to population in the Commons but that regional equality would prevail in the Senate. Thus, each of the three original regions—the Maritimes, Quebec, and Ontario—was to receive 24 senators, appeasing smaller provinces that could be easily outvoted in the lower chamber.

Confederation was more than just a union of provinces; it was also a uniting of two cultural groups, English and French. Thus, the fifth aspect of the Confederation Settlement might be called *cultural guarantees*. Considering the anxiety of French Canadians about the preservation of their language and culture, these guarantees were surprisingly minor. Section 133 of the 1867 act made French and English official languages in the federal Parliament and federal courts as well as in the Quebec legislature and Quebec courts—but nowhere else. At the time, religion was probably of greater concern than language, so existing separate school systems in the provinces (especially Ontario and Quebec) were guaranteed by allowing the federal government to step in to restore them, if necessary. French Canada was also protected by giving power over property and civil rights to the provinces so that Quebec could maintain certain cultural particularisms, including its civil law system.

Of these five components of the Confederation Settlement, only three relate directly to the relationship between federal and provincial governments. This chapter will therefore proceed to track the development of the Settlement in these three aspects: the division of powers, financial resources, and federal controls. In discussing the evolution of Canadian federalism, a key concern will be to explain how the very centralized federation created in 1867 became the highly decentralized Canada of today. This trend is apparent in all three areas.

Division of Powers

The evolution of the *division of powers* between federal and provincial governments can be examined in two respects: formal constitutional amendments that altered the division of powers, and judicial decisions that interpreted sections 91 and 92 of the Constitution Act, 1867.

Since 1867, only four formal constitutional amendments have been adopted that directly affected the division of powers. In 1940, unemployment insurance was added to the list of federal powers in section 91 after the courts had earlier declared it to belong to the provinces. In 1951, old age pensions were made a concurrent power, allowing the federal government into this area as well, and in 1964 Ottawa's jurisdiction was enlarged to include widows' and survivors' benefits and disability pensions. In 1982, the new section 92A increased provincial jurisdiction over natural resources, while the Charter of Rights and Freedoms generally reduced the powers of both levels of government. Thus, in the first three cases, the net result was a slight increase in federal powers, but this increase was accomplished with the unanimous consent of the provinces. The 1982 amendment was the only formal constitutional amendment that in any way increased provincial powers at the expense of Ottawa. Formal constitutional amendments, therefore, do little to explain the more powerful provinces of today.

Judicial interpretation of the federal and provincial powers in the 1867 act is a much more complicated and significant subject. Before 1949, the Judicial Committee of the Privy Council (JCPC) in London was Canada's final court of appeal, and its decisions had a major impact in transforming Canadian federalism from a centralized to a decentralized system. The significant JCPC decisions related primarily to the federal *peace, order, and good government clause* as opposed to the provincial power over property and civil rights.

Section 91 of the 1867 act has two parts. First, the peace, order, and good government clause says that all powers not given to the provinces in section 92 are left with the federal government. This is also known as "POGG" or the residual clause. Then, for greater certainty, a list of 29 examples of federal powers is included. In the course of its judgments, the Judicial Committee drove a wedge between these two parts of section 91, deciding that the 29 enumerations were the *real* federal powers rather than just examples and ignoring the peace, order, and good government clause except in cases of national emergency. In times of national emergency, as determined by the JCPC, federal powers were almost unlimited. (How it managed to transform the residual clause into an emergency power is very difficult to fathom.) In normal times, on the other hand, the JCPC gave an extremely broad interpretation to section 92-13, property and civil rights in the province, finding that almost any matter that was the subject of a federal– provincial constitutional dispute could be incorporated within this provincial power.[2] That is why so little was left over for the federal residual clause.

The effect of the judicial interpretation of the peace, order, and good government clause, along with other clauses such as trade and commerce and treaty powers, was to reduce significantly the intended dominance of the federal government, and, given its complementary broad interpretation of property and civil rights, to increase substantially the scope of provincial powers. This influence has been very controversial in political, judicial, and academic circles because it was clearly contrary to John A. Macdonald's conception of Canadian federalism and because it did not permit Ottawa to take initiatives that centralist advocates often wished.[3]

Other observers contend, however, that the Judicial Committee's line of interpretation was consistent with the increasing size and distances that characterized the country as time went on, as well as with societal forces and public orientations, at least outside Ontario. They argue that the provincial bias pervading so many of the JCPC's decisions was "in fundamental harmony with the regional pluralism" of the federal, decentralized, diversified nature of Canadian society. However desirable centralization may have seemed at the outset, it was inappropriate in the long run "for the regional diversities of a land of vast extent and a large, geographically concentrated, minority culture."[4]

Federal–Provincial Finance

In the Confederation Settlement, the federal government was given the power to levy any kind of tax, while the provinces were restricted to direct taxation.[5] The federal government was also committed to pay the provinces small annual grants. While the intention was thus to create a highly centralized federation, the financial factor also ultimately contributed to the increased power of the provinces. This situation came about because the provinces levied direct taxes that they were not expected to use, such as income taxes; because the provinces successfully lobbied for larger federal grants, mostly unconditional in nature; and because some provincial revenues, such as those from natural resources, turned out to be more significant than anticipated.

Provincial revenues proved to be inadequate from the beginning, and it did not take long for the provinces to begin levying their own direct personal and corporate income taxes or for them to demand larger sums from Ottawa. With both levels of government taxing the same personal and corporate incomes, but in a totally uncoordinated fashion, and with the two levels increasingly intertwined in shared-spending programs, the federal–provincial financial situation became very complicated. This muddied state of affairs worsened with the advent of the Depression, when even fewer funds were available to go around. As a result, Mackenzie King appointed the Rowell–Sirois Commission, officially the Royal Commission on Dominion–Provincial Relations, in 1937. Its only recommendation to be immediately implemented was that the costly responsibility for unemployment insurance be transferred to the federal government.

Before 1940, therefore, the two levels of government were relatively independent on both the taxation and expenditure sides of public finance. Since the Second World War, on the other hand, they have become intimately intertwined, and Ottawa has taken the lead (sometimes with provincial encouragement) in coordinating the various ingredients of the financial relationship. The complicated federal–provincial financial situation since 1940 might be simplified somewhat by taking three aspects separately: taxation agreements; conditional and block grants; and equalization payments.

Since 1942 the taxation side has been characterized by a series of five-year federal–provincial agreements. The name and terms of the agreements have changed over the years, but the basic objective has been the same: to effect a degree of coordination in the field of federal–provincial taxation. The main taxes in question were personal and corporate income taxes. While the federal personal income tax is standard across the country (except for Quebec), each province determines its own rate as a percentage of the federal tax, so that the provincial portion varies widely. Except for Quebec, all personal income taxes are collected by Ottawa in the first instance, after which the provincial portion is transferred back, an arrangement found generally satisfactory to all concerned. Quebec collects its own personal income tax, so that its residents complete two separate income tax forms. All provinces except Ontario, Quebec, and Alberta also have tax collection arrangements with Ottawa with respect to provincial corporate income taxes.

Federal–provincial shared-cost programs expanded considerably after 1940 in the joint development of a welfare state. The most important shared-cost social programs were postsecondary education (1952), hospital insurance (1957), the Canada Assistance Plan (CAP) (1966), and medical insurance (1968). Health insurance later replaced the two earlier measures in this field.

Federal grants for postsecondary education have always been of a *block grant* variety, that is, a sum of money given to each province for the operating costs of postsecondary educational institutions but without any conditions or strings attached. The other major shared-cost programs originally fell into the conditional grant category. The usual pattern here was for the federal government to pay approximately 50 percent of the cost of each program provided the provinces met Ottawa's conditions. For example, Ottawa would fund half of any provincial health-care program that was comprehensive (covering all necessary health services provided by hospitals and medical practitioners), universal (covering the whole population), portable (covering the costs of provincial residents while temporarily absent from the province), accessible (not impeding or precluding reasonable access to services by extra charges), and publicly administered. Under the Canada Assistance Plan, Ottawa similarly provided half the funding for almost any provincial or municipal program that provided social assistance and welfare services to persons in need.

While a combination of provincial pressure and federal political and bureaucratic expansionism inspired most of these programs, the provinces often criticized the federal conditions attached as being out of place in areas of provincial jurisdiction. Quebec in particular took this point of view in the early 1960s. In 1965, the Pearson government allowed provinces to opt out of certain conditional grant programs and continue to receive federal funding as long as they maintained an equivalent program. Then, in the 1970s, Ottawa became upset at the rapidly escalating costs of many of these programs and its commitment to finance 50 percent of whatever the provinces spent on them.

In 1977 the federal government transferred health insurance from the conditional to the block grant category, under the Established Programs Financing Act. This transformation had two major implications. First, Ottawa removed the detailed conditions attached to the health-insurance programs, as many provinces wished, but in return, the federal government no longer felt obliged to pay 50 percent of the provincial program costs. The federal grants now took the form of tax transfers as well as cash, and henceforth, Ottawa would only increase its funding of such programs by a certain annual percentage that would not necessarily cover one-half of their overall costs. Removing the conditions from health-insurance grants, however, led to problems with hospital user fees, doctors' double-billing, and provinces using health-care funds for other purposes.

To much provincial condemnation, therefore, the federal government passed the Canada Health Act in 1984. The act resurrected the five earlier conditions and penalized those provinces permitting user fees and double-billing. At the same time, especially after 1982, the federal share of such programs fell below 50 percent, and the 1990s saw a progression of freezes and cuts in funding. For a time, the Canada Assistance Plan remained a conditional grant program, with Ottawa continuing its 50 percent contribution, but the Mulroney government put a ceiling on its CAP contributions to the three richest provinces in the early 1990s, and the Liberals repealed the plan completely.

The 1994 federal budget brought in by Finance Minister Paul Martin announced a freeze on all major federal transfers except equalization payments, and the 1995 budget inaugurated a major transformation of federal–provincial transfers. Established Program Funding (postsecondary education and health insurance) and the Canada Assistance Plan (social assistance and welfare services) were combined into one block grant beginning in 1996–97 called the Canada Health and Social Transfer (CHST). It would be a combination of cash payments and tax points, but would represent a significant reduction in previous amounts. As a block grant, the CHST would not contain the conditions of CAP nor would Ottawa's expenditures be driven by provincial costs. The only condition on welfare transfers would be that provinces not impose a minimum residency requirement. Despite the protests of almost all social reformers, who did not trust provincial governments to provide adequate social assistance programs, Ottawa felt it could not retain such conditions when it was reducing its contributions. On the other hand, the federal Liberal government continued to enforce the principles of the Canada Health Act and fought with Alberta over the funding of private health clinics that charged "facility fees."

The third aspect of federal–provincial finance consists of equalization payments. In 1957, the federal government began to pay unconditional grants to have-not provinces based on provincial need, so that all could offer a relatively equal standard of services. The essence of equalization payments was to bring the have-not provinces up to the national average tax yield per capita. Typically, Ontario, British Columbia, and Alberta have been above the national average and have not received equalization payments, while the other seven provinces receive an annual payment based on the per capita shortfall multiplied by the province's population. Equalization payments were not touched by the federal reforms of 1995.

Combining these major federal contributions to the provinces, Table 12.1 shows that in 1994–95 Ottawa paid the provinces a total of $37 billion, but that the total declined by $3.5 billion four years later.

In addition to their grants from Ottawa, the provinces have levied over 30 forms of direct taxation that were unanticipated in 1867. The enormous natural-resource revenues that some provinces receive on top of direct taxation and federal contributions are also significant.[6] Some idea of the balance among federal transfers, natural resource revenues, and provincial taxes and other revenues can be gathered from Table 12.2.

TABLE 12.1 MAJOR FEDERAL TRANSFERS TO PROVINCES, 1994–95 AND 1998–99, (OCTOBER 1997 ESTIMATED ENTITLEMENTS)

| | ($ Millions) | | | | | |
| | 1994–95 | | | 1998–99 | | |
	EPF/CAP	Equalization	Total	CHST	Equalization	Total
Newfoundland	624	958	1 502	511	976	1 401
P.E.I.	135	192	311	118	201	299
Nova Scotia	954	1 065	1 934	822	1 211	1 930
New Brunswick	760	927	1 610	651	891	1 454
Quebec	8 048	3 965	11 658	6 923	4 108	10 609
Ontario	10 536	—	10 536	9 468	—	9 468
Manitoba	1 130	1 085	2 133	976	1 065	1 947
Saskatchewan	985	413	1 293	848	135	874
Alberta	2 506	—	2 506	2 269	—	2 269
B.C.	3 574	—	3 574	3 312	—	3 312
Total	29 252	8 607	37 056	25 898	8 587	33 564

Notes:

– Totals may not add due to rounding.

– Equalization associated with tax point transfers under CHST appears in both the Equalization and CHST figures. Totals are adjusted to avoid double counting.

* As per the forthcoming revision to the CHST legislation (i.e., $12.5 B cash floor).

Source: Federal–Provincial Relations Division, Finance Canada. Used with permission.

TABLE 12.2 ESTIMATED FEDERAL TRANSFERS, NATURAL-RESOURCE REVENUES,
PROVINCIAL TAXES AND OTHER REVENUES, AND TOTAL REVENUE, 1994–95

| | | ($ Millions) | | |
| | | Provincial Taxes | | |
	Federal Transfers	& Other Provincial Revenues	Natural Resource Revenue	Total Provincial Revenues
Newfoundland	1 507.4	1 943.0	31.2	3 481.6
P.E.I.	301.3	506.5	0.6	808.4
Nova Scotia	1 750.8	2 780.7	10.5	4 542.0
New Brunswick	1 588.2	2 830.8	50.2	4 469.2
Quebec	7 751.6	33 691.5	96.0	41 539.1
Ontario	7 186.5	41 836.7	364.6	49 387.8
Manitoba	1 830.4	4 590.7	63.2	6 484.3
Saskatchewan	1 642.2	4 216.0	407.7	6 265.9
Alberta	2 455.5	9 254.1	2 687.8	14 397.4
B.C.	2 336.5	17 204.6	1 687.0	21 228.1
Total	28 350.4	118 854.6	5 398.8	152 603.8

Source: Adapted from Statistics Canada, Public Sector Finance 1994–95, Financial Management System, Cat. No. 68-212 (March 1995). Reproduced with the permission of the Minister of Supply and Services Canada, 1997.

Thus, the combination of unanticipated federal grants, direct taxes, and natural-resource revenues has contributed significantly to the enhanced status of the provinces in the Canadian federal system. It should also be reiterated that the two levels of government began by operating more or less independently of each other, taxing and spending in different areas, with federal grants being unconditional in nature. Now, the federal and provincial governments are closely intertwined by taxation agreements on the revenue side and by conditional and block grant programs in terms of expenditures, although less so since 1995.

Federal Controls

The 1867 Constitution Act contained three specific federal controls over the provinces: reservation, disallowance, and the declaratory power. In the first 30 years after Confederation all three controls were actively used, and this had the effect of keeping the provinces subordinate to Ottawa. Their use has gradually declined since then—the reservation and declaratory powers were last used in 1961, while disallowance was last exercised in 1943. As these were the federal powers that originally precluded Canada from being classified as a true federation, their disuse has meant that the provinces have shrugged off their subordinate status. Canada is now a genuine federation, and a highly decentralized one at that.

Canadian Federalism Today

Federal–provincial relations in Canada have gone through many different phases since 1867, depending on shifting attitudes of federal and provincial governments, states of war and peace, and variations in judicial interpretation. In fact, Canadian federalism has experienced pendulum-like swings between centralization and decentralization: the evolution from a centralized to a decentralized federal system has not been a unilinear process.

Cooperative Federalism

Canadian federalism today is still in the phase that began after the Second World War and might be called *cooperative federalism*. The essence of this concept is that while neither level is subordinate to the other, the federal government and the provinces are closely intertwined rather than operating independently. Here the crucial variable is financial relations. As noted in that connection earlier, the post-1945 period has been marked by federal–provincial taxation agreements on the revenue side and a host of shared-cost programs in terms of expenditures.

Cooperative federalism results from several developments.[7] First, federal and provincial objectives must often be harmonized if public policy is to be effective. Second, public pressure forces the federal government to establish minimum standards throughout the country in certain public services within provincial jurisdiction such as health care. In the third place, the two levels of government compete for tax revenues and need to coordinate these efforts to some extent, at least for the convenience of taxpayers. Fourth, given a generally vague division of powers, federal and provincial ministers and bureaucrats usually seek to maximize their jurisdiction and eventually overlap with the other level of government.

Cooperative federalism is made operational by hundreds of federal–provincial conferences at all levels—first ministers, departmental ministers, deputy ministers, and even lesser officials—who engage in almost continuous consultation, coordination, and cooperation. Cooperative federalism can be conducted on a multilateral basis, involving the federal government and several or all provinces, or alternatively, on a bilateral basis in which Ottawa interacts with individual provinces. Since the ministers and bureaucrats involved are all part of the executive branch of government, cooperative federalism is sometimes called *executive federalism*. Two main implications of executive federalism are that legislatures, political parties, and the public at large are not given much role to play in decisions that emerge from the secrecy of such meetings, and that federal–provincial conflicts are worked out in conferences or meetings rather than being referred to the courts.

Executive federalism can therefore be defined as "relations between elected and appointed officials of the two levels of government."[8] When it is practised at the level of first ministers, it is often called "federal–provincial summitry." The first ministers' conference—that is, a conference of premiers and the prime minister—is not provided for anywhere in the written Constitution and rests upon a conventional base. Nevertheless, especially since 1945, this institution has made many significant policy decisions, especially with respect to constitutional issues, shared-cost programs, and taxation and fiscal arrangements. Some of these had to be ratified later by federal and provincial legislatures, but except on constitutional matters, legislative ratification was usually a formality. Such agreements could rarely be altered in any legislature because they would then have to be changed in all 11. First ministers' conferences have become more elaborate and institutionalized over time. They are usually held in the Government Conference Centre in Ottawa, the refurbished old train station across from Parliament Hill. They can be televised, in whole or in part, but it is generally agreed that any serious negotiation has to take place behind closed doors. The prime minister functions as chair, in addition to representing the federal government, and individual ministers from either level of government are usually allowed to speak as well. Every delegation brings along a host of advisers. After the collapse of the Charlottetown Accord, however, such first ministers' conferences fell into disrepute.

Executive federalism conducted at the level of departmental ministers and leading bureaucrats is sometimes labelled "functional" or "bureaucratic" federalism. This form of executive federalism is usually more successful than federal–

provincial summitry, partly because the officials involved often share certain professional norms, and once they reach a consensus, these experts may be able to "sell" it to their departmental ministers.

Variations in Cooperative Federalism

Canadian federalism between 1945 and 1960 may have been "cooperative" in the sense that the two levels of government were closely intertwined, but it continued to be highly centralized in the immediate postwar period. The ministers and bureaucrats in Ottawa who had almost single-handedly run the country during the Second World War were reluctant to shed their enormous power. Moreover, they had discovered Keynesian economics, which prescribed a leading role for the central government in guiding the economy. The Diefenbaker government after 1957 was more sensitive to provincial demands, and the whole picture was increasingly complicated from about 1960 onward by the Quiet Revolution in Quebec. This period still manifested an intertwined, nonsubordinate relationship between the two levels of government, but cooperation was sometimes harder to come by, with Quebec regularly rejecting federal initiatives. The concept of opting out was a hallmark of this phase of federalism, which saw a significant degree of decentralization take place.

Between about 1970 and 1984, federal–provincial relations became even less cooperative. Quebec and the other provinces were more aggressive than ever, but the Trudeau government was not prepared for any further decentralization. Thus, taxation agreements were now accompanied by more provincial unhappiness, and block funding replaced conditional grants in important areas, leaving the two levels less intertwined than before. Moreover, especially at the level of first ministers, federal–provincial conferences frequently failed to come to any agreement and Ottawa often chose to act unilaterally. In this phase, federal–provincial conflicts were more frequently referred to the courts, resulting in a renewed emphasis on the division of powers.

The Trudeau era was characterized by years of federal–provincial discord over resource and energy policies, especially the National Energy Program, conflict with Newfoundland over offshore oil, and conflict with Saskatchewan over the regulation and taxation of that province's oil and potash industries. When these disputes coincided with Trudeau's attempt to unilaterally amend the Constitution and entrench official bilingualism as a national policy, many Western Canadians began to re-examine their place in the federation. Some of the heat was reduced when Trudeau conceded the new section 92A, which recognized enhanced provincial jurisdiction over natural resources, in order to secure federal NDP support for the 1982 constitutional package and as a peace-offering to the West.

When Brian Mulroney came to power in 1984, he was determined to improve federal–provincial relations and embark on another period of decentralized, genuinely cooperative federalism. During his first term many would say he succeeded, for much of the federal–provincial animosity of the Trudeau years seemed to dissipate. Western and Eastern concerns about energy resources were respectively resolved to a large extent in the 1985 Western and Atlantic Accords. During its second term, however, the Mulroney government increasingly aroused provincial anger, especially as it became obsessed with deficit reduction and cut back on grants to the provinces. To the surprise of many observers, the Mulroney government enforced the Liberals' Canada Health Act, imposing penalties on provinces that allowed doctors to extra-bill or permitted hospitals to charge user fees. The major federal–provincial dispute of the Mulroney years concerned the Goods and Services Tax (GST). To some extent it was just "good politics" for provincial premiers to jump on the anti-GST bandwagon because of widespread popular opposition. Most provinces refused to integrate their sales taxes with the new federal tax, even though many mutual advantages would have accrued from doing so.

The Chrétien Liberals were initially popular with provincial governments in offering funds under the national infrastructure program, and were somewhat successful in negotiating a reduction in provincial barriers to the free movement of people, goods, services, and capital across the country. They had only partial success in implementing their promise to replace the GST (in reality, they harmonized it with the provincial retail sales tax in three Atlantic provinces), and angered the provinces with reductions in their transfers, especially after 1995. The principal complaints included severe reductions in health, postsecondary education, and welfare transfers, although provinces also joined in to protest the cuts to almost every other aspect of federal government operations, such as a wide range of transportation subsidies. Ottawa did not cut equalization payments, however, and most provinces were realistic enough to recognize the desirability of reducing the federal deficit.

Canada has thus passed the apex of cooperative federalism. For many reasons, both levels of government increasingly desire to extract themselves from such programs. Since a certain amount of duplication probably increases program costs, federal and provincial governments' strained fiscal positions are largely responsible. In some cases, when Ottawa is no longer funding programs so generously, it cannot impose standards on them. In other cases, each side simply wants to do things in its own way.

NOTES

1. Donald Smiley, *The Canadian Political Nationality* (Toronto: Methuen, 1967).
2. Peter Russell et al., *Federalism and the Charter* (Ottawa: Carleton University Press, 1989); Peter Hogg, *Constitutional Law of Canada*, 2nd ed. (Toronto: Carswell, 1985).
3. V.C. MacDonald, "Judicial Interpretation of the Canadian Constitution," *University of Toronto Law Journal* 1 (1935–36): 260–85; the *O'Connor Report*, Senate of Canada, 1939. It is ironic that judicial interpretation contributed to decentralizing a centralized Canadian federation but centralized a decentralized federation in the United States. See Roger Gibbins, *Regionalism* (Toronto: Butterworths, 1982), ch. 4.
4. Alan C. Cairns, "The Governments and Societies of Canadian Federalism," *Canadian Journal of Political Science* (December 1977): 695–725; Cairns, "The Judicial Committee and Its Critics," *Canadian Journal of Political Science* (September 1971): 301–45.
5. Direct taxes are derived from the very people who are intended to pay them, while indirect taxes are extracted from one person in the expectation that they will be passed on to someone else.
6. G.V. La Forest, *The Allocation of Taxing Powers under the Canadian Constitution*, 2nd ed. (Toronto: Canadian Tax Foundation, 1981); Canadian Tax Foundation, *Provincial and Municipal Finances* (1989), 12: 1.
7. Donald Smiley, *Canada in Question: Federalism in the Seventies* (Toronto: McGraw-Hill Ryerson, 1972), 56.
8. Ibid.

FURTHER READING

Banting, Keith. *The Welfare State and Canadian Federalism*. Kingston: McGill–Queen's University Press, 1982; 2nd ed., 1987.

Canada: The State of the Federation. Kingston: Institute of Intergovernmental Relations, Queen's University, annual.

Canadian Tax Foundation. *The National Finances*. Toronto, biennial.

Heard, Andrew. *Canadian Constitutional Conventions*. Toronto: Oxford University Press, 1991.

Hogg, Peter. *Constitutional Law of Canada*. 2nd ed. Toronto: Carswell, 1985.

Mallory, J.R. "The Five Faces of Canadian Federalism." In P.-A. Crépeau and C.B. Macpherson, *The Future of Canadian Federalism*. Toronto: University of Toronto Press, 1965.

Mellon, Hugh, and Martin Westmacott, eds. *Challenges to Canadian Federalism*. Scarborough: Prentice-Hall Canada, 1997.

Milne, David. *Tug of War: Ottawa and the Provinces under Trudeau and Mulroney*. Toronto: Lorimer, 1986.

Russell, Peter, et al. *Federalism and the Charter*. Ottawa: Carleton University Press, 1989.

Smiley, D.V. *The Federal Condition in Canada*. Toronto: McGraw-Hill Ryerson, 1987.

Stevenson, Garth, ed. *Federalism in Canada: Selected Essays*. Toronto: McClelland and Stewart, 1989.

Stevenson, Garth. *Unfulfilled Union*. 3rd ed. Toronto: Gage, 1989.

Swinton, Katherine. *The Supreme Court and Canadian Federalism: The Laskin–Dickson Years*. Toronto: Carswell, 1990.

PART 4

Governing

Having examined the societal context of the political system and the means of linking people to government in the "politics" part of this book, and the constitutional context as the first part of the "government" section, we can now focus on governing itself. This section, therefore, examines the individual institutions of government in detail. These institutions consist of the executive, including the Crown, the prime minister, and the cabinet; the bureaucracy; Parliament, including the House of Commons and the Senate; and the judiciary. The functions and operations of each branch of government are outlined, as are the kinds of outputs or authoritative decisions each makes. Initially, however, these institutions are put into the context of the "policymaking process," providing an overview of how they interact with each other in order to produce public policies.

Chapter 13

The Executive

The prime minister and cabinet constitute the political executive and are the key players in the Canadian policymaking process. Their decisions are sometimes overturned by the courts and occasionally even by Parliament, and are usually based to a considerable extent on advice from the bureaucracy. But in the end, the prime minister and cabinet do make and are responsible for making the biggest political decisions in the country. This chapter begins with a brief discussion of the policymaking process and the Crown, and then concentrates on the prime minister and cabinet.

The Policymaking Process

The analyses of the individual institutions of government that follow in this and subsequent chapters will be more meaningful if they are first put in the context of the policymaking process. This section provides an overview of that process, indicating in a general way how the various institutions interact with each other in the making of public policy. *Public policy* can be defined as "a course of action or inaction chosen by public authorities to address a given problem or interrelated set of problems."[1]

Chapter 1 contained a model of the whole political system that included such components as demands, authorities, outputs, and feedback. Now imagine focusing in more detail on the "authorities" part of that model. The result would be an enlargement of that part of the system directly involved in the policymaking process and would look something like Figure 13.1.

As this model suggests, the actual policymaking process can be divided into six phases: initiation, priority-setting, policy formulation, legitimation, implementation, and interpretation. Not all policies or decisions involve such an elaborate process; indeed, many can be made unilaterally by the prime minister, the cabinet, the bureaucracy, or the courts. But the model shows the policymaking process in its broadest form, that is, a policy that requires the passage of a new law, or an amendment to an existing law and whose constitutionality is later challenged in the courts.

Figure 13.1   The Canadian Policymaking Process

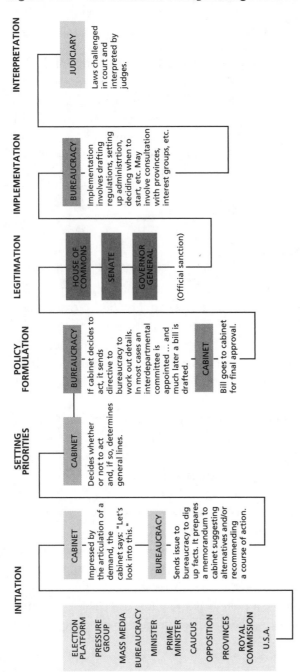

INTERPRETATION

JUDICIARY

Laws challenged in court and interpreted by judges.

IMPLEMENTATION

BUREAUCRACY

Implementation involves drafting regulations, setting up administrtion, deciding when to start, etc. May involve consultation with provinces, interest groups, etc.

LEGITIMATION

HOUSE OF COMMONS

SENATE

GOVERNOR GENERAL

(Official sanction)

POLICY FORMULATION

BUREAUCRACY

If cabinet decides to act, it sends directive to bureaucracy to work out details. In most cases an interdepartmental committee is appointed ... and much later a bill is drafted.

CABINET

Bill goes to cabinet for final approval.

SETTING PRIORITIES

CABINET

Decides whether or not to act and, if so, determines general lines.

INITIATION

CABINET

Impressed by the articulation of a demand, the cabinet says: "Let's look into this."

BUREAUCRACY

Sends issue to bureaucracy to dig up facts. It prepares a memorandum to cabinet suggesting alternatives and/or recommending a course of action.

ELECTION PLATFORM
PRESSURE GROUP
MASS MEDIA
BUREAUCRACY
MINISTER
PRIME MINISTER
CAUCUS
OPPOSITION
PROVINCES
ROYAL COMMISSION
U.S.A.

The authorities are bombarded daily with hundreds of demands. These demands emanate from many different sources, but the policymaking process is set in motion when the prime minister and cabinet decide to look into a matter further. On a smaller scale, a single minister may also make such a decision. It is at this point that a demand is sometimes said to become an issue. An issue, therefore, is a demand that has made it onto the public agenda and that is under serious consideration by the authorities.

The second phase of the policymaking process involves the prime minister and cabinet again, this time in their priority-setting capacity. They decide which of the proposals they have previously selected for consideration are worthy of adoption. In other words, the prime minister and cabinet (or on lesser issues an individual minister) must decide whether or not to take action on the issue, and if they decide to act, they must determine the general lines of the new initiative.

The limited number of projects that have been given the green light by the cabinet in the priority-setting phase then enter the policy formulation phase. Once the cabinet has approved a proposal in principle, it usually sends a directive to the bureaucracy to work out the details. This is often a very time-consuming process requiring coordination among many federal government departments. It may also involve consultation with provincial governments, interest groups, and others. Questions may be referred back to the cabinet for further direction, but eventually a Memorandum to Cabinet is submitted, outlining the policy in detail.[2] Assuming the proposal requires legislative action, the policy formulation stage culminates in a bill being drafted on the basis of the Memorandum to Cabinet.

The proposal then enters the legislative arena. The relevant minister may accept technical alterations to the bill as it proceeds through the House of Commons and the Senate, but the main intent or principle of the bill cannot be changed without being approved by the cabinet. The legislative stage is referred to as "legitimizing" the bill because it is put under the scrutiny of the democratically elected representatives of the people and made legitimate by their approval. The cabinet and members of Parliament contribute political expertise to the process, but given the shortage of time and limited technical expertise characteristic of the legislative branch, most such bills are passed in "skeletal" form, with details and regulations to be added later. The legitimation stage ends with the token approval of the governor general, signifying that the policy has been officially sanctioned.

Royal assent is by no means the end of the policymaking process. Few laws attain any significance just by sitting on the statute books; they must be implemented in order to be made effective. Implementation almost always involves the drafting of detailed regulations by the bureaucracy, to add meat to the skeleton of the statute. Even though they have the same legal standing as if they were part of the enabling statute itself, the regulations a law authorizes the executive to make are given only the scarcest scrutiny by either ministers or Parliament, and thus are almost the exclusive preserve of the bureaucracy. Implementation normally requires the setting up of new administrative machinery—new staff, agencies, field offices, and operational manuals, among other things. It is therefore not surprising that most legislation does not automatically take effect upon royal assent; it is not "proclaimed" or made operational until the government is ready to implement it.

The policymaking process may well end, at least for the time being, with the implementation phase. But if new legislation is involved, its constitutionality may be challenged in the courts, especially if it appears to violate the Charter of Rights and Freedoms in any way. Thus, especially since 1982, it is appropriate to add a sixth phase to the policymaking process, that of judicial interpretation. If a statute is challenged in the courts, the judiciary must interpret the law and decide whether its provisions are contrary to the Charter or to the division of powers between federal and provincial governments.

The Crown

To classify Canada as a *constitutional monarchy* essentially means that it is a democracy headed by a king or queen. In other words, the Queen is the Canadian head of state, but she reigns according to the Constitution. Canada is also said to have a "dual executive," meaning that the formal and largely symbolic executive powers are given to the Queen, but the effective executive is made up of the prime minister and cabinet.

The concept of *the Crown* revolves around the head of state and can be defined as the collectivity of executive powers exercised by or in the name of the monarch. Although the Crown is largely irrelevant to the effective functions of government, many government operations are performed in the name of the Queen or governor general.[3] Moreover, the Crown does perform useful functions in the political system that are largely of a symbolic and ceremonial nature.

The Crown is not only the collectivity of executive powers; it also represents the entire state and embodies what belongs to the people collectively. This can be seen in Crown corporations (state-owned corporations) or Crown lands (state-owned lands). The Crown is also central to the legal system: Crown attorneys, those who prosecute crimes on behalf of society; court cases initiated in the name of the Queen, for example, *R.* (for Regina) *v. Canadian Newspapers Co.*, or cases against the government (*Russell v. The Queen*); branches of the judiciary called the Court of Queen's Bench; and lawyers awarded the title of Queen's Counsel (Q.C.). The term "royal" is also widely used in Canada to refer to institutions that function for the advantage of all in the name of the Queen: royal commissions, investigating problems for the general good, and the Royal Canadian Mounted Police, charged with capturing violators of society's laws. Three important aspects of Parliament also reflect the existence of the monarchical system: royal assent, the Speech from the Throne, and Her Majesty's Loyal Opposition. "Loyal Opposition" demonstrates that criticism of the government has been legitimized and institutionalized in the name of the Queen.

The Queen of Canada, Elizabeth II, is also Queen of other countries, and normally resides in England. That means that she needs a local representative in Canada, the governor general, who may perform any of her functions and exercise any of her powers in her absence. Until 1926 the governor was a double agent: besides being the representative of the monarch, he was an agent of the British government, and as long as Canada was a British colony, the governor general exercised authority over Canada on behalf of the British cabinet. Today, the governor general has no connection whatsoever to the British government. The Canadian prime minister nominates the governor general, who, upon appointment by the Queen, serves a term of approximately five years.

Despite the impressive theoretical list of powers possessed by the Queen and governor general, there is no doubt that in a democratic age almost all of them must be exercised on the advice of the government—the prime minister and cabinet—of the day. The most important *prerogative power* of the governor general is the appointment of the prime minister, but this must be performed on the basis of constitutional convention. In ensuring that the office of prime minister is never vacant, the governor general normally relies on the operation of political parties and elections, and does not have far to look. On two occasions in the 1890s, however, the governor had to help find a person to be prime minister. Political parties are better organized today, and prefer to choose their own leader. Thus, if the position should suddenly become vacant, such as through the death of the prime minister, the cabinet and/or government caucus would usually name an acting leader pending a leadership convention.

The two most controversial discretionary acts of governors general took place in 1896 and 1926 when the governors not only acted on their own initiative but refused the advice of the prime minister and cabinet. The first concerned the question of making government appointments. Many appointments such as senators and judges are announced by the governor general, even though they are decided by the cabinet. But the Charles Tupper government chose to retain office after it lost the 1896 election (awaiting defeat in the House of Commons), and during that interim period presented a list of several recommended appointments to the governor general which he refused to make.

The second famous case of refusing government advice, the King–Byng dispute, had to do with the dissolution of Parliament. The governor general normally dissolves Parliament on the advice of the prime minister, but in 1926 Lord Byng refused Mackenzie King's request to do so and call an election. In this case, the governor general was primarily influenced by the fact that a motion of censure against the government regarding a scandal in the Customs Department was under debate in the House of Commons. The request for a dissolution appeared to be an attempt to avoid defeat in the Commons. In addition, the opposition Conservatives actually had more seats than the governing Liberals (who had been kept in power with the support of the Progressives), and an election had been held only eight months before. Thus, it seemed logical to Lord Byng to try to avoid an election when an alternative government might be available.

Whether any discretionary action of the governor general is constitutional today as a check on unconstitutional behaviour by prime ministers and cabinets remains an open question. Everyone is agreed, however, that in normal circumstances governors general must act on the advice of the prime minister and cabinet. Before they invoke such emergency powers, "they must be sure they have reached the danger point, and that their actions will stand up to the subsequent judgment of other institutions and the people."[4] The governor general has been called a "constitutional fire extinguisher" whose emergency powers can only be used "when normal controls cannot operate and a crisis gets out of hand."[5] Andrew Heard adds that "governors should intrude into the democratic process only to the minimum extent absolutely required for the basic functioning of Parliamentary government."[6] Since the governor general is intended to function as an impartial symbol of unity, any act that could remotely be interpreted as partisan must be avoided.

The Prime Minister and Cabinet
Powers of the Prime Minister and Cabinet

The prime minister and cabinet have the power to make the most significant governmental decisions. Given their importance, it is ironic that they are not provided for in the written parts of the Constitution, their functions and powers resting instead on custom and convention.[7] What *is* provided for in the 1867 Constitution Act is a Privy Council to advise the governor general in the exercise of the powers of that office. In fact, the cabinet acts as a committee of the Privy Council, but rather than merely advising the governor general, it actually makes the decisions in question. With rare exceptions, the prime minister and cabinet exercise whatever powers are given to the Queen or the governor general in the Constitution.

Thus, after an election, the governor general calls upon the leader of the party with most members elected to the House of Commons to become prime minister and to form a government. The prime minister assumes the title "Right Honourable" and selects the cabinet ministers, all of whom are sworn into the Privy Council. This allows them to use the title "Honourable" as well as the initials "P.C." (Privy Councillor, not to be confused with Progressive Conservative). Since these are lifelong appointments and titles, members of former cabinets remain in the Privy Council, but only those in the cabinet of the day are invited to cabinet meetings.

In normal circumstances, then, the prime minister and cabinet exercise the powers of the Crown. These powers include summoning and dissolving Parliament, the pardoning power, and the appointment of senators, judges, other officials, and royal commissions. The prime minister and cabinet recommend money bills to Parliament, and all international acts and the general conduct of foreign relations are the prerogative of the cabinet, including declarations of war and peace, signing treaties, appointing ambassadors, and recognizing foreign governments. The cabinet may feel it politically advantageous to have Parliament debate declarations of war and may need to submit legislation to Parliament to make treaties effective, but unlike the system in the United States, such international acts are essentially within the purview of the executive, not the legislature.

Exercising the powers of the Crown is only a small part of the reason that the prime minister and cabinet are the centre of gravity in the Canadian political system, however. More importantly, they have the responsibility for providing political leadership and determining priorities for the country. That is, the prime minister and cabinet decide which problems to deal with, establish the general thrust and direction of new policies, and determine the spending priorities of the government. In the British and Canadian systems, the responsibility for initiating legislation rests primarily with the cabinet. As seen in Chapter 15, opportunities do exist for other members of Parliament to introduce bills, but most of the time of the House of Commons is set aside for government business. The Speech from the Throne provides the cabinet with an opportunity to outline its legislative program at the beginning of the session. The cabinet's virtual monopoly over the passage of legislation should ensure coordination among government policies, while its total monopoly over financial legislation is designed to guarantee a close relationship between policies adopted and the funds to make them effective. Such strong executive leadership, based on tradition, necessity, and the Constitution Act, has evolved over many centuries, and has generally proven itself to be an effective way to run a country.

Beyond the powers of the Crown and this general leadership function, cabinet power is also derived from specific acts of Parliament. Almost every law delegates to a minister or the Governor in Council (i.e., the cabinet) the power to make decisions of many kinds. Similarly, it is largely based on acts of Parliament that individual ministers are charged with supervising the administration of their departments. They provide direction and leadership, establish priorities, and transmit their personal, party, and cabinet perspectives, all in an effort to ensure that public servants remain accountable to democratically elected leaders and public opinion. Ministers are also given quasi-legislative power to issue regulations under a law, sometimes called delegated or subordinate legislation, which flesh out the bare bones of the statute. In addition, ministers are involved in Parliament, answering questions about the department's operations, defending departmental spending proposals, and piloting bills emanating from the department.

The principle of ministerial responsibility—each minister being held responsible to Parliament for everything that goes on in his or her department— was once thought to entail a minister's resignation over public servants' errors, even those the minister knew nothing about.[8] In an age of big government, however, the principle has lost most of its meaning. Ministers can still be criticized for departmental failures and are expected to correct them, but they rarely resign except for monumental personal mistakes and conflicts of interest. Much depends on the personal ethical code of the minister to do the "proper thing,"[9] and the power to sanction error rests more with the prime minister (demotion or forced resignation) than with Parliament.

The Prime Minister

The system of government that Canada inherited from Britain has traditionally been called *cabinet government*, but most observers argue that such a label does not do justice to the modern pre-eminence of the prime minister. Political scientists disagree as to whether cabinet government has been completely transformed into a system of prime ministerial government, but no one doubts that the prime minister has enormous power and should be singled out for special attention. The pre-eminence of the prime minister over cabinet colleagues can be seen in 10 of the PM's principal powers, rights, or responsibilities. In many cases, these relate to the different arenas in which the prime minister must operate, such as cabinet, Parliament, party, media, federal–provincial relations, international diplomacy, and the economy, and are as follows:[10]

- cabinet-maker
- chair of cabinet meetings
- party leader
- chief policymaker
- dominates House of Commons
- holds power of appointment
- controls government organization
- advises governor general
- chief diplomat
- public persuader

First, the prime minister is the cabinet-maker.[11] Prime ministers select their own ministers, subject to certain conventions discussed below, and decide what portfolios to assign each of them. Ministers thus owe allegiance to the prime minister, who may sometimes dictate to them the policies they must adopt. The prime minister also promotes and demotes ministers, asks for their resignation, or, if necessary, dismisses them.

Chairing cabinet meetings is a second main source of the prime minister's power. To start with, the prime minister determines the agenda of such meetings, but in addition to the usual advantages of a chair, the prime minister benefits from the peculiar way in which cabinet decisions are arrived at. Rather than by motions and votes, the decision is reached when the PM summarizes the discussion and articulates the "consensus"—either by extracting a real consensus from the meeting or by imposing his or her own viewpoint. Ministers who do not agree with this interpretation either keep quiet or resign. Even though many decisions are now made by cabinet committees, the prime minister decides which committees will be struck, who will chair them, who will sit on them, and which matters will be sent to them, so that this delegation of power from the full cabinet does not necessarily reduce the PM's control.

In the third place, the prime minister is the leader of the party, and the PM's pre-eminence has probably increased over the years as political parties have become more cohesive and as election campaigns have come to focus on party leaders. In fact, many ministers may have been elected on the leader's coattails. As leader, the prime minister can control party organization, personnel, strategy, and policy.

Fourth, the prime minister could be called chief policymaker. The PM has the last word on government policy, whether in personal interaction with individual ministers, within the cabinet chamber, in Parliament, or in other forums such as the media. Modern government, of course, is too complex for one person to have an active role in formulating all policies, but the prime minister "can play a critical role in problem definition."[12]

In the fifth place, the prime minister is the central player in the House of Commons, although some prime ministers have had greater impact there and been better performers than others. Even though they now delegate control of the parliamentary agenda to the government House leader, they are still expected to be there for the oral Question Period every day.

A sixth source of prime ministerial pre-eminence is an enormous power of appointment. This includes the appointment of ministers, senators, Supreme Court judges, deputy ministers, and heads of a wide range of government agencies.

Given the extent and power of the bureaucracy today, the prime minister's seventh power, control over government organization, is also significant. Subject to usually routine parliamentary approval, the PM can decide to create new departments and set out their mandates, reorganize government departments, abolish departments or agencies, or privatize Crown corporations.

In the eighth place, the prime minister personally advises the governor general on such matters as when to call the next election. Furthermore, in an era of summit diplomacy, the prime minister often overshadows the minister of Foreign Affairs on the world stage, functioning as Canada's chief diplomat in annual bilateral meetings with the U.S. president, annual meetings of the Group of Seven leading industrialized countries, Commonwealth Conferences, meetings of the Francophonie, and occasional appearances at the United Nations.

The prime minister is also the chief "public relations officer" of the government, or "public persuader."[13] Television has become the main instrument for transmitting the prime minister's message to the party, the government, and the public. Survival in the battleground of media relations "threatens to become the key determinant of prime ministerial success."[14]

Given all these powers as well as a deferential majority in the House of Commons, the PM can usually succeed in controlling the policy and personnel of government. In many respects, in fact, the Canadian prime minister is more powerful than the American president, except of course in international clout. In order to get his agenda adopted, the latter must bargain with Congress in which party discipline is not strong, whereas prime ministers can normally count on a disciplined majority to back their measures. Indeed, the expansion of prime ministerial staff, the holding of prime ministerial news conferences, the making of televised addresses to the nation, luxurious travel arrangements, and other conspicuous trappings of power have led many observers to criticize the "presidentialization" of the office of prime minister.[15]

Others continue to emphasize the restraints on the power of the prime minister, such as financial constraints, opposition from the provinces, international influences, and the limits within which government policy of any kind can effect societal change. The prime minister is often at the mercy of events, which may bring about a fall in public support and a loss of much overall influence in turn. A list of prime ministers ranked by tenure reveals the variations in prime ministerial political fortunes.

PRIME MINISTERS OF CANADA, RANKED BY TENURE (YEARS)

Mackenzie King	22	Alexander Mackenzie	5
John A. Macdonald	19	Jean Chrétien	5+
Pierre Elliott Trudeau	15	John Thompson	2
Wilfrid Laurier	15	Arthur Meighen	2
Brian Mulroney	9	John Abbott	1
Robert L. Borden	9	Mackenzie Bowell	1
Louis St. Laurent	9	Joe Clark	9 mos.
John Diefenbaker	6	Kim Campbell	4 mos.
R.B. Bennett	5	John Turner	2 mos.
Lester Pearson	5	Charles Tupper	2 mos.

Composition of the Cabinet

In theory, all cabinet ministers are equal, although in practice this is far from being the case. All recent PMs, for example, designated one minister as deputy prime minister. In some cases, this title seemed to carry more prestige than any real power, but as deputy PM to Brian Mulroney, Don Mazankowski exercised general administrative control of the government and created a small deputy prime minister's office to support him. When Herb Gray replaced Sheila Copps in this capacity in 1997, the position was seen as becoming significant again.

Below the deputy PM are the regular departmental ministers, each normally in charge of a single department. An informal ranking of these departments may result in variations in influence among this group of ministers, with Finance, Foreign Affairs, Justice, International Trade, Treasury Board, and Human Resources usually being among the key portfolios. One rank lower than departmental ministers were the ministers of state who were members of the cabinet from the early 1970s to the early 1990s. They were junior ministers in charge of small agencies (e.g., Fitness and Amateur Sport), had responsibility for a particular constituency (e.g., women, youth, or seniors), or were assigned to assist a senior minister (e.g., Finance). In any case, somewhat similar to ministers without portfolio, they did not have regular departments to administer, but they did attend cabinet meetings. The list is completed with the government leaders in the House of Commons and the Senate.

Since the cabinet occupies such a central position in the Canadian policy-making process, every interest in the country would like to be represented in its deliberations. This desire alone creates pressure to expand its size. In general, the cabinet contained about 13 or 14 ministers before 1911, then rose to around 20 until about 1960, increasing to the 30 mark under Trudeau and to around 40 in the Mulroney period. Until Jean Chrétien, the Canadian tradition was that all ministers, even ministers of state, were included in the cabinet, so that, unlike Britain, no distinction existed between the cabinet and the ministry. Chrétien reduced the cabinet's size to 23 in 1993, supplemented by 9 junior ministers, called secretaries of state, who were part of the ministry but not invited to cabinet meetings. The secretaries of state each had a small staff and operating budget, and received 75 percent of a cabinet minister's pay. After the 1997 election, however, Chrétien's cabinet grew to 28, with 8 secretaries of state also sitting in the ministry.

Several conventions have developed to constrain the PM's prerogatives in the selection of ministers.[16] In the first place, reflecting the fact that Canada is a democracy and that the ministers represent the people, all cabinet ministers must have a seat in Parliament. Ministers sit in the legislative branch of government at the same time as they form the executive. Almost all ministers therefore have a seat in the House of Commons. It is possible for the prime minister to name someone to the cabinet who has not won election to the Commons, but convention dictates that such a person run in a by-election as soon as possible in order to obtain a seat. This sometimes happens when a PM chooses to appoint someone of unusual qualifications from outside parliamentary life, rather than a sitting backbencher, as Jean Chrétien did with Stéphane Dion and Pierre Pettigrew in 1996. The modern tradition is to include only one senator in the cabinet, usually serving as government leader in that chamber and having no departmental responsibilities.

The next constraint on the prime minister is the convention that each province be represented in the cabinet. This flows from the fact that Canada is a federation and that the Senate has never performed its intended role of representing provincial interests in Ottawa. Thus, with the occasional exception of Prince Edward Island, every province that has elected a member to the government side of the chamber has been awarded a cabinet position. This convention usually results in some ministers being appointed only because their province needs cabinet representation, rather than on their merits, leaving worthy MPs from other locations excluded. In both the Trudeau and Clark governments, the prime minister chose to appoint senators to the cabinet to represent provinces that had not elected any or enough government members (the three Western provinces in the former case and Quebec in the latter). That such a practice breaks the modern convention of having only one senator in the cabinet attests to the importance of provincial representation. In 1997, Chrétien responded to the absence of Liberal MPs from Nova Scotia by choosing his one senator from that province.

It is not only that residents of a province feel more secure if one of their number is in the cabinet; it is also very useful for the cabinet itself to have such provincial representation.[17] In fact, ministers essentially wear two hats: they speak for their department as well as for their province. This arrangement is functional for patronage as well as policy purposes: appointments and contracts awarded on a partisan basis in any province will be the responsibility of the resident minister, often called the "political minister" for that province.

Larger provinces are not content with a single minister, of course, and in a cabinet of 30 or 40 members, Ontario and Quebec have sometimes exceeded 10.

In such cases the ministers can be distributed so that each region within the province gains its own representative. Prior to 1984, however, Quebec was usually underrepresented in the cabinet when the Conservatives were in power, while the West was inadequately represented in the Pearson and Trudeau cabinets.

The next convention of Canadian cabinet-making is a recognition of the need for a balance of ethnic representatives. A proper balance of anglophone and francophone ministers—that is, about one-third francophone and two-thirds anglophone—may result almost automatically from the carefully constructed provincial representation. French-Canadians were underrepresented even in Liberal governments before 1963, however, and often grossly underrepresented in Conservative cabinets. It was only in the Pearson, Trudeau, and Mulroney cabinets that francophone ministers achieved or exceeded the one-third benchmark. Those of other ethnic origins were not proportionately represented except in the Clark and Mulroney cabinets.

As for other social divisions, religion was much more important in the pre-1900 period than it is today. Prime ministers are now more concerned to appoint women to the cabinet. Since it was difficult to include representatives of all social groups in a cabinet of only 23, Chrétien tried to appease others in the appointment of his 1993 secretaries of state: three women, one member from P.E.I., one Aboriginal, and one Asian.

The cabinet is therefore another locus of *elite accommodation*, and Matheson writes of a representative cabinet as follows:

> Adherence to the representation principle first introduced by Sir John A. Macdonald in 1867 has brought together the elites from the various subcultures and provided them with a means whereby they can work together to stabilize the Canadian political system. Thus in the Canadian context the cabinet has filled a dual role, for in addition to exercising the usual functions of executive leadership, the cabinet has provided an arena in which the elites may counter the dysfunctional and unstabilizing effects of cultural, regional, and religious fragmentation.[18]

Once the PM has chosen the people who will form the cabinet, they must be assigned portfolios, that is, departmental responsibilities. It is not normally expected that ministers will be expert in the field to which they are appointed, partly because the electorate is not likely to furnish the prime minister with members of Parliament having such credentials. Indeed, an argument can be made that a semi-expert is more dangerous than a total amateur since the latter will have enough sense to listen to the real experts within the department, while the former might try to substitute his or her limited knowledge for theirs. Thus, apart from the minister of Justice's normally being a lawyer, there is no necessary relationship between ministers' training or pre-political occupation and their departmental assignment.

Operation of the Cabinet

CABINET SOLIDARITY AND CABINET SECRECY

The cabinet is usually considered to be a collective decision-making body. Exceptions to this notion include the prime minister's making some decisions single-handedly, and decisions taken by cabinet committees or by individual ministers. Regardless of which or how many ministers are involved in making such decisions, however, the cabinet operates on the principle of *cabinet solidarity*, meaning that all ministers must publicly defend all cabinet policies or else resign. The most extreme manifestation of cabinet solidarity can be seen in terms of the annual budget, usually the most important government policy statement of the year. Only the Finance minister and PM know much about it until the budget is delivered in Parliament, yet all must support it. Ministerial resignations because of policy differences are rare in Canada, perhaps only 28 since 1867,[19] suggesting that the thought of giving up the perks of office engenders considerable flexibility in ministers' principles.

Cabinet solidarity and collective responsibility are also linked to a third principle, that of cabinet secrecy or confidentiality. Cabinet operations are shrouded in secrecy and ministers are not supposed to disclose information about its deliberations. Such confidentiality protects state secrets, protects the cabinet against opposition and media exploitation of ministerial discord, and protects senior civil servants from identification and public criticism. Cabinet documents are not normally made public for 30 years, and, as a result, we do not know as much about how the cabinet operates as about decision-making bodies that meet in public. On the other hand, clever ministers are conscious that information represents power and that a well-timed "leak" can sometimes be of benefit when involved in a battle within cabinet.

CABINET PROCEDURE

Before 1960 or so, perhaps especially in the Mackenzie King and St. Laurent eras, ministers and departments were largely autonomous. Each developed its own policies and programs with little regard for central coordination and with only minimal prime ministerial interference. Strong ministers could make many decisions and policies without consulting their colleagues, and such ministers tended to remain in charge of a single department for long periods of time. Such autonomous departmental ministers often doubled as strong regional ministers, who were also allowed to handle regional responsibilities on their own. In addition, senior bureaucrats usually served their careers within a single department and became "carriers of the interests, traditions, skills and memories of these particularized bureaucratic organizations."[20]

Despite what has been said above about collective cabinet decision-making, the change from autonomous ministers to collegial cabinet decisions is really a product of the post-1960 period and the enormous expansion of government activity in the following 30 years. As society and its problems became more complex, individual ministers and departments could no longer make decisions and policies in isolation. The policies of one department almost inevitably affected those of another. More consultation and coordination were called for, with the result that ministerial collegiality replaced departmental autonomy. To some extent the need for policy coordination coincided with the view that cabinet ministers should have greater control over the bureaucracy; another stimulus was the development of techniques for more rational government decision-making. The Pearson era was transitional in this respect, and the major change was adopted in the Trudeau period.

Much has been written on the Trudeau approach to increase the rationality of government policymaking, an approach involving five main elements.[21] First, the priorities and planning committee of cabinet established the overall priorities of the government. Second, the Prime Minister's Office and the Privy Council Office were expanded and strengthened so as to provide policy analysis to the prime minister and cabinet independent of other government departments. The Department of Finance and the Treasury Board also became more effective central agencies, advising the cabinet on its financial decisions. In the third place, to avoid cabinet overload and to enhance specialization and policy coordination within it, most of the cabinet's work was done in committees. Fourth, cabinet procedures were rigidly adhered to, including agendas, advance notice of issues, and advance circulation of background documents. Finally, new techniques of policy analysis, especially at the bureaucratic level, provided ministers with a more rational basis for their decisions. All of these measures tended to render cabinet decisions more coordinated, organized, disciplined, political, and rational, hence the term "institutionalized cabinet."[22]

The cabinet as a whole normally meets for about three or four hours once a week. An agenda is prepared under the prime minister's supervision and circulated in advance, together with background documents and cabinet committee decisions and recommendations. The cabinet usually tackles four or five major issues and several minor matters at each session. Rather than resolving questions by a formal vote, the prime minister sums up the discussion on each item and articulates the consensus arrived at. A handful of senior officials is on hand to take note of the discussion and decisions, and to circulate minutes afterward. Given the demands on the time of those involved, meetings are conducted in a very businesslike manner.

As mentioned, since the mid-1960s more and more of this work has been done by cabinet committees rather than by the full cabinet. Each committee also normally meets once a week; ministers are likely to be members of one or two committees. Unlike cabinet meetings, as such, ministers may bring advisers along to cabinet committees, so they are less reliant on their own personal resources. Between the Pearson and Mulroney regimes, the Priorities and Planning Committee was clearly the most important cabinet committee. Its special functions included setting priorities, allocating budgets, reviewing other committee decisions, making many important decisions itself, and supervising federal–provincial relations. Being chaired by the prime minister and containing the most important ministers (including the chairs of other cabinet committees) also added to its significance.

Jean Chrétien reverted to the St. Laurent model of a cabinet in which individual ministers and departments were allowed to look after their own affairs. The maze of cabinet committees was reduced, leaving only four (using post-1997 election names): Economic Union, Social Union, Treasury Board, and the Special Committee of Council.[23] Chrétien curtailed the scope of many other coordinating, central agencies, and departments were allowed more leeway in moving funds from one program to another. Even in an era of government downsizing, however, many observers felt that the complexity of issues required greater coordination and consultation, and that the 40-year-old model was no longer adequate. The Finance Department began to fill the gap, partly because the budget and the deficit were the driving forces of the day, but also because some kind of coordinating device was needed. Not everyone was satisfied with deficit reduction becoming the basis for policy coordination, however.

After the 1997 election, Chrétien altered the cabinet decision-making system to some extent. Cabinet itself would increase its focus on setting the government's overall agenda and spending priorities, as well as coordinating the work of its committees. Cabinet committees were given new responsibilities in overseeing specific areas of the government's agenda. The Treasury Board, for example, was reoriented to play an enhanced role as the government's management board, while the special committee of council expanded its jurisdiction to include management of legislative issues and planning.

Cabinet Support Agencies

In addition to regular departments that advise individual ministers, the subject of Chapter 14, four main agencies exist to support the prime minister and/or the cabinet as a whole:

- Prime Minister's Office
- Privy Council Office
- Finance Department
- Treasury Board

The Prime Minister's Office handles the prime minister's correspondence, media relations, partisan appointments, public appearances and speeches, and briefs the PM on legislative proceedings. It monitors political developments and offers policy advice from a partisan point of view. Jean Chrétien's PMO of about 85 bodies was headed by chief of staff Jean Pelletier. Its other principal officials were Eddie Goldenberg, senior policy adviser; Chaviva Hosek, policy and research director; Peter Donolo, director of communications; and Jean Carle, director of operations. The PM usually meets daily with the head of the PMO to be briefed on developments from a partisan perspective.

The Privy Council Office has served several unique purposes since it was recognized as the cabinet secretariat and since cabinet meetings became more businesslike in 1940 due to the pressures of war. First, it provides logistical support for the cabinet—organizing meetings, preparing agendas, writing and distributing background material ("briefing notes"), taking and circulating minutes, and communicating cabinet decisions. In these ways the PCO is engaged in the coordination of overall government policy. It also performs the same services for cabinet committees; in fact, a branch of the PCO serves as a secretariat for each cabinet committee (except for Treasury Board, which is supported by the Treasury Board Secretariat). Other sections of the Privy Council Office have responsibility for the machinery of government, the appointment of senior public service personnel, and federal–provincial relations. The head of the PCO, called the Secretary to the Cabinet and Clerk of the Privy Council, is regarded as the government's highest-ranking public servant. The Clerk meets daily with the prime minister to review problems and render nonpartisan advice. The PCO under Jean Chrétien was headed by Jocelyne Bourgon, the first woman to occupy this prestigious post. She and other PCO officials brief cabinet committee chairs and the prime minister even on the strategy of conducting their meetings, all of which helps the PCO obtain the kind of decisions that it considers best. Another example of its influence is in its detailed strategy notes for the prime minister when meeting important people or making critical telephone calls.

The Department of Finance and the Treasury Board primarily supply financial information to the cabinet, and have historically exercised a cautioning, restraining influence on new program proposals. The role of the Finance Department is to look at the government's overall revenue and expenditure situation, including its accumulated debt and annual deficit, and to advise on allocations among departments. Under the powerful deputy minister, it is also the chief adviser on taxation policy and on transfer payments to the provinces. While reporting directly to the minister of Finance and in that sense an ordinary department of government, Finance has a special responsibility of advising the cabinet collectively on such matters, being incorporated into the process of developing memoranda to cabinet as well as preparing the budget. In an age of government restraint and retrenchment, the influence of Finance necessarily increases, and in the Chrétien regime, that department basically determined the government's whole agenda.[24]

The Treasury Board is a committee of cabinet chaired by the minister called President of the Treasury Board, who is in turn in charge of a full-fledged government department, the Treasury Board Secretariat. This secretariat has the overall responsibility for controlling regular departmental spending, being involved in the detailed development of departmental budgets—the Estimates— and overseeing the actual expenditure of funds. The Treasury Board is also in charge of labour relations in the public service and issues policies on personnel, administration, and finance. In particular, Treasury Board approval is required for

Figure 13.2   The Expenditure Management System

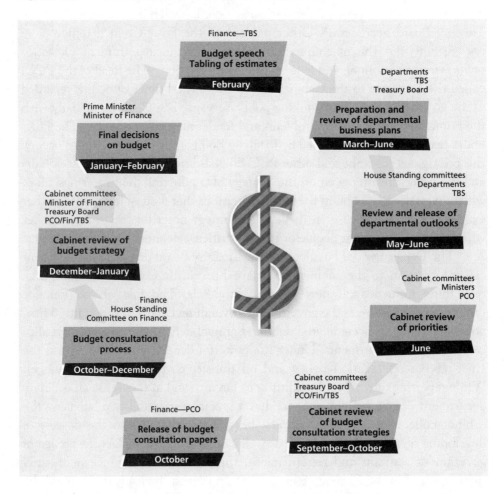

Source: Treasury Board of Canada Secretariat, The Expenditure Management System of the Government of Canada, 1995, cat. no. BT22-371/1995. Reproduced with permission of the Minister of Public Works and Government Services Canada, 1997.

the hiring of any new personnel. Although its perspective is more detailed than that of Finance, the two agencies usually see things in a similar light, and Treasury Board's influence also increases when a government is obsessed with its deficit.

Figure 13.2 outlines the expenditure-management system in the Chrétien government, which constituted the central core of its decision-making process.

NOTES

1. Leslie A. Pal, *Public Policy Analysis: An Introduction* (Toronto: Methuen, 1987), 4.
2. Department of Justice, *The Federal Legislative Process in Canada* (Ottawa: Supply and Services, 1987).
3. David E. Smith, *The Invisible Crown* (Toronto: University of Toronto Press, 1996).
4. Frank McKinnon, *The Crown in Canada* (Calgary: McClelland and Stewart West, 1976), 124.
5. Andrew Heard, *Canadian Constitutional Conventions* (Toronto: Oxford University Press, 1991), 123.
6. Ibid., 47.
7. Ibid., ch. 3.
8. Kenneth Kernaghan and David Siegel, *Public Administration in Canada: A Text*, 2nd ed. (Scarborough: Nelson Canada, 1991), 379–85.
9. Heard, *Canadian Constitutional Conventions*, 52–56.
10. Leslie Pal and David Taras, eds., *Prime Ministers and Premiers: Political Leadership and Public Policy in Canada* (Scarborough: Prentice-Hall Canada, 1988); Peter Aucoin, "Prime Ministerial Leadership: Position, Power, and Politics," in Maureen Mancuso et al., *Leaders and Leadership in Canada* (Toronto: Oxford University Press, 1994).
11. W.A. Matheson, *The Prime Minister and the Cabinet* (Toronto: Methuen, 1976), ch. 3; R.M. Punnett, *The Prime Minister in Canadian Government and Politics* (Toronto: Macmillan, 1977), ch. 4.
12. Leslie Pal, "Hands at the Helm? Leadership and Public Policy," in Pal and Taras, *Prime Ministers and Premiers*, 25.
13. Frederick Fletcher, "The Prime Minister as Public Persuader," in Thomas A. Hockin, ed., *Apex of Power*, 2nd ed. (Scarborough: Prentice-Hall Canada, 1977); Punnett, *The Prime Minister in Canadian Government and Politics*, 22.
14. David Taras, "Prime Ministers and the Media," in Pal and Taras, *Prime Ministers and Premiers*.
15. Denis Smith, "President and Parliament: The Transformation of Parliamentary Government in Canada," in Hockin, *Apex of Power*, 315.
16. Heard, *Canadian Constitutional Conventions*.
17. Herman Bakvis, *Regional Ministers* (Toronto: University of Toronto Press, 1991); "Cabinet Ministers: Leaders or Followers," in Maureen Mancuso, *Leaders and Leadership in Canada*.
18. Matheson, *The Prime Minister and the Cabinet*, ix, 22–23.
19. S.L. Sutherland, "Responsible Government and Ministerial Responsibility: Every Reform Is Its Own Problem," *Canadian Journal of Political Science* (March 1991): 101.
20. Donald Smiley, *The Federal Condition in Canada* (Toronto: McGraw-Hill Ryerson, 1987), 88.
21. Bruce Doern and Peter Aucoin, eds., *The Structures of Policy-Making in Canada* (Toronto: Macmillan, 1971), and *Public Policy in Canada* (Toronto: Macmillan, 1979); Colin Campbell and George Szablowski, *The Superbureaucrats* (Toronto: Macmillan, 1979); and several articles in Hockin's *Apex of Power*.
22. J. Stefan Dupré, "Reflections on the Workability of Executive Federalism," in Richard Simeon, ed., *Intergovernmental Relations* (Toronto: University of Toronto Press, 1985).
23. On the Chrétien changes, see *The New Face of Government: A Guide to the New Federal Government Structure*, 2nd ed. (Ottawa: Canada Communication Group, 1994).
24. Edward Greenspon and Anthony Wilson-Smith, *Double Vision: The Inside Story of the Liberals in Power* (Toronto: Doubleday Canada, 1996).

....

FURTHER READING

Bakvis, Herman. *Regional Ministers*. Toronto: University of Toronto Press, 1991.

Greenspon, Edward, and Anthony Wilson-Smith. *Double Vision: The Inside Story of the Liberals in Power*. Toronto: Doubleday Canada, 1996.

Heard, Andrew. *Canadian Constitutional Conventions*. Toronto: Oxford University Press, 1991.

Mancuso, Maureen, et al., eds. *Leaders and Leadership in Canada*. Toronto: Oxford University Press, 1994.

Matheson, W.A. *The Prime Minister and the Cabinet*. Toronto: Methuen, 1976.

McKinnon, Frank. *The Crown in Canada*. Calgary: McClelland and Stewart West, 1976.

Pal, Leslie, and David Taras, eds. *Prime Ministers and Premiers: Political Leadership and Public Policy in Canada*. Prentice-Hall Canada, 1988.

Punnett, R.M. *The Prime Minister in Canadian Government*. Toronto: Macmillan, 1977.

Smith, David E. *The Invisible Crown*. Toronto: University of Toronto Press, 1996.

Chapter 14

The Bureaucracy

Most citizens encounter public servants as providers of services, but the bureaucracy is probably even more significant in its advisory role. Modern government is so pervasive and complex that cabinet ministers hardly make a move without the advice of their permanent, expert staff. In fact, the bureaucracy has become so large and indispensable that many observers wonder whether it can be kept under political control.

This chapter begins by examining the functions and powers of the bureaucracy. It then deals in turn with the three main kinds of bureaucratic organization: the government department, the Crown corporation, and the regulatory agency. The chapter concludes with a discussion of controlling the bureaucracy and recent attempts to reform it.

Functions and Powers of the Bureaucracy

The significance of the bureaucracy can be demonstrated by examining its presence in the model of the policymaking process presented in Chapter 13. First, it plays a crucial part in the initiation phase. The bureaucracy may be a source of demands, since administrators of any program may be among the first to recognize its inadequacies. Even if a demand reaches the cabinet from other sources, once the politicians decide to look into an issue further, the public service will usually be asked to provide them with additional information and advice.

If the cabinet decides to take action at the priority-setting stage, the bureaucracy is then centrally involved in the policy formulation phase. With its concentration of technical information and experience, the public service spends a great deal of its time in formulating policies, since the details of such policies are usually beyond the grasp of the politicians.

Once the policy, program, or law has received political authorization by Parliament, implementation is almost exclusively a bureaucratic responsibility. In today's complex society, the politicians are forced to leave wide discretionary powers to the public service to carry out their general, abstract goals.[1] Because of the time and informational constraints on Parliament, most bills are passed in rather general or skeletal form, and the real meat or substance of the law is expressed in the regulations issued under it. These are published under the authority of the minister or cabinet in the *Canada Gazette*. A considerable lag often exists between the political approval of a law and its effective implementation, during which time the public service drafts such regulations, sets up new administrative machinery, and hires new personnel. The implementation phase may involve time-consuming negotiations with the provinces or with relevant interest groups. Once the date arrives for the start of a new program, it is the bureaucracy again that actually provides the service, does the regulating, or performs whatever other functions are involved. Implementation also requires the bureaucracy to disseminate information to the public about new policies or programs, and may even involve exercising quasi-judicial powers.

Given its role in almost all phases of the policymaking process, reference to "bureaucratic power" in political science or contentions that the bureaucracy is more powerful than the legislature or even the prime minister and cabinet should not be surprising. While it is more conventional to say that the cabinet makes the most important decisions in the political system and that it theoretically controls the bureaucracy, this is not to deny the extent of bureaucratic power in the modern state. The government of Canada currently employs about 500 000 people in the public service.

Government Departments

The most common forms of bureaucratic operations are regular government departments, Crown corporations, and regulatory agencies. Government departments are created and reorganized by acts of Parliament that also set out the responsibilities of each. But the cabinet can determine the internal structure of the department and can even transfer responsibilities from one department to another.

A major consolidation of departments took place in 1993, reducing the overall number from 25 to 20. As of 1997, the following departments existed:

- Agriculture and Agri-Food
- Canadian Heritage
- Citizenship and Immigration
- Environment

- Finance
- Fisheries and Oceans
- Foreign Affairs and International Trade*
- Health
- Human Resources Development
- Indian Affairs and Northern Development
- Industry
- Justice
- Labour
- National Defence
- National Revenue
- Natural Resources
- Public Works and Government Services
- Solicitor General
- Transport
- Treasury Board
- Veterans Affairs

The government department assumes a pyramidal shape, with the minister at its apex. Since ministers in this system (unlike the United States) are chosen from among the politicians elected to Parliament, it is too much to hope that they will be experts in the work of the department. All that is expected is that they have intelligence, ideas, common sense, and an ability to relay government priorities and public opinion to departmental experts as well as to relate expert advice from the department to Parliament and the public. Ministers will naturally develop some expertise if they stay in one cabinet position for any length of time, but nowadays they are often shuffled to another department just as they are getting the hang of it. Jean Chrétien reverted to the earlier practice of leaving ministers in place if moves could be avoided.

Ministers are responsible for their department in the sense that they are expected to provide overall direction and must accept criticism for its faults. In other words, ministers take most of the credit or blame for what the department does, whether or not they know what is going on within it. As pointed out in Chapter 13, the principle of ministerial responsibility was once thought to mean

---

* One department, but two separate ministers.

that ministers had to resign for serious mistakes made by their public servants. But no cases of this occurring have been recorded since 1867, and in this age of big government it is not a realistic proposition.[2] What does ministerial responsibility mean today? First, ministers occasionally resign over their personal mistakes. Second, they must take political responsibility and answer to Parliament for all actions of their officials. The minister must explain and defend the actions of the department in Parliament, especially during Question Period, and when a bureaucratic error is made, the minister must apologize and promise to correct the mistake. Third, although ministers may discretely discipline the offender, they should not violate the traditions of public-service anonymity.[3]

The more permanent head of the department is the deputy minister. Even though appointed by the prime minister (on the advice of the Secretary to the Cabinet), "deputies" or "DMs" are usually career public servants. Deputy ministers have two principal roles: they act as chief policy adviser to the minister and function as manager of the department. Such officials used to spend a lifetime working their way toward the top of a single department and became great experts in its subject matter. Over the past 35 years, however, emphasis in the appointment of deputy ministers has switched to managerial skills that can be applied in any administrative setting. Even though DMs are now frequently shuffled from one department to another, they are still usually there longer than the minister, and are thus likely to develop greater knowledge of the department's work. Deputy ministers also interact regularly with DMs in other federal departments, provincial DMs in corresponding departments, and the heads of pressure groups particularly interested in the department's work.

The relationship between the minister and the deputy minister is of great interest and concern to political science and public administration.[4] Ideally, the minister sets the priorities for the department while the DM provides a number of options among which the minister can choose. The deputy should give the minister advice based on administrative, technical, and financial considerations, but that is also sensitive to the political context. Evidence exists that the reality of the relationship sometimes approaches this theoretical ideal. On the other hand, weak ministers may be mere puppets of their bureaucratic advisers, and even strong ministers may encounter bureaucratic resistance to new initiatives, such as in being denied relevant information, having it delayed, or having new policies implemented without enthusiasm.[5]

It is not easy for a single, solitary, temporary, amateur minister to impose his or her will on thousands of expert, permanent public servants who have established departmental attitudes, values, policies, and procedures. Ministers are allowed to appoint a small personal staff, but it is primarily engaged in promoting the image and reputation of the minister. While the staff may provide partisan policy advice, any effort to interfere in the administration of the department will be strongly resented by the deputy minister. In the Mulroney regime, ministers set up large offices headed by a powerful chief of staff, and these were, among other things, the target of most lobbying efforts. As in other ways, Chrétien reverted to an earlier era by reducing the size and significance of ministerial offices and eliminating the chief of staff position. One sign of the lesser importance of such offices was that lobbyists transferred their attention to the bureaucracy.[6]

Under the deputy minister, the department is typically divided into several branches, each headed by an assistant deputy minister (ADM). The hierarchy broadens out below them. Those divisions of a department that actually carry out services and interact with the public are said to be performing "line" functions. Except for the top managerial posts, most of the line positions in any department will be located in the "field"—in local offices in communities across the country. But every department will also have "staff" divisions serving internal needs: policy development and research, personnel, financial, information, and legal divisions. These positions are normally located in Ottawa along with the heads of the line divisions.

Hundreds or thousands of public servants in the department are ranged in descending levels of authority under the deputy minister and share four basic characteristics: they are expert, permanent, impartial, and anonymous. First, they are chosen on their merits—ability, knowledge, training and/or experience—for the duties their position entails. Second, they are career public servants, normally remaining within the public service until retirement. Third, they are nonpartisan and expected to serve whichever party comes to power with equal loyalty and enthusiasm. Fourth, bureaucrats are not normally identified in public; instead, the minister speaks for the department and takes responsibility for its performance.

The federal public service is divided into six main occupational categories: management or executive; scientific and professional; administrative and foreign service; technical; administrative support; and operational. The first four categories are called "officer" categories, generally requiring postsecondary education, while the last two are called "support." University graduates are normally hired in the administrative and foreign service or scientific and professional groups and work their way up from there. Within each group are many levels or steps that determine one's salary level. It is an extremely complex operation to draw up a job description for so many positions and to evaluate and classify them for purposes of determining necessary qualifications and salary.

Relations with Other Departments and Central Agencies

The operation of a government department is complicated by the necessity of interacting with other departments as well as by the authority of various central bureaucratic agencies to intervene in its affairs. Since almost any law, policy, or program affects a variety of departments, many interdepartmental committees exist. Among the permanent ones are two Coordinating Committees of Deputy Ministers, one on management and the other on policy. Whenever any new policy is under active consideration, an ad hoc interdepartmental committee is appointed to look into it. Not only must the problem be examined from a number of departmental perspectives, but it is also subject to considerable bureaucratic "politics" and territorial claims.

The central agencies that complicate the life of a department include the Public Service Commission (PSC), the Treasury Board Secretariat (TBS), the Privy Council Office, the Department of Finance, and the Prime Minister's Office, most of which were mentioned in Chapter 13.

The Public Service Commission is a three-member board theoretically in charge of all hiring, promotions, and dismissals. In practice, however, the PSC delegates much of its authority to individual departments. It is primarily concerned to police the merit system and prevent appointments and promotions from being made on partisan or discriminatory grounds.

The Treasury Board Secretariat has responsibility for personnel, financial, and expenditure management. The TBS determines the terms and conditions of employment for the public service, approves the creation and classification of new positions, and represents the employer in the collective bargaining process. On the financial-management side, the TBS is responsible for the preparation of the Estimates, which normally involves cutting back on departmental spending proposals, especially when the government's priority is to reduce the deficit. It also issues all sorts of administrative policies such as on purchasing, contracts, and travel. The Department of Finance is normally allied with the TBS as an opponent of new departmental spending programs.

The Privy Council Office's relations with regular government departments primarily arise in connection with policy development and coordination, reallo-cation of programs between departments, reorganization of departments, and senior management appointments. The Prime Minister's Office, on the other hand, does not often interact with departments except with respect to new pol-icy initiatives or political problems that engage the prime minister. Government-wide services such as purchasing and accommodation are provided by the Public Works and Supply and Services Department.

Staffing the Bureaucracy

The Canadian public service originally operated on the *spoils system*, under which the party that won an election replaced those holding civil service positions with its own friends and supporters. One of the main motives for entering the politi-cal arena was to reward family and friends with political patronage—government jobs and contracts.[7] Such partisan, amateur personnel proved to be increasingly inadequate as government operations grew more complex after the turn of the century, leading to the creation of the Civil Service Commission, predecessor to the Public Service Commission, in 1908. Henceforth, public servants in Ottawa were supposed to be hired on merit, and after passage of the 1918 Civil Service Act, field positions were also to be based on merit. Politicians were reluctant to give up their traditional right to reward their supporters with government jobs, however, and the foundations of the modern merit system in Ottawa were not really laid until the 1930s.[8]

Even if patronage was virtually eliminated in the public service, there remained considerable scope for partisan appointments in other areas. Senators, the boards of regulatory agencies and Crown corporations, certain diplomatic posts, the PMO and ministers' offices, lieutenant governorships, citizenship judgeships, and some real judgeships were all positions where partisan appoint-ments still prevailed. The Liberals accused Brian Mulroney of excessive patron-age, but the Chrétien government, despite its reputation, was no more restrained.

Almost as soon as the merit system was fully effective, people began to demand that the bureaucracy be more representative of the society that it served. Given the power of the public service, many critics argued that the public service could be responsive to all parts of society only if it included a proportional rep-resentation of various groups in the population. The senior levels of the public service had always overrepresented males, anglophones, the middle and upper classes, the well educated, and Ontarians. Thus it was claimed that policy recommendations and implementation reflected an insensitivity to women, the working class, the poor, francophones and other ethnics, and the peculiarities of hinterland regions.

The first main concerns in this connection were the small number of francophones in the higher reaches of the bureaucracy and the virtual absence of the use of the French language at policymaking levels. The passage of the Official Languages Act in 1969 essentially bilingualized the executive branch of government. It gave both English- and French-speaking citizens the right to deal with head offices of government departments in either official language, as well as with local offices where numbers warranted. It also expanded language-training programs, made recruitment and promotion of francophones a higher priority, and designated certain positions as bilingual. It was fortunate that the Quebec educational system had improved by this time so that the new policy involved little or no loss of quality in government appointments and promotions. It did, however, ignite a backlash against the preference given to French Canadians and to bilingualism. As of March 31, 1996, 31 percent of public-service positions had been designated as bilingual, 58 percent as English essential, 6 percent as French essential, and 4 percent as requiring either official language. Table 14.1 shows the language designation of actual public servants by category. The figures in the table bear a reasonably close approximation to census statistics (French mother tongue just under 25 percent), although francophones are overrepresented in the administrative and foreign service and administrative support categories.

TABLE 14.1 LANGUAGE DESIGNATION OF PUBLIC SERVANTS BY CATEGORY

	Anglophone		Francophone		
	Number	%	Number	%	Total
Management	2 168	76	684	24	2 852
Scientific & professional	18 096	76	5 714	24	23 810
Administrative & foreign service	46 039	68	21 665	32	67 704
Technical	18 417	78	5 195	22	23 612
Administrative support	36 307	66	18 704	34	55 011
Operational	21 270	77	6 354	23	27 624
Total	142 459	71	58 188	29	200 647

Source: Treasury Board of Canada Secretariat, Official Languages in Federal Institutions, Annual Report 1995–1996 (Ottawa: Supply and Services, 1996). Reproduced with the permission of the Minister of Public Works and Government Services Canada, 1997.

Women also began to be targeted for increased representation in the higher levels of the public service in the 1960s and 1970s.[9] In addition, the pay equity program of the 1980s and 1990s was primarily designed to ensure that women received equal pay for doing work having the same value as that done by men. Many occupational groups made up largely of women have had their salaries increased as a result.

The next stage of making the public service more representative of society came in 1983 when an explicit affirmative action program was adopted for women, Aboriginals, and the disabled, and two years later visible minorities were added to the list. Once again, this did not necessarily result in a decline in the quality of appointments and promotions, but it sparked opposition from those who did not fall into the designated categories, such as able-bodied, anglophone, white males. Table 14.2 provides 1996 figures by equity categories.

TABLE 14.2 PUBLIC SERVICE BY EMPLOYMENT EQUITY CATEGORIES, 1996

	Women		Aboriginals		People with Disabilities		Visible Minorities		
	Number	%	Number	%	Number	%	Number	%	Total
Executive	725	21.3	54	1.6	71	2.1	78	2.3	3 399
Scientific & professional	7 212	30.2	328	1.4	447	1.9	2 165	9.1	23 917
Administrative & foreign service	35 709	50.1	1 633	2.3	2 479	3.5	3 106	4.4	71 237
Technical	4 662	19.9	315	1.3	431	1.8	637	2.7	23 477
Administrative support	45 096	84.6	1 559	2.9	2 268	4.3	2490	4.7	53 301
Operational	3 390	13.2	776	3.0	595	2.3	505	2.0	25 678
Total	96 794	48.2	4 665	2.3	6 291	3.1	8 981	4.5	201 009

Source: Treasury Board of Canada Secretariat, Employment Equity in the Public Service, Annual Report 1995–1996 (Ottawa: Supply and Services, 1996). Reproduced with the permission of the Minister of Public Works and Government Services Canada, 1997.

Collective Bargaining

Until they were granted collective-bargaining rights in 1967, public servants had little input into determining their level of salary or other terms and conditions of employment. Seventy or so occupational groups now constitute bargaining units whose representatives engage in negotiations with the Treasury Board. These separate collective agreements involve 16 different unions, the largest being the Public Service Alliance of Canada (PSAC), representing about 165 000 employees. When renegotiating their contract, the bargaining agent must specify in advance whether it wishes to have a possible impasse resolved by referral to binding arbitration or to a conciliation board, leading, if necessary, to a strike. Most bargaining units choose the latter option, and several public-service strikes have occurred, especially among postal workers. The severe limitation on public service salary increases announced in the 1991 budget resulted in a 33-day strike by the PSAC involving about 70 000 workers.

Certain subjects are recognized as rights of the employer and are not negotiable, and certain groups of public servants are excluded from the collective bargaining process. Moreover, on several occasions the government has suspended collective bargaining on monetary matters as well as the right to strike. Public-service salaries were repeatedly frozen during the 1990s.

The Estimates System

As noted earlier, the authorities spend a great deal of their time discussing the expenditure of public funds. Members of Parliament want money allocated to their constituencies, premiers and federal ministers press to get funds allocated to their provinces, and bureaucrats seek funding for their programs and departments. In addition, much of the pressure from interest groups and corporations consists of demands for federal funds. In earlier eras, such spending was the prerogative of individual politicians or governing parties and was carried out on a patronage basis. Nowadays, the spending process has been highly bureaucratized, and it is the function of the Estimates system to decide how such funds will be allocated in any fiscal year.

On the advice on the Finance Department, the Treasury Board, and the Privy Council Office, the cabinet decides what the government's financial priorities and overall levels of government revenue and expenditure will be, as well as approving any new spending initiatives. The preparation of the Estimates involves projections of the cost of new and existing programs at the departmental level within these limits and guidelines. A great deal of interaction takes place between departments and the Treasury Board Secretariat as deputy ministers and ministers try to maximize their departmental allocations while Treasury Board personnel engage in cutting them back. At the end of the process, the Estimates are consolidated for cabinet approval and introduced into Parliament by the President of the Treasury Board before the beginning of the next fiscal year.

Interaction with Provinces and Pressure Groups

Much of the interaction between federal and provincial governments takes place at the bureaucratic level. Because the division of powers is often vague and because both federal and provincial personnel usually try to maximize their jurisdiction, the two levels end up operating programs in the same fields. Limitations on provincial finances have also prompted the provinces to request federal financial assistance, to which Ottawa has usually attached conditions, making it even more intertwined with provincial governments.

At the height of cooperative federalism, federal and provincial program administrators would often interact harmoniously in the design and operation of such integrated programs as the Canada Assistance Plan.[10] In many federal departments, line officials still interact regularly with their provincial counterparts. Nowadays, however, with federal funding in short supply, they are less likely to be engaged in developing new initiatives and are more often trying to disengage.

The close relationship between pressure groups and the bureaucracy was discussed in Chapter 10. Groups wishing to influence either the formulation or the implementation of policies and programs are active in taking their message to the relevant government department. Sometimes public servants resist the approach of self-seeking groups, but the department will be more receptive if the group has vital, reliable information that will lead to the development of a more effective program or can help muster support for the departmental initiative among other key players in the policymaking process.

These mutually advantageous contacts between a group and a department may result in a symbiotic, *clientele relationship*. It will generally be in the interest of both the department and the group to keep their relationship somewhat confidential so that they can present a united front in case central agencies and cabinet committees become involved.

Crown Corporations

The second-most important form of bureaucratic organization is the Crown corporation. Crown corporations may be private firms that have been nationalized by the government by buying their shares, or they may be transformed from regular departments or created from scratch. Several hundred Crown corporations exist at the federal level. The largest in terms of employees in 1996 were Canada Post (44 107), CBC (8181), VIA Rail (3178), and AECL (3881).

MAJOR FEDERAL CROWN CORPORATIONS, 1997

- Atomic Energy of Canada Ltd.
- Bank of Canada
- Business Development Bank of Canada
- Canada Mortgage and Housing Corporation
- Canada Ports Corporation
- Canada Post Corporation
- Canadian Broadcasting Corporation
- Canadian Wheat Board
- Cape Breton Development Corporation
- Export Development Corporation
- Farm Credit Corporation
- Marine Atlantic Inc.
- National Capital Commission
- Royal Canadian Mint
- St. Lawrence Seaway Authority
- VIA Rail Canada Inc.

One major difference between a Crown corporation and a regular government department can be seen in its structure. A Crown corporation includes a board of directors, president, vice-presidents, and general manager. The cabinet appoints the board of directors, which theoretically sets the general policy of the corporation, as well as the president.

A second distinguishing feature of the Crown corporation is that it is not subject to day-to-day political direction. The statute that creates it sets out its objectives to some extent, and the cabinet may issue general policy guidelines, but the corporation otherwise operates more or less independently. The cabinet minister to whom the Crown corporation is attached acts largely as a channel of communication between it and Parliament, passing on answers to parliamentary inquiries but not being held responsible for the corporation in the same way as for a regular department. On the other hand, because the government created the Crown corporation, appoints its leading personnel, and usually provides some of its funds, the minister and cabinet cannot avoid complete responsibility for its actions. In some cases the cabinet can issue a directive to the corporation if informal persuasion to change its ways has not been effective. A government obsessed with its deficit can make deep cuts in a Crown corporation's budget, as the CBC found throughout the Mulroney and Chrétien periods.

In the third place, Crown corporations are freer of bureaucratic controls than ordinary government departments. They are not usually subject to the same personnel supervision by the Public Service Commission, for example, or quite the same financial control by the Treasury Board. They can therefore operate more flexibly, especially if they are in competition with private firms. The Financial Administration Act lists different categories of Crown corporations, ranged in order of increasing independence from government control; as a general rule, the greater the financial self-sufficiency of the corporation, the greater its autonomy.

The Crown corporation is a logical structure for a governmental operation of a commercial or industrial nature. It may also be used in politically sensitive areas such as broadcasting, and the case for a Crown corporation rather than a department is always stronger if the operation has private-sector competition. More specifically, Crown corporations have been created to promote national integration (VIA Rail, and previously Air Canada and CN), national identity (CBC and Canada Museums), economic development (Cape Breton Development Corporation), a particular industry (Canadian Wheat Board), and to save the jobs of a failing company (the temporary nationalization of Canadair and de Havilland Aircraft).

Like other government operations, then, Crown corporations have a public policy purpose. They are created where, for one reason or another, the private sector has not met public needs. The basic objective of Crown corporations is to provide a public service, not to make a profit, but because most Crown corporations need annual public subsidies, they are often criticized for being inefficient. In fact, however, they may be just as efficient as private companies; the subsidies are necessary because many Crown corporations operate in areas where no profit is feasible.

The 1980s witnessed a worldwide trend toward the privatization of public enterprises, led by Margaret Thatcher in Britain, and the Mulroney government happily jumped on the bandwagon. Privatizations were largely made for two ideological reasons: the government had an instinctive preference for the private sector, and the sale of Crown corporation shares helped to reduce the national deficit. Privatizers also argued that such Crown corporations no longer served a public-policy purpose and that they would operate more efficiently as private companies. As of 1995, the federal government estimated that it had carried out at least 23 privatizations, raising some $4 billion and transferring 52 000 employees to the private sector.

The new Liberal government claimed that privatization was no longer an ideological issue. Finance Minister Paul Martin said: "If the government doesn't need to run something, it shouldn't. And in future, it won't." He argued that privatization freed up scarce resources for deficit reduction or new initiatives, that government was rethinking its role in society, that privatization reduced the scope of government to essentials, and that it improved service delivery, exposed government organizations to competitive business pressures, and broadened ownership of the Canadian economy. Against this background, the Chrétien government announced that it would privatize the second-largest Crown corporation, the Canadian National Railway Company, and had other cases under consideration.

MAJOR FEDERAL PRIVATIZATIONS, 1984–1997

- Air Canada
- Canada Development Corporation
- Canadair
- Canadian Arsenals Ltd.
- Canadian National Railway and subsidiaries
- Co-Enerco Resources
- de Havilland Aircraft
- Eldorado Nuclear (Cameco)
- Fishery Products International
- Nordion International Inc.
- Northern Canada Power Commission
- Northern Transportation Company
- Petro-Canada
- Teleglobe Canada
- Telesat

··

Regulatory Agencies

Regulatory agencies are the third basic form of bureaucratic organization. Such agencies regulate many aspects of our daily lives. Some of the most important are listed below.

LEADING REGULATORY AGENCIES

- Atomic Energy Control Board
- Canadian Human Rights Commission
- Canadian Labour Relations Board
- Canadian Radio-television and Telecommunications Commission (CRTC)
- Canadian Transportation Authority
- Immigration and Refugee Board
- Investment Canada
- National Energy Board
- National Parole Board

In structure, regulatory agencies bear considerable resemblance to Crown corporations. They are made up of a chair and board appointed by the cabinet and are advised by a permanent, expert staff. The incidence of partisanship in appointments to the chair and board is unfortunately quite large; indeed, regulatory agencies remain one of the last refuges of patronage in the political system. Regulatory agencies typically receive policy guidelines from the cabinet, but as with Crown corporations, ministers are kept at arm's length from their day-to-day operations.

Regulatory agencies may make *quasi-legislative* rules and regulations, such as in the case of the Canadian content regulations of the CRTC. A typical regulatory agency also makes *quasi-judicial* decisions based on the cabinet's policy guidelines and its own regulations. They recognize unions (Canadian Labour Relations Board), approve foreign investment (Investment Canada), decide contentious immigration cases (Immigration and Refugee Board), and review transportation rates (Canadian Transportation Authority).

These functions could presumably be performed by regular government departments, but they are given to semi-independent regulatory agencies in order to divorce them from political and partisan considerations. Such adjudicative functions could also be performed by the courts. But these kinds of decisions demand a technical expertise not expected in judges, and given the backlog in the court system, it is hoped that the decisions of regulatory agencies will be made more quickly and more cheaply than those of the courts.

At the same time, however, regulatory agencies are expected to provide an impartial, court-like hearing, and in many cases lawyers are present in the same capacity as in court. Decisions of such agencies are normally appealable to the courts on procedural grounds, but not on the substance of the case. Some are appealable to the cabinet on the merits of the case.

Not all government operations fall into the three categories discussed above. "Structural heretics"[11] include central agencies, royal commissions, task forces, advisory councils, funding bodies, and other one-of-a-kind agencies (Elections Canada, the RCMP, and the Canadian Security Intelligence Service).

Task forces are an informal means of quickly acquiring information and recommendations. They may be composed of members of Parliament, ministers, public servants, outsiders, or some combination thereof. Task forces were used most extensively in the early Trudeau years: the new prime minister came to power with a desire to do things differently but without much knowledge of many issues and with typical suspicion of public service resistance to change. The most prominent was probably Herb Gray's Task Force on Foreign Investment.

Royal commissions are a much older instrument, about 450 having been appointed since 1867. They are formal, in-depth inquiries set up by the cabinet to investigate some difficult problem for which the resources of the regular public service are considered inadequate. Royal commissions may be headed by up to 10 commissioners, usually people of stature and expertise, and normally involve extensive public hearings and an elaborate research program. They are often regarded somewhat cynically because of their cost and the length of time it takes them to produce a report. Cynics also point out that governments have not had a good record of implementing royal commission recommendations, and that such commissions often appear to be appointed to take the heat off of a particular issue. Sometimes they are also seen as devices with which to educate the public to the government's way of thinking or to generate support for a policy the government already had in mind. Nevertheless, many royal commissions have served a useful purpose and many public policies such as equalization payments, medicare, bilingualism, and free trade owe their existence, at least in part, to royal commission reports. Whatever their formal name, they are often referred to by the name of their chair, such as Rowell–Sirois (Federal–Provincial Relations, 1940), Hall (Health Services, 1964–65), and Macdonald (Economic Prospects, 1985).

Controlling the Bureaucracy

Given the enormous influence and considerable power of the bureaucracy in the modern state, democracies are understandably concerned about keeping the public service under control. A number of means of doing so can be identified.

In the first place, individual ministers and the cabinet as a whole are supposed to provide political control of the bureaucracy. The minister gives direction to the public service and has the power to veto any of its proposals. Ministers have provided varied accounts of what happens in practice: some argue that they do control their departments, while others feel that they are manipulated by their public servants. Even where the minister in charge is weak or manipulated, however, the cabinet as a whole may step in to reject bureaucratic advice and opt for a proposal whose political implications are more favourable.

In the second place, the power of some bureaucrats is controlled by other bureaucrats, such as the financial control of the Treasury Board and the Finance Department, the personnel control of the Public Service Commission, and the policy control of the Privy Council Office. To some extent the central agencies operate on the orders of the cabinet or cabinet committees, so that these agencies supplement the political control mentioned above.

The third line of defence against bureaucratic power is the House of Commons. One principle of parliamentary government is that the executive (cabinet or bureaucracy) is not allowed either to raise or to spend money without Parliament's approval. In practice, proposals for tax changes as well as spending proposals all originate with the executive, they are rarely altered in the legislative process, and the taxing and spending usually begins before Parliament has given its consent. Examining the Estimates, however, gives the House of Commons an opportunity to question and criticize ministers and deputy ministers about all aspects of their departmental spending, programs, and policies. Furthermore, once the money has been spent, an official of Parliament, the Auditor General, inspects the Public Accounts and informs Parliament in an annual report of instances where funds were spend unlawfully or unwisely.[12] Considerable controversy raged in the 1980s over the size of the Auditor General's staff, their ability to gain access to cabinet documents, and whether they should function narrowly as auditors or make broader policy recommendations. The Public Accounts Committee of the House (chaired by an opposition member) goes through the Auditor General's report and calls onto the carpet those ministers or deputy ministers who have committed the worst financial faults.

The House of Commons has several other means of exercising some control over the bureaucracy, the first being the daily, oral Question Period. In this case, the Commons acts through the intermediary minister who is theoretically responsible for everything the department does. While the minister is expected to take the blame for bureaucratic errors, public servants seek to avoid bringing such embarrassment or disrepute upon their minister and department. In addition, members of Parliament receive requests on a daily basis from their constituents to intervene on their behalf to speed up or correct bureaucratic decisions. MPs and their staff normally handle such problems with a telephone call or a letter to the public servant or minister concerned. Another aspect of parliamentary control of the bureaucracy is exercised by the Standing Joint Committee on the Scrutiny of Regulations, which attempts to review the reams of regulations that the bureaucracy produces annually.

A fourth kind of control of the bureaucracy is provided by the judiciary. The power of the courts to overturn decisions of bureaucrats in regular government departments is essentially restricted to cases of breaches of the law or actions taken beyond the public servant's jurisdiction. The Charter of Rights provides more scope for this kind of judicial review than has existed in the past, and in the *Singh* case, for example, the Supreme Court ruled that the Immigration Department had to provide an oral hearing for refugee claimants. Regulatory agencies are usually expected to operate in a court-like manner, and their decisions can be overturned by the courts for procedural abuses as well as for exceeding their jurisdiction. The Federal Court of Canada, discussed in Chapter 16, specializes in hearing appeals from such regulatory agencies.

Finally, of several independent watchdog agencies, perhaps the most important is the Information Commissioner. Canadian governments have traditionally functioned under a thick cloak of secrecy at both the cabinet and bureaucratic levels. This tradition prevented the opposition and the public from knowing what alternative policies were considered, what kind of public opinion polling was done, or what advice was actually offered by the bureaucracy. The 1983 Access to Information Act considerably improved the situation, although the many exemptions in the act mean that it is not entirely effective. If a citizen, journalist, company, or pressure group is denied access to a desired piece of government information, they can appeal to the Information Commissioner, who can overrule the department in the matter, with a final appeal to the Federal Court.

Dysfunctions and Reform of the Bureaucracy

Apart from the problem of keeping the bureaucracy under some kind of democratic control, three other problems or dysfunctions are often identified. First, from the public's perspective, the bureaucracy is accused of being bound up in "red tape." This generally includes a collection of sins that characterize the behaviour of all large organizations, not only governmental ones, including delays, a multitude of forms, excessive rules and regulations, difficulty in finding the appropriate official to solve a problem, and lack of helpful, personal attention. If these dysfunctions are more characteristic of government than of large private firms, it is primarily because governments are required to operate according to the law and the regulations issued under the law. Government must treat everyone in exactly the same way, and unlike private firms, cannot show favouritism or make individual deals. Delays are usually the result of public servants wanting to be certain their decision is absolutely right, because mistakes may be criticized in Parliament or in the media.

A second general criticism of bureaucracy is that it is inefficient because it lacks the profit motive of the private sector. Officials in private firms are said to move more quickly because they are in greater danger of losing their jobs and because minimizing costs is a higher priority. To some extent this is true. Given that the essential difference between the public and private sectors is that the bureaucracy is charged with providing a public service, however, it should be judged primarily on the adequacy of that service. Nevertheless, the widespread belief that there is much "fat" and inefficiency within the bureaucracy led both the Mulroney and Chrétien governments to impose severe financial restraints on government departments and some Crown corporations, leading them to make across-the-board cuts, terminate programs, lay off staff, freeze hiring, charge user fees, and contract out certain services.[13]

From a management point of view, the main dysfunction of the public service is that deputy ministers and other managerial personnel are too hemmed in by rules and regulations and their authority is too limited by central agencies. In consequence, in 1986 the Mulroney government introduced the Increased Ministerial Authority and Accountability (IMAA) process. The objective of IMAA was to provide more autonomy and managerial flexibility to deputy ministers by relaxing some of the detailed rules and reporting requirements.

Three other recent bureaucratic reforms also related to these dysfunctions.

First, as mentioned, Prime Ministers Mulroney and Campbell undertook a major restructuring of government departments in 1993. The second is the establishment of Special Operating Agencies (SOAs). These are units that function with relative autonomy within government departments. In most cases they have the potential to become self-financing, and the basic objective is to deliver a service along private-sector lines—that is, in a manner that is more sensitive to client requirements, promotes a more creative, entrepreneurial working environment, and brings savings to government. These units have a minimal role in advising on policy, and their autonomy is based on a framework agreement with the department. The head of the unit reports to the deputy minister, and the departmental minister retains political responsibility. The Passport and Patent (Canadian Intellectual Property) Offices are examples of the 19 SOAs created by 1997. More are likely in the future.

In the third place, the minister of Finance in his 1995 budget declared his intention to eliminate 45 000 public service jobs by 1998. Some public servants would be eligible for buyouts and early retirement packages, and some would be able to swap jobs with those who wished to leave but whose jobs were secure. Eleven departments were identified for the most drastic cuts—especially Transport, many of whose operations were privatized—but the policy was service-wide. The announcement aroused great opposition from public-sector unions, especially the PSAC, which had earlier suggested alternative ways of saving government money. That budget also reflected the government's intention to reduce its costs and commitments by shifting responsibility for many programs to the provinces in order to eliminate overlap and duplication. Provincialization, commercialization, contracting out, establishing more autonomous operational units, reducing transfers, and laying off staff are all part of the new focus on "alternative service delivery" or ASD.

During the first half of the 1990s, then, politicians made rather drastic changes in the Canadian federal public service. These served primarily to help the government reduce its deficit, but they do not exhaust the reforms that would make it a more effective public service for all concerned.

. . . .

NOTES

1. Kenneth Kernaghan and David Siegel, *Public Administration in Canada: A Text*, 2nd ed. (Scarborough: Nelson Canada, 1991), 137. A third edition was published in 1995.
2. S.L. Sutherland, "Responsible Government and Ministerial Responsibility: Every Reform Is

Its Own Problem," *Canadian Journal of Political Science* (March 1991): 91–120.
3. Kernaghan and Siegel, *Public Administration in Canada*, 379–85; S.L. Sutherland, "The Al-Mashat Affair: Administrative Responsibility in Parliamentary Institutions," *Canadian Public Administration* (Winter 1991): 573–603.
4. Gordon Osbaldeston, *Keeping Deputy Ministers Accountable* (Toronto: McGraw-Hill Ryerson, 1990).
5. See the exchange between Flora Macdonald and Mitchell Sharp in Paul Fox and Graham White, eds., *Politics: Canada*, 7th ed. (Toronto: McGraw-Hill Ryerson, 1991), and between Flora Macdonald and Don Page in Mark Charlton and Paul Barker, eds., *Crosscurrents: Contemporary Political Issues*, 2nd ed. (Scarborough: Nelson Canada, 1994).
6. Interview with John Chenier, editor of *The Federal Lobbyists*.
7. Jeffrey Simpson, *Spoils of Power* (Toronto: Collins, 1988); S.J.R. Noel, "Leadership and Clientelism," in David Bellamy et al., eds., *The Provincial Political Systems* (Toronto: Methuen, 1976).
8. J.L. Granatstein, *The Ottawa Men: The Civil Service Mandarins 1935–1957* (Toronto: Oxford University Press, 1982).
9. Kathleen Archibald, *Sex and the Public Service* (Ottawa: Queen's Printer, 1970); Task Force on Barriers to Women in the Public Service, *Beneath the Veneer*, Vol. 1 (Ottawa: Supply and Services, 1990).
10. Rand Dyck, "The Canada Assistance Plan: The Ultimate in Cooperative Federalism," *Canadian Public Administration* (Winter 1976).
11. J.E. Hodgetts, *The Canadian Public Service: A Physiology of Government, 1867–1970* (Toronto: University of Toronto Press, 1973).
12. S.L. Sutherland, "On the Audit Trail of the Auditor General: Parliament's Servant, 1973–80," *Canadian Public Administration* (Winter 1980): 616–44; S.L. Sutherland, "The Politics of Audit: The Federal Office of the Auditor General in Comparative Perspective," *Canadian Public Administration* (Spring 1986): 118–48.
13. Kernaghan and Siegel, *Public Administration in Canada*, 498–502.

FURTHER READING

Adie, Robert, and Paul Thomas. *Canadian Public Administration*. 2nd ed. Scarborough: Prentice-Hall Canada, 1987.
Kernaghan, Kenneth, and David Siegel. *Public Administration in Canada: A Text*. 2nd ed. Scarborough: Nelson Canada, 1991; 3rd ed., 1995.
Osbaldeston, Gordon. *Keeping Deputy Ministers Accountable*. Toronto: McGraw-Hill Ryerson, 1989.
Plumptre, T.W. *Beyond the Bottom Line: Management in Government*. Halifax: Institute for Research on Public Policy, 1988.
Savoie, Donald. *The Politics of Public Spending in Canada*. Toronto: University of Toronto Press, 1990.

Chapter 15

Parliament

In popular parlance, the word "Parliament" is often synonymous with the House of Commons, by far its most important part. Hence members of the House of Commons are called members of Parliament or MPs. The House of Commons is the central link between the public and the government in Canadian democracy; it is where the elected representatives of the people meet in daily open, verbal combat, making it the furnace of national politics. This chapter examines the House of Commons from a number of perspectives, and later explores the role of the other branch of the legislature, the Senate.

Functions and Powers of the House of Commons

The Westminster model of government employed by Canada begins with a bicameral legislature—an elected lower house with primary legislative powers answerable to the people through elections, and an upper house with limited legislative powers. The executive is part of the lower house and through the cabinet drives or "energizes" the legislative process. The government or cabinet is in charge of and responsible for the conduct of parliamentary business, while an institutionalized opposition has the right and duty to criticize the government. This model therefore promises potent government and political stability through the cabinet, along with political accountability through open debate. MPs can thus be divided into three main groups: those who serve as cabinet ministers, those who support the cabinet (government backbenchers), and those who oppose the government (the opposition).[1]

Historically, the sovereignty or supremacy of Parliament has been a basic principle of Canadian government; that is, apart from interfering in provincial jurisdiction and with other minor exceptions, Parliament could pass laws that were virtually beyond review by any other organ of government, including the courts. With the adoption of the Canadian Charter of Rights and Freedoms in 1982, however, this principle was considerably transformed. The courts have now been given the power to review both federal and provincial legislation in terms of the Charter, and to invalidate such legislation to the extent of any contradiction. On the other hand, the courts have often suggested that the legislation be redrafted to fit within the boundaries of the Charter, and the notwithstanding clause allows for the reassertion of Parliamentary sovereignty on many points.

In discussing the functions of the House of Commons it is instructive to examine its role in the chart of the policymaking process outlined in Chapter 13. In the first place, Parliament may be involved in the initiation phase by raising issues in the daily Question Period and in general debates, in criticizing existing spending programs, or by means of private members' bills. It is then virtually nonexistent in the priority-setting and policy-formulation phases. Where the Commons dominates the picture is in the legitimation stage. Whether or not bills are refined in the process, cabinet proposals are made legitimate by their passage through the formal, authorized, democratic channels of the Commons. The House may not make many significant changes, but it does subject bills to extended debate and publicizes their advantages and disadvantages before converting them into laws or statutes. The legislative stage serves to inform the public of the content of new policies, and out of this "prolonged warfare," consent or acceptance is eventually obtained. This debate essentially prepares the electorate for its decision on how to vote in the next election.

Composition of the House of Commons

The basic principle of representation in the House of Commons is that each province is represented in proportion to its population. Chapter 8 outlined how the 301 seats in the Commons are distributed among the provinces, with the following results: Ontario, 103; Quebec, 75; B.C., 34; Alberta, 26; Manitoba, 14; Saskatchewan, 14; Nova Scotia, 11; New Brunswick, 10; Newfoundland, 7; P.E.I., 4; N.W.T., 2; and Yukon, 1.

Even if members of Parliament other than cabinet ministers have only a limited role in the policymaking process, ordinary members are important enough to justify an inquiry into their social background characteristics. Since they are elected to represent territorial units and usually live in or near their constituencies, MPs almost automatically become representative of the population in a geographic sense. An increasing proportion of MPs are elected without any previous service at the municipal or provincial levels.

They are also representative in terms of English and French ethnic background, but less so of other ethnic groups. The Constitution Act, 1867, required from the beginning that all House documents be printed in English and French, but the absence of simultaneous interpretation until 1958 and the unilingualism of most MPs served to limit interaction between the two linguistic groups.

Members of Parliament do not reflect the population very well in terms of education, occupation, class, or gender. Although not as exclusive in these respects as cabinet ministers, MPs have higher educational levels and higher-status occupations than the general population. Historically the legal profession has furnished the largest single group in the Commons, but the number of MPs with a business background equalled or exceeded the number of lawyers in the 1984 and 1988 Conservative victories. The occupational distribution of members of Parliament after 1993 was roughly 20 percent each for business, law, education, other professions, and others.[2] Relatively few women are elected to the House of Commons, although the number is on the increase, reaching 53 out of 295 in 1993 and 62 out of 301 in 1997.

What is probably most striking about Canadian MPs, especially compared to members of other legislatures around the world, is their rapid turnover in office. The proportion of new members after each election averages 40 percent, and the typical MP serves less than 10 years.[3] Few members remain in Parliament long enough to develop an understanding of the institution or to stand up to a long-serving prime minister. The 1993 turnover was over 75 percent, as a result of the decimation of the Conservatives and NDP.

The Parliamentary Timetable

Perhaps the best way to get an overview of the work of the House of Commons is by examining the parliamentary timetable—the agenda of a typical session and a typical week. A session of Parliament normally lasts one year, but sometimes extends longer.

The Typical Session

A session begins with the *Speech from the Throne*, prepared by the prime minister and read by the governor general. Its function is to outline the government's legislative plans for the session, and it introduces the Throne Speech debate, a six-day debate in which MPs can talk about anything that comes to mind. Party leaders and cabinet ministers may use the occasion to articulate their priorities, while backbenchers often expound on the wonders or troubles of their constituency.

The second major event of the session is the budget and the budget debate. The budget itself is a statement delivered by the minister of Finance chiefly concerned with tax changes (the revenue side of the government's books) but also dealing with government finances in general. Among other things, the budget usually fleshes out the promises of the Speech from the Throne. So that no one can take advantage of tax changes beforehand, the budget is shrouded in secrecy until its delivery, and real or apparent "budget leaks" always generate great controversy. The budget sets the stage for a four-day freewheeling debate and provides the opposition with a second opportunity to try to defeat the government. Majority governments need not worry, but the Trudeau and Clark minority governments were defeated on their budgets in 1974 and 1979 respectively. Legislation incorporating the specific tax changes mentioned in the budget comes along later, although the changes usually take effect as of budget night.

The other side of the financial picture is the government's spending proposals for the next fiscal year, the *Estimates*. Their presentation is the third major item of business in the session. Once tabled, however, the Estimates are transmitted to standing committees of the House for scrutiny, so that they actually occupy little time of the Commons as a whole.

A fourth element of the session consists of the 20 *opposition days* when the opposition parties choose the subject of debate and the government in turn responds. These are divided proportionally among the opposition parties and distributed throughout the session.

Other than these four components, the time of the House of Commons is essentially taken up with the discussion of bills, and most of that time with bills introduced by the government. Indeed, it is partly because of the volume of government legislation that some sessions of Parliament exceed a year in length. Since bills not passed die at the end of the session, governments are tempted to allow sessions to continue beyond one year until all current legislation is disposed of. The number of sitting days is about 135 per year.

When the government wishes to take a break within a session, it *adjourns* the House; when it wants to bring a session to an end, it *prorogues* the Commons; and when the government decides to call an election, Parliament is *dissolved*.

The Typical Week

The House begins its sessions at 11:00 a.m. on Monday and meets at 10:00 a.m. on the other four weekdays. The weekly schedule as of mid-1997 can be seen in Figure 15.1.

Figure 15.1   Weekly Order of Business

HOURS	MONDAY	TUESDAY	WEDNESDAY	THURSDAY	FRIDAY	HOURS
10:00–11:00		Routine Proceedings		Routine Proceedings	Government Orders	10:00–11:00
11:00–11:15	Private Members' Business (3)				Members' Statements	11:00–11:15
11:15–12:00					Oral Questions	11:15–12:00
12:00–1:00					Routine Proceedings (1)	12:00–1:00
1:00–1:30	Government Orders	Government Orders (2)	Review of Delegated Legislation (4)	Government Orders (2)	Government Orders (2)	1:00–1:30
1:30–2:00						1:30–2:00
2:00–2:15	Members' Statements	Members' Statements	Members' Statements	Members' Statements	Private Members' Business	2:00–2:15
2:15–2:30	Oral Questions	Oral Questions	Oral Questions	Oral Questions		2:15–2:30
2:30–3:00						2:30–3:00
3:00–5:30	Routine Proceedings (1) Government Orders (2)	(1) Government Orders (2)	Routine Proceedings (1) Notices of Motions for the Production of Papers Government Orders (2)	(1) Government Orders (2)		3:00–5:30
5:30–6:30		Private Members' Business (3)	Private Members' Business (3)	Private Members' Business (3)		5:30–6:30
6:30–7:00	Adjournment Proceedings (2)	Adjournment Proceedings (2)	Adjournment Proceedings (2)	Adjournment Proceedings (2)		6:30–7:00

(1) Possible extension of Routine Proceedings to complete Introduction of Government Bills pursuant to Standing Order 30(4).

(2) Possible extension or delay pursuant to Standing Order 33(2) respecting Ministerial Statements.

(3) Possible delay or rescheduling pursuant to Standing Order 30(7) to compensate for a delay or an interruption of more than 30 minutes, and pursuant to Standing Order 33(2) respecting Ministerial Statements.

(4) If required, House to sit at 1:00 p.m. for the review of Delegated Legislation pursuant to Standing Order 128(1).

Source: Reproduced with permission of the Clerk of the House.

The highlight of the day is the 45-minute Question Period. It is this period that offers the opposition its best opportunity to criticize and embarrass the government, as it grills cabinet ministers about their deficiencies and faults. Ministers are not given notice of such questions, but before going into the chamber they are briefed by aides who try to anticipate what questions might be asked. Even greater daily effort goes into the preparation and rehearsal of questions by opposition party leaders and their staff. The Leader of the Opposition and the leader of any other recognized party begin the attack, and the Speaker of the House distributes questions to various opposition parties in a rough proportion to their numbers. Since ministers often respond in a deliberately vague manner, several supplementary questions are allowed, but the objective of the opposition is not so much to elicit information as to portray the government in a negative light. Such exchanges, along with corridor interviews and hallway "scrums" based on Question Period, find their way onto the television news and form the backbone of media reporting on the House. Government backbenchers are also allowed to participate, but they usually ask "planted" questions to which ministers give prepared and self-serving replies.

Immediately before Question Period, 15 minutes are set aside for *members' statements*, during which individual MPs have 60 seconds to get something off their chests. After Question Period, unless the House is involved in one of the special events—the Throne Speech or budget debates or an opposition day—the regular business is the discussion of *government orders*, usually government bills. These debates are the basic routine of Commons life. At this point in the day most of the press gallery and MPs leave the chamber in search of more pressing or more interesting activity. The speeches in these debates are generally dull and boring; the public and media can hardly be blamed for paying so little attention to them when MPs themselves rarely listen to each other. The few members assigned to make up quorum on any day are more likely to be answering their mail or reading the newspaper.

Only five hours a week are reserved for *private members' bills* and motions, at the normal rate of one hour per bill. These are bills and motions, introduced either by government supporters not in the cabinet or by opposition members, are usually of little interest to anyone else, and are virtually assured of being dropped to the bottom of the pile when their hour on the stage has elapsed.

Finally, the *adjournment proceeding* is a half-hour opportunity at the end of the daily sitting (6:30 to 7:00 p.m.) four times a week to pursue issues that MPs feel were inadequately answered in the Question Period. Five members have four minutes each to restate their question and a parliamentary secretary representing the minister has two minutes to respond.

Given the sharply adversarial nature of Question Period and the dullness of the rest of the parliamentary day, television coverage of the House of Commons does little to enhance the public's support of the government or politicians in general. On the other hand, "the all-consuming ritual of adversarial combat completely dominated by political parties"[4] has its defenders. It serves the functions of keeping government conduct under constant surveillance and of providing an alternative, and it presents a clear-cut picture to the electorate of which party is responsible for everything that has been done.

Party Discipline and the Caucus

Probably the most significant aspect of the operation of the House of Commons is that everything is organized along party lines and that party discipline is so rigid. Almost all members belong to one party or another, and with rare exceptions, the MPs of each party vote together. Why is it that members of Parliament so consistently toe the party line?

The most obvious reason for party discipline, at least on the government side of the House, is the system of responsible government. It is generally believed, both inside and outside Parliament, that if the cabinet is defeated on a major measure, it must resign or call an election; therefore, its backbenchers must always ensure that cabinet proposals are passed. Until such time as the principle of responsible government is interpreted more flexibly, government supporters will always have to put party loyalty ahead of their own views or those of their constituents. That kind of reform could be accomplished by regarding a limited number of nonconfidence motions as really critical and then allowing the cabinet to carry on in spite of the occasional defeat of a piece of legislation.

Several other reasons can also be cited to explain why MPs stick together with party colleagues in parliamentary votes. One is the tendency of people who belong to a political party to see things in a similar light—a natural cohesiveness common to most organized groups. Related to this cohesiveness is an equally natural deference to the leadership of the party and a desire to present an image of party unity to the public. In addition, MPs are encouraged to support the party line because of the prospects of promotion. Government backbenchers who are well behaved can become committee chairs, parliamentary secretaries, or cabinet ministers, while even opposition party members can be moved up to more important responsibilities. Members also want to participate in the distribution of perks available in parliamentary life, especially opportunities to travel at public expense, which are generally in the control of the *party whips*. Another inducement is to receive full support of the party organization in the next election, including campaign funds and a visit by the party leader. Moreover, many MPs depend on the government to provide them with employment if they suffer defeat. The ultimate sanctions for disloyal behaviour are expulsion from the party caucus and denial of the party label in the next election. For all these reasons, parties vote as blocs and a government with a majority of seats in the Commons feels confident that it can get parliamentary approval for almost anything it wants.

In recent years, three Conservative MPs were expelled from the caucus and two were denied the party's candidacy.[5] Despite concessions made to Liberal dissenters and other opponents of the Chrétien government's gun-control bill, many backbenchers absented themselves from the vote and three voted against it. The PM quickly retaliated by removing them from their committee assignments. When veteran MP Warren Allmand voted against the 1995 budget because it dismantled historic Liberal social programs, the prime minister removed him as a committee chair. The prime minister even threatened not to sign the nomination papers of Liberal candidates in the next election if they had voted against government measures. When John Nunziata did so, based on the claim that they violated Red Book campaign promises, he was quickly booted out of the party.

It is fashionable to advocate more *free votes* and greater opportunity for MPs to represent the interests of their constituencies rather than slavishly following the dictates of the party. Rare free votes have been held on such subjects as capital punishment and abortion, and while few would argue against a little more autonomy and freedom for the individual MP, free-vote advocates sometimes fail to appreciate the merits of an executive-centred system. Forcing MPs to toe the party line has allowed the executive to pursue a collectivist public interest beyond the narrow interests of constituencies, provinces, parties, pressure groups, and lobbyists, and has permitted Canadian governments to be more activist and welfare-oriented than legislature-centred systems such as the United States.[6] Party discipline protects MPs individually and collectively from the blandishments and threats of single-interest pressure groups and promotes the accountability of the government party to the electorate. It also frees the prime minister from time-consuming negotiations with individual MPs.

The other side of this public display of party discipline is that MPs are allowed to speak their mind in the secrecy of the *party caucus*.[7] The caucus consists of all the elected members of each party (and such senators who choose to attend) who meet behind closed doors on Wednesday mornings. As in the case of cabinet secrecy, however, members occasionally "leak" caucus information for their own benefit. Provincial and regional caucus meetings of each party are held before the general caucus meeting, and caucus committees are often appointed. In the case of the government party, the prime minister and cabinet ministers attend such meetings, unlike the practice in Britain.

Stages and Kinds of Legislation

The great bulk of legislation introduced takes the form of *public bills*. These are general bills, such as the Income Tax Act or the Employment Insurance Act, that affect all Canadians. Most public bills (and all that involve the raising or spending of money) are sponsored by the government and introduced by a cabinet minister, thereby being titled *government bills*. As noted earlier, most of the weekly and yearly agenda is taken up with such government business. However, a certain amount of time (now normally five hours per week) is set aside for members who are not in the cabinet to introduce legislation and motions of their own. Since these MPs (on whichever side of the House) are private members, their proposals are called *private members' bills*. These bills are still of a general nature, such as those attempting to restore capital punishment, but they almost never reach the statute books because the government arranges to have them "talked out." The government ensures that a backbencher is still talking when the time for their consideration expires and they therefore do not come to a vote. Historically, the most private members could hope for was that the cabinet might incorporate their ideas into a government bill. Since 1992, however, provision has been made for a more in-depth examination of a random sample of 30 private members' bills and motions. A committee decides which ones are "votable" and up to 10 of these get expanded debate and can come to a vote. Then, if successful, they could continue in the regular legislative channels. Lynn McDonald's 1988 private member's bill on nonsmokers' rights was a rare example of one that made it to the statute books; others included the bill to change the name of Trans-Canada Airlines to Air Canada, and the act that recognized the beaver as a symbol of Canadian sovereignty.[8]

Private bills, on the other hand, refer to a specific person or corporation. Certain divorces used to be effected by act of Parliament and took the form of private bills, although today this category consists mostly of bills incorporating companies. Private bills now originate in the Senate, and occupy very little of the Commons' time.

Turning to the stages of the legislative process, the first requirement is for three readings in each chamber. Most government bills originate in the Commons, although with the exception of money bills, they may be first introduced in the Senate. *First reading* simply means that a bill has been introduced—it is tabled, printed, and made public—and may be briefly explained. Some days later, the bill comes up for *second reading*. This stage involves a debate on the principle of the bill and may last several days, or even weeks if it is controversial. A favourable vote at the end of the second-reading debate means that the bill has been approved in principle.

Even if the opposition has little chance of defeating a bill, it may hope that prolonged exposure of the flaws in the legislation will persuade the government to amend it. Failing that, public opinion can be aroused via media coverage so that the electorate will remember the incident when the next election occurs. Excessive opposition debate is called "filibustering," but government and opposition rarely agree on what is excessive. In 1913, during protracted opposition to its Naval Bill, the Borden government introduced *closure*, a rule allowing a majority government to cut off debate. This device was used sparingly until the pipeline debate of 1956, and it is widely believed that the abusive resort to closure helped to defeat the Liberals a year later. Although the closure rule has been used more routinely in recent years, a more civilized procedure is for the government to negotiate with the opposition over the time to be allocated to debating various issues.

After second reading a bill goes to committee, where it is examined in detail. In the small, informal confines of a Commons committee, the bill is scrutinized and voted on clause by clause, while ministers, public servants, interest groups, and other experts may be called upon for explanations or criticisms. After being approved, sometimes with amendments, the bill is reported back to the House in what is called the *report stage*. This gives all members of the House, not just those on the committee, an opportunity to move amendments. Once the bill is concurred in, it goes to *third reading* for a final, overall appraisal.

Assuming that the bill started in the Commons, it must then go through the same procedure in the Senate. In the rare case that the Senate amends a bill already approved by the Commons, the bill will have to go back to that house to see if it is acceptable in its amended form. Once a bill is passed in identical terms by both houses, it is given royal assent by the governor general or a Supreme Court judge acting as "deputy governor general" and then becomes a law or statute, although it may not be immediately proclaimed.

Although this may seem like an overly complicated process, each stage has a distinctive purpose and most bills must be debated for some time before the media and public begin to pay attention to them. Besides being necessary to engender eventual public knowledge of and consent to the law, reasonably lengthy consideration of the merits and faults of the bill serves to help the electorate gradually make up its mind about whether to re-elect the government that introduced such legislation or to opt for an opposition party that criticized it effectively.

Officers and Procedure in the Commons
The Speaker

The leading official of the House of Commons is the presiding officer, the *Speaker,* for whom deputy or acting speakers can substitute in the chair. In addition to ceremonial and administrative functions, the Speaker interprets and enforces the written rules of the Commons, called the *Standing Orders,*[9] plus unwritten traditions, practices, conventions, and usages. The powers of the Speakership include recognizing which member can speak and ruling on whether motions are in order, whether debate is relevant, whether questions are urgent, and whether an unruly MP should be expelled. It is therefore important for the person selected to be competent as well as totally impartial. Unfortunately, Speakers were in the past chosen by prime ministers from among their party's MPs and thus carried the suspicion of being biased in favour of the government. In seeking eventual reward beyond the Speakership such as promotion to the cabinet, some also feared displeasing the prime minister. In 1986, a major change was adopted that allowed MPs to choose their own Speaker by secret ballot. In 1988, the Speaker was given new authority to "name" (i.e., suspend) a member for the rest of the day and for a period of five days for a second breach of the rules.

Speakers can vote only in the case of a tie and cannot articulate the needs of their constituency or constituents in the Commons as such. In compensation for this silence, ministers and bureaucrats are especially sensitive to the concerns that the Speaker discusses with them outside the Chamber.

House Leaders, Party Whips, and Clerks

From within their ranks, each party selects a *House leader* and a *party whip*. The government House leader is a cabinet minister who manages the government's business in the Commons. This minister seeks to work out an agenda for House business with the opposition House leaders, who function as procedural strategists for their parties and often speak for their parties if their leaders are absent. Party whips, on the other hand, are responsible for ensuring that their members are present for important votes and that their members vote the right way.[10] Whips must therefore know the whereabouts of all their members at all times. They also distribute members' offices, assign members to parliamentary committees, and line up the order of party speakers in Question Period and debates. It is largely through the whips that party leaders impose discipline on their members. Members' opportunities to speak, to serve on the committee of their choice, and to travel as part of parliamentary delegations are largely influenced by their degree of party loyalty. In return, whips seek out backbench opinion on various matters and transmit it to the party leadership. Given the power of the party whips and House leaders to organize the business of the House, independent MPs and those belonging to parties with fewer than 12 members find little opportunity to participate.

The chief permanent official of the Commons is the Clerk of the House, a position analogous to a deputy minister in a government department. As chief procedural adviser to the Speaker and manager of the support staff attached to the Commons, the Clerk is also required to act in a totally nonpartisan manner. The Clerk is assisted at the table by the deputy clerk and several principal clerks. Figure 15.2 shows the layout of the Commons chamber.

Procedure in the Commons

Votes in the Commons are in the first instance taken orally when the Speaker invites members to say "aye" or "nay." When either side wants a formal recorded vote it will request a *division*. In this case the division bells ring until the government and Official Opposition party whips agree that all their available members have arrived, at which time a standing vote is conducted. It used to be that if either whip refused to give the go-ahead, the bells could ring indefinitely, but after the two-week "bell-ringing incident" of 1982, a 30-minute limit was adopted in 1986. A new procedure in 1994 allowed for deferred divisions with all-party consent.

Figure 15.2 The House of Commons

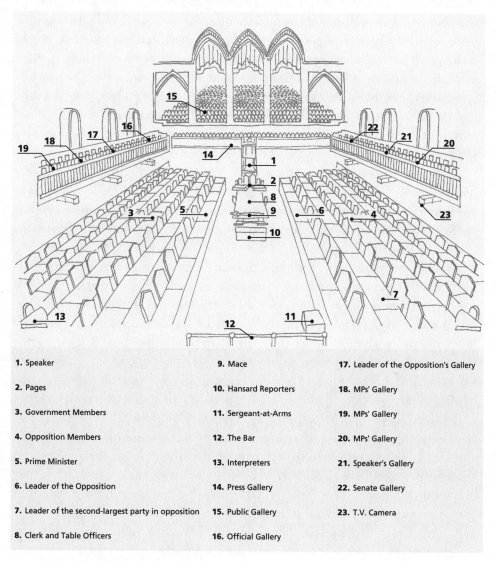

1. Speaker	9. Mace	17. Leader of the Opposition's Gallery
2. Pages	10. Hansard Reporters	18. MPs' Gallery
3. Government Members	11. Sergeant-at-Arms	19. MPs' Gallery
4. Opposition Members	12. The Bar	20. MPs' Gallery
5. Prime Minister	13. Interpreters	21. Speaker's Gallery
6. Leader of the Opposition	14. Press Gallery	22. Senate Gallery
7. Leader of the second-largest party in opposition	15. Public Gallery	23. T.V. Camera
8. Clerk and Table Officers	16. Official Gallery	

Source: Reproduced with permission of the Clerk of the House.

The length of MPs' speeches has been severely curtailed over the past 15 or so years. The 1982 reforms generally shortened them from 40 minutes to 20, but this depends on who is speaking, in what debate, and at what stage of the debate. As a debate drags on, the maximum length is reduced to 10 minutes.

The Committee System

Much important legislative work of the House takes place outside the Commons chamber in a variety of committees. Committees allow a small number of people to develop expertise in a particular field and to examine proposals in depth; moreover, if several committees operate simultaneously, a greater volume of business can be accomplished. Committees could allow private members to make constructive contributions to the governing of the country and to do so in a consensual rather than adversarial atmosphere, but the Canadian Commons committee system did not function well during the first 100 years after Confederation. Repeated reforms since 1968 have made it more significant.

Standing committees are set up more or less permanently in most of the substantive areas of government policy, such as agriculture and transport. They have two principal functions: to peruse the Estimates, that is, the government's spending proposals, and to examine legislation at the committee stage. The Estimates of the Department of Agriculture, for example, are scrutinized by the Standing Committee on Agriculture, and the examination can now go beyond the spending plans of the current year. In studying bills clause by clause after second reading, committees question ministers, public servants, pressure groups, and other expert witnesses. As a result of the 1986 changes, standing committees have new functions and resources. Since they largely parallel government departments, they are authorized to investigate any aspect of the department with which they are associated, including a review of nonjudicial government appointments. They also have a budget to hire a clerk, supporting staff, and researchers, and thus to develop independent expertise. The Standing Committee on Finance is perhaps most important, and now engages in pre-budget consultations.

Standing committees have been reduced to between 7 and 15 members, and because they often have a number of different issues on their agenda, they may also set up sub-committees. Representation on all committees is proportional to party standings in the House; committee chairs are elected by committee members, but are usually pre-selected by the PMO. Thus, in a majority situation, the government will have a majority on each committee and its own designated choice as chair. The one exception to this government control is the Public Accounts Committee, which normally has a government majority but has been chaired by an opposition MP since 1958. It has the important function of examining the report of the Auditor General, the official of Parliament who audits the government's accounts.

Special committees are set up temporarily for some specific, special purpose. They usually have an investigatory function—to examine an issue before the government has made up its mind on how to deal with it.

In addition to the standing and special committees of the House of Commons alone, the Commons and Senate sometimes work together in joint committees. Joint committees avoid duplication and give senators a chance to get involved at an earlier stage of the process than is usually the case. The most important joint standing committee is that on the Scrutiny of Regulations. It has the vital but unenviable responsibility of scrutinizing the mounds of regulations and other subordinate legislation issued by the executive branch each year, and can recommend rescission of offensive delegated legislation.

Finally there is the *committee of the whole*. This is simply the entire Commons membership sitting in the chamber as a committee. In such a case, the Speaker is replaced in the chair by the deputy speaker, and the rules are somewhat relaxed. This committee is used only to debate appropriation bills (once the Estimates have been approved) and certain noncontroversial bills, preference otherwise being given to smaller committees that can meet simultaneously in rooms outside the Commons chamber.

The transformation of the committee system in recent years has enhanced the position of backbench MPs in the legislative process. As committees have become smaller, more stable in their membership, and more expert in their field, and as their members developed greater collegiality, they have shed a good deal of their partisanship. Since 1986, for example, many standing and legislative committees have developed a consensus on the issues before them that cuts across party lines. Such committees have become newly independent sources of power in the legislative system. This has led to the acceptance of an unprecedented number of committee amendments to government bills.

Members' Services and Roles

As of 1997, ordinary MPs received $64 400 in salary plus $21 300 in a tax-free expense allowance (for which they did not have to submit receipts). Since the equivalent taxable value of the expense allowance would be about double, the total remuneration package is worth approximately $100 000. On top of this basic income, a large number of MPs received additional payments for supplementary responsibilities. These supplementary payments are as follows:

- Prime minister $69 920
- Speaker and Leader of the Opposition   49 100
- Ministers   46 645
- Secretaries of State   34 984
- Leaders of other recognized parties   29 500
- Deputy speaker   25 700
- Opposition House leader   23 800
- Chief government whip and chief opposition whip   13 200
- Parliamentary secretaries and assistant deputy speakers   10 500
- Other party House leaders   10 100
- Other party whips, deputy government and
  opposition whips   7 500

In addition to this basic pay, backbench MPs receive many benefits and services at public expense. Equipment and supplies are provided for their parliamentary and constituency offices; they have a staff allowance of approximately $170 000; they are allowed 64 return trips between Ottawa and their constituency, with partial provision for family and staff, and travel within the constituency; and they have unlimited telephone and mailing privileges. Members who reside at least 100 km from Ottawa are also entitled to a $6000 accommodation allowance. Recognized parties in the House—that is, groups of at least 12 members—receive substantial annual funding for research purposes, the loss of which was a major blow to the Conservatives and NDP after the 1993 election.

The MPs' pension plan has raised much controversy. Although contributory, many observers felt that it was too generous because it was indexed to the cost of living and because, regardless of age, members became eligible for the pension immediately upon leaving the Commons after six years of service. Moreover, those subsequently appointed to a government position continued to receive the pension on top of their new salary. In 1995, the Liberals removed some of these provisions for newly elected MPs: they would have to wait until age 55 to collect, they could not "double-dip," and they could opt out entirely.

The roles that members of Parliament perform can be seen in two different lights. First, in terms of how they vote, MPs can be classified as trustees, constituency delegates, or party delegates. *Trustees* are MPs who feel obliged to vote according to their own conscience, their own understanding of the issue in question, or their own conception of the national interest. *Constituency delegates*, on the other hand, are MPs who vote the way they think a majority of their constituents want them to or in their conception of the best interests of their constituency. In practice, MPs rarely deviate from the party line, and they could all be labelled *party delegates*. If the party caucus determines a position that conflicts with either their own views or those of their constituents, MPs are almost always obliged to put the party position first. Public pressure for more free votes seems to be increasing, however, and such discipline may also be in decline at the committee stage.

The other way to examine the roles of MPs is in terms of how they spend their time or what their priorities are. The first role in this respect is the *lawmaker*—devoting attention to the legislative process by introducing, amending, and debating legislation. MPs are supported in these tasks by the Research Branch of the Library of Parliament.[11] This role is usually irrelevant to their constituents, and MPs are more likely to spend time promoting their constituency to bring it public favours in what could be called a *representational* role. These members lobby ministers and public servants for new public buildings, roads, wharves, and other facilities so that they will have something concrete to show for themselves by the time of the next election. Finally, MPs function as *ombudsmen* or social workers for their individual constituents, intervening with ministers or public servants to hasten administrative decisions, correct bureaucratic errors, and repair governmental injustices. There will always be constituents with passport, immigration, employment insurance, pension, and many other kinds of problems. This "caseload" of MPs is now so heavy that they are provided with considerable administrative assistance in their Ottawa and constituency offices.

The Government–Opposition Balance and Parliamentary Reform

An objective look at Parliament reveals a basic dilemma: the government wants legislation passed expeditiously, but the opposition must have the time to criticize government proposals in order to make the public aware of their defects and to articulate constituency needs.

When the government has a majority of seats in the Commons, the cabinet operates as a virtual dictatorship until it has to face the electorate again some four or five years down the road. Many observers who deplore the arrogance of a majority government and regret that so much opposition talent and so many opposition ideas ordinarily go to waste prefer a minority government.

In a *minority government* situation—where the government is outnumbered by opposition members—it may have to negotiate with opposition parties to some extent, such as to amend its proposals, abandon them, or even accept opposition initiatives. Between 1867 and 1997 there were eight minority governments in Canada; few of these could have been called weak and indecisive. Many, such as the 1957–58 Diefenbaker government, were more active and courageous than the majority governments that preceded or followed them. Some were exceptionally bold and decisive, especially the Pearson governments and the Trudeau minority, the latter being particularly sensitive to opposition demands. While minority governments admittedly did not last as long as majority governments, not all of them ended by being defeated; some, for example, ended when the prime minister decided to call an election.

Because of the imbalance between government and opposition in a majority situation and because the legislative role of ordinary MPs has been so ineffective, parliamentary reform is never far from the minds of political scientists and politicians alike. Reform proposals are designed to remedy excessive partisanship, cabinet domination, and private members' lack of influence. Those adopted are summarized below.

RECENT PROCEDURAL CHANGES IN THE HOUSE OF COMMONS

1970s   Improvement in members' services
        Televised proceedings
1980s   Elimination of night sittings
        Speeches limited to 20 minutes
        Members' statements before Question Period
        Committees reduced in size, allowed to examine any aspect of government policy, to hire staff, and to review order-in-council appointments
        20 private members' bills looked at seriously and 6 voted on
        30-minute maximum on ringing of division bells
        Speaker elected by secret ballot
1990s   Reduction in length of Throne Speech and budget debates
        Most speeches limited to 10 minutes
        Opposition days reduced to 20
        Some bills permitted to go to standing committees after first reading
        Deferred divisions
        Pre-budget consultations by Finance Committee

The question of reforming the House of Commons leads to a discussion of the principle of responsible government, which declares that the cabinet must have the confidence of the Commons or else call an election or resign. It is not always clear whether the cabinet is required to take such drastic action. In a majority situation the problem is most unlikely to arise, but when the government is in a minority position, does it have to resign or call an election over any and every defeat? If there was any doubt about this point, it was probably resolved by the 1968 incident in which the Pearson government was defeated on a piece of financial legislation. Pearson argued that the defeat was a fluke and that his government should be able to carry on. In that case the matter was decided when the cabinet subsequently survived an explicit nonconfidence motion. Any other case of dispute about whether or not a government has been defeated should probably be settled in the same manner.[12]

The Senate
Purposes and Powers

The ideal of democracy was still not enthusiastically accepted in the 1860s and the Fathers of Confederation felt it advisable to provide for an appointed body that would exercise "sober second thought" with respect to measures emanating from the popularly elected House of Commons. Thus the Senate was to be the equivalent of the British House of Lords, an older, conservative influence, with a minimum age of 30, appointment for life, and a relatively high property qualification.[13]

In the second place, the smaller provinces would agree to join Confederation and accept representation by population in the House of Commons only if they were overrepresented in the Senate. The Fathers settled on a chamber that would be based on equal regional representation. Such a system gave the Maritimes and Quebec a limited amount of protection against the voting power held by Ontario in the House of Commons. It followed that senators were supposed to represent their regions and provinces within the national policymaking system.

A third function of the Senate, not explicitly provided for in 1867 but that can also be seen as part of the concept of sober second thought, is to improve legislation from a technical point of view. The Senate often acts as a nonideological, routine revising chamber, picking up on flaws in legislation that have not been noticed during its passage through the busy Commons.

As far as powers were concerned, the Senate was given a veto over all legislation, a power that was not restricted as in the case of the British House of Lords. The only point of Senate inferiority to the Commons was that "money bills"—legislation involving the raising or spending of money—had to be introduced in the lower chamber. Nothing in law prevented the Senate from delaying, amending, or vetoing any bills, whether or not they involved money.[14]

It was not until 1982 that the Senate's power was in any way reduced, and that had to do only with constitutional amendments, not ordinary legislation. According to the Constitution Act, 1982, the Senate can only delay a constitutional amendment for 180 days. If the Senate has not approved such an amendment by then, it can be repassed by the Commons, and bypasses the Senate in the process of ratification.

Composition of the Senate

Ontario, Quebec, and the Maritimes originally received 24 senators each. When Prince Edward Island joined Confederation, it received 4 of the 24 Maritime senators, reducing Nova Scotia and New Brunswick to 10 each. In a general reform in 1915 the West was designated as a senatorial region with 24 senators, preserving the principle of equal regional representation, with 6 being allocated to each Western province. In 1949, Newfoundland was awarded 6 senators in addition to the 96 already allotted, so as to leave the Maritime contingent intact. Finally, in 1975, the Yukon and Northwest Territories were given 1 senator each, so that the total became 104 $(4 \times 24 + 6 + 2)$.

The 1867 Constitution Act gives the governor general the power to appoint senators, but by convention this is done on the advice of the prime minister. Prime ministers have almost always chosen partisan supporters, such as MPs seeking a safe haven, defeated MPs or candidates, those who have served the party organization well, retired premiers or other provincial politicians, and federal cabinet ministers who have outlived their usefulness. Hence, almost all of those appointed could be called "party hacks." In addition to rewarding faithful service to the party in the past, many appointments were made on the assumption that the new senator would continue to promote the party in the future. Such senators carried on as party fundraisers, party presidents, organizers, election campaign strategists or managers, or in other partisan capacities.

Senators have traditionally been English or French male lawyers or businessmen, and have maintained active business connections after their appointment. Most saw nothing wrong with continuing as directors of various corporations or even being appointed to new ones at the same time as they held public office. Colin Campbell has detailed and condemned such senatorial corporate connections in his book *The Canadian Senate: A Lobby from Within*. He accuses the chamber of systemic corruption as its members "bargain and negotiate on business's behalf" and provide business with "preferential access to the policy process."[15]

The Constitution Act, 1867, speaks of "qualified persons" being eligible for appointment to the Senate, language originally understood to include only men. In one of the most famous court cases in Canadian history, however, an enterprising group of women challenged this interpretation of "persons," and in 1929 the Judicial Committee of the Privy Council decided that "persons" did include women![16] Thus gender has joined ethnic and religious considerations in Senate appointments, for many senators have been appointed as representatives of various ethnic communities.

Senators originally served for life, and many lived to a ripe old age before they died. Lester Pearson had a constitutional amendment passed in 1965 to the effect that incumbent senators could stay until death (all gone by 1997) or retire at 75 with a pension; all subsequent appointees have had to retire at 75.

Operation of the Senate

Today's senators try to justify their existence primarily in terms of the routine revision of bills, and some observers support their claim.[17] In addition to this function, the Senate sometimes undertakes detailed and protracted examination of complex legislation, such as the Bankruptcy Act or the Criminal Code. Similarly, bills are sometimes introduced simultaneously in both chambers so that the Senate can engage in an unhurried "pre-study" of the bill rather than wait until it has passed three readings in the Commons.

Senators also seek to emphasize other important aspects of their work, such as their consideration of private bills. These concern individuals, companies, churches, professional associations, and other institutions, and are a nuisance to a busy House of Commons. Since 1934, almost all private bills have been introduced in the Senate where the background work can be done so that the Commons can approve them routinely at a later date. This practice does help the Commons, but private bills are not numerous and do not absorb much of anyone's time.

Another kind of work not originally provided for is the study of various public problems by Senate committees in what Colin Campbell calls "social investigations."[18] Senators often have the expertise and time to conduct inquiries that relieve the pressure on the House of Commons and are cheaper than royal commissions. Among the issues investigated by the Senate over the years were poverty, aging, unemployment, the mass media, science policy, land use, national defence, Canadian–American relations, and the Canadian Security Intelligence Service.

Finally, the Senate reviews regulations issued by various government departments. The Standing Joint Committee on the Scrutiny of Regulations has the responsibility of reviewing the great quantity of subordinate legislation issued every year.

In the 1990s, Senators were paid $64 400 plus a non-taxable expense account of $10 100, for a total value of approximately $80 000. The Senate timetable is very lax, and a small group of 15 or 20 does most of its work.

The periodic partisanship of the institution is most striking when considering the Senate's vetoing of Commons legislation. In almost all such cases, a Liberal majority in the Senate has obstructed a Conservative majority in the Commons, or vice versa.[19] Brian Mulroney had considerable difficulty with the Senate between 1984 and 1991, for example, when a Liberal majority in that chamber coincided with a Conservative majority in the Commons. The Senate repeatedly passed amendments to the government's drug patent bill, only retreating at the last minute;[20] its amendments to the Meech Lake Accord had to be overridden by the Commons after the expiry of the 180-day limit on constitutional amendments. Then, in mid-1988, at John Turner's direction, the Liberal majority in the Senate held up the Canada–U.S. Free Trade Agreement until the electorate had a chance to express its will on this important measure. After the 1988 election, the Senate bowed to the popular will and passed the Free Trade Agreement, but later dug in its heels on other measures, especially the Goods and Services Tax (GST). At this point, Mulroney invoked an obscure clause in the 1867 Constitution Act that allowed him to appoint eight additional senators (two for each of the four senatorial regions) to tip the balance in favour of the Conservatives.[21] After the GST passed in an atmosphere of great bitterness on both sides, the Senate defeated the government's compromise abortion bill (on a tie vote). This became the first measure in 30 years that the Senate actually defeated, but it was a peculiar case in that the government allowed a free vote and some cabinet ministers were probably secretly relieved that the Senate had exercised its rare veto.

By the time the Liberals came to power in 1993, the Conservatives had established a clear majority in the Senate, so positions were reversed and the Liberals began to pay for their earlier intransigence. The Conservative majority in the Senate was particularly incensed about the Liberal bill cancelling privatization of Toronto's Pearson Airport. The PC-controlled Senate was also reluctant to agree to the bill designed to redistribute seats in the House of Commons even after forcing the Liberals to abandon their objective of postponing the whole operation. Several other government bills were amended by the Senate, and a number were abandoned there when the 1997 election was called. Shortly afterward, a Liberal majority in the chamber was restored.

Senate Reform

Given the limited value of the Senate as it currently operates, its reform is high on the political agenda. All sorts of proposals have been made, ranging from abolition, to election, to having provinces choose some or all of its members. Many reformers have advocated reactivating the Senate's role of representing regional and provincial interests at the federal level. To legitimize its existence in a democratic age, there is an increasing consensus that Senators should be elected.

In the 1980s, Alberta began pushing its *Triple-E* proposal for Senate reform: elected, effective, and equal.[22] The government of Alberta felt so strongly about an elected Senate that it held a "senatorial election" in 1989 when a vacancy occurred and Brian Mulroney asked for a list of provincial nominees in the spirit of the Meech Lake Accord. The Reform Party candidate, Stan Waters, won the province-wide contest, and Premier Don Getty forwarded his name to the prime minister, who after some delay reluctantly complied. No other province has yet followed this precedent, but Senate reform was a prominent part of the 1992 Charlottetown Accord.

That Accord would have provided for a new 62-member Senate, with 6 representatives from each province and 1 from each territory. They would be popularly elected at the same time as MPs, except in Quebec where they would be chosen by the National Assembly. To reinforce their new role as independent, provincial representatives in Ottawa, they would not be eligible to sit in the cabinet. Defeat of a government bill in the Senate would not be considered a vote of nonconfidence; instead, when the Senate rejected a Commons bill, a joint sitting of both houses would be held and a combined vote taken in which the Commons would outnumber the Senate 337 to 62. However, legislation dealing with the taxation of natural resources, as in the case of the National Energy Program, could be killed by a simple majority in the Senate. It could also veto government appointments to national institutions such as the governor of the Bank of Canada. Bills dealing with the French language and culture would have to be approved by a majority of francophone senators as well as by the Senate as a whole. Any kind of legislation except government money (supply) bills could be initiated in the Senate, but a Senate vote against a supply bill could be simply overridden by reintroducing it in the Commons. When the Charlottetown Accord went down to popular defeat, the Senate remained unreformed, and little has been heard on the subject since.

····················

NOTES

1. C.E.S. Franks, *The Parliament of Canada* (Toronto: University of Toronto Press, 1987); John B. Stewart, *The Canadian House of Commons: Procedure and Reform* (Montreal: McGill–Queen's University Press, 1977).
2. P.G. Normandin, ed., *Canadian Parliamentary Guide* (Toronto: INFO GLOBE, annual).
3. Franks, *The Parliament of Canada*, 73.
4. Ibid., 142.
5. Andrew Heard, *Canadian Constitutional Conventions* (Toronto: Oxford University Press, 1991), 83–84.
6. Franks, *The Parliament of Canada*, 6, 29, 96, 268.
7. Paul Thomas, "The Role of National Party Caucuses," in Peter Aucoin, ed., *Party Government and Regional Representation in Canada* (Toronto: University of Toronto Press, 1985).
8. Most of the others that passed dealt with changes to the name of an MP's constituency. Heard, *Constitutional Conventions in Canada*, 78.
9. *Standing Orders of the House of Commons* (September 1994) and *Précis of Procedure* (4th ed., 1991), both published by the House of Commons; Alistair Fraser, W.F. Dawson, and John Holtby, eds., *Beauchesne's Rules and Forms of the House of Commons of Canada*, 6th ed. (Toronto: Carswell, 1989).
10. Martin Westmacott, "Whips and Party Cohesion," *Canadian Parliamentary Review* (Autumn 1988).
11. The Research Branch of the Library of Parliament regularly publishes excellent summaries of topical political issues for the benefit of MPs and senators; they are also found in many post-secondary libraries under the titles *Background Papers* and *Current Issue Review*.
12. Other defeats that did not cause much fanfare are noted in Franks, *The Parliament of Canada*, 139.
13. Quoted in R.A. MacKay, *The Unreformed Senate of Canada*, rev.ed.(Toronto: McClelland and Stewart, 1967), 47–48.
14. MacKay, *The Unreformed Senate*, 91–95; F.A. Kunz, *The Modern Senate of Canada 1925–1963: A Re-Appraisal* (Toronto: University of Toronto Press, 1965), 337–47. Andrew Heard argues that a constitutional convention is emerging that the Senate may not insist on altering the financial provisions of money bills. See *Canadian Constitutional Conventions*, 94.

15. Colin Campbell, *The Canadian Senate: A Lobby from Within* (Toronto: Macmillan, 1978).
16. Kunz, *The Modern Senate*, 53–56. The case was officially referred to as *Edwards v. Att. Gen. of Can.* [1930] AC 124.
17. MacKay, *The Unreformed Senate*, 110; Kunz, *The Modern Senate*, 186.
18. Campbell, *The Canadian Senate*, 12–19, 147.
19. MacKay, *The Unreformed Senate*, 96–112.
20. Lorna Marsden, "Doing Its Thing—Providing 'Sober Second Thought': The Canadian Senate, 1984–1990," in Paul Fox and Graham White, eds., *Politics: Canada*, 7th ed. (Toronto: McGraw-Hill Ryerson, 1991).
21. In 1873 Alexander Mackenzie had asked the British government to summon additional senators but was refused on the ground that it was not necessary at the time.
22. Peter McCormick, "Canada Needs a Triple E Senate," in Fox and White, *Politics: Canada*; H. McConnell, "The Case for a 'Triple E' Senate," *Queen's Quarterly* (Autumn 1988).

• •

FURTHER READING

Campbell, Colin. *The Canadian Senate: A Lobby from Within*. Toronto: Macmillan, 1978.

Fleming, R.J., and J.E. Glenn, eds. *Fleming's Canadian Legislatures, 1997*. Toronto: University of Toronto Press, 1997.

Franks, C.E.S. *The Parliament of Canada*. Toronto: University of Toronto Press, 1987.

Heard, Andrew. *Canadian Constitutional Conventions*. Toronto: Oxford University Press, 1991.

Kunz, F.A. *The Modern Senate of Canada 1925–1963: A Re-Appraisal*. Toronto: University of Toronto Press, 1965.

Mackay, R.A. *The Unreformed Senate of Canada*. Rev. ed. Toronto: McClelland and Stewart, 1967.

Normandin, P.G., ed. *The Canadian Parliamentary Guide, 1994*. Toronto: INFO GLOBE, 1994 (annual).

Stewart, John. *The Canadian House of Commons: Procedure and Reform*. Montreal: McGill–Queen's University Press, 1977.

Chapter 16

The Courts

Canadian political science was traditionally interested in the judiciary or court system primarily in terms of its interpretation of the federal–provincial division of powers. Now that the Charter of Rights and Freedoms has catapulted the courts into the midst of many heated political issues, however, political scientists are giving this fourth branch of government much more attention.

This chapter examines the judiciary as an institution of government, discussing the function of adjudication, categories of laws, the structure of the courts, the operation of the Supreme Court of Canada, and the appointment, retirement, removal, and independence of judges. Chapter 11 considered the role of the courts in interpreting the Charter of Rights and Freedoms.

Functions and Powers of the Courts

The judiciary has always been associated with the *rule adjudication* function in the political system. Adjudication can be defined as interpreting the law in case of dispute, settling disputes by applying the law to them, or making a judgment based on the law. Peter Russell defines the term as "providing authoritative settlements in disputes about the law."[1]

The function of the judiciary therefore is to render formal, impartial, authoritative judgments in the case of legal disputes between two parties that cannot be settled otherwise. It is a process that generally relies on the adversarial system, with lawyers representing each side. The judge, clothed with the authoritative powers of the state, acts as an independent referee and decides which of the disputants is legally right. As a result, the process usually culminates in the designation of a winner and a loser, rather than in the achievement of some acceptable middle ground.

Apart from the *civil law* system in Quebec, the Canadian legal system operates in the tradition of the English *common law*. The basis of that system is the accumulation over the centuries of judicial precedents, both in England and more recently in Canada. Thus, in a typical court case, the two sides seek to find precedents—previous court decisions—favouring their respective points of view. The judge (and sometimes the jury) have to decide which precedents most closely resemble the case currently before the court. The principle that precedents are binding on successive decisions is called *stare decisis*.

If the law were always comprehensive and crystal clear, and if the situations to which it applied were always simple and straightforward, rule adjudication would be fairly routine and the judiciary would not have much discretion. The real world is more complex, and the law may not be clear on all points or provide for every conceivable situation. Russell refers to the "inescapable generality of the law" such that, while judges theoretically settle disputes according to pre-existing law, they actually shape and develop the law in the very process of settling disputes about it. Judges at least establish priorities among competing legal rules and principles, and in this process they "put flesh on the bare skeleton of the law and shape its substance."[2]

The judiciary and the function of judicial interpretation were included in the chart of the policymaking process in Chapter 13. Rather than taking place subsequent to policymaking, where it once was placed, adjudication or judicial interpretation can now be considered as part of the policymaking process. Unlike Americans, Canadian observers have not given much recognition to the concept of judicial involvement in this process. But Russell argues that this Canadian approach "wrongly assumes that all important public policies are expressed in statutes passed by legislatures ... and overlooks the extent to which [such] policies ... are shaped through the process of being applied in particular cases by judges and administrators."[3] In the course of adjudicating disputes, the courts are inherently involved in policymaking.

Rather than merely interpreting laws with discretion, *judicial review* is the power of the courts to declare them invalid. The original Constitution Act, 1867, did not contain any such provision, although the courts soon appropriated this power in one respect. Chapter 12 detailed the extent to which the courts invalidated federal and provincial legislation as violations of the division of powers. In rendering federal or provincial legislation void if either encroached on the jurisdiction of the other, the decisions of the courts had a significant effect on the shape of Canadian federalism. The courts' power of judicial review was greatly enhanced with the adoption of the Canadian Charter of Rights and Freedoms in 1982; the effects of the first 15 years of that review were discussed in Chapter 11. Peter McCormick writes in this connection:

> We should recognize that judges have always had power, have always affected our society by the decisions they make (and by

the way they decide to decide and *how* to decide). The Charter has simply made a longstanding reality more immediately visible and directed us belatedly to an assessment of the implications of judicial power.[4]

Access to and Costs of Justice

Many people cannot afford to hire a lawyer to defend themselves in a criminal (or even civil) case, yet the objective of the court system must be the search for truth and the obtaining of justice, goals which have traditionally rested on the adversarial system. To ensure that those without the financial resources have a fairer chance to achieve justice, legal aid programs financed jointly by the federal and provincial governments have been established. Although these vary in detail from one province to another and do not cover every kind of legal work, they go some way to meet the fairness objective. Community legal clinics serve a similar function.

A related means of reducing the costs of the administration of justice are the practices of plea bargaining and pretrial conferences. Plea bargaining involves discussions between defence and Crown attorneys with the aim of achieving agreement on charges to be pursued, typically by having the accused plead guilty to one charge and the Crown drop other charges. This practice is routine at the provincial court level and avoids a lengthy, costly trial. In the higher trial courts it is increasingly common for the judge to hold a pretrial conference with the lawyers for each side. Such conferences can result in a negotiated settlement or at least a time-saving clarification of the issues involved. They have also proven useful at the level of family and small claims courts. While plea bargaining and pretrial conferences must not be allowed to subvert justice, they are valuable devices that cut costs for everyone involved (including the public) and reduce the workload of the usually congested court system.

Categories of Laws

The law can be defined as "society's system of binding rules."[5] Laws are commonly divided into different categories, primarily between "civil" and "criminal." A *civil law* regulates relationships between two private parties such as individuals or corporations, and if private agreement cannot be reached in the case of dispute, one party may take the other to court. Most aspects of civil law in Canada are within provincial jurisdiction, largely based on the provincial power over property and civil rights. Civil cases often involve disputes over commercial contracts or property; such cases are normally resolved by the court's ordering one party to pay damages to the other. Civil cases are decided on the basis of the "balance of probabilities" of the merits of each side.

Criminal law, on the other hand, is primarily a federal responsibility; it is thus more or less uniform throughout the country, and has been consolidated in the *Criminal Code*. In this case, the commission of a crime such as murder, sexual assault, or theft is considered to be a wrong against society as a whole, and the state takes the initiative to bring the suspect to justice by means of the police and Crown attorneys. In criminal cases, judges may impose fines or prison sentences if the accused is found guilty, such guilt having been proven "beyond a reasonable doubt."

One of the peculiarities of Canadian federalism is that while criminal law is within federal jurisdiction, it is usually the provincial attorneys general and their agents, the Crown attorneys, who are responsible for initiating proceedings against the person who is charged. This situation has come about because the provinces have jurisdiction over the administration of justice. Sometimes a case contains both civil and criminal elements, such as a drunken driver who does damage to another person's car. The state pursues the violation of the Criminal Code, but the victim's insurance company would have to take the initiative to sue for property damage.

Instead of this basic division between civil and criminal law, a distinction is sometimes made between public and private law.[6] Private law is essentially the same as civil law described above, that is, law that primarily involves private interests. Beyond the contracts and property mentioned, private law includes torts, wills, company law, and family law. Public law, involving the public interest or the government, goes beyond criminal law to include constitutional, administrative, and taxation law. Constitutional law has traditionally involved questions about federal or provincial jurisdiction, and governments themselves have often been the parties to a constitutional case. With the adoption of the Charter of Rights and Freedoms, a whole new aspect of constitutional law in Canada has emerged. Administrative law concerns the operation of government departments and agencies, and with the expansion of government activity over the years this branch of law has also increased in significance.

By giving the provinces jurisdiction over property and civil rights, the Fathers of Confederation allowed the province of Quebec to retain its distinctive private or civil law system, called the *Code Civil du Québec*. The private law system in the other provinces is based on the English common law tradition. The theoretical distinction between the two systems in terms of form is that while the common law consists of a hodge-podge of judicial precedents, the Civil Code is a single comprehensive document. As Gall puts it, "in a common law system, the courts extract existing principles of law from decisions of previous cases, while in the civil law system, the courts look to the civil code to determine a given principle and they then apply the facts of an instant case to that principle."[7]

Structure of the Courts

Because the provinces that formed Confederation in 1867 already possessed a court system, and because the Judicial Committee of the Privy Council continued to function as a court of appeal for the whole British Empire, it was not necessary to devote much attention to the judiciary in the Constitution Act, 1867. The new federal government was allowed to establish a general court of appeal and any additional courts, but the provinces were given responsibility for the establishment of a provincial court system. McCormick describes the logic of the court structure as follows:

First: Identify the more routine cases and those that involve less serious possible outcomes and assign them to an accessible high-volume, low-delay court, preferably one that sits in many different centres.

Second: Assign the less routine and more serious cases to a lower-volume court that can devote more time and more focused attention to each individual case.

Third: Establish a court of appeal to correct simple errors and to promote uniformity in the application of the law within each province.

Fourth: Establish a "general court of appeal" to promote uniformity in the application of the law within the country as a whole and to provide judicial leadership.

Fifth: Create a system of federal courts for cases directly involving the federal government as a party or raising issues concerning the administrative law applied by federal departments.[8]

Figure 16.1· **The Court Structure in Canada**

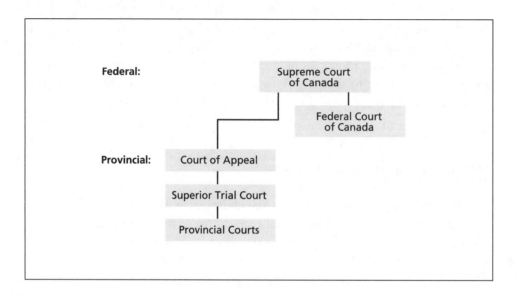

As seen in Figure 16.1, the court systems within each province developed into a reasonably uniform three-level hierarchy. At the top are two "superior" courts—the superior trial court and the court of appeal, although they go by different names from province to province. At the bottom are provincial courts.

Because of the assumption that provinces could not be trusted to make worthy appointments to superior, district, and county courts, the Fathers of Confederation provided that the judges of these courts would be appointed by the governor general, conventionally meaning the federal cabinet. Such judges were also paid by the federal government. Thus, in another peculiarity of Canadian federalism, each province determines how many superior court judges it needs, but they are appointed and paid by Ottawa. Since these courts and their judges were provided for in section 96 of the 1867 document, they are often called "section 96 courts" and "section 96 judges." Judges of the provincial courts are appointed by the provincial cabinet.

Provincial Courts

Whatever their structure or name, provincial courts generally have the following functions:

1. summary offences including less serious crimes, provincial and municipal offences

2. most aspects of indictable offences, some mandatory and others optional

3. preliminary hearings for most serious crimes

4. bail hearings

5. Young Offenders Act offences

6. family law, except divorce and proceedings flowing from divorce

7. small civil cases

Provincial courts have a monopoly on summary offences except in provinces where this responsibility has been given to lower tribunals such as justices of the peace. More serious crimes, called indictable offences, can be subdivided into three categories. Some, like murder, are reserved for superior courts; others, like theft, are assigned to provincial courts; and those in an intermediate category can be tried in either section 96 or provincial courts. The federal Young Offenders Act covers offences committed by those aged 12 to 18, and in some provinces these offences are tried in special youth courts.

Family law is another area of great federal–provincial complexity. Since divorce is a federal responsibility, divorces are dealt with in section 96 courts and any proceedings flowing from the divorce must also be dealt with there. On the other hand, as long as divorce is not involved, such matters as custody, access, maintenance, alimony, adoption, guardianship, and protection of children are handled in provincial courts, sometimes called family courts. Several provinces have tried to overcome the problem of the fragmentation of family law with a "unified family court" presided over by a section 96 judge.

Provincial courts, sometimes in a civil division and sometimes called small claims courts, also have jurisdiction over disputes involving small amounts of money. Each province determines the monetary limit for cases that can be considered at that level, with disputes involving larger sums being initiated at the section 96 court level. Some provinces have also tried to remove the adversarial nature of small claims or other civil cases by instituting various mediation services.

The Superior Trial Court

The functions of the superior trial court in the province, whatever its name, are as follows:

1.   some mandatory and other elective indictable offences

2.   civil matters over a given monetary amount

3.   divorces and proceedings flowing therefrom

4.   appeals from lower courts re summary convictions, juvenile and family cases

5.   administrative law cases

Provincial Courts of Appeal

Provincial courts of appeal hear criminal, civil, and other appeals. Although some of these courts' judgments can be appealed to the Supreme Court of Canada, decisions of the provincial courts of appeal are usually final, adding to the significance of this level of court.[9] The basic function of an appeal court is to correct errors or injustices that were made in a lower court, so that an appeal court is primarily interested in legal rather than factual issues. The second function of the appeal court is to render an opinion in a *reference case*, that is, on a constitutional issue referred to it by the provincial cabinet. Russell thus speaks of the "law-making" role of appeal courts because their legal interpretations have a "creative legislative dimension."[10] Decisions of the court of appeal are binding on all courts below it in the same province and are "strongly persuasive" for trial courts in other provinces. Courts of appeal normally sit in banks of three judges, but these panels can be increased to five for very important cases. Each side of a case submits a brief or "factum" in advance summarizing its arguments, and lawyers then engage in oral argument.

The Federal Court of Canada

The Federal Court of Canada was established in 1971 with trial and appeal divisions. It was intended to relieve the Supreme Court of Canada of routine appeals from certain federal administrative tribunals and to strengthen judicial review of federal administration by developing a more unified and cohesive body of federal administrative law.[11] The Federal Court has the following functions:

1. cases involving admiralty law and copyright, trademark, and patent disputes

2. citizenship and immigration appeals

3. appeals from other federal administrative tribunals

4. civil cases involving the federal government

5. cases involving bills of exchange, promissory notes, aeronautics, and interprovincial works and undertakings

6. appeals from boards of referees under the Employment Insurance Act

7. prerogative writs (e.g., injunctions) applying to agencies of the federal government

8. appeals re Access to Information and Privacy Acts

9. issuance of Canadian Security Intelligence Service warrants

The work of the Federal Court is dominated by cases involving the Immigration Act and Immigration and Refugee Board, employment insurance, penitentiaries and the Parole Board, the Public Service Commission and Public Service Staff Relations Board, and the Ministry of National Revenue. It has recently seen a growth in Aboriginal cases dealing with monetary and constitutional issues, land entitlements, and natural resources. Of great interest to political science, the Federal Court also hears appeals regarding the Access to Information Act and the Privacy Act and decides on requests for warrants from the Canadian Security Intelligence Service in order to plant bugs, open mail, and engage in other surreptitious activities.

The Federal Court consists of a chief justice and 10 other judges on its appeal division and the associate chief justice and 19 other full-time and assorted part-time judges on its trial division. The appeal division judges sit in panels of at least three members.

....

The Supreme Court of Canada

The Supreme Court of Canada sits at the apex of the Canadian court system. It hears appeals from the provincial courts of appeal in civil and criminal cases and from the appeals division of the Federal Court of Canada in administrative law matters. That part of its work of most interest to political science involves constitutional law, whether in terms of the division of powers or the Charter of Rights and Freedoms. Besides hearing actual appeal cases from lower courts, the Supreme Court can be asked by the federal cabinet to give opinions, usually on constitutional matters, in what are called *reference cases*. While the Supreme Court hears fewer cases per year than any lower court, it is interested almost exclusively in questions of law. Thus, of all courts, it is the most heavily engaged in a "law-making" role, and its decisions are binding on all lower courts.

Until 1949, the Supreme Court was a seriously deficient institution. First, its decisions could be appealed to Canada's pre-1949 final court of appeal, the Judicial Committee of the Privy Council (JCPC) located in London, and it was bound by JCPC precedents. But even more humiliating, appeals could go directly to that Empire court from provincial appeal courts, completely bypassing the Supreme Court of Canada. This weakness in authority was exacerbated by the generally poor quality of judges appointed to it in that earlier period, with some notable exceptions.[12]

Canada could have cut off appeals to the Judicial Committee after obtaining complete independence in 1931, but it was unclear whether the provinces would have to agree to this measure, since their appeals could already go directly to the JCPC. By the late 1940s it was determined that Ottawa could unilaterally curtail all such appeals, and it promptly did so. The Supreme Court of Canada has not been formally bound by Judicial Committee decisions since 1949 and has explicitly overruled them on occasion.

The Supreme Court used to have little discretion in deciding which cases it heard, but since 1974 it has basically controlled its own agenda. Such discretion considerably enhances the stature of the institution. Today, only two categories of cases have an automatic right of appeal to the Supreme Court: provincial reference cases, and murder cases in which the provincial court of appeal was split on a question of law. Applications for leave to appeal discretionary cases are normally handled in writing by a panel of three judges, but sometimes the panel hears them live. Public law cases, especially criminal and constitutional, now clearly predominate over private law disputes on the Supreme Court docket.

Although an increasingly important institution of government, the Supreme Court rests primarily on the Supreme Court Act rather than being embedded in any constitutional act as such. That act now provides for a nine-member court, three of whom must come from Quebec with its distinctive civil law system. Convention dictates that of the other six, three normally come from Ontario, two from the West, and one from Atlantic Canada. The act requires that at least five judges constitute a quorum, with the result that civil law cases from Quebec can be heard by a five-member panel including a majority from the civil law system. The position of chief justice normally alternates between francophone and anglophone members, simultaneous interpretation is available, and Supreme Court judges are now expected to be at least functionally bilingual. The judges hold office during good behaviour until the age of 75. One of the merits of the Meech Lake and Charlottetown Accords would have been to "constitutionalize" the Supreme Court in order to give it a firmer foundation and to clarify how it could be changed.

The Court holds three sessions of about two months' duration each per year, and then adjourns to write up its decisions. As much as possible, the Court tries to hear cases with a full complement of nine. Judges study the lower court proceedings and judgments in advance, along with the written arguments of the lawyers for each side. Oral arguments normally last only two hours, during which time the judges often ask trenchant questions. In some instances the Court also grants "intervenor status" to provincial governments and interest groups that are concerned about a case but not directly party to it. Once the arguments are completed, the judges usually "reserve judgment" and meet in private conference to discuss the case. Each gives his or her tentative conclusion and one or more draft opinions are prepared. These are later circulated and evoke comments before being revised. Each Supreme Court judge is assisted by a number of outstanding new law school graduates called law clerks. They help the busy judges search for and sift through precedents and other relevant material on the issues involved. So much effort is put into the process of preparing their opinions that a decision is typically not issued until about six months after the Court hears the case, and it has occasionally taken over a year for all members of the Court to make up their mind. The Court tries to come to a unanimous decision, but if this is not possible, majority and minority opinions will be issued. Membership of the Supreme Court of Canada in recent years can be seen in Table 16.1.

TABLE 16.1 MEMBERSHIP IN THE SUPREME COURT OF CANADA, 1984–1997

Appointment	Name	Retirement (Death)
1973	Brian Dickson CJ[1]: 1984–90	1990
1974	Jean Beetz	1988
1977	William Estey	1988
1979	William McIntyre	1989
1979	Jean Chouinard	(1987)
1980	Antonio Lamer CJ: 1990–	
1982	Bertha Wilson	1990
1984	Gerald Le Dain	1988
1985	Gerald La Forest	1997
1987	Claire L'Heureux-Dubé	
1988	John Sopinka	(1997)
1989	Peter Cory	
1989	Charles Gonthier	
1989	Beverley McLachlin	
1990	William Stevenson	1992
1991	Frank Iacobucci	
1992	John Major	
1997	Michael Bastarache	
1998	Ian Binnie	

[1] *Chief Justice*

. . . .

The Appointment of Judges

As has already been established, Supreme and Federal Court of Canada judges as well as judges of provincial superior courts are appointed by the federal cabinet, while provincial court judges are appointed by provincial cabinets. The former number about 750, and the latter, about 1250. All of the first group must be qualified lawyers of at least 10 years' standing, as must provincial court judges in Ontario and Quebec. Elsewhere, provincial court judges have to be members of the bar for a minimum of five years.

In a high proportion of cases over the years, Canadian cabinets at both federal and provincial levels have used judicial appointments to reward faithful party supporters, often defeated candidates.[13] Such party patronage raises three main problems: unsuitable individuals are appointed because of their partisan connections; well-qualified candidates are overlooked because of their lack of service to the party in power; and partisan judges may favour their former political colleagues.[14] This patronage system of appointing judges is still alive, although it is on the decline.

At the federal level, Pierre Trudeau as minister of Justice instituted an informal practice of submitting names of potential judicial appointments to the National Committee on the Judiciary of the Canadian Bar Association (CBA). Trudeau sullied his own government's record in this field, however, with the appointment of six high-profile Liberal partisans, several to the Federal Court of Canada, in 1984. After an even more partisan record of judicial appointments during its first term,[15] the Mulroney government established a somewhat more satisfactory appointment system in 1988 for all "federal" judges except those on the Supreme Court of Canada, and modified it slightly in 1991. An independent Commissioner for Federal Judicial Affairs now maintains a record of those interested in federal judicial appointments. This official then submits such names to a seven-member committee set up in each province, including a section 96 judge, one nominee of each of the provincial law society, the provincial branch of the CBA, and the provincial attorney general, and three nominees of the federal minister of Justice. This committee ranks each candidate as "highly recommended," "recommended," or "not able to recommend," and the minister makes the final decision, still being entitled to choose from those "not recommended."[16] On the other hand, party service or legislative experience should not automatically disqualify a worthy candidate from a judicial appointment.[17]

The prime minister chooses the chief justice in each province, almost always from the existing bench, as well as new members of the Supreme Court of Canada. Prime ministers consult widely before making such appointments, and have managed to overcome their penchant for partisanship in this one area. Patronage has therefore not been much of a problem on the Supreme Court for nearly 50 years.

At the provincial court level, the attorney general now usually consults with the provincial judicial council or equivalent in making such appointments. A central nonpartisan nominating commission consisting largely of nonlawyers was established in Ontario in 1988, originally headed by political scientist Peter

Russell. It screens judicial applicants on their merits and leaves the attorney general little or no discretion.

Another controversial aspect of judicial appointments concerns the Supreme Court of Canada alone. Because this court must adjudicate federal–provincial disputes, concern has been expressed that all of its members are federally appointed. In theory, once appointed, judges act with total impartiality and their independence is protected in various ways. Nevertheless, it may not *appear* as if justice has been done in such a situation. The ill-fated Meech Lake and Charlottetown Accords provided for Ottawa to make Supreme Court of Canada appointments from lists provided by the provinces. The 1992 Accord also proposed federal and provincial consultation with Aboriginal peoples in the appointment process.

If a proper geographic balance is characteristic of Canadian judges, what can be said of their other socioeconomic characteristics? Partly as a consequence of geography, judicial appointments have balanced francophone and anglophone origins at both federal and provincial court levels, especially in recent years as provinces have made more French-language court services available. Those of other origins have generally been excluded, but names such as Laskin (Jewish), Sopinka (Ukrainian) and Iacobucci (Italian) are now appearing on the Supreme Court of Canada and increasingly on lower courts as well. Thus the most serious aspects of judicial underrepresentation relate to women and the working class.[18]

Just as in the case of "other ethnics," however, more female and working-class law school graduates are becoming available for judicial appointments, and governments have at least begun to recognize the necessity of appointing greater numbers of female judges. The Supreme Court finally saw its first woman member in 1982, and for a time had a total of three women out of nine. Such female judges have sometimes used their position to point out the male bias in legislatures, judiciaries, and laws.

As noted in Chapter 4, Aboriginal Canadians have even more serious reservations about the Canadian judicial system, feeling that it discriminates against them at every turn. They argue that an increase in the number of Native judges would not substantially improve this situation, and therefore advocate the establishment of a parallel justice system to deal with Aboriginal defendants (at least where they did no harm to non-Aboriginals), reflecting their own distinctive concepts of guilt and punishment.

....

Retirement, Removal, and Independence of Judges

Whatever the process involved in making judicial appointments, judges are expected to abide by the principle of *judicial independence* or impartiality once they are on the bench. They are supposed to adjudicate without fear or favour with respect to private or political interests, and without any incentive to give preference to the government side where it is involved.

The independence of judges is primarily based on security of tenure, and it is difficult for the government to remove judges before their scheduled date of retirement. Judges on the Supreme and Federal Courts of Canada and provincial superior courts have a mandatory retirement age of 75 years, and provincial court judges of 65 or 70. The general rule is that they serve on "good behaviour"—that is, they cannot be removed unless they have been guilty of misbehaviour. While the meaning of these terms has never been definitively established, judges are certainly removable for serious criminal acts and possibly for reasons of infirmity or incapacity, failure to execute their duties, or bringing the judicial system into disrepute.[19] On the other hand, they cannot be removed merely because the government regards their decisions as erroneous or contrary to government policy, nor because they ruled against the Crown.

The process of removing a judge varies with the level of the position, the degree of difficulty increasing with the court's ranking in the hierarchy. Except in Ontario, where legislation is required, provincial court judges can be removed by an order-in-council of the provincial cabinet but only after an inquiry has been conducted by one of the judge's peers or by the provincial judicial council. It is even more difficult to remove judges of the provincial superior courts and the federal courts. In that situation, the Canadian Judicial Council conducts an inquiry and reports to the minister of Justice, after which the passage of a joint address of both houses of Parliament is required.

The Canadian Judicial Council was created in 1971 and consists of all the chief justices and associate chief justices of courts staffed by federally appointed judges, chaired by the Chief Justice of the Canadian Supreme Court. Like the provincial judicial councils, its primary purpose is to deal with complaints raised against individual judges, but it also has a role in the continuing education of judges, provides a forum for developing consensus among its members, and makes representations to government with respect to judicial salaries and benefits.

While a number of judges have been reprimanded by judicial councils, the issue of judicial removal has rarely arisen. Several provincial court judges have been removed over the years, a practice that is increasingly common as the public becomes less tolerant of their faults. But only four judges of the old county and district courts met this fate, and not a single superior court judge has been removed from office. Such proceedings were initiated in four cases, but the judges either died or resigned during the removal process.

Besides security of tenure, judicial independence involves financial, administrative, and political independence.[20] Salaries and pensions are fixed in such a way that neither individually nor collectively can judges be intimidated by government threats to reduce them, although some judges went to court to challenge freezes or reductions in their salaries as part of recent provincial government restraint programs. In addition, judges are increasingly in control of the administration of the court system. Judges must also be able to function without political pressure—from cabinet ministers, legislators, bureaucrats, or other judges—whether in public or in private. At both federal and provincial levels, many cases have occurred of cabinet ministers contacting judges, but however innocent their questions might seem, this must not be done.

It is sometimes thought that the prospect of promotion from one court to another might bias a judge's decisions, but no evidence has been found to justify this fear. On the other hand, judges are not supposed to make public speeches that could compromise their impartiality. For example, when Tom Berger of the B.C. Supreme Court publicly criticized the 1982 Constitution Act for its omission of Quebec and virtual neglect of Aboriginals, certain highly placed opponents of his views brought him before the Canadian Judicial Council. Although its recommendation was not to dismiss him, he resigned to protest the process employed.[21]

....

NOTES

1. Peter Russell, *The Judiciary in Canada: The Third Branch of Government* (Toronto: McGraw-Hill Ryerson, 1987), 5.
2. Ibid., 14.
3. Peter Russell, "The Effect of a Charter of Rights on the Policy-Making Role of the Canadian Courts," *Canadian Public Administration* (Spring 1982): 2.
4. Peter McCormick, *Canada's Courts* (Toronto: James Lorimer and Company Limited, 1994), 3.
5. Russell, *The Judiciary in Canada*, 6.
6. Gerald L. Gall, *The Canadian Legal System*, 3rd ed. (Toronto: Carswell, 1990), 23–28.

7. Ibid., 30.
8. McCormick, *Canada's Courts*, 23.
9. Ibid., 56,
10. Russell, *The Judiciary in Canada*, 290.
11. Ibid., 313, 319–27; Peter Hogg, *Constitutional Law of Canada*, 2nd ed. (Toronto: Carswell, 1985), 142–48.
12. James G. Snell and Frederick Vaughan, *The Supreme Court of Canada: History of the Institution* (Toronto: The Osgoode Society, 1985); Russell, *The Judiciary in Canada*, 337.
13. Carl Baar quotes an oft-repeated maxim that "to become a judge in the United States, you must be elected; to become a judge in Canada, you must be defeated," in "The Structure and Personnel of the Canadian Judiciary," in Paul Fox and Graham White, eds., *Politics: Canada*, 7th ed. (Toronto: McGraw-Hill Ryerson, 1991), 513.
14. Andrew Heard, *Canadian Constitutional Conventions* (Toronto: Oxford University Press, 1991), 135.
15. During the Mulroney government's first term, 48 percent of all judges appointed were known Conservative supporters compared to 7 percent who supported opposition parties. Peter Russell and Jacob Ziegel, "Federal Judicial Appointments: An Appraisal of the First Mulroney Government's Appointments and the New Judiciary Advisory Committees," *University of Toronto Law Journal* 41 (1991).
16. Commissioner for Federal Judicial Affairs, *Judicial Appointments: Information Guide and A New Judicial Appointments Process* (Ottawa: Supply and Services, 1988).
17. McCormick, *Canada's Courts*, 112.
18. Dennis Olsen, *The State Elite* (Toronto: McClelland and Stewart, 1980), ch. 3; Russell, *The Judiciary in Canada*, 164–65.
19. Heard, *Canadian Constitutional Conventions*, 124; Russell, *The Judiciary in Canada*, 176; Gall, *The Canadian Legal System*, 227–39.
20. *Valente v. the Queen* [1985] 2 SCR 673; Perry S. Millar and Carl Baar, *Judicial Administration in Canada* (Montreal: McGill–Queen's University Press, 1981).
21. Heard, *Canadian Constitutional Conventions*, 131; Russell, *The Canadian Judiciary*, 85–89; Gall, *The Canadian Legal System*, 236–38; McCormick, *Canada's Courts*, 130–31.

FURTHER READING

Baar, Carl. "The Structure and Personnel of the Canadian Judiciary." In Paul Fox and Graham White, eds. *Politics: Canada*. 7th ed. Toronto: McGraw-Hill Ryerson, 1991.

Canadian Bar Foundation. *The Independence of the Judiciary in Canada*. Ottawa: Canadian Bar Association, 1985.

Commissioner for Federal Judicial Affairs. *A New Judicial Appointments Process*. Ottawa: Supply and Services, 1988.

Commissioner for Federal Judicial Affairs: *Judicial Appointments: Information Guide*. Ottawa: Supply and Services, 1988.

Gall, Gerald. *The Canadian Legal System*. 3rd ed. Toronto: Carswell, 1990.

Heard, Andrew. *Canadian Constitutional Conventions*. Toronto: Oxford University Press, 1991.

Hogg, Peter. *Constitutional Law of Canada*. 2nd ed. Toronto: Carswell, 1985.

Mandel, Michael. *The Charter of Rights and the Legalization of Politics in Canada*. Toronto: Wall and Thompson, 1989; rev. ed., 1994.

McCormick, Peter. *Canada's Courts*. Toronto: Lorimer, 1994.

McCormick, Peter, and Ian Greene. *Judges and Judging: Inside the Canadian Judicial System*. Toronto: Lorimer, 1990.

Russell, Peter. *The Judiciary in Canada: The Third Branch of Government*. Toronto: McGraw-Hill Ryerson, 1987.

To the owner of this book

We hope that you have enjoyed *Canadian Politics,* Concise Edition, and we would like to know as much about your experiences with this text as you would care to offer. Only through your comments and those of others can we learn how to make this a better text for future readers.

School _____ Your instructor's name _____

Course _____ Was the text required? _____ Recommended? _____

1. What did you like the most about *Canadian Politics?*

_____
_____
_____

2. How useful was this text for your course?

_____
_____
_____

3. Do you have any recommendations for ways to improve the next edition of this text?

_____
_____
_____

4. In the space below or in a separate letter, please write any other comments you have about the book. (For example, please feel free to comment on reading level, writing style, terminology, design features, and learning aids.)

_____
_____
_____

Optional

Your name _____ Date _____

May ITP Nelson quote you, either in promotion for *Canadian Politics* or in future publishing ventures?

Yes _____ No _____

Thanks!

You can also send your comments to us via e-mail at
college_arts_hum@nelson.com

PLEASE TAPE SHUT. DO NOT STAPLE.

TAPE SHUT

TAPE SHUT

- - - FOLD HERE - - -

MAIL POSTE
Canada Post Corporation
Société canadienne des postes
Postage paid   Port payé
if mailed in Canada si posté au Canada
Business Reply   Réponse d'affaires
0066102399   01

Nelson

TAPE SHUT

TAPE SHUT

0066102399-M1K5G4-BR01

ITP NELSON
MARKET AND PRODUCT DEVELOPMENT
PO BOX 60225 STN BRM B
TORONTO ON M7Y 2H1